SELF PUBLISH, BE HAPPY

A DIY Photobook Manual and Manifesto
by Bruno Ceschel

aperture

Table of Contents

The Self Publish, Be Happy Manifesto by Bruno Ceschel

Self Publish, Be Happy is not a survey of recent photobooks. It is not a best-of. It is a call to arms—a rallying cry to take part, to act, to share.

The self-publishers featured in this book are all part of a long tradition of people finding means to communicate via printed matter. In doing so, they have often challenged the modus operandi of production and distribution.

It is a tradition based on resistance and defiance—to power, ideology, the status quo, and the market. Political and religious pamphlets, erotic novels, futurist manifestos, Dadaist journals, punk and skate zines: these publications have not only disseminated ideas via alternative channels, but also created a social space around them. Their circulation has been an agent of aggregation, of social interaction and exchange.

Books are both social and utopian places.

While in the past self-published books were necessary for spreading ideas in censorious environments, in today's free-for-all digital era, one might believe that they'd been made obsolete—that their raison d'être had ceased to exist. Why bother with something as laborious, non-immediate, and costly as a publication?

Because today, more than ever, we need to rise against the homogeneous globalized culture in which we are (un)knowingly trapped—a culture dictated by the market and absorbed via social media.

The act of making publications subverts the diktat that the digital must be substituted for the analog, the sensorial, the physical. The pleasure of making, consuming, and exchanging books is at the core of *Self Publish, Be Happy*. This book reasserts human experience, bridging knowledge and history across time and space.

The artists featured in this book defy the system first and foremost by giving the finger to the godlike profit paradigm, choosing to do not one, but two unprofitable things: make art and publish.

DIY culture is by its nature an ethic in opposition to society's rules at large. It flourishes in environments of communitarian support, collaboration, and even informal barter economies. It is rooted in self-affirmation against a conformist and normative system.

It is no coincidence that, like the old mole—as Marx and Hegel called the revolution that lies in wait underground—the DIY ethic in art and society at large has popped out again in the last decade, coinciding with financial and political crises and emerging in response to a white-cube and auction-house-driven art market, elitist institutions, and tastemakers.

Grassroots collectives and individual enterprises have been powered by technological possibilities that offer cheap and approachable means of making art and books. An army of young artists is undermining the greed-run system at its foundations, one page at a time.

Self Publish, *Be Happy* is not about any one book, any single endeavor, but rather the energy created by collective effort—the (dis)harmony of the whole.

Self Publish, *Be Happy* is a state of mind.

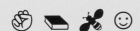

New Old Media
by David Senior

In the March 1964 issue of *Artforum*, Ed Ruscha took out an advertisement for his new self-published book, *Twentysix Gasoline Stations*. Ruscha had done some design work for the magazine, and took his payment for those services in the form of this ad. It featured an image of the book's front cover, with the caption: "REJECTED Oct. 2, 1963 by the Library of Congress, Washington 25, D.C." Ruscha had sent the book to the library of record for all publications originating in the United States, and instead of adding it to its collection, the library had returned it to him. It looked like a book and was bound like a book, but there must have been something about its content or structure that caused a librarian to send it back. Perhaps it was its lack of identifiable publisher, or the opaqueness of its intent in regards to photographic imagery and sequencing, but *Twentysix Gasoline Stations* was officially categorized as a non-book.

This anecdote helps convey the awkwardness of these kinds of experimental books at that historical moment. There really was no established vocabulary to identify what this kind of gesture was: an artist using new printing tools—in this case, new, cheap offset technology—to produce an informal printed work independent from a publishing house. Now this might not seem all that profound, but it is important to remember that this printing activity was part of a conceptual turn in the early 1960s, and a very pragmatic response to newly available technology. Images were cheaper to reproduce in print than ever before, and Ruscha, having worked at a print shop, seized on this by creating his own taxonomies of images in the now-celebrated book series that started with *Twentysix Gasoline Stations*.

Roughly ten years later, the notion of artists as publishers had been established to the degree that an artists' magazine such as *Art-Rite*, based in New York, could publish a themed issue on artists' books in 1976. The issue collected responses from artists who made self-published books about why they published. ("Art becomes pure for a moment and disconnected from money," wrote John Baldessari.

"And since a lot of people can own the book, nobody owns it. Every artist should have a cheap line.") Places like Printed Matter and Franklin Furnace in New York, or Art Metropole in Toronto, popped up around this time, as distribution points for self-published artists' books. This increased distribution correlated with increased discourse on the subject of artists' publications, with related exhibitions, critical commentary, and recognition of various genres within this expanded field of publishing.

Of course, the historical avant-garde produced a large number of little magazines and books in the first half of the twentieth century, and most canonical modern art movements can be linked to related experimental publications of art, design, and photography. In many ways, the published experiments with chance, collage, appropriation, and montage of images that we find in these pages can certainly be related to this lineage. Perhaps, though, two specific historical phenomena from the second half of the twentieth century can connect most directly to *Self Publish, Be Happy*'s contemporary survey and living archive.

First, as for Ruscha, a maverick sensibility toward new printing tools drew artists, writers, and designers to produce printed work independent of "the establishment." The introduction of cheap web offset printing, mimeograph printing, or new typesetting tools such as the IBM Selectric typewriter coupled with a critical look at how media was produced. Developing alternative strategies to produce and distribute print media, and publishing outside the settings of larger publishing houses, was part of a larger trend to subvert conventional patterns of media production and distribution. Like underground cinema, new kinds of video production, and guerrilla television, artists' publications proposed a means through which images and ideas could be distributed cheaply and directly. In the 1960s and '70s, conceptual art movements were often defined by the networks created by little books.

For these generations of artists and designers, who published books, posters, magazines, and journals, the idea of a self-directed broadcasting medium is the substantial legacy of their efforts. In many exceptional and wide-ranging projects of the era, we have this idea of the publication as a broadcast device, a new media tool. To self-publish, to decentralize the production of print media, created a new type of printed object—one in which artists and designers bent the rules, played with conventions of the format, and created new containers for communication. This new publishing, as with other new media formats, permitted artists and designers to have a practice completely on their own terms, and to connect with others using this format.

In the context of art-making, self-publishing proposed one alternative for having a public practice, navigating around a reliance on the gallery and museum system through innovative use of materials and alternative networks of distribution. As curator and activist Lucy Lippard stated in the above-mentioned issue of *Art-Rite*, "I'm talking about communication, but I'm also talking about propaganda. Artists' books spread the word, whatever word that may be."

Lippard was a member of the group of artists and art workers that founded New York's Printed Matter in 1975, around which time there was a flowering of artist-run initiatives, mostly exhibition spaces, taking place in cities across North and South America and Europe. This led to the second historical phenomenon through which we can contextualize contemporary self-publishing. Initiators of these spaces clearly conceived that existing institutions were not responsive and supportive of new forms of art production, of socially and politically engaged practices that addressed social-justice issues, or of feminist or queer discourses. Disused urban spaces such as old industrial buildings, lofts, and makeshift studios served as informal exhibition halls, screening rooms, performance venues, and community meeting points.

The alternative space movement included not only initiatives such as Printed Matter and Franklin Furnace to foster the distribution of artists' publications, but the artists' publications themselves were also viewed as another type of alternative space. In her 1977 article "Alternative Space: Artists' Periodicals," curator and artist Howardena Pindell made the connection that self-published projects were operating in the same way as alternative galleries and performance spaces, but within the space of a book or magazine. They served as a creative shelter for projects whose content might have been too edgy or less clearly commodifiable for the gallery system, or for projects by younger artists looking for their first break. In this way, the flourishing of self-published projects from this time parallels the intentions and energy of the alternative space movement, and represents innumerable little alternative spaces for the dispersal of art, ideas, and images.

This idea of the self-published book as an alternative art space is not lost in the contemporary context. In fact, this is exactly what I'm interested in when we think about contemporary artists' publishing or self-publishing: the book as a self-run artist's space. The conditions and setting are different for sure, but I still see the self-published photobooks included in this volume as a functional alternative to certain alienating aspects of the art market—as an opening for young artists, especially, to experiment, collaborate, and put their work out into the world. As an excessive art market spins in its own gaudy orbit and affordable space in our cities becomes a nostalgic tale, it makes sense that people would turn to this kind of self-directed practice to create space for something new to happen. The idea of opting out of a context that one doesn't feel completely comfortable with, of looking for other answers, does become political.

This is something that is clear to me as I elbow my way through the teeming NY or LA Art Book Fairs, or through the other fairs that are increasingly popping up around the globe, and meet the individuals sitting at their tables behind stacks of new books. There is directness in this interaction between artist and audience that runs counter to other kinds of art production and exchange, and there are many people reacting positively to it, sensing that it is different. There is a clear sense in this contemporary self-publishing community that people are always seeking out new networks for distribution, and playing with possibilities for their materials to travel to new places.

There are tremendous amounts of other recent media experiments also following this trajectory. They often reside in a completely other territory of digital networks and social media, and provide new platforms to distribute images, video, and text. One of the open questions for me as I work with this genre of print publishing is: "Why so many new, self-published projects when there are other media available?" Public discourse incessantly refers to new digital futures for publishing; the mass-market publishing industry is moving into digital formats for newspapers, magazines, and books, both fiction and nonfiction. But then there's this weird, little island of art and photo publishers that are persisting and seemingly growing. It runs counter to the overarching idea that everything, everywhere, is going digital.

A part of this paradox is the degree to which digital images are now being recirculated within self-published books. Many artists are using the idea of Internet image appropriation or accumulation to create a printing practice, distilling the crazy amount of images that one encounters online into the space of a book—through reproduction, collage, or by making taxonomies of the images. There is a dialogue between these different media languages, in which artists and designers use the digital sphere as a place to harvest images, then push them onto the printed page. From one perspective, this might be a weird mixture, but for a younger generation, this extreme hybridity of media languages is not challenging; they are fluent in the lingua franca of images and media forms that is increasingly shared across the world.

Whether their books' content relates to this call-and-response with digitally distributed images, or whether they are more focused on the texture and surface of the printed image, or on the craft of sequencing a series of photographs, there is a growing network of individuals and publishing collectives who are in communication and are aware of each others' practices. This self-publishing community has found ways to share skills and information, often in regards to new methods of distribution, or cheap places to print, bind, and source paper or other types of materials. Beyond what can be seen on websites and in online discussions, an international network of book fairs allows for this community to see itself, and for more exchanges of information and books. In this volume, we can read along with the community-in-print that Self Publish, Be Happy has represented and articulated over its five-year history.

Instructions for Use

This book presents fifty publications that are part of the collection of the London-based organization Self Publish, Be Happy. The collection now comprises more than three thousand publications, donated by the self-publishers themselves, beginning in June 2010. The creation of this collection coincides with the rise of the self-published photobook, a phenomenon that has reshaped the publishing landscape, prompting the language of the photobook to evolve and for photobooks to reach a much broader audience than ever before.

The publications included here are not meant to be a subjective grouping together of the best self-published photobooks published in the last five years, but are rather a select sample of a much bigger group of fantastic publications released over the course of the collection's existence.

This book is divided into five chapters, each of which groups ten books with similar themes, aims, or conceptual frameworks:

1. Self Publish, Be Playful—play as photographic subject, methodology, or spirit
2. Self Publish, Be Yourself—photographers turn their cameras toward their own lives and environments
3. Self Publish, Be a Storyteller—photographers turn their cameras outward, employing various documentary strategies
4. Self Publish, Be a Team—collaboration as the foundation of bookmaking
5. Self Publish, Be Crafty—the book as handcrafted object

The chapters are meant to be a navigational tool, not a strict index of the books. In fact, most books featured could easily fluctuate from one chapter to another, as they are ambiguous and multifaceted both in form and content.

Self Publish, Be Happy is also a manual that offers ideas and information for you to learn from and get inspired by to make your own photobook. Each entry comes with a detailed book specification sheet, with editorial and technical information. This includes the very important "cost per unit," which means how much it cost to print, bind, and otherwise physically produce each individual copy of the publication. (It doesn't include costs related to the production of the content, design fees, or marketing, etc.)

A key to costs per unit:

$	Less than $5
$$	$5–10
$$$	$10–15
$$$$	$15–30
$$$$$	More than $30

Each entry also captures the voices of the community with quotations from the self-publishers themselves, who offer tips or tell the stories of how their books came to be.

Self Publish, Be Playful

Title: As Long As It Photographs, It Must Be a Camera

Artists: Taiyo Onorato and Nico Krebs

Designers: Megi Zumstein and Claudio Barandun

Editors: Taiyo Onorato, Nico Krebs, Megi Zumstein, and Claudio Barandun

Printer: DZA, Altenburg, Germany

Publication date and place: November 2011 / Berlin, Germany, and Zurich, Switzerland

Edition: 700

Format and binding: softcover, two volumes / saddle stitched

Size: 11 6/8 x 16 1/2 in. (29.7 x 42 cm)

Number of pages and images: various / various

Type of printing and paper: offset / Fly 150gsm

Retail price: 20 EUR / 25 USD

Cost per unit: $$

Book soundtrack: "Hungry Eyes" by Eric Carmen

Humor and a sense of play have long been parts of the photographic practice of Swiss artists Taiyo Onorato and Nico Krebs. In the two-volume *As Long As It Photographs*, *It Must Be a Camera*, they playfully question the act of photographing. The first volume features images of cameras they have constructed from various objects and materials: one is made from essay books published by Aperture—the idea being to literally photograph through knowledge—while another is made from a turtle shell. The DIY cameras, which become sculptures in their own right, question what a camera is or could be. The artists include screenshots of messages from potential buyers on eBay, where they advertised the cameras for sale. The second volume features images taken by the pair, including abstract studies of light and objects. These books' dialogue gets inside the nature of photography itself.

1. Find yourself a studio close to—or, even better, above—a post office.
2. If you can't find a studio above a post office, buy a good granny cart.
3. Usually the best time to queue at the post office is between 3 and 5 p.m., when you'll be surrounded by elderly people. Your granny cart is the perfect conversation piece.
4. When it comes to selling, the best way is the direct way: money comes in, publication goes out. Beware of bookstores: only work with the ones you trust. (Some of the people reading this still owe us money!)
5. Your book doesn't sell? Keep a few copies and start all over again.
—Taiyo Onorato and Nico Krebs

IT MUST BE
A CAMERA

AS LONG AS IT
PHOTOGRAPHS

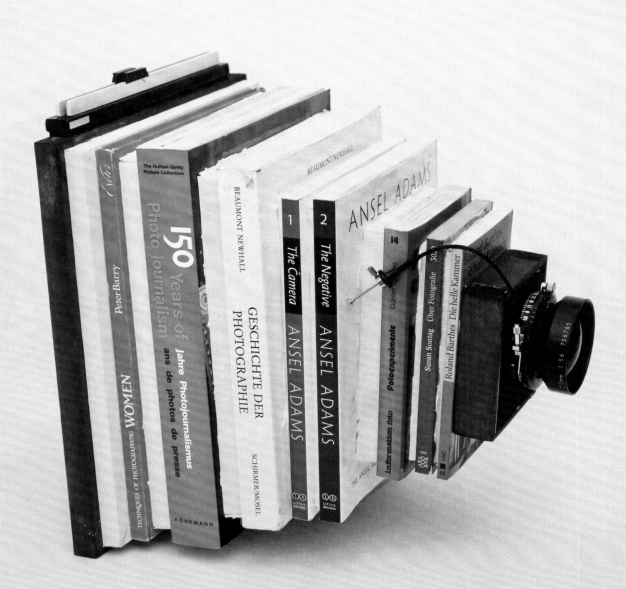

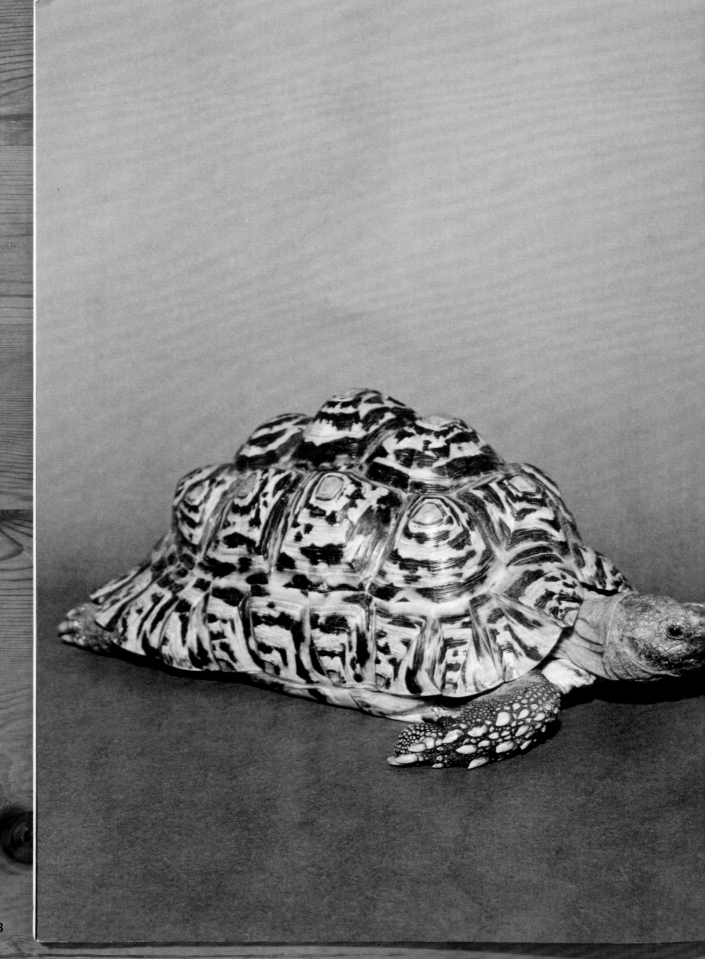

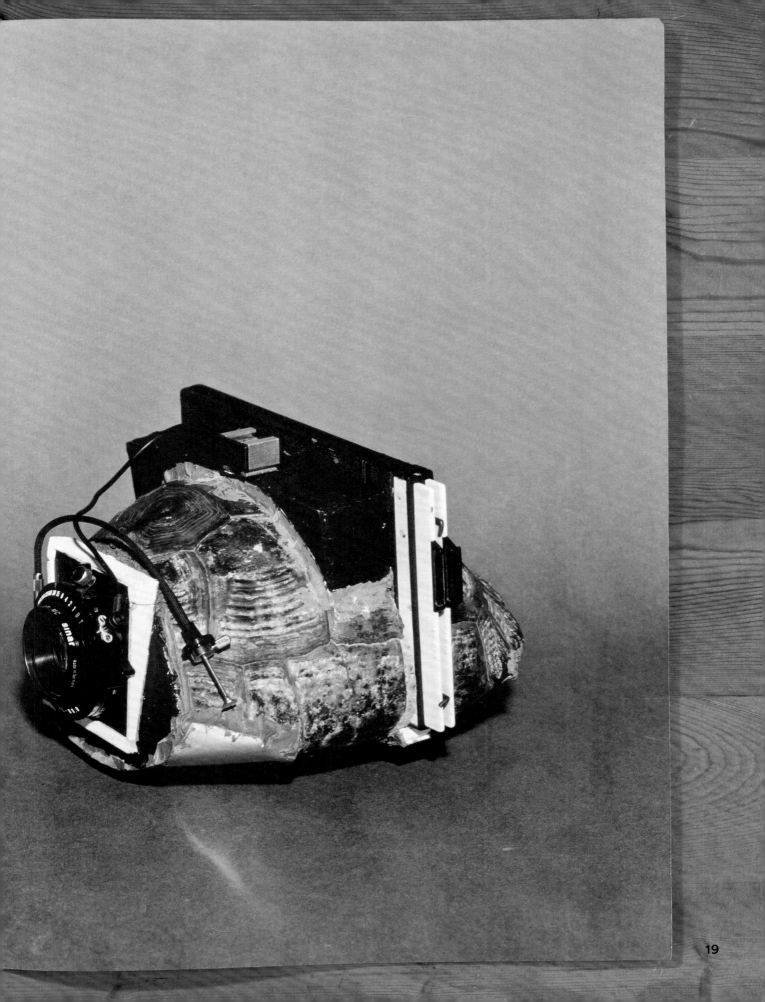

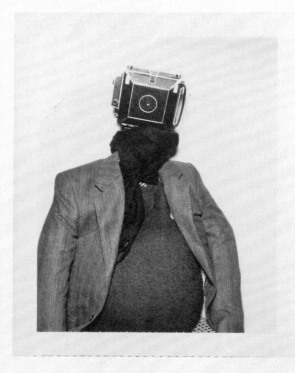

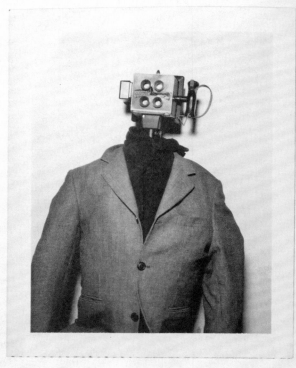

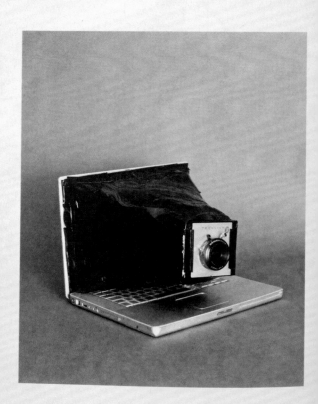

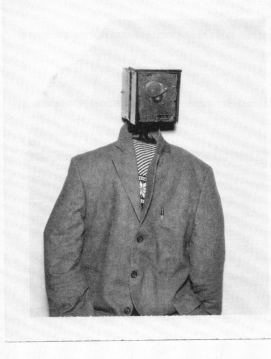

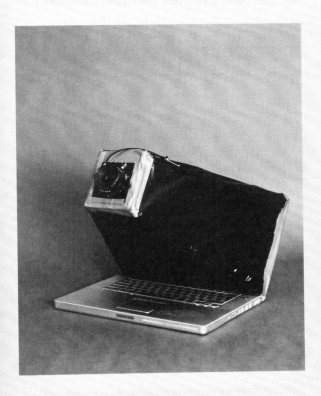

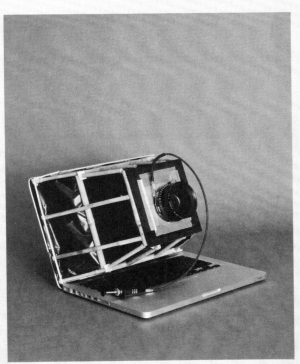

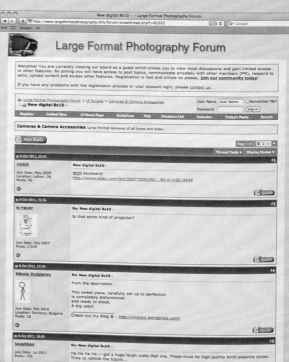

Large Format Photography Forum

Welcome! You are currently viewing our board as a guest which allows you to view most discussions and gain limited access to other features. By joining you will have access to post topics, communicate privately with other members (PM), respond to polls, upload content and access other features. Registration is fast and simple so please, **join our community today**!

If you have any problems with the registration process or your account login, please contact us.

Large Format Photography Forum > LF Forums > Cameras & Camera Accessories
Every Camera has a SOUL (?)

Cameras & Camera Accessories Large format cameras of all types and sizes.

Page 1 of 3 1 2 3 >

14-Oct-2011, 11:34 — #1
Honour & Crab
Join Date: Oct 2011
Posts: 3

Every Camera has a SOUL (?)

Good Day Everyone,

We have noticed that one of our recent Camera Auctions on Ebay have been discussed in this forum. We'd like to take up the opportunity today to discuss one of our main concerns in contemporary Camera Construction.

We have a strong belief at the Honour & Crab Workshop: EVERY CAMERA HAS A SOUL.
Im sure most of you would agree on this.
Some cameras become dear over the years, they are like pets or partners, sharing lifetime and experiences. The same goes for Photography. We dont see it as a simple outcome of a physical / mechanical / chemical process, its much more a question of what we see, what we are, how we feel and beyond.

We decided to take this thought one level further and are currently experimenting with a more metaphysical approach. Therefore I'd like to post the most recent experiment from our workshop, the Tortoise Cam?

As you can see the Body of the Camera was crafted with a real body, the remains of our dear neighbours tortoise that recently deceased and was kindly donated to us by its caretaker.
The tortoise shell was carried around by a living and seeing creature for many years. If transformed into a Camera, we hope it merges memory, or soul, and a newly acquired function. Apart from the technical characteristics, we are aiming at unpredictable and new results in the photographic output.

Has anyone of you made similair experiences or has a special bond to his / her camera, that goes beyond the notions of material possession?

We'd be more than happy to get this discussion started and share thoughts.
This might sound a little strange, but we are looking forward to a serious discussion.

All the best,
Honour & Crab

14-Oct-2011, 12:08 — #2
cdholden
back in the saddle again
Join Date: Sep 2008
Location: Nashville, TN
Posts: 776

Re: Every Camera has a SOUL (?)

I've been known to roll in the dirt and hug a tree from time to time. I get the whole thing with the turtle. Call it art if you like. It's all open to interpretation. At least your tortoise cam has a crude (functional?) film back. I could see this possibly working.
For the life of me, I can't figure out the logic in the bamboo, laptop and duct taped lens in the other auction. Most folks expect something functional when bidding on a "camera" from that section of auction items on Ebay.
I would recommend you to look for the section of holistic items if you're selling zen enlightenment.

Best of luck,
Chris

14-Oct-2011, 13:00 — #3
Frank Petronio
dip 'n dunk
Join Date: Jun 2002
Location: Upstate New York
Posts: 7,268

Re: Every Camera has a SOUL (?)

Go for the skull-cam next, that will really get attention.

Smart People Live Upwind from Kodak

BLOG http://www.frankpetronio.com
FLASH http://www.frankpetronio.net

14-Oct-2011, 13:34 — #4
unixrevolution
Join Date: Apr 2011
Location: Waldorf, MD
Posts: 48

Re: Every Camera has a SOUL (?)

Quote:
Originally Posted by Frank Petronio
Go for the skull-cam next, that will really get attention.

With the eye sockets each housing a lens for stereo photography.

Please, call me Erik.
Find me on: Flickr Pentaxforums RangeFinderForum
Omega View 45F Monorail, Super Graphic, 75, 90, 135, 150, 265 lenses.

14-Oct-2011, 13:40 — #5
Two23
Foamer
Join Date: Oct 2010
Location: South Dakota
Posts: 367

Re: Every Camera has a SOUL (?)

Needs a Petzval lens, otherwise you can't focus it.

Kent in SD

Gud blessi Island!

14-Oct-2011, 13:43 — #6
Mark Sampson
Join Date: Mar 2002
Location: Rochester NY USA
Posts: 1,463

Re: Every Camera has a SOUL (?)

Tortoise shell? perfect place for a slow lens.

14-Oct-2011, 14:12 — #7
sanchi heuser
Anti Heuser
Join Date: Jun 2008
Location: Düsseldorf,Germany
Posts: 265

Re: Every Camera has a SOUL (?)

Hi,
what do you mean with soul?

The term is used by some people to describe the inner being of a human (sometimes also animals or plants, or even the earth 'the earth soul'), they give the soul a metaphysical or spiritual meaning - the soul is something different from the material world, a (very little) part of a higher being that is in the centre of a human.

Others describe the soul as emotional center of humans or animals, plants.

Last edited by sanchi heuser : 14-Oct-2011 at 14:19. Reason: typo

14-Oct-2011, 14:15 —

John Kasaian
Join Date: Dec 2001
Location: San Joaquin Valley, California
Posts: 4,883

Re: Every Camera has a SOUL (?)

I tried to make a pinhole frozen turkey once. I think the turtle cam rocks!

"Tradition is not the worship of ashes, but the preservation of fire"---GKC

14-Oct-2011, 14:16 — #9
Jim Michael
Join Date: Nov 2008
Location: Atlanta, GA
Posts: 452

Re: Every Camera has a SOUL (?)

Who would shell out good money for such a hare brained idea?

14-Oct-2011, 14:21 — #10
Steve Hamley
Join Date: Mar 2002
Location: Knoxville, Tennessee
Posts: 1,622

Re: Every Camera has a SOUL (?)

The tortoise apparently "shelled out" for it...

Cheers, Steve

14-Oct-2011, 15:21 — #13
E. von Hoegh
Join Date: Feb 2006
Posts: 530

Re: Every Camera has a SOUL (?)

Well, lets see. Mahogany once was alive, as was the sheep the bellows leather came off. Then the textiles in the rest of the bellows, (all those silkworms!), trees the pulp for the pasteboard stiffeners came from....the hide glue came from the hide and hoofs of who-knows-what. I'd say my V8 has many souls bound up in it.

Anyone have contact info for a competent exorcist??

Exceptio probat Regulam.

14-Oct-2011, 15:23 — #14
codex0
Join Date: Jan 2011
Location: State College, PA
Posts: 18

Re: Every Camera has a SOUL (?)

It's an interesting enough camera, but the execution (craftsmanship) leaves something to be desired in my opinion.

The only other cameras I've seen in this vein are here : http://boyofblue.com/cameras.html

14-Oct-2011, 15:28 — #14
Honour & Crab
Join Date: Oct 2011
Posts: 3

Re: Every Camera has a SOUL (?)

Thank you everyone for a promising start.

cdholden: Most folks expect something functional when bidding on a "camera" from that section of auction items on Ebay.

This is true. Maybe its about time to rethink the general definition of what a "camera" actually is. But obviously ebay is the wrong place for such a discussion. you wouldnt want to know what kind of names we were called by the guy who actually bought the 2 cameras (officially of course).

frank: thank you for the idea with the skull cam, i put someone from the team on research. will keep you updated!

sanchi heuser: by using the general word of "soul" i meant the spirit, the energy that (in some beliefs) inhabits everything, be it stone, machine or human being. the source of power that holds everything together, keeps everything in flux . rereading your post, i realize you answered it yourself.
do you know the days when a camera does what it wants? when it wants you to know how it feels?

john: a frozen turkey pinhole? very interesting! also the idea of using a transitional material.

in the meantime, an update on the current test arrangement

16-Oct-2011, 11:29 — #19
Honour & Crab
Join Date: Oct 2011
Posts: 3

Re: Every Camera has a SOUL (?)

Thank you for all your comments!

We'd like to use the opportunity of this post to present our latest model, the BookCam (the Heritage and Technique Edition), specially designed to photograph through 2142 pages of essential Photohistory, Theory and Techniques: Roland Barthes, Susan Sontag, Günther Spitzing, Ansel Adams, Beaumont Newhall, the Hulton Getty Collection and last but not least, Peter Barry.

Also we were welcoming the honest critiques concerning craftsmanship. It was handed over to the technical department and we are happy to present a beautifully executed and flawless construction this time.

Further comments are very much appreciated.

16-Oct-2011, 12:16 — #20
jb7
joseph
Join Date: Jan 2007
Location: Dublin
Posts: 940

Re: Every Camera has a SOUL (?)

You can't be accused of producing a one-liner this time, I suppose-
or even that your cameras lack focus....
You could add another hefty volume on Macro Photography for the close up version-

16-Oct-2011, 12:56 — #21
Jim Michael
Join Date: Nov 2008
Location: Atlanta, GA
Posts: 452

Re: Every Camera has a SOUL (?)

I think this signals a new chapter in camera design.

Page 2 of 3 < 1 2 3 > »

Large Format Photography Forum

Welcome! You are currently viewing our board as a guest which allows you to view most discussions and gain limited access to other features. By joining you will have access to post topics, communicate privately with other members (PM), respond to polls, upload content and access other features. Registration is fast and simple so please, **join our community today**!

If you have any problems with the registration process or your account login, please contact us.

Large Format Photography Forum > LF Forums > Cameras & Camera Accessories
New digital 8x10

Cameras & Camera Accessories Large format cameras of all types and sizes.

Page 1 of 2 1 2 >

9-Oct-2011, 13:41 — #1
civich
Join Date: May 2008
Location: Luther, OK
Posts: 92

New digital 8x10 -

With keyboard!
http://www.ebay.com/itm/320772091991...84.m1438.l2649

9-Oct-2011, 15:56 — #3
ic-racer
Join Date: Feb 2007
Posts: 2,519

Re: New digital 8x10 -

Is that some kind of projector?

9-Oct-2011, 17:34 — #4
Nikola Dulgiarov
Join Date: Feb 2010
Location: Sevlievo, Bulgaria
Posts: 18

Re: New digital 8x10 -

from the description

This sweet piece, carefully set up to perfection is completely disfunctional
and ready to shoot.
A big catch
Check out my blog @ : http://nickdul.wordpress.com/

9-Oct-2011, 18:05 — #5
Jayabbas
Join Date: Jul 2011
Location: ??
Posts: ??

Re: New digital 8x10 -

Ha Ha He He -- got a huge laugh outta that one. Those must be high quality birch popsicle sticks. Time to rethink the future...

9-Oct-2011, 18:07 #6

jayabbas
Join Date: Jul 2011
Posts: 105

Re: New digital 8x10 -
My mistake - high quality bamboo sticks !!!

Quote

10-Oct-2011, 12:44 #7

ImSoNegative
Large Format Rocks
Join Date: Oct 2008
Location: Georgia
Posts: 233

Re: New digital 8x10 -
you can take the bamboo sticks off and you will have a bag bellows. Sweet deal lol

"WOW! Now thats a big camera. By the way, how many megapixels is that thing?"

Quote

10-Oct-2011, 19:50 #9

Sdrubansky
M
Join Date: Jul 2010
Location: Italy
Posts: 54

Re: New digital 8x10 -
Bidders should make sure there's an instruction manual included.

M

Quote

11-Oct-2011, 10:10 #11

turtlecam
Join Date: Oct 2011
Posts: 1

Re: New digital 8x10 -
you havent seen nothing yet, check out this one for sale on ebay as well

http://www.ebay.com:80/itm/ws/eBayIS...:L:LCA:US:1123

Quote

11-Oct-2011, 15:50 #14

ghe67
the nuts
Join Date: Jul 2011
Location: Torino
Posts: 53

Re: New digital 8x10 -
oh well, leather from Tanzania...this will change things!!

Quote

11-Oct-2011, 21:27 #16

Michael E
Join Date: Apr 2011
Location: Leipzig, Germany
Posts: 91

Re: New digital 8x10 -
Somebody actually bid on these things...

Quote

13-Oct-2011, 02:28 #17

Richard Rau
Join Date: Mar 2004
Location: MO
Posts: 23

Re: New digital 8x10 -
It looks too small to be an 8x10 to me. The back is a trapezoid. At best it's a 4x7x5!

Quote

Post Reply — Page 2 of 2 < 1 2

Großformatfotografie – Die Seite für Großformatfotografen • Thema anzeigen – RATLOS, bitte um Kritik/Kommentare/Tips

http://forum.grossformatfotografie.de/viewtopic.php?f=26&t=8704

Großformatfotografie – Die Seite für Großformatfotografen

das Forum rund um die Großformatfotografie

Abmelden [turtle] 0 neue Nachrichten — FAQ Suche Mitglieder Persönlicher Bereich

Dein letzter Besuch: 17.10.2011, 15:21 — Aktuelle Zeit: 18.10.2011, 22:52

Unbeantwortete Themen | Aktive Themen — Ungelesene Beiträge | Neue Beiträge | Eigene Beiträge

Foren-Übersicht » Fotogalerie » Kritikbereich — Alle Zeiten sind UTC + 1 Stunde [Sommerzeit]

RATLOS, bitte um Kritik/Kommentare/Tips

Moderator: Site-Admins

neues Thema — antworten — **Seite 1 von 1** [13 Beiträge]

Thema beobachten | Lesezeichen setzen | Druckansicht | Thema weiterempfehlen — Vorheriges Thema | Nächstes Thema

Autor — Nachricht

niconico79
offline
Registriert: 10.12.2010, 22:34
Beiträge: 2

Betreff des Beitrags: RATLOS, bitte um Kritik/Kommentare/Tips — **Verfasst:** 09.10.2011, 18:13

Hallo liebe Grossformatfreunde,

ich habe vor ein paar Tagen mit meiner 8x10 Eigenkonstruktion ein neues Bild gemacht. Ich bin ziemlich ratlos, weil es nicht so aussieht wie ich es mir vorgestellt hatte . Ich wollte eine Szene fotografieren, die träumerisch und romantisch wirkt. Der Traum des Klavierspielers soll es heissen. Hat jemand von euch einen Kommentar (wie gefällt euch das Bild?) oder Tips und Vorschläge bezüglich Technik, Ausschnitt, Licht, Komposition?
Bin für jeden Post dankbar!
Liebe Grüsse,
Nico

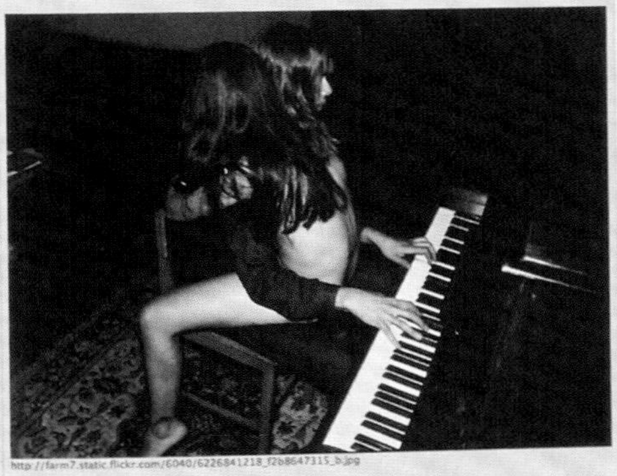

http://farm7.static.flickr.com/6040/6226841218_f2b8647315_b.jpg

Fotografiert mit einer 8x10 Eigenbau, Schneider Symmar S 240mm, Metz CT45
auf Ilford HP5, Schalenentwicklung mit Kodak D76

Nach oben — Profil PN E-Mail — zitieren

johnars
offline
Registriert: 28.04.2005, 00:30
Beiträge: 2663
Wohnort: Zentralschweiz nähe Luzern

Betreff des Beitrags: Re: RATLOS, bitte um Kritik/Kommentare/Tips — **Verfasst:** 09.10.2011, 18:36

Das Licht ist nicht gerade der Bringer hier, einfach frontal draufblitzen ergibt selten spannendes Licht! Zudem würde ich es glaub im Hochformat ablichten!

Gruss Armin

____
" You push the button and we do the rest."
Kodak Werbespruch!
Today
"You push the button and the pixels do the rest"

Nach oben — Profil PN — zitieren

EOTS
online
Registriert: 06.02.2011, 18:42
Beiträge: 147
Wohnort: Linz, Österreich

Betreff des Beitrags: Re: RATLOS, bitte um Kritik/Kommentare/Tips — **Verfasst:** 09.10.2011, 18:39

Weil ich mich gerade mit Soft Focus Optiken auseinandersetze,
Rodenstock Imagon oder ähnliches für träumerischen, leicht surrealen Look?

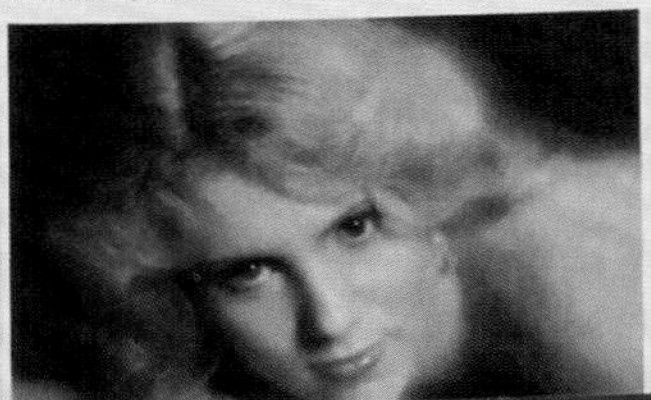

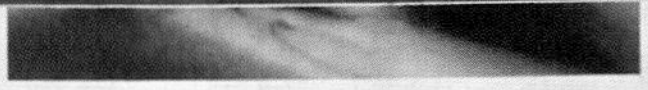

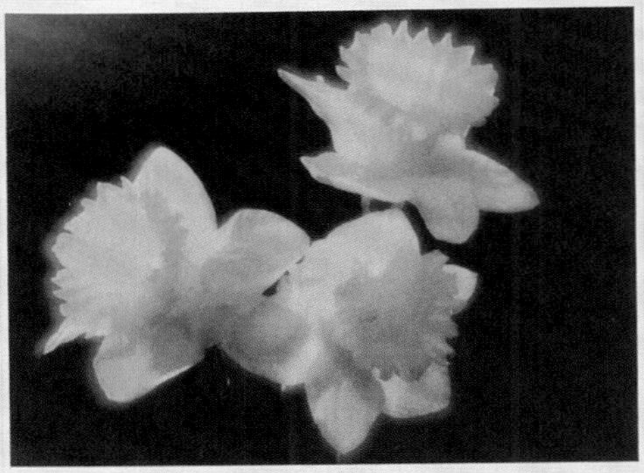

Die Ausleuchtung gefällt mir nicht so, recht viel Schatten, und harte Reflexe?
Da könnte man sicher noch viel machen...
Ist das ein einzelner frontaler Blitz?

____
Martin Jan Köhler
http://www.flickr.com/photos/martinjankoehler

Nach oben — Profil PN — zitieren

Unes
offline
Registriert: 09.11.2003, 18:59
Beiträge: 820
Wohnort: Essingen/Württ.

Betreff des Beitrags: Re: RATLOS, bitte um Kritik/Kommentare/Tips — **Verfasst:** 09.10.2011, 19:11

Also ich muss sagen mir gefällts. Wie Araki in seiner Frühphase in den Tokioter Bordellen. Hart und ehrlich. Ich würde es ins Quadrat setzen. Damit wäre der auf linken Seite dann auch nicht mehr im Bild und rechts nicht soviel von dem dunklen Klavier. Also vergiss Hamilton, vertrau Araki und mach weiter so.

Gruss Sven.

____
www.so-froehlich.de

Nach oben — Profil PN E-Mail — zitieren

turtle
online
Registriert: 09.10.2011, 17:15
Beiträge: 2

Betreff des Beitrags: Re: RATLOS, bitte um Kritik/Kommentare/Tips — **Verfasst:** 09.10.2011, 19:38

Ein Hallo an alle Fotofreunde, ich bin ja ganz neu hier im Forum.

Ich Finde Deine Idee recht originell, und auch das die haare von den beiden so ineinader verschmelzen finde ich toll.
Kannst Du noch einiges mehr zur Kamera sagen die Du selber gebaut hast sagen?

Nach oben — Profil PN E-Mail — zitieren

niconico79
offline
Registriert: 10.12.2010, 22:34
Beiträge: 2

Betreff des Beitrags: Re: RATLOS, bitte um Kritik/Kommentare/Tips — **Verfasst:** 10.10.2011, 18:39

DANKE FÜR EURE KOMMENTARE.
JA, es ist ein einzelner Frontal Blitz, viel mehr hab ich leider nicht im Sortiment.
Soft Aesthetik ist schon ziemlich experimentell, da muss ich mich erst mal rantasten.

Hier das Bild der Kamera, mit der ich das Bild fotografiert habe.
Sie braucht noch etwas Liebe, aber funktioniert nicht schlecht.
Hier wird sie gerade im Aussenbereich installiert.

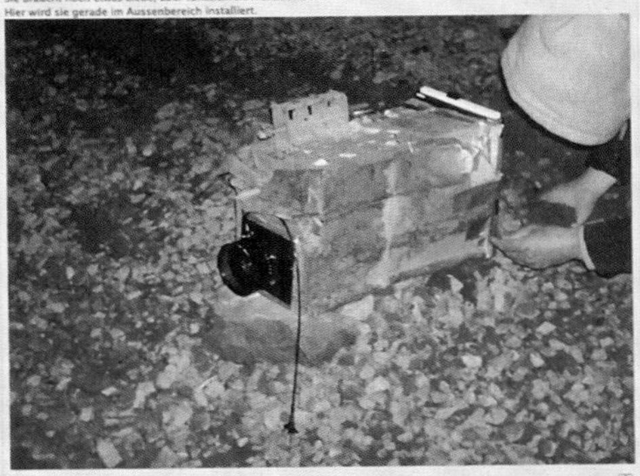

Nach oben — Profil PN E-Mail — zitieren

Cartochrom
offline
Registriert: 26.12.2007, 23:29
Beiträge: 430
Wohnort: Weil am Rhein

Betreff des Beitrags: Re: RATLOS, bitte um Kritik/Kommentare/Tips — **Verfasst:** 10.10.2011, 20:20

Ähm,

fallen da keine Rostkrümmel auf den Film, wenn du den Schieber ziehst?

Nach oben — Profil PN E-Mail — zitieren

turtle
online
Registriert: 09.10.2011, 17:15
Beiträge: 2

Betreff des Beitrags: Re: RATLOS, bitte um Kritik/Kommentare/Tips — **Verfasst:** 11.10.2011, 09:30

Also einen Schönheitswettbewerb gewinnt die auf jedenfall nicht, eigenartiges Teil.

Aber ja, so lange du bilder damit machen kannst, warum nicht.

Nach oben — Profil PN E-Mail — zitieren

klausesser
offline
Benutzeravatar
Registriert: 02.01.2007, 15:18
Beiträge: 3641
Wohnort: Düsseldorf

Betreff des Beitrags: Re: RATLOS, bitte um Kritik/Kommentare/Tips — **Verfasst:** 11.10.2011, 17:40

[quote="niconico79"]
Sie braucht noch etwas Liebe, aber funktioniert nicht schlecht.
Hier wird sie gerade im Aussenbereich installiert.

Geil! Solange es fotografiert isses ´ne Kamera!

Gruss, Klaus

Nach oben — Profil PN E-Mail — zitieren

henningr
offline
Registriert: 03.09.2008, 00:05
Beiträge: 126
Wohnort: Südbayern

Betreff des Beitrags: Re: RATLOS, bitte um Kritik/Kommentare/Tips — **Verfasst:** 12.10.2011, 08:33

Hallo Nico,

einen Traum mit hoher Bildschärfe – das find ich schon bei Hitchcock super.
Das Schlaglicht ist es nicht, was hier schwierig ist. Das ist o.k.

Klavierspieler sind immer schwierig mit dem hohen Kasten vor dem Gesicht: Entweder die Tasten + Spielerrücken oder irgendwie schräg rein.

Hier finde ich könnte der Spieler einen kleinen Tuk männlicher und der nackte Rücken etwas weniger wie ein dicker Bauch aussehen. (Zumindest, wenn man das nur als Ausschnitt nimmt). Vielleicht weniger gekrümmt? oder ein anderes Instrument? Vielleicht muss das Mädel gar nicht nackt sein?
Oder den Knaben weniger lässig, mehr gerade und konzentrierter sitzend und den Hintern des Mädels etwas weiter Richtung Klavier damit es nicht so hängt?

Die Haarvermischung gefällt mir.

Das sind aber nur so Gedanken von mir.

Die Kamera ist jedenfalls nicht ohne Schärfe, wie man an den Kratzern an deiner Hand sieht!

Gruss Henning

Nach oben — Profil PN E-Mail — zitieren

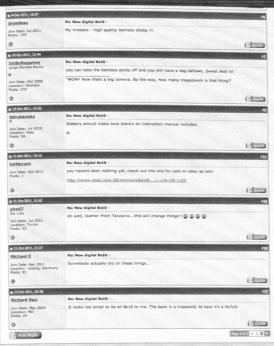

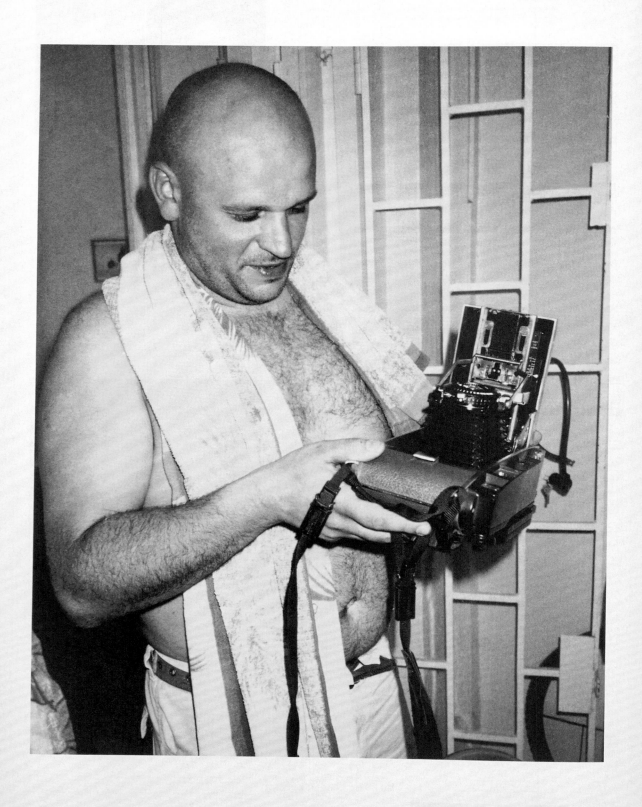

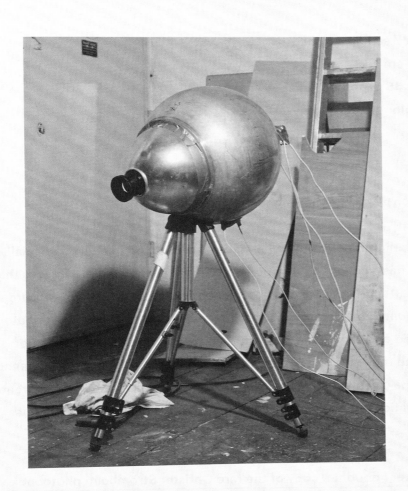

Title: Handicraft

Artist: Thomas Mailaender

Designer: Myriam Barchechat

Editor: Thomas Mailaender

Imprint: Fun Archive Publications

Printer: off7passion, Nîmes, France

Publication date and place: June 2010 / Paris, France

Edition: 500

Format and binding: softcover / saddle stitched

Size: 7 7/8 x 10 5/8 in. (20 x 27 cm)

Number of pages and images: 36 pages / 23 images

Type of printing and paper: color offset / glossy

Retail price: 15 EUR / 17 USD

Cost per unit: $

Book soundtrack: "Big Girls Don't Cry" by Mr. Pregnant

Thomas Mailaender is a French multimedia artist who makes use of found imagery, especially photographs found online. He has a collection of around eleven thousand amateur images that he refers to as his "Fun Archive," and with each new project he finds new, ever-more-absurd ways to exploit the material. *Handicraft* details ceramics made by the artist, each with photographs from the archive worked into them. The book shifts between the documentation of material pieces he's created and related pictures from the archive that inspired them. Mailaender makes a lot of books. Though he often takes on the role of the mischievous prankster to create his humorous or bizarre publications, they nearly always deliver a message about typologies or sociological patterns.

This book was self-financed after I bought a copy of the rare Christer Strömholm photobook *Poste Restante* (inscribed by Strömholm to his best friend) at a flea market for 8 euros, and sold it for 2,500 euros at the Pierre Bergé auction house. —Thomas Mailaender

HANDI-CRAFT

THOMAS MAILAENDER

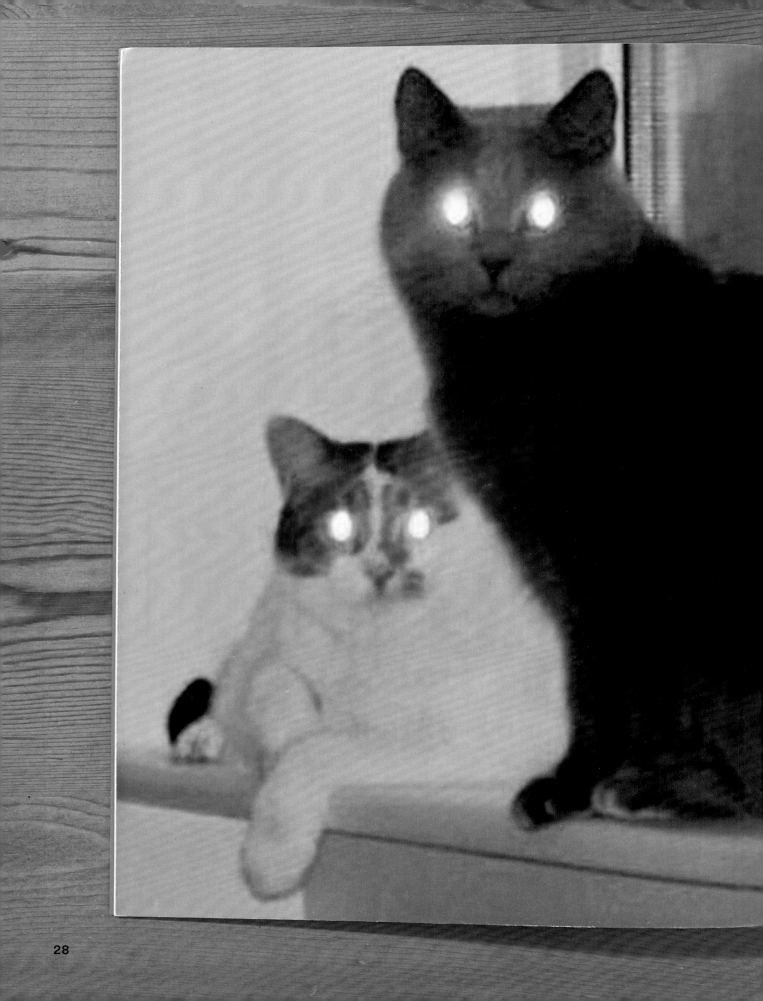

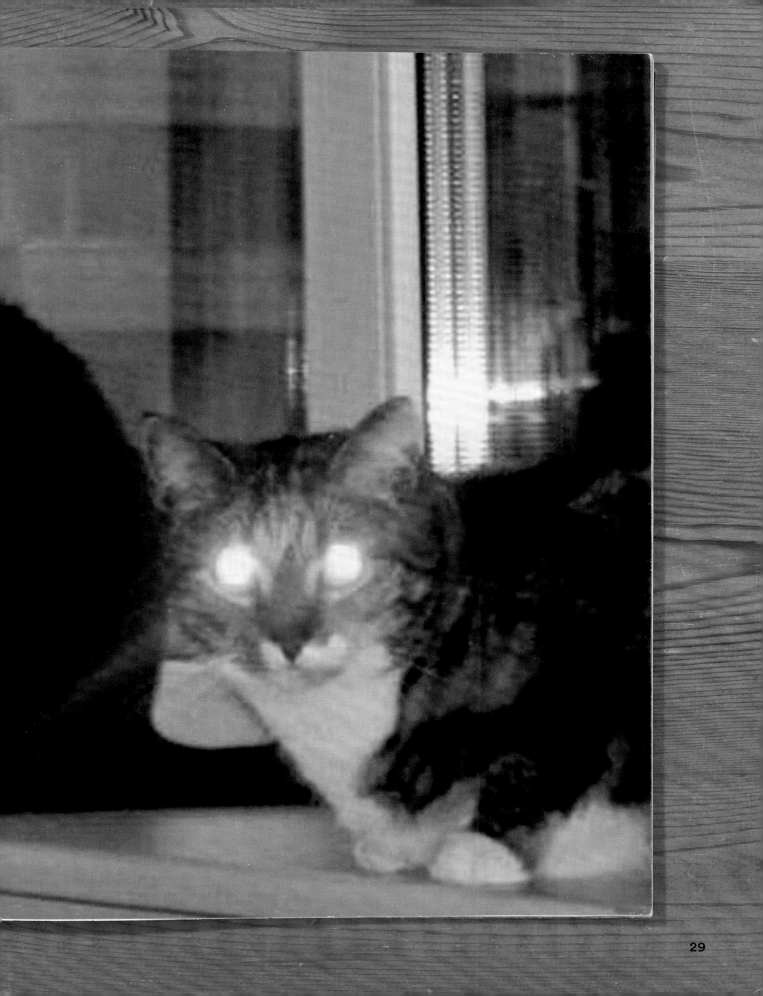

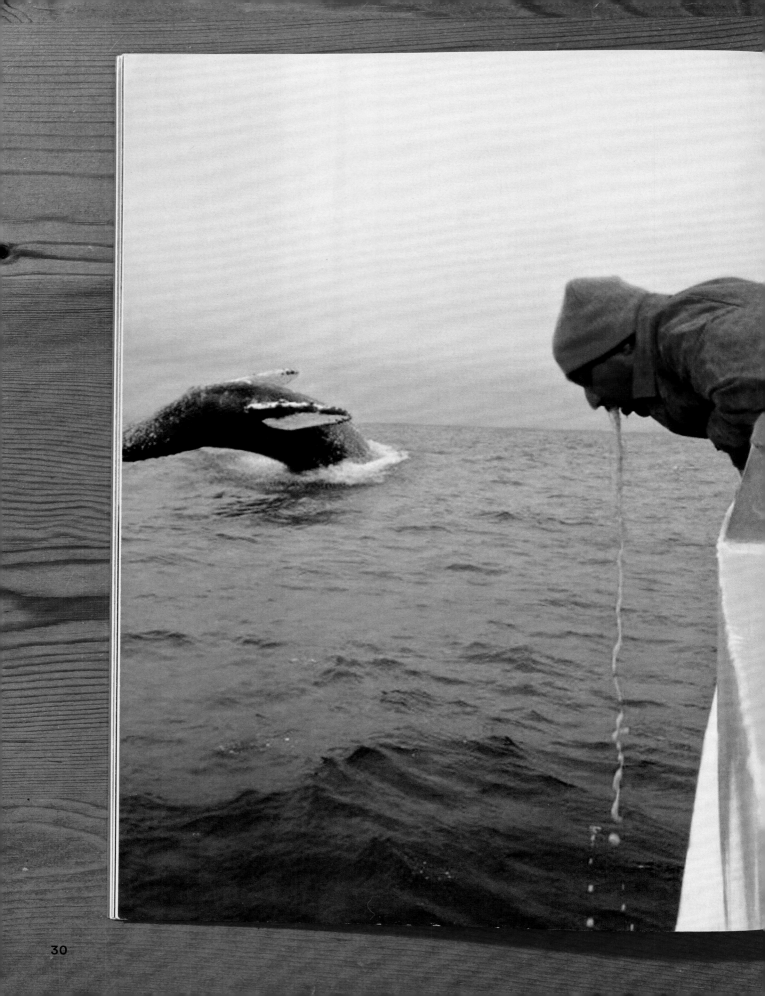

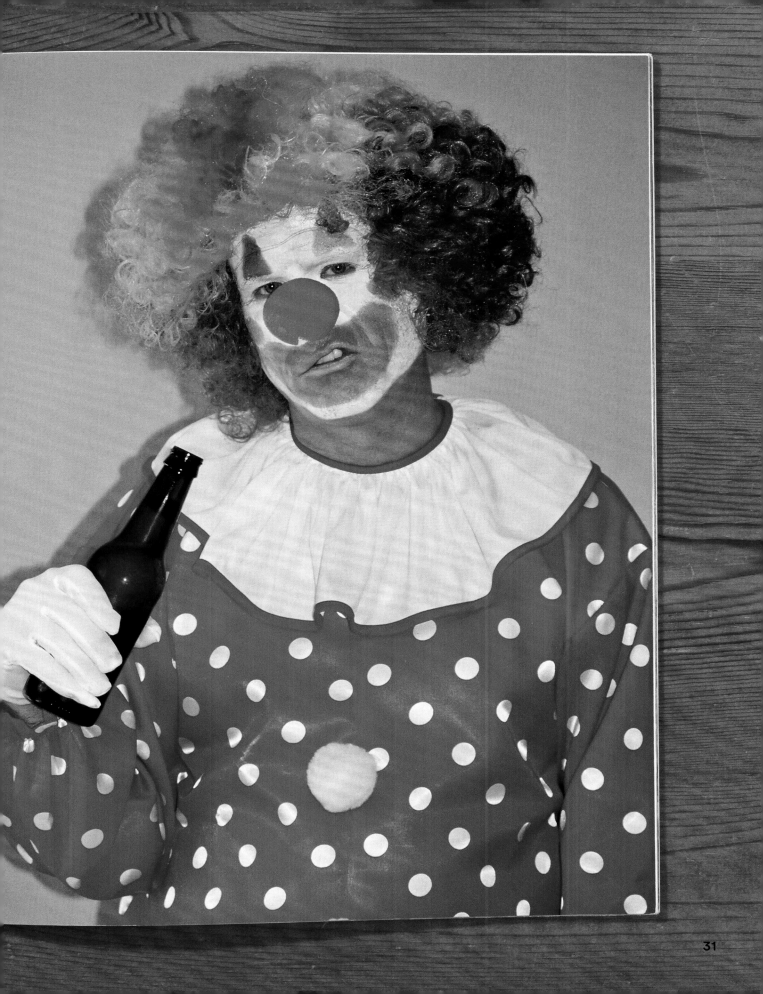

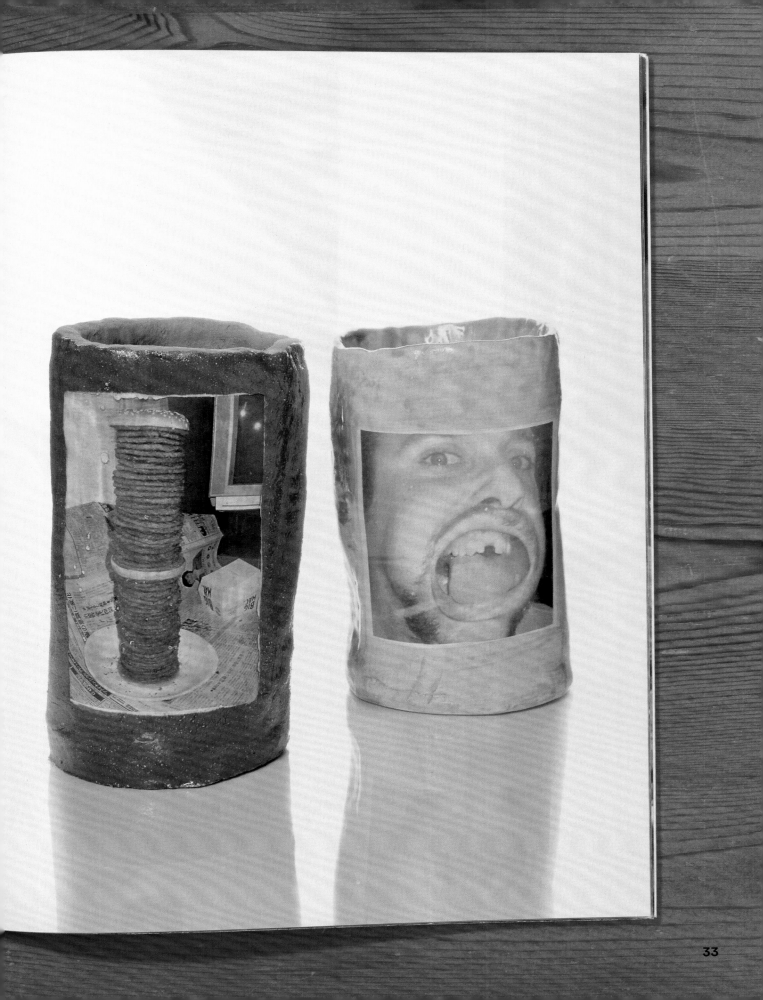

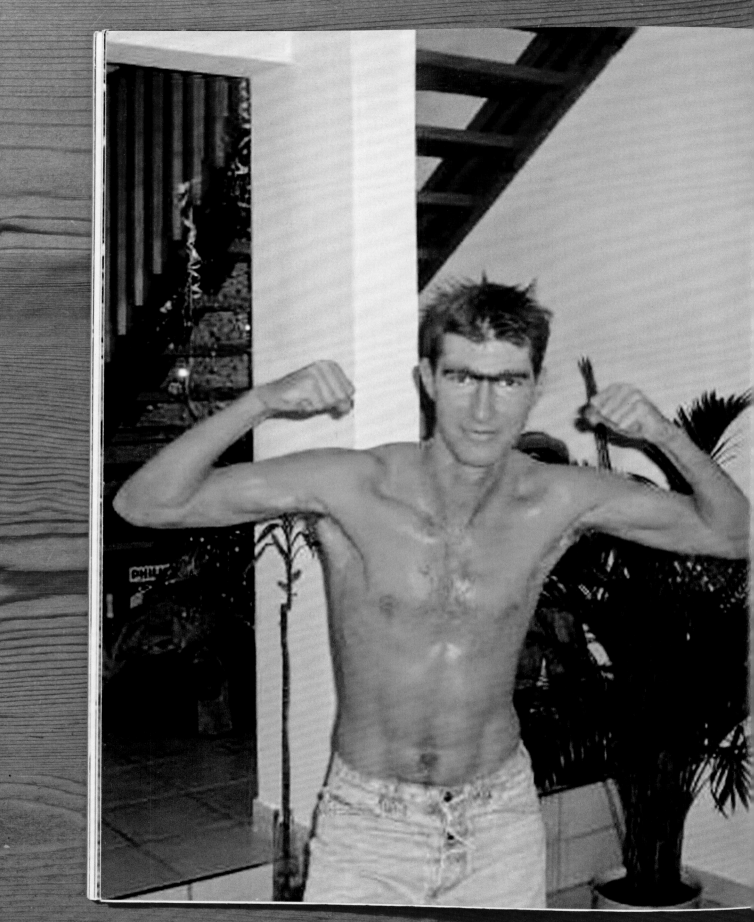

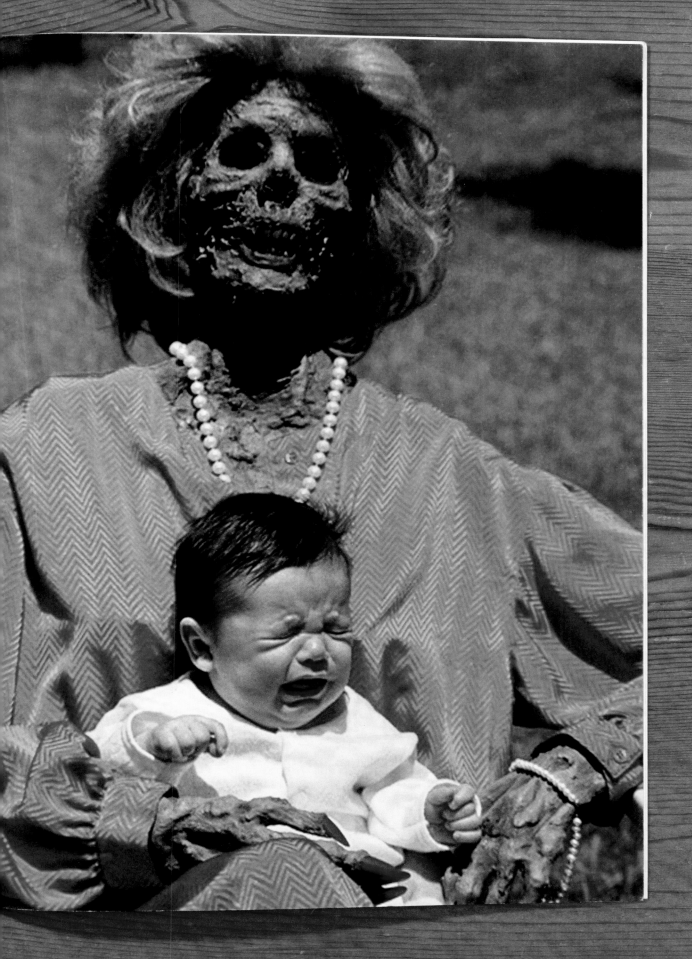

Title: Nude

Artist: Ren Hang

Designer: Ren Hang

Editor: Ren Hang

Imprint: none

Printer: Unknown, Shenzhen, China

Publication date and place: 2012 / China

Edition: 500

Format and binding: hardcover / case bound

Size: 4 1/4 x 6 in. (10.7 x 15.2 cm)

Number of pages and images: 94 pages / 92 images

Type of printing and paper: offset / unknown

Retail price: 29 USD / 180 RMB

Cost per unit: unknown

Although it is not Ren Hang's first book, *Nude* was perhaps the first to cross borders in a significant way and begin finding an international audience for his work. Self-published and printed at a friendly print shop which agreed to work on it afterhours, the book is distinctly out-of-bounds of Chinese content standards, which prohibit anything that violates "public morality" or that is detrimental to the "physical and mental health of youth and young people." The book offers a series of nudes that are both playful and provocative; each image is presented full-bleed and suggestively paired. Bodies are often interwined with groups of other bodies, as well as props ranging from chickens to knives, plastic dinosaurs, hot-dog buns, and strawberries—strategically placed, but hiding nothing.

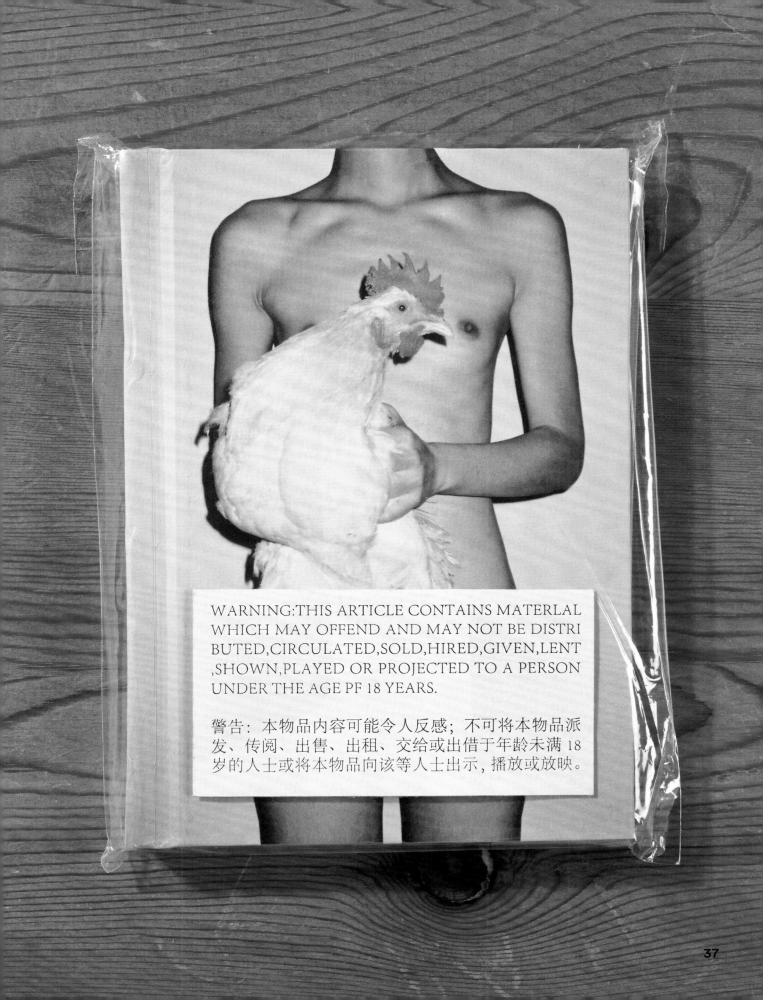

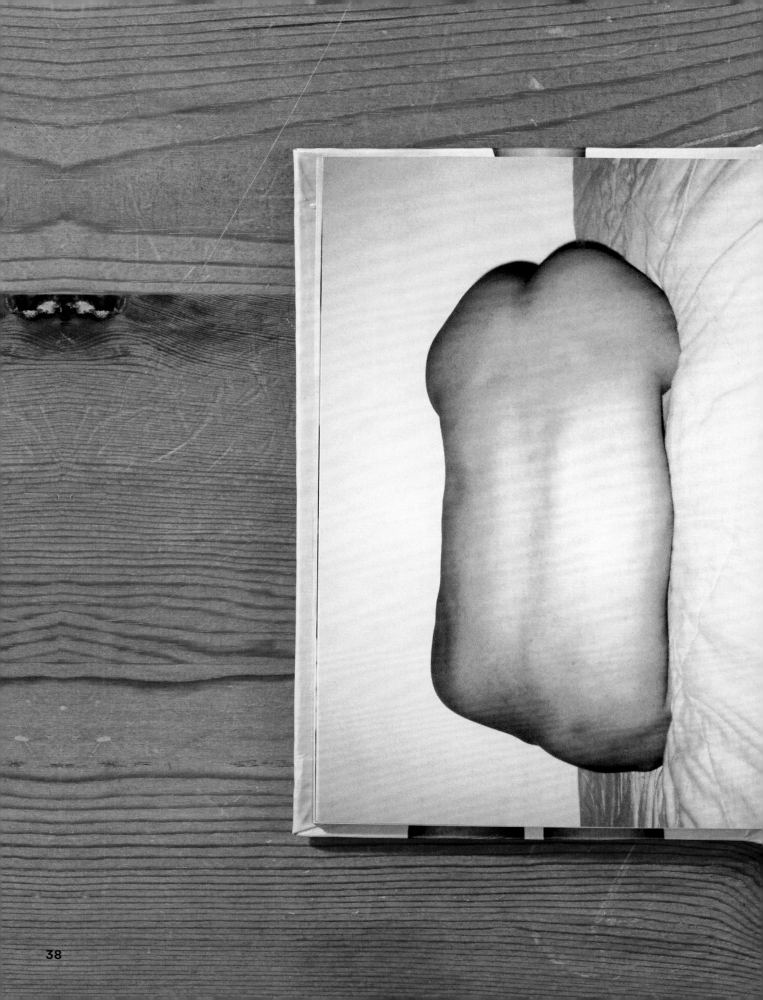

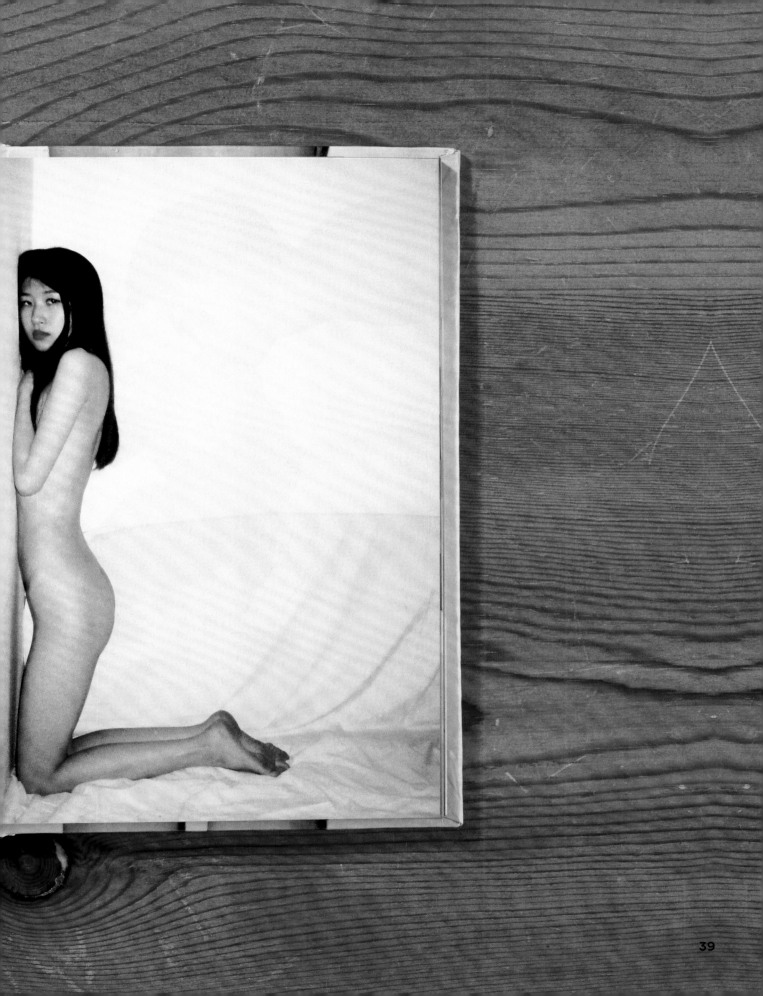

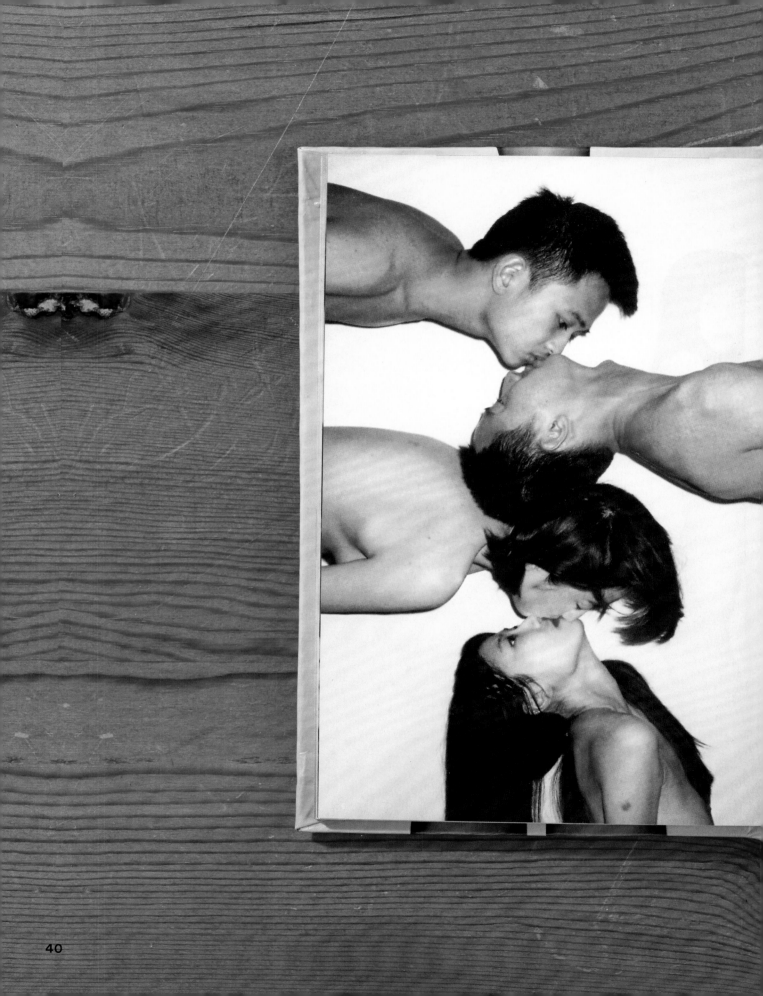

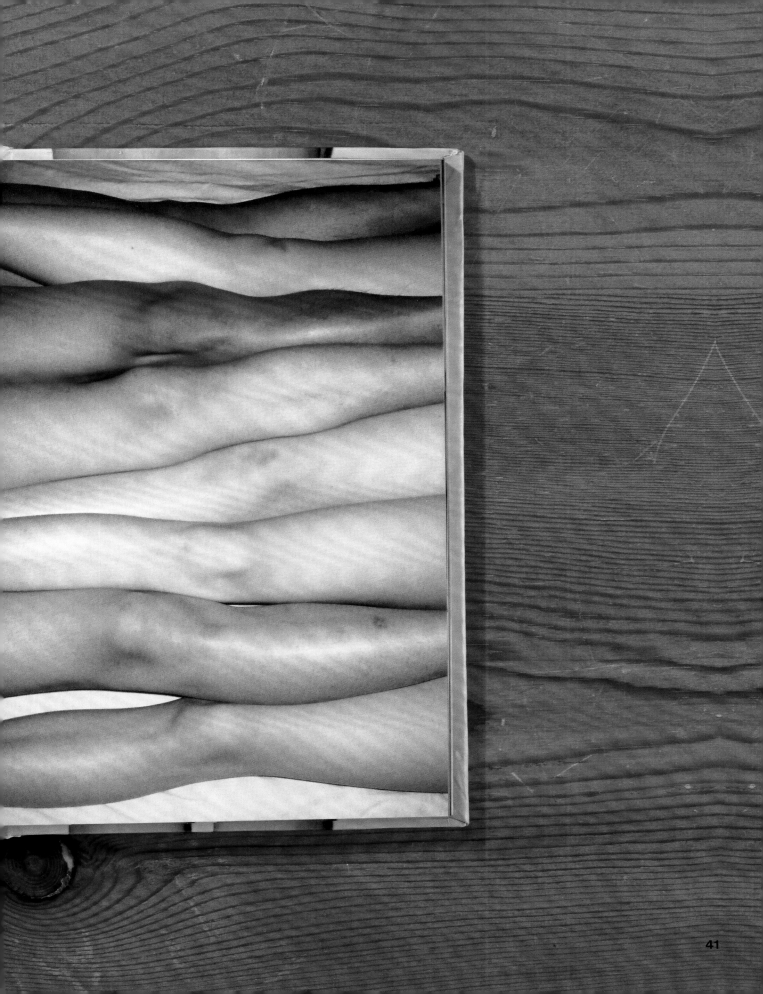

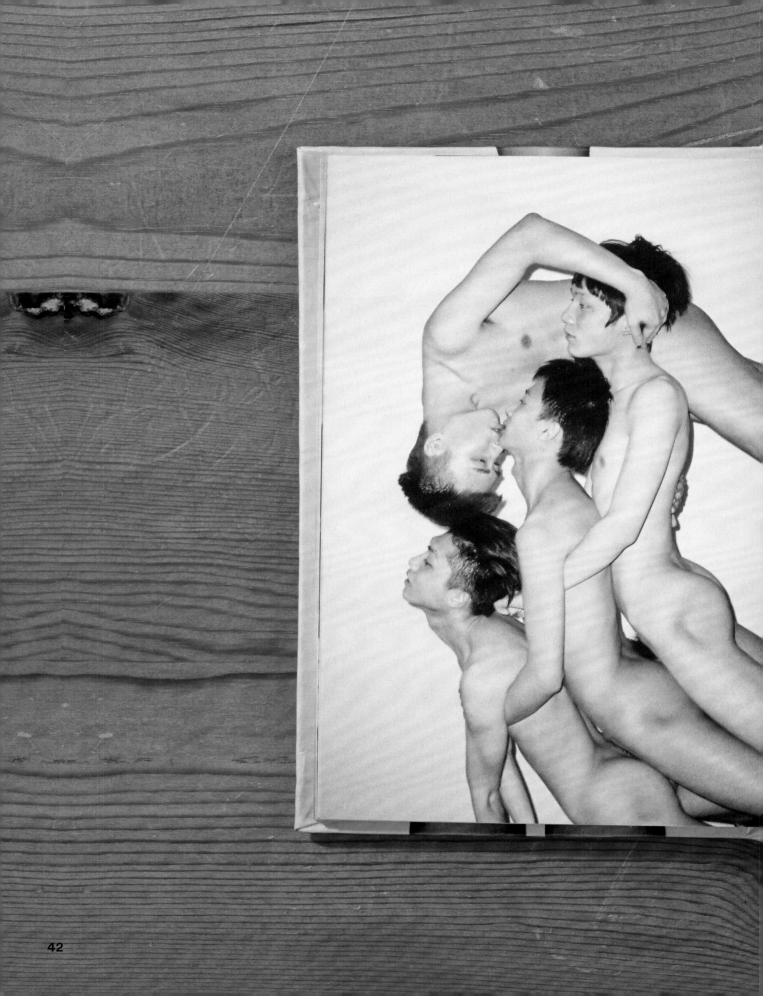

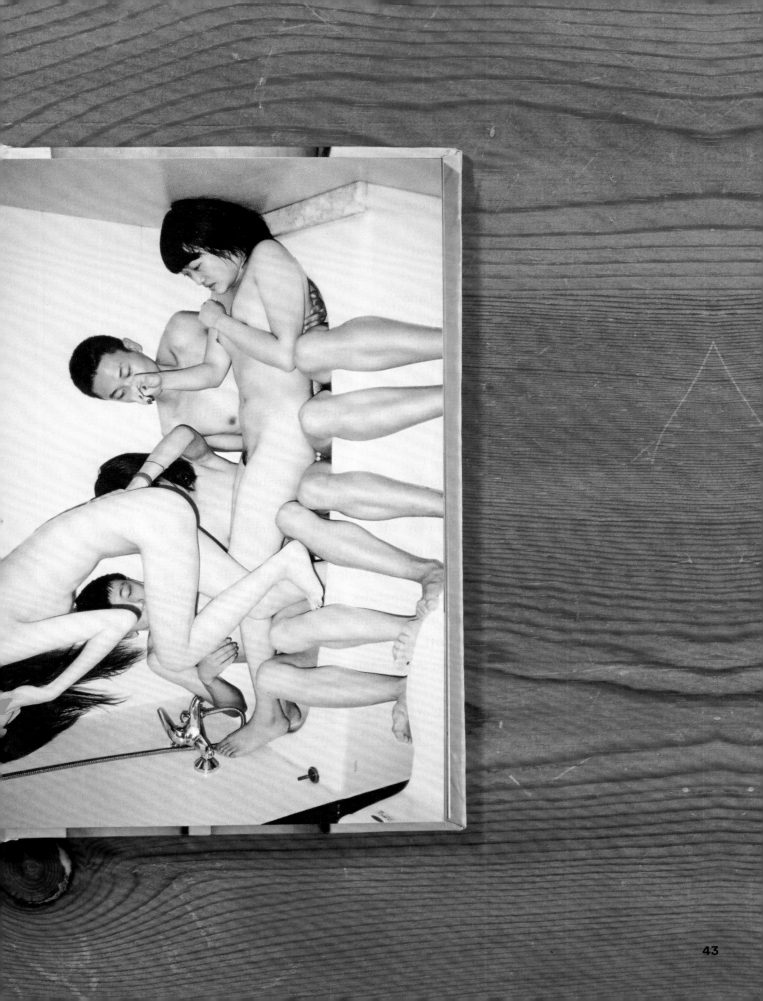

Title: Color Cocktail

Artist: Isabelle Wenzel

Designer: Isabelle Wenzel

Editor: Isabelle Wenzel

Imprint: none

Printer: Xerox color photocopier

Publication date and place: May 2011 / Amsterdam, the Netherlands

Edition: 30

Format and binding: softcover / perfect bound

Size: 8 1/4 x 11 6/8 in. (21 x 29.7 cm)

Number of pages and images: 44 pages / 41 images

Type of printing and paper: color photocopy / white and colored paper, 100gsm

Retail price: 35 EUR / 39 USD

Cost per unit: $

Book soundtrack: The buzzing of the copier machine and people passing by in the lobby of Gerrit Rietveld Academie, Amsterdam

Isabelle Wenzel makes work that surveys the human body as a malleable object, often photographing herself or a model contorting on surreal sets. *Color Cocktail* was shot mainly in Wenzel's studio in Amsterdam and in her native Germany, and visualizes a dream she had about flying and bodies turning into machines. Using a remote shutter release with her camera, she was able to position herself in the frame and use her body as a sculpture. She also built rockets and other flying objects which she photographed and incorporated into the narrative, alongside research material and images from her archive. The book accompanied an exhibition of Wenzel's work at Gerhard Hofland Gallery, Amsterdam, in 2011, and was made from work prints on a photocopier, then hand-bound into an edition of thirty on the same day.

I like to work in the instant, so I took a stack of prints and did the edit for this book while I made the copies. I think it can be very refreshing to be spontaneous—to trust one's inner logic.
—Isabelle Wenzel

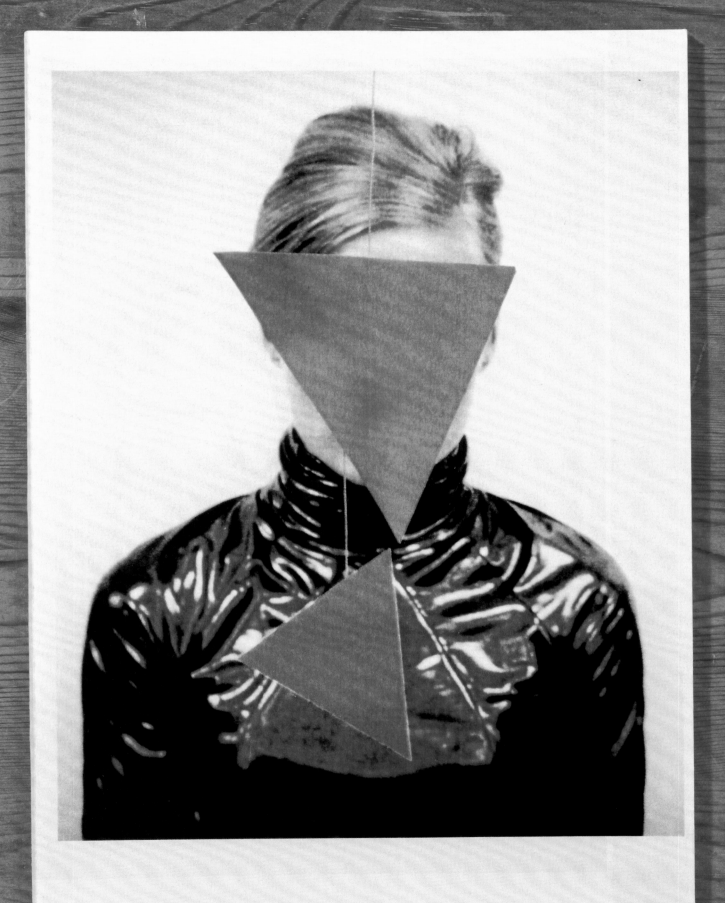

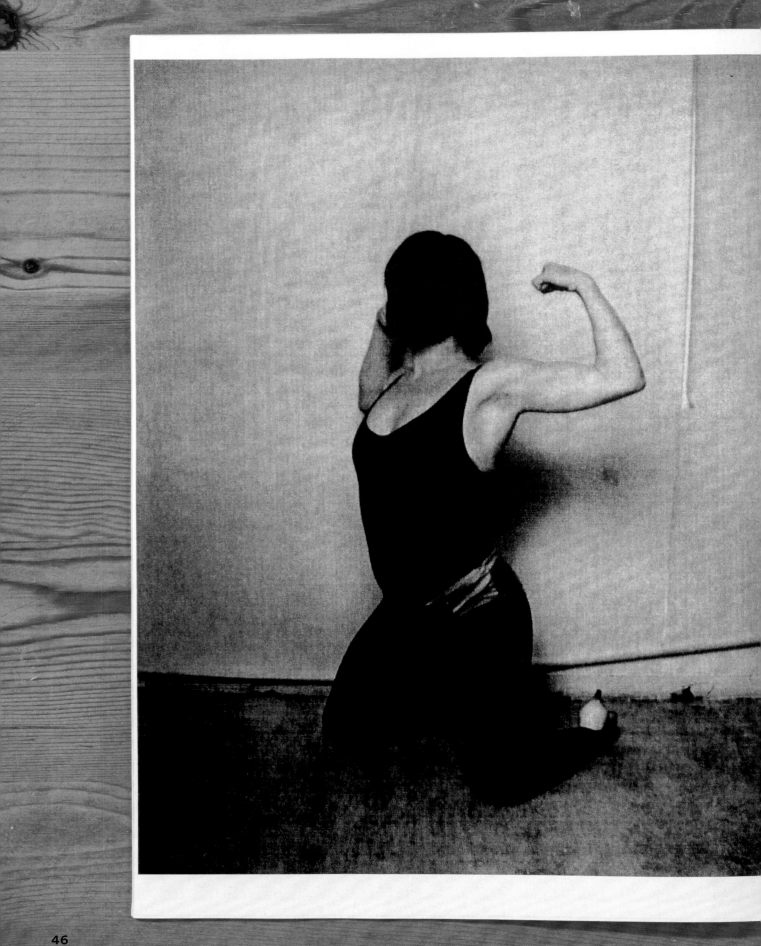

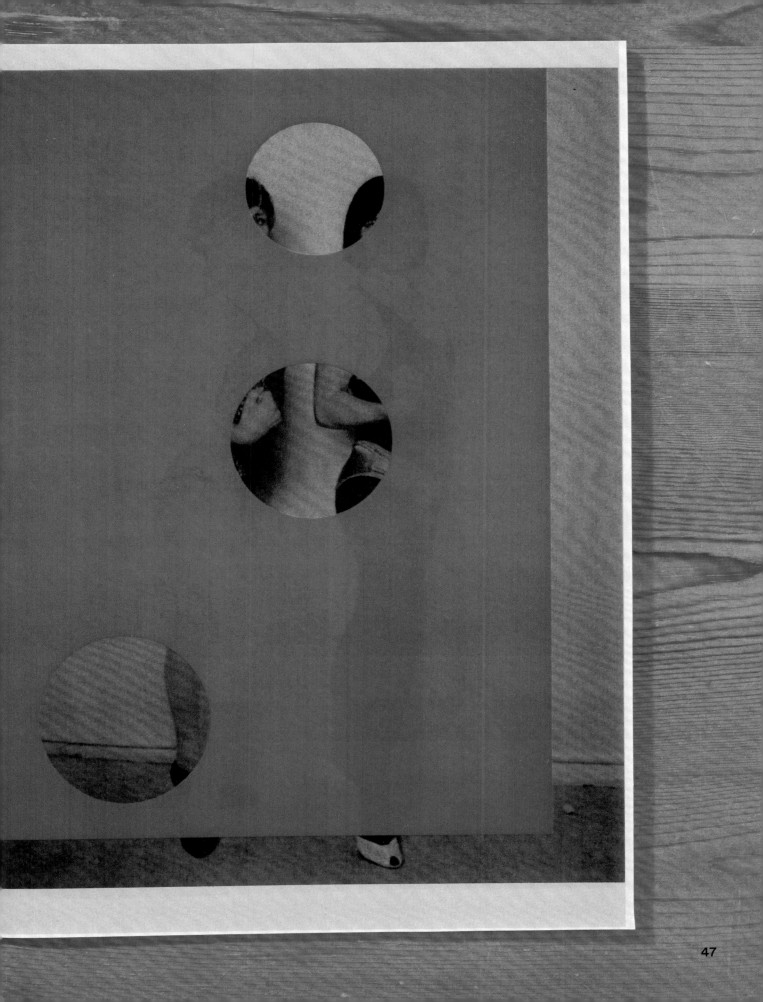

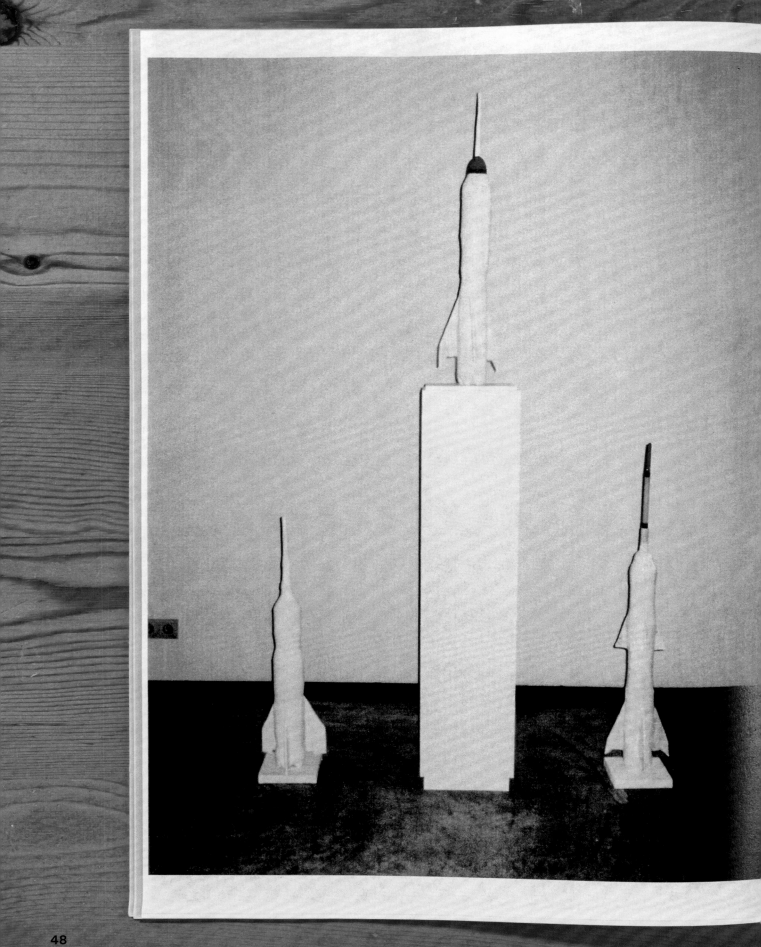

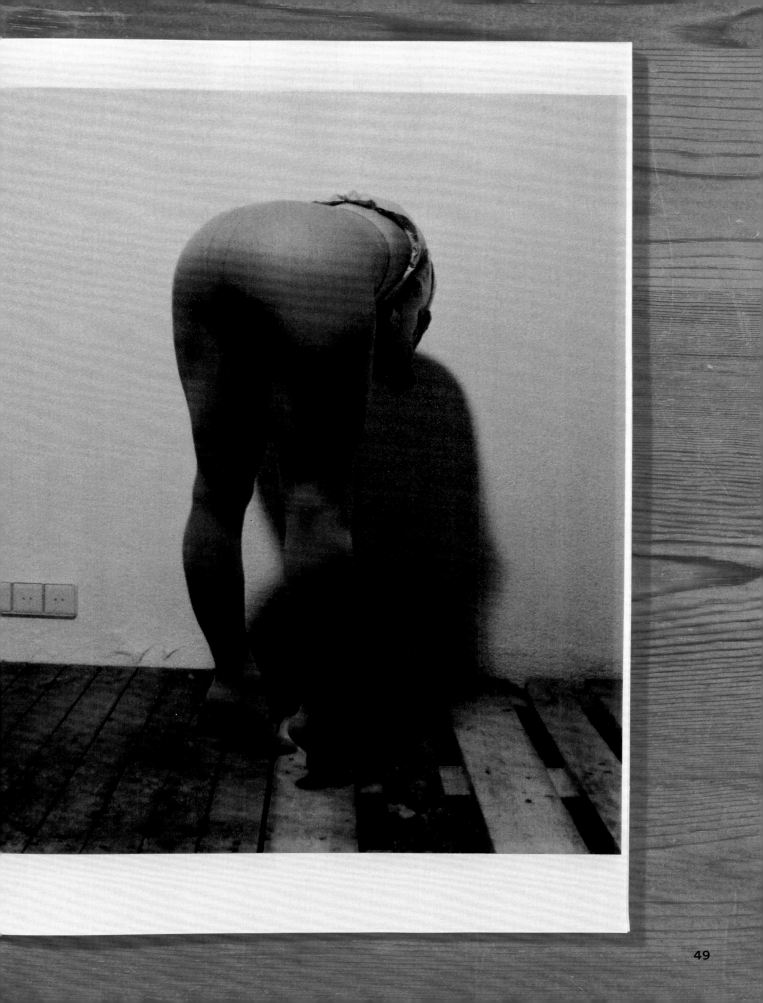

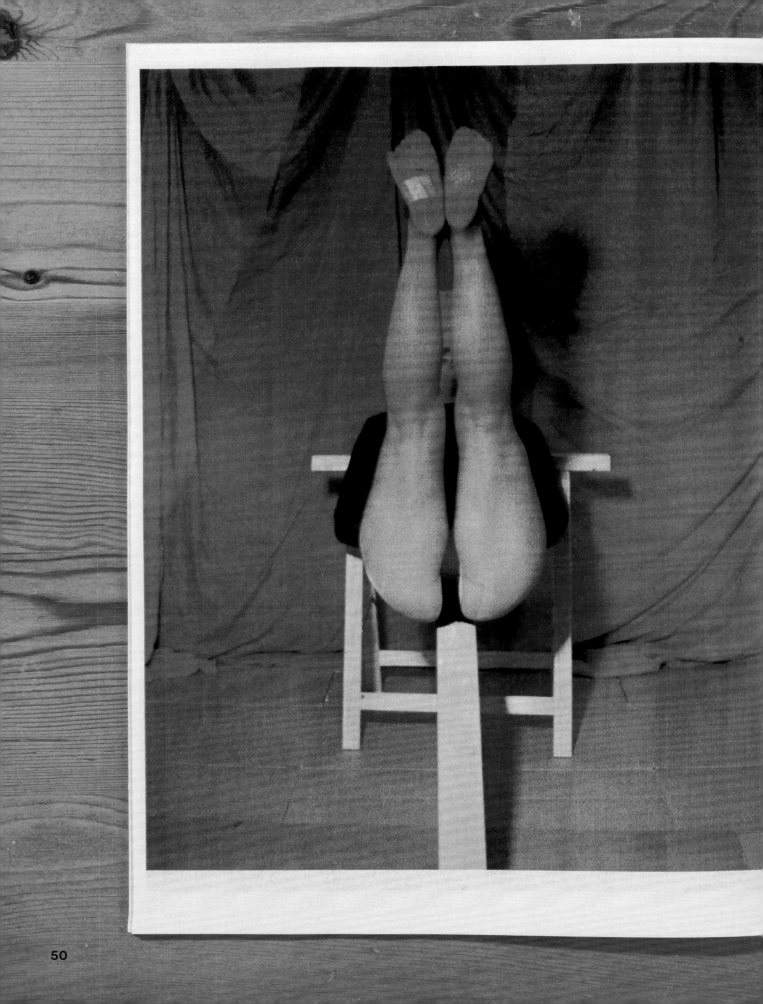

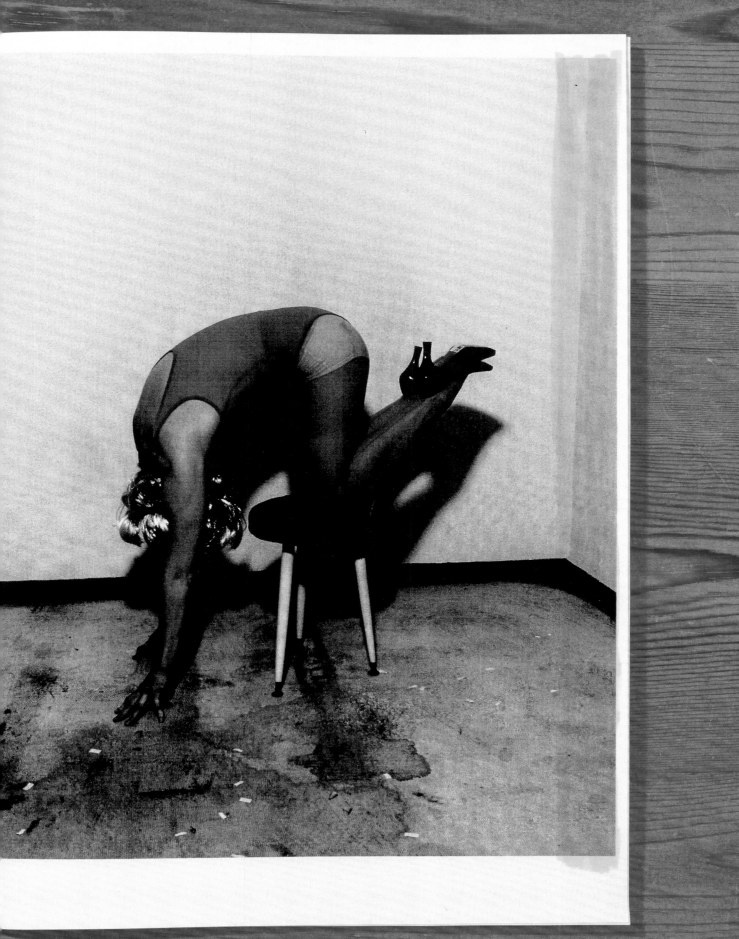

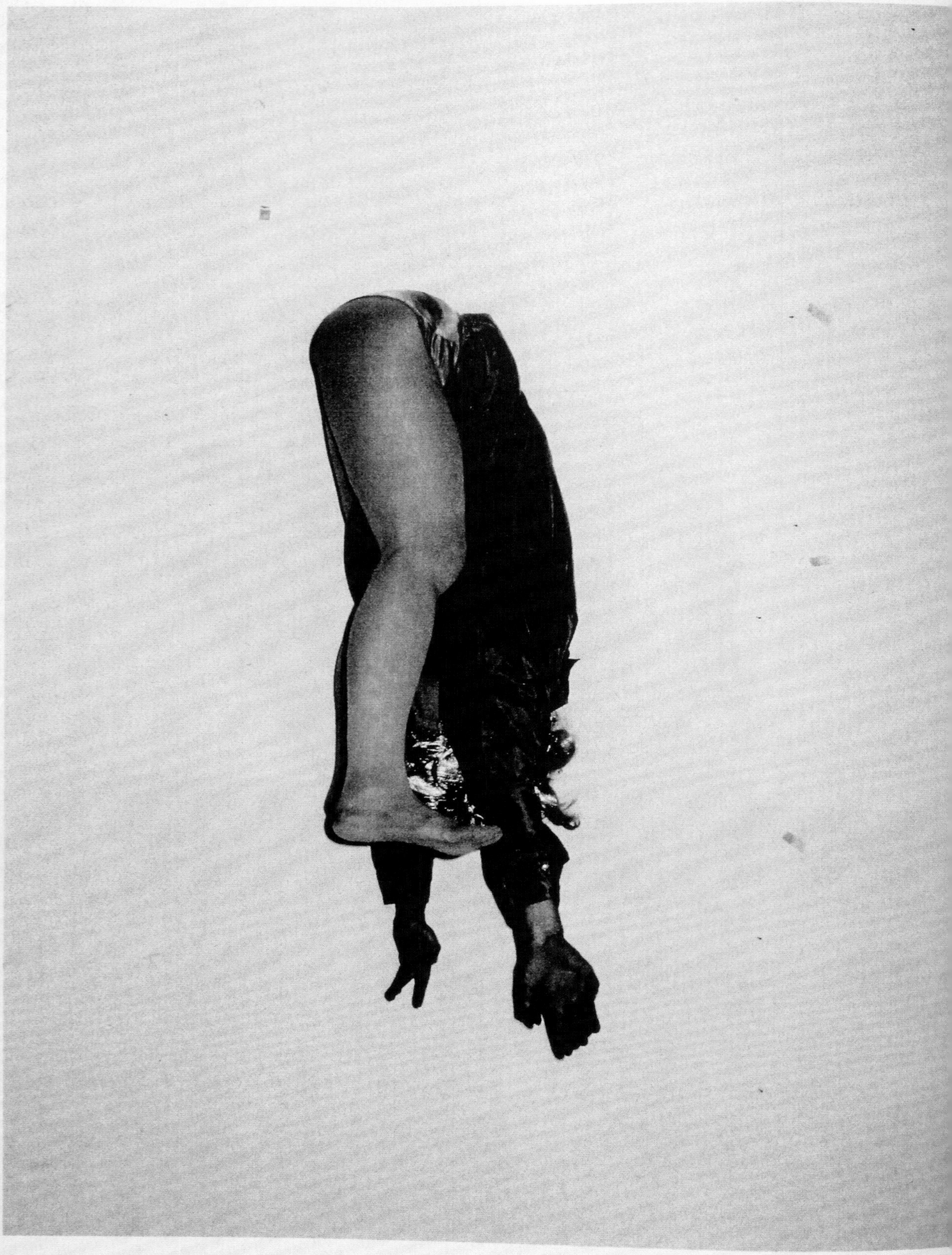

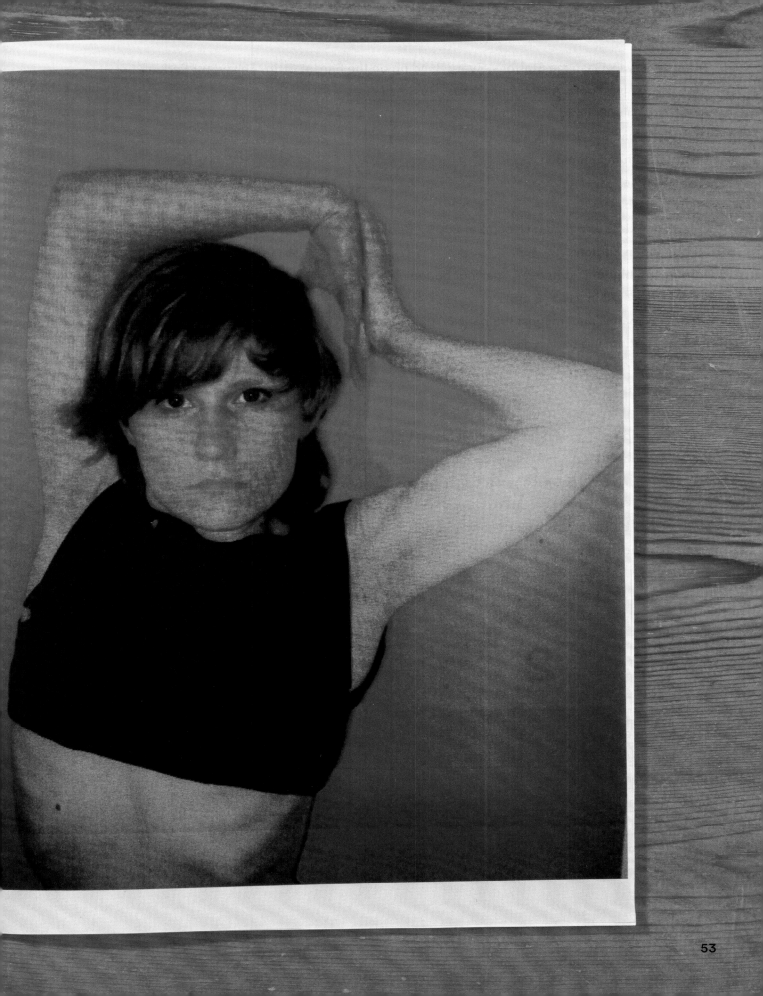

Title: Twentysix Gasoline Stations, Every Building on the Sunset Strip, Thirtyfour Parking Lots, Nine Swimming Pools, A Few Palm Trees, No Small Fires

Artist: Joachim Schmid

Designer: Joachim Schmid

Editor: Joachim Schmid

Imprint: none

Printer: Blurb

Publication date and place: December 2009 / Berlin, Germany

Edition: open edition

Format and binding: softcover / perfect bound

Size: 7 1/8 x 7 1/8 in. (18 x 18 cm)

Number of pages and images: 198 pages / 113 images

Type of printing and paper: digital / semi-matte

Retail price: 40 EUR / 45 USD

Cost per unit: $$$$

Archiving and selling his books through his website, German artist Joachim Schmid has produced around 180 publications using mostly found photographs to observe and comment on the way we live. *Twentysix Gasoline Stations*, *Every Building on the Sunset Strip...* is a playful homage to Ed Ruscha, who is credited with reinventing the artist book in the 1960s. Schmid's book features full-bleed aerial shots of car parks and highway interchanges collected from Google Earth. Similarly to Ruscha, who embraced the mechanics of photographic reproduction, Schmid engages with print-on-demand services, bringing Ruscha's ideas up to date. He also founded Artists' Book Cooperative, a collective of artists working with on-demand books, in 2009, although he is no longer part of it.

The arrival of print-on-demand providers such as Blurb or Lulu had a major impact. It meant the end of prohibitive cost barriers, as artists were able to make books in small editions. The result was a plethora of books and a very playful approach to bookmaking—but the limited choice of formats, paper, and binding options were disenchanting, and the prices per copy even more so. After a while all the books looked the same, and all of them were too expensive to sell. When I started working with these companies I was aware I was signing a pact with the devil, but then the devil turned out to be even worse than I expected. Fortunately, digital printing has become a viable option with local printers, making it easy to find a printer that's more suitable than any of the international top dogs. —Joachim Schmid

Joachim Schmid

Twentysix Gasoline Stations,
Every Building on the Sunset Strip,
Thirtyfour Parking Lots,
Nine Swimming Pools,
A Few Palm Trees,
No Small Fires

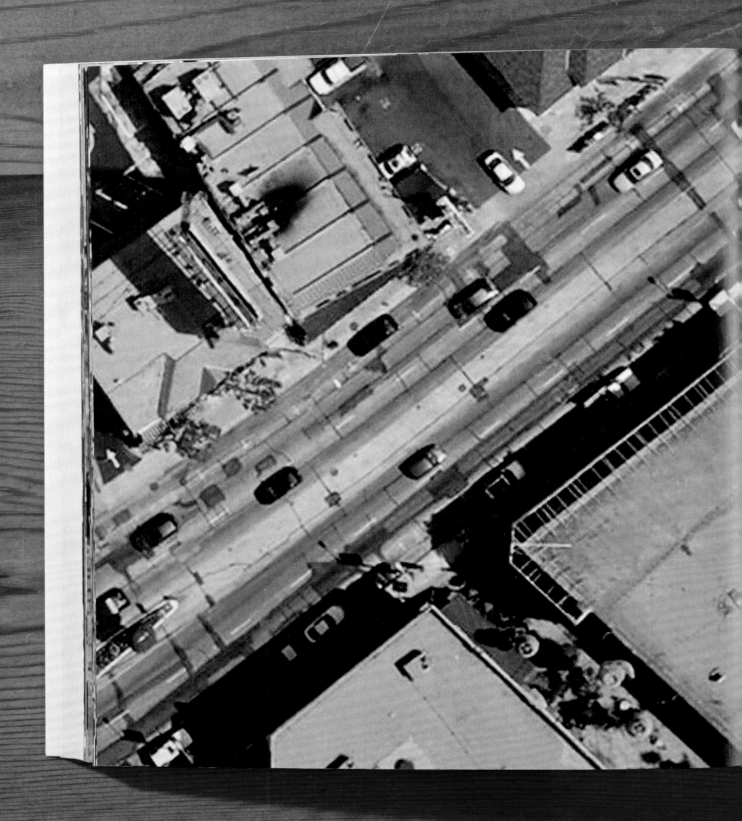

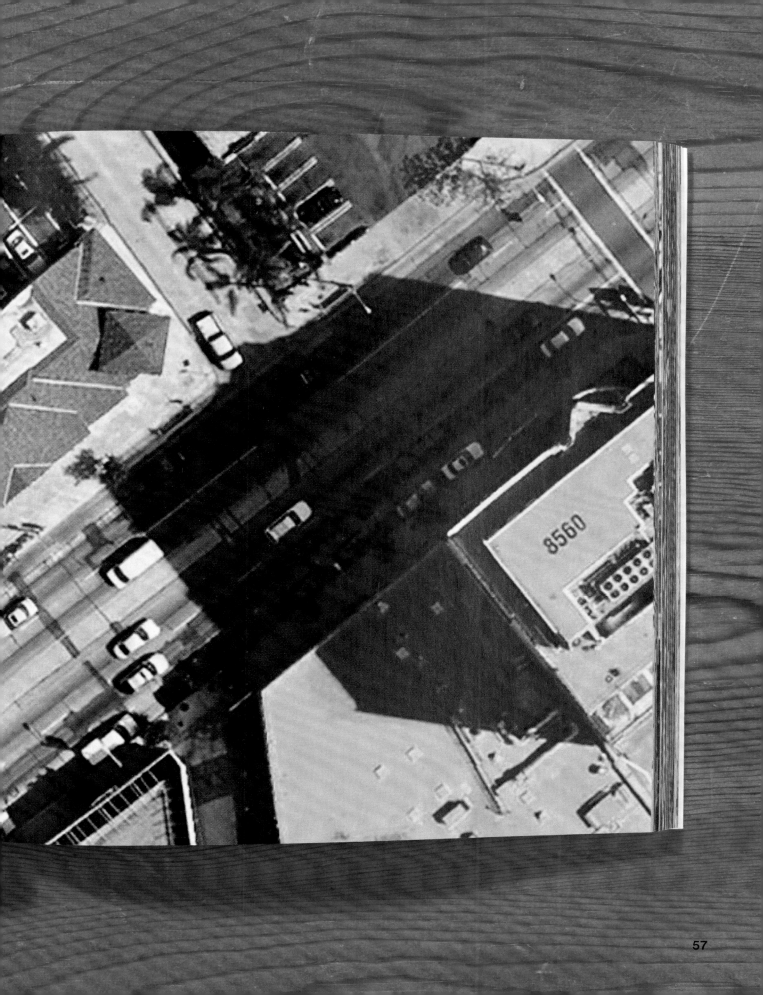

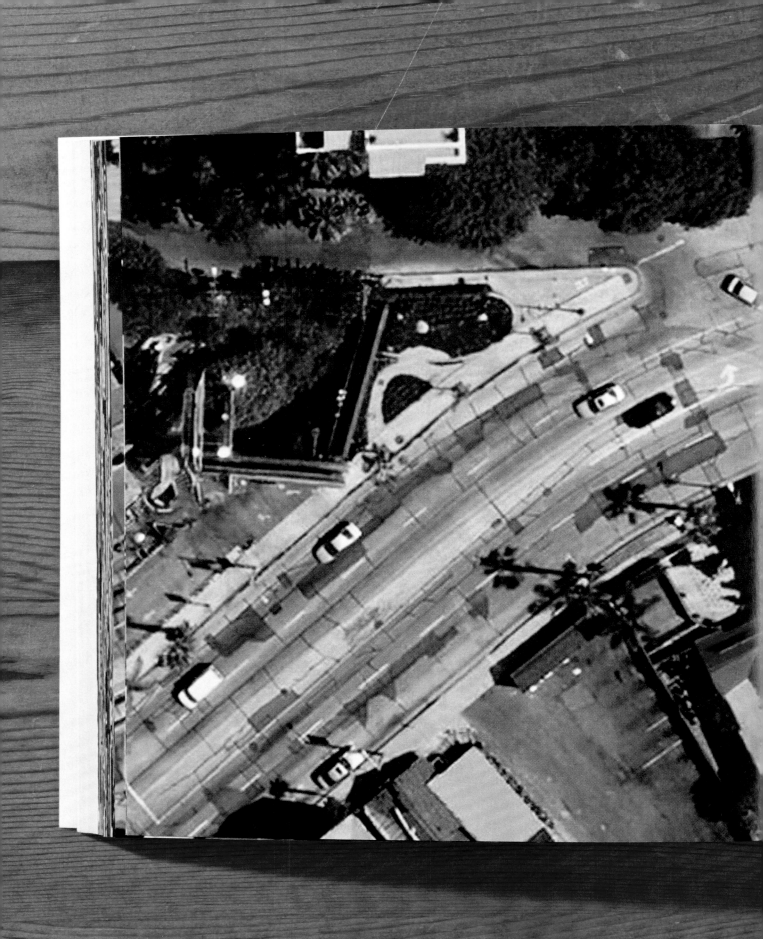

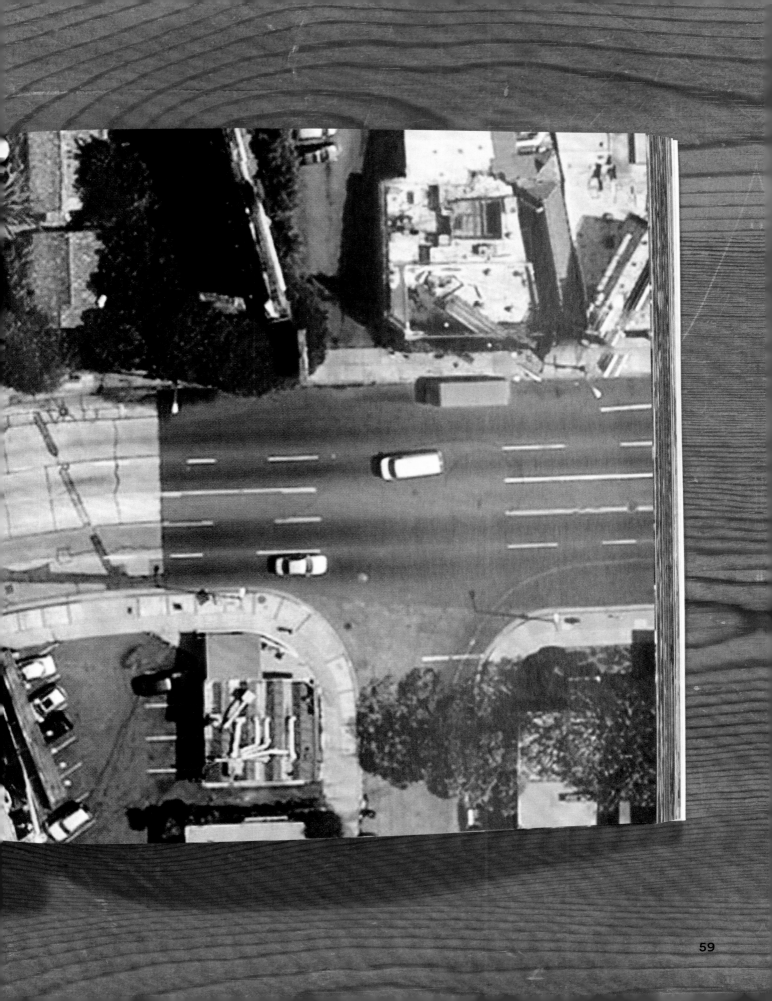

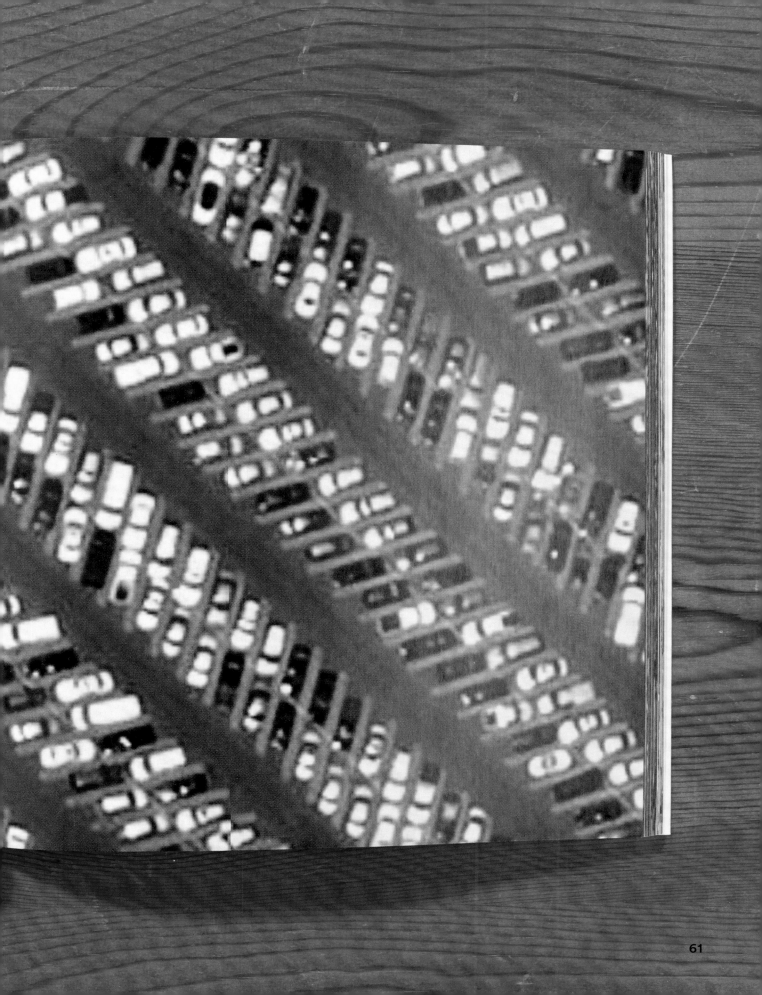

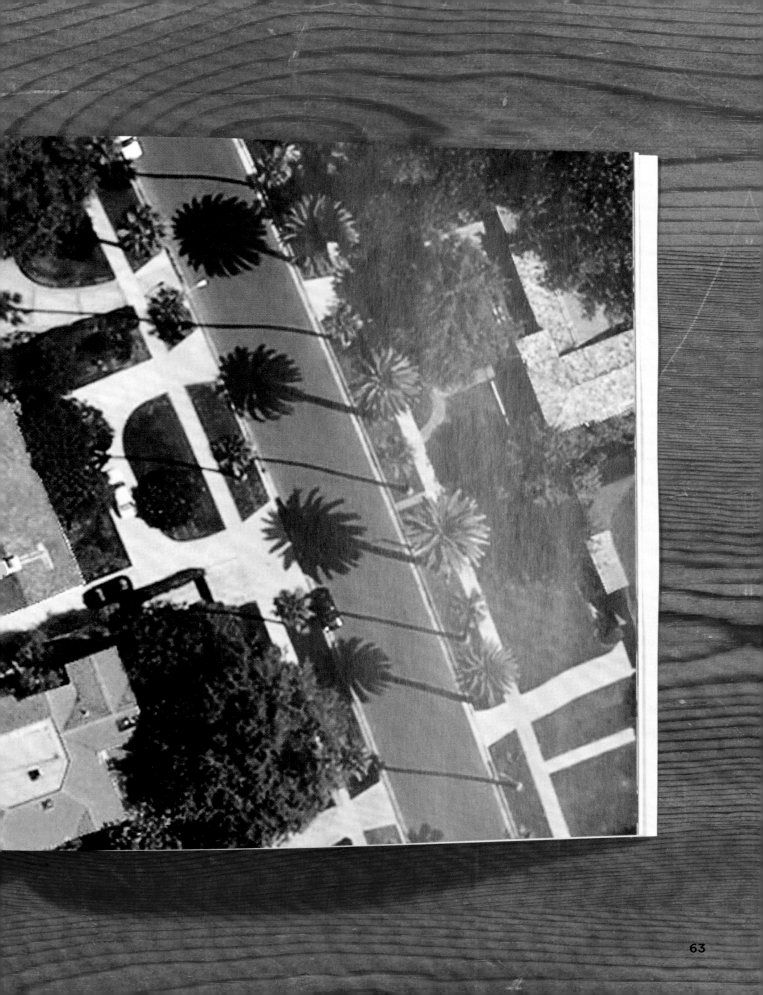

Title: La Montagne Dorée

Artist: Myriam Ziehli

Designer: Pierre Girardin

Editor: Myriam Ziehli

Imprint: none

Printer: Artgraphic Cavin, Grandson, Switzerland

Publication date and place: September 2012 / Lausanne, Switzerland

Edition: 150

Format and binding: softcover / heat-sealed binding

Size: 7 1/2 x 10 5/8 in. (19 x 27 cm)

Number of pages and images: 74 pages / 66 images

Type of printing and paper: digital / Bio Top 3 Extra 80gsm

Retail price: 42 CHF / 48 USD

Cost per unit: $$$$

Book soundtrack: anything by Buvette

Part classically Swiss, obsessively ordered index, part surrealist retelling of a traditional fairy tale, *La Montagne Dorée* takes an unusual approach to exploring a real-estate project in the Alpine village of Andermatt, on the brink of being developed into high-end apartments and hotels, exclusive ski slopes, and a golf course. This region is also the site of a well-known fairy tale about the construction of a bridge involving a devil's bargain. Ziehli sketches the basic facts and retells the fable in a brief introductory text. The rest of the book is broken into the categories Props, Casting, Costumes, and Set. The images that follow introduce the characters and other essential ingredients for what the artist calls "a fictitious play." The reader is given all the elements to create their own narrative for the situation—save for the script, which remains open to interpretation.

The book was designed by Pierre Girardin, a friend of mine, who I gave the whole project without explanation. I was really happy when I saw the final result! —Myriam Ziehli

La

Montagne

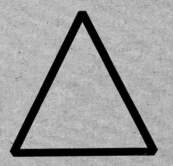

Dorée

by   Myriam   Ziehli

A   Fictitious   Play

In La Montagne Dorée (The Golden Mountain) :
From "The Devil's Bridge", a proposal for a fanciful
setting, I explore the development of real estate
projects in the Swiss Alps. In a village in central
Switzerland called Andermatt, an Egyptian investor
intends to build a series of hotels, a number of
cottages, some retail spaces and a golf course for
about 1.8 billion Swiss francs.

> In a steep valley not far from Andermatt, is the setting for a
> Swiss mythological story "The Devil's Bridge". The story goes
> that one day, while the villagers were complaining about not
> being able to build a bridge linking two valleys, the devil
> enters the stage in the form of a newcomer. He offers to build
> the bridge in one night. The residents agree. In exchange for
> his endeavor, he asks for the soul of the first person who
> crosses the bridge. The next day, it is erected and the villagers
> cunningly send a goat instead of a human being. The devil
> is so angry that he tries to demolish his work.

In La Montagne Dorée, I propose to revisit this
myth through the lens of a contemporary situation
in the form of a fictitious play. The bridge will
operate as a metaphor. I cast my players and put
thought into the sets. I produced a number of
photographs but I also collected existing images.
The book is an inventory of all my character
studies, sets, props and costumes. The captions
are carefully fabricated and sometimes enhanced
with additional details allowing the viewer to
create their own story. They hold all the elements
to become the director of this play, performing their
own imaginary edits, choosing studies that could
become a proposal for a story. The ambiguity
of this position (that of both being a passive
onlooker as well as an influential director), echoes
the contemporary issues related to tourism in
the Alps. An issue as philosophical as political.
Should we preserve an attractive industry or leave
the mystical landscapes untouched ?

3

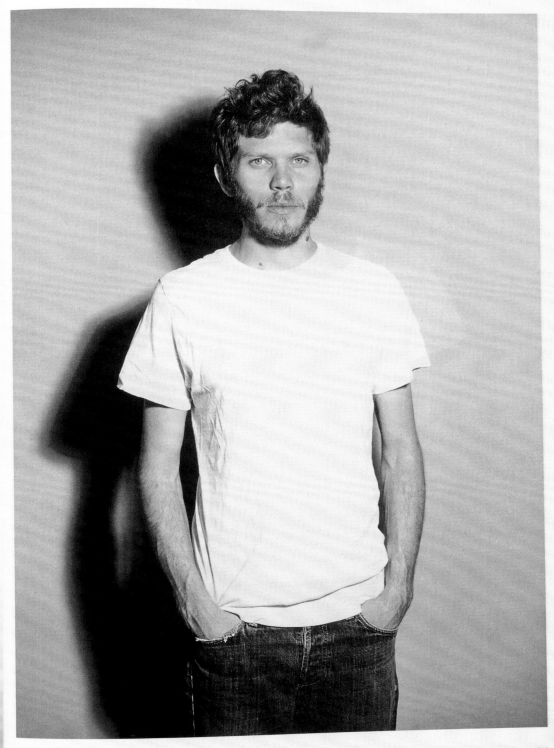

The citizens 2 (the shepherds)

25

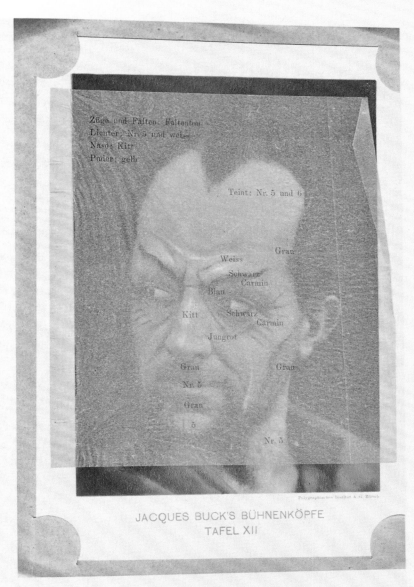

JACQUES BUCK'S BÜHNENKÖPFE
TAFEL XII

The devil 3

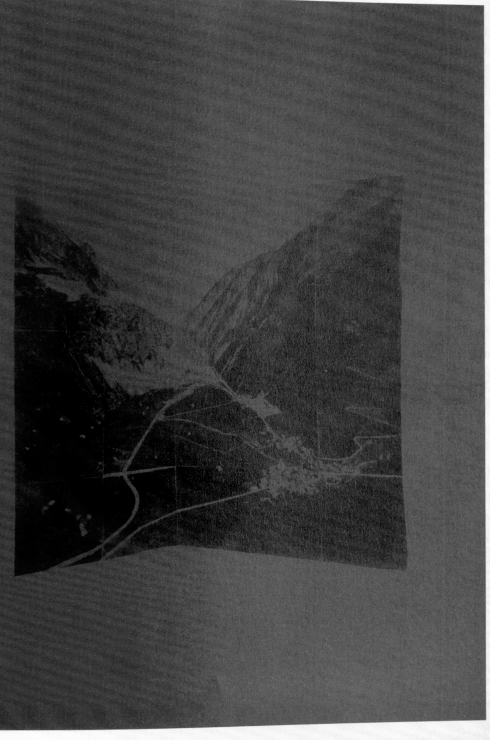

Background 4

Title: I Believe You, Liar

Artist: Lucas Blalock

Imprint: iceberg, iceberg, iceberg

Printer: Paper Chase Press, Los Angeles, USA

Publication date and place: January 2009 / New York, USA

Edition: 500

Format and binding: softcover / perfect bound

Size: 8 x 8 in. (20.3 x 20.3 cm)

Number of pages and images: 36 pages / 25 images

Type of printing and paper: digital / unknown

Retail price: 25 USD

Cost per unit: $$$

Book soundtrack: "Ode to Joy" by Ludwig van Beethoven

I Believe You, Liar is Lucas Blalock's first publication, and is grounded in the capabilities of photography to challenge its own comprehension. Blalock's work is often defined by content that points to something entirely outside itself. This book's name derives from Jean-Luc Godard's film *Pierrot le Fou*, and *I Believe You, Liar* shares Godard's aspirations for innovation through deconstruction. Throughout the publication, Blalock's edit and sequence of the photographs echo the gags and jump cuts of Godard's films, including the failure to fully contextualize subject matter.

At the time when I made this book (2007–8), Godard's films were a really significant touchstone for me. Godard is famous for inventing the jump cut, which introduced all of these strange juxtapositions. But he also had a way of bringing together really heterogeneous content—references to film history, politics, psychology, the character's personal lives—that gave his films a distinct character. I was really impressed by this and wanted to do something like it with the book, except I felt that the conventions I had to play with were photography's, not cinema's.

—Lucas Blalock

I BELIEVE YOU, LIAR.

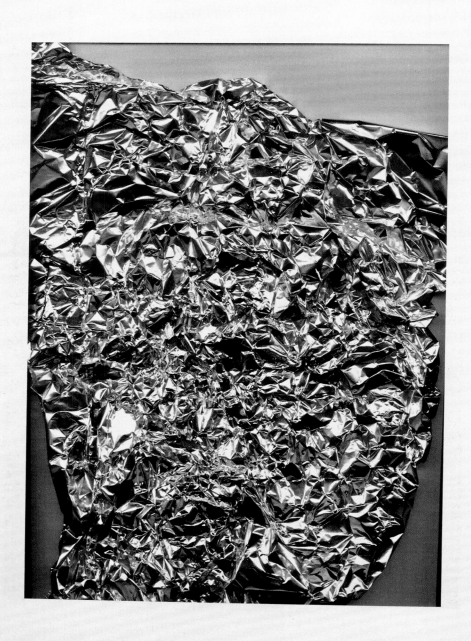

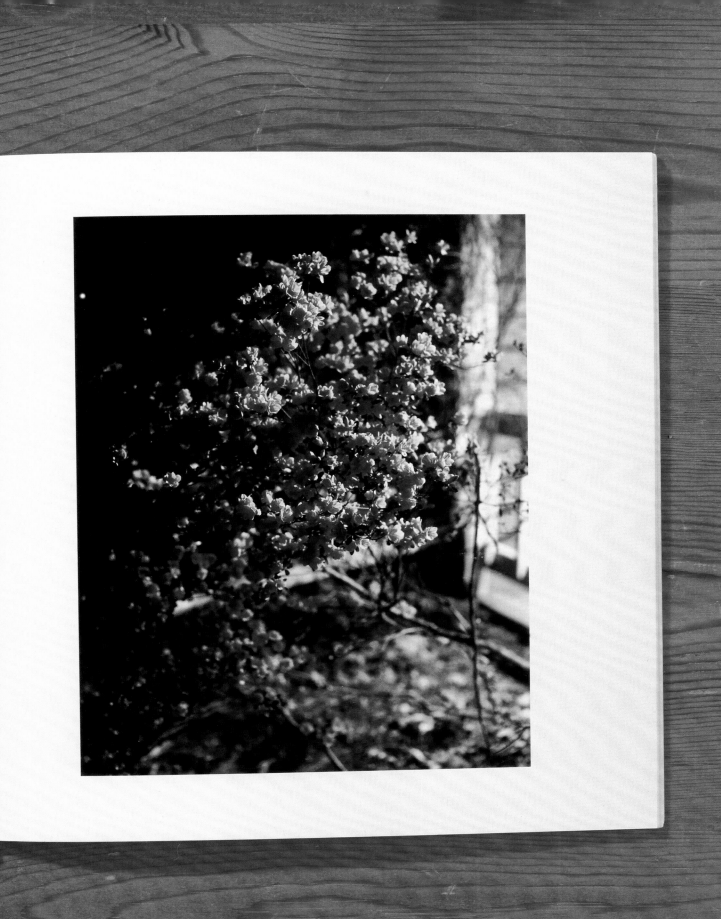

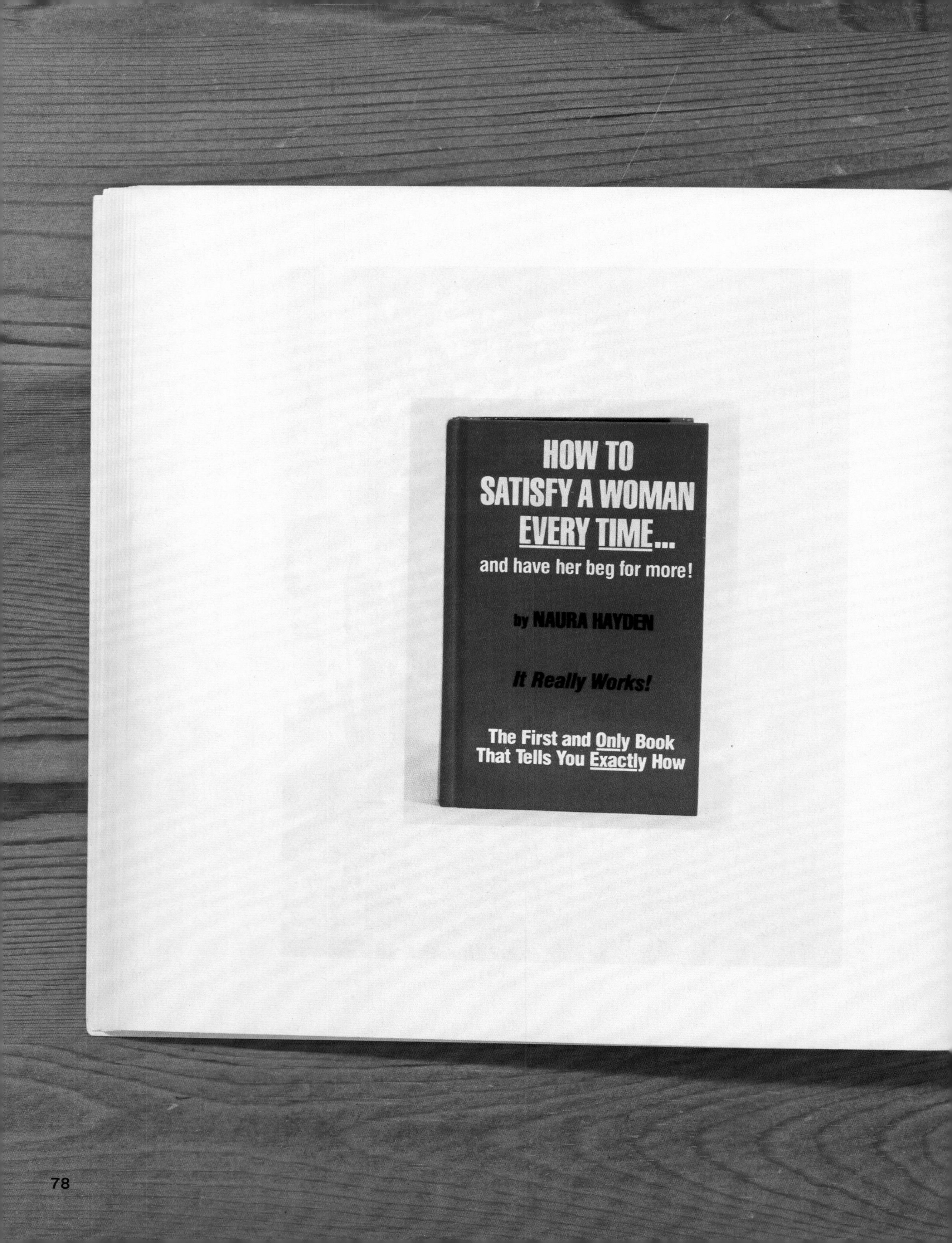

HOW TO SATISFY A WOMAN EVERY TIME...
and have her beg for more!

by NAURA HAYDEN

It Really Works!

The First and Only Book
That Tells You Exactly How

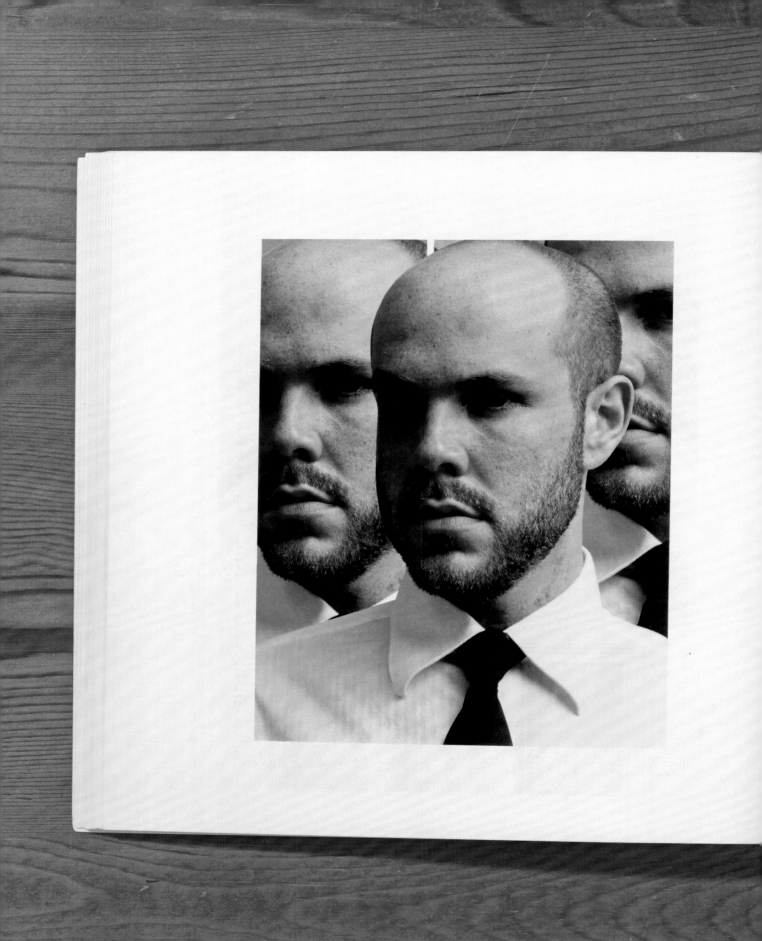

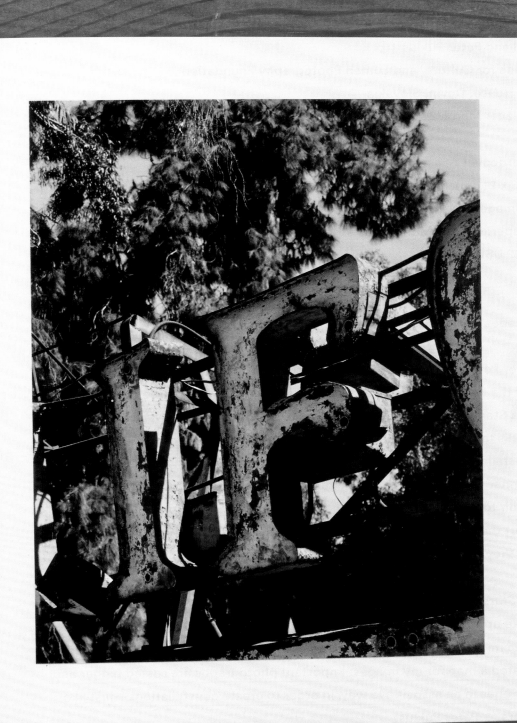

Title: Handbook to the Stars

Artist: Peter Puklus

Additional contributors: Claudia Küssel and Svätopluk Mikyta

Designers: Palo Balík and Peter Puklus

Editors: Claudia Küssel and Peter Puklus

Imprint: Štokovec, Space for Culture, and Lumen Photography Foundation

Printer: Devin Printing House, Devin, Slovakia

Publication date and place: March 2012 / Banská Štiavnica, Slovakia

Edition: 300

Format and binding: hardcover / case bound

Size: 6 1/4 x 8 1/4 in. (16 x 21 cm)

Number of pages and images: 64 pages / 50 images

Type of printing and paper: offset / Munken Pure 110gsm

Retail price: 28 EUR / 32 USD

Cost per unit: $$$$

Book soundtrack: "Decades" by Joy Division

Hungarian photographer Peter Puklus is preoccupied with what can be done with photography beyond the confines of the frame. *Handbook to the Stars* emerged during a three-month artist residency at the Banská Stanica cultural center in Slovakia. Locking himself away in his studio, Puklus was alone with his thoughts as he began to play with materials in the space, creating a series of sculptural installations and readymades and photographing them. The book is an attempt to visualize the inner workings of the human mind, with its endless associative tendencies and connections; the edit follows no linear sequence or chronology. Single images exist mostly in fragments throughout the book, and it's only when multiple copies of the publication are arranged together that they can be seen whole.

Since *Handbook to the Stars* is mostly about the endless capacity of the human mind to connect unrelated things to make up stories, I was pretty sure I did not want to make a "classic" photobook, with images in the middle of white spreads. This is when the title became handy. I started to play around and created a map for my images: important photographs are scaled bigger and connected with smaller ones in an associative way, in order to create constellations—just like when we look at the stars. —Peter Puklus

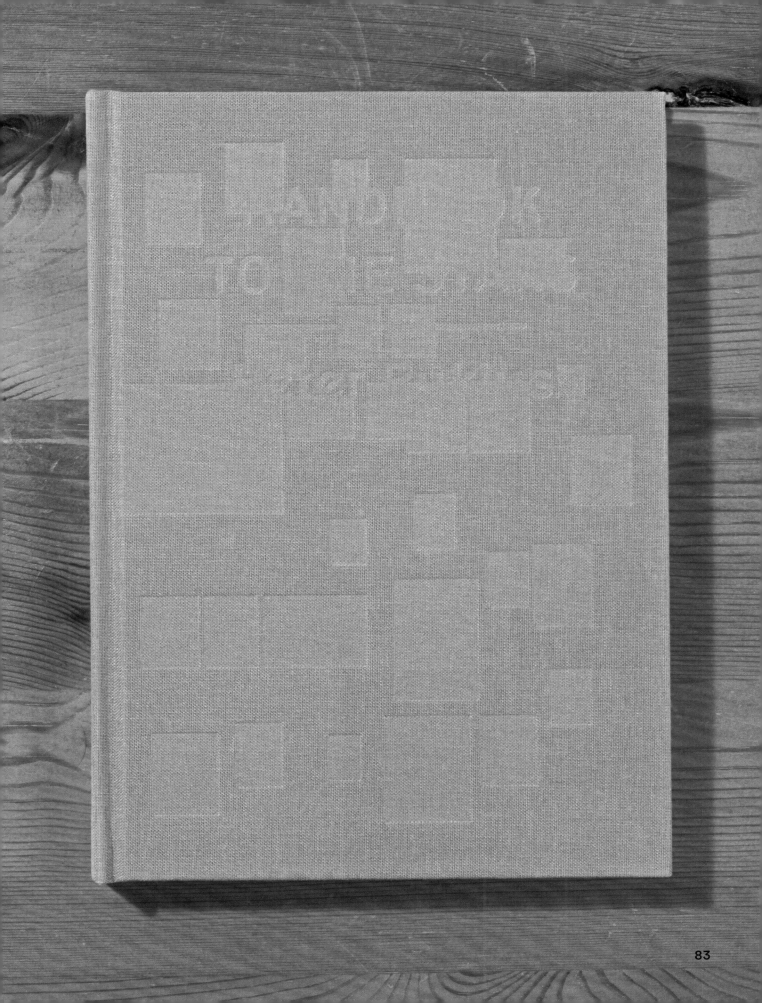

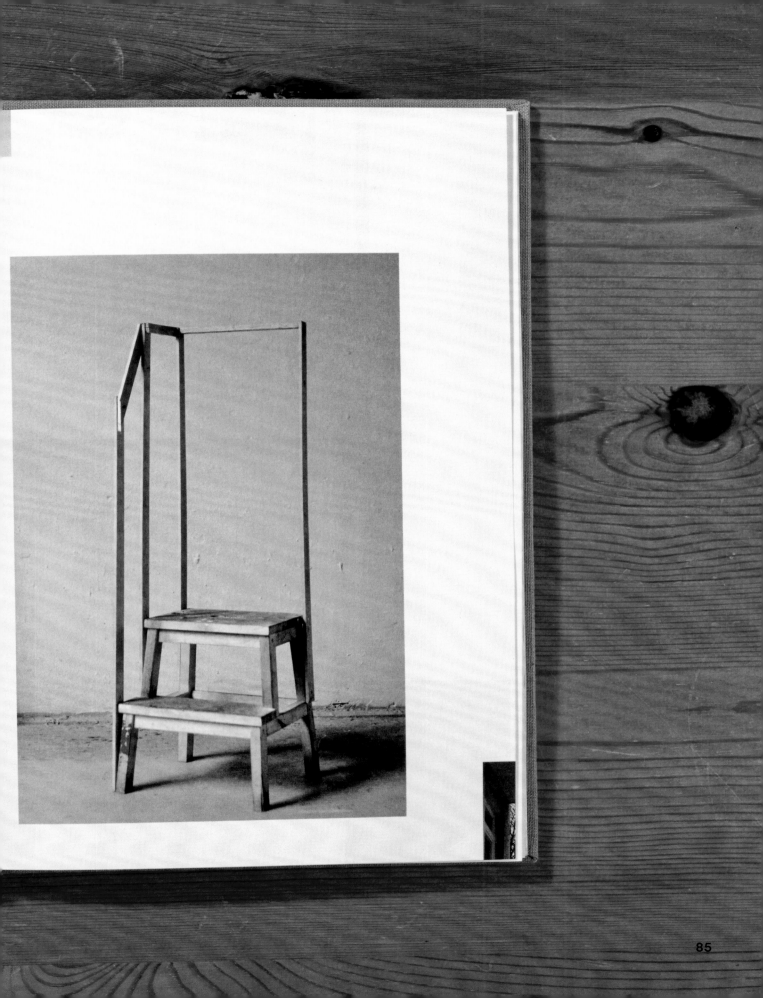

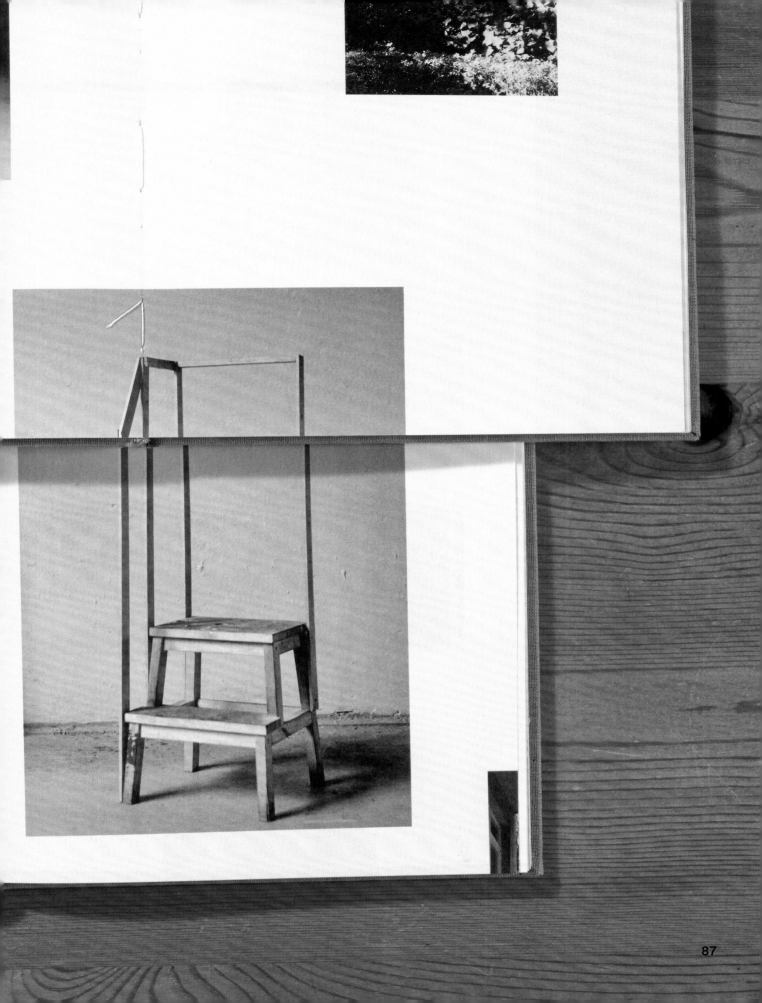

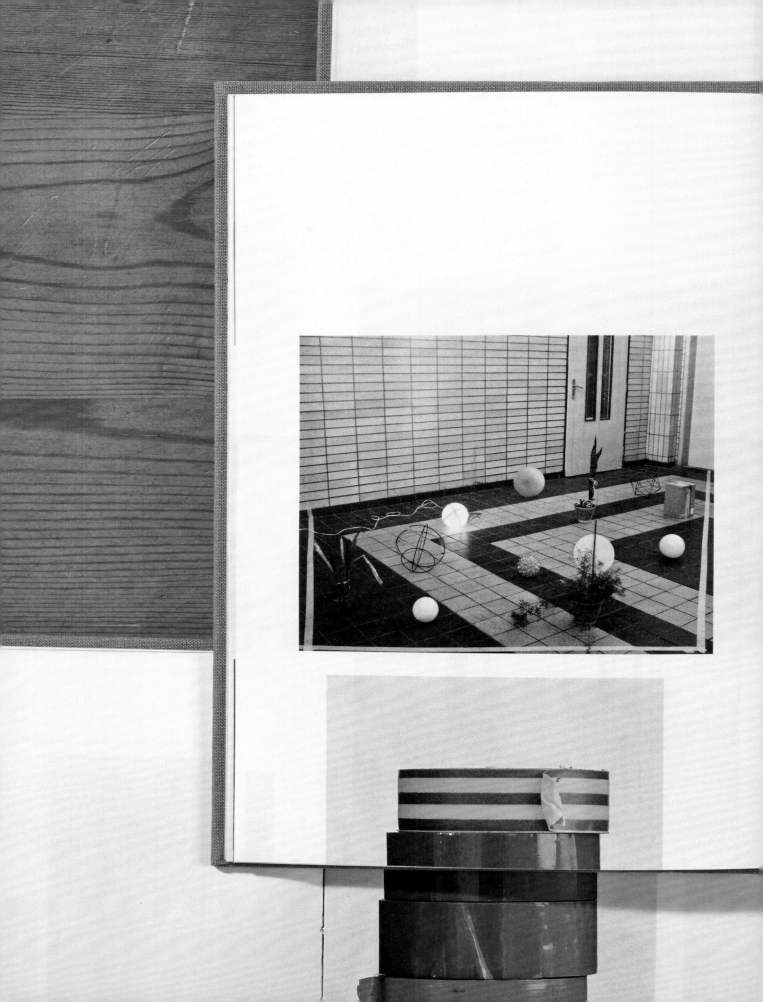

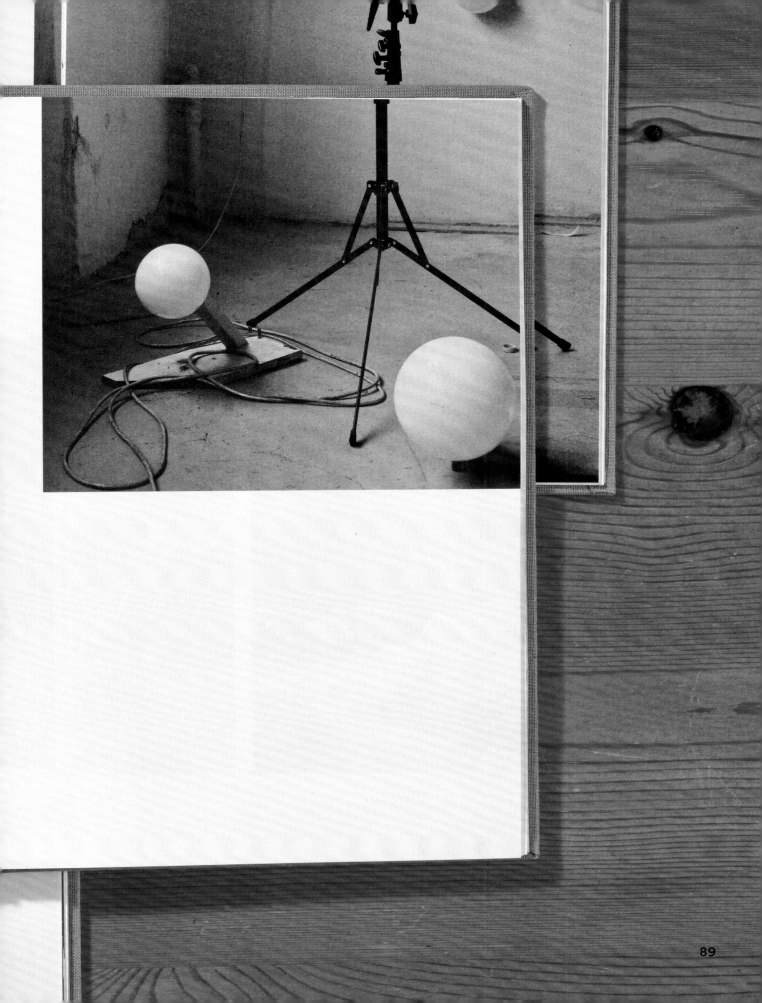

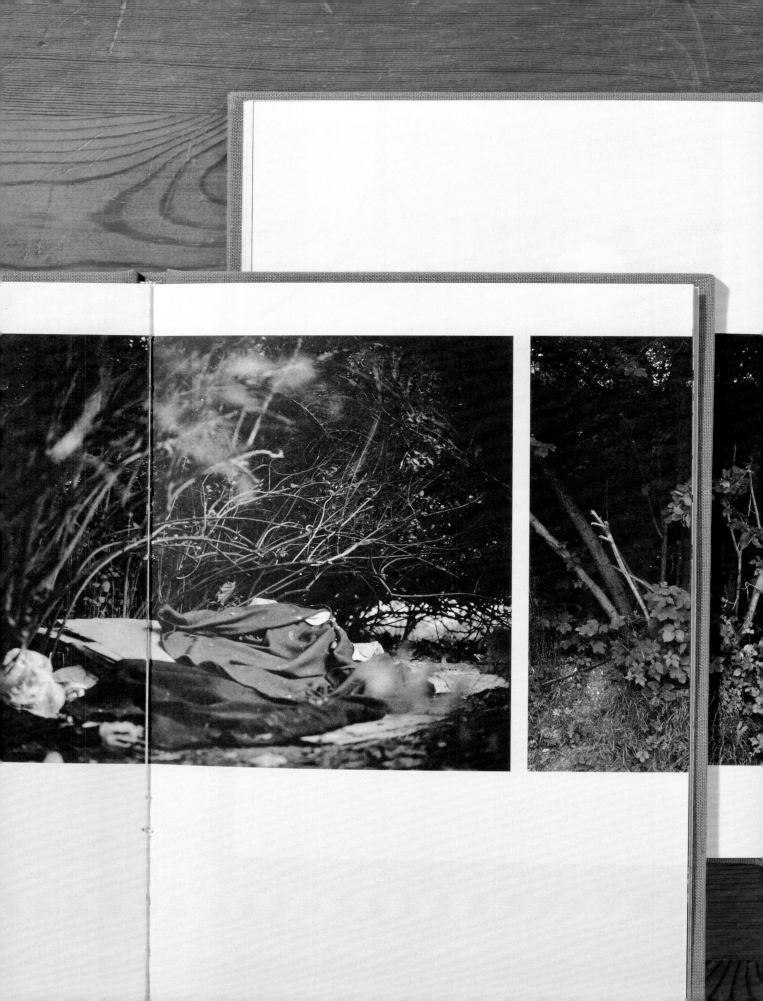

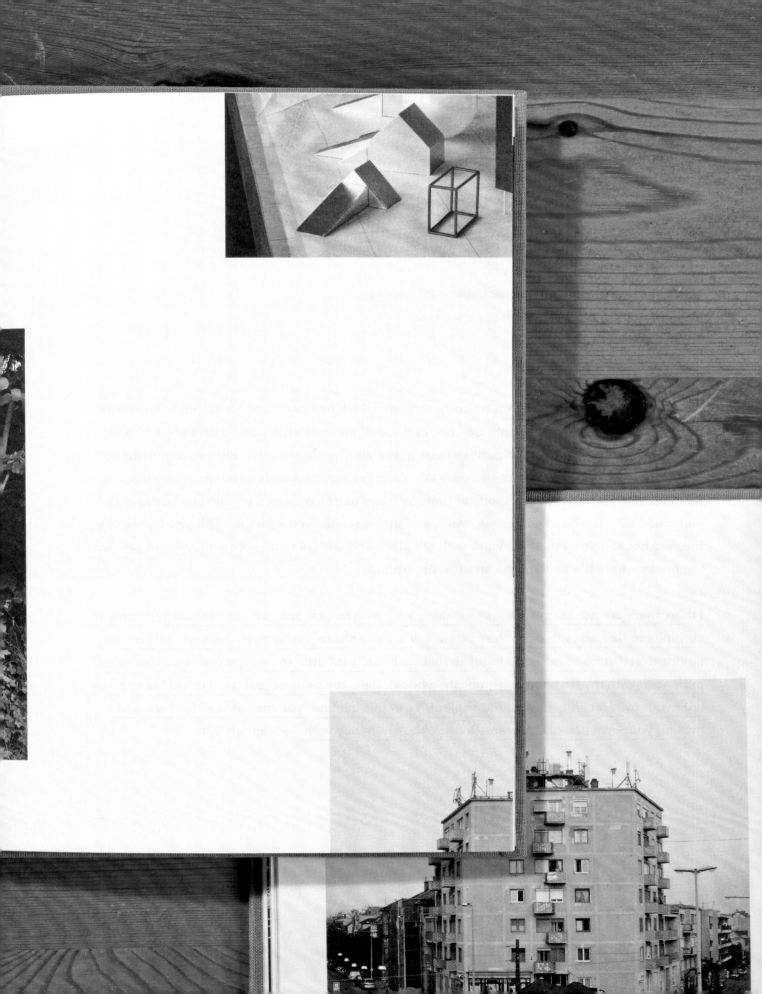

Title: Buried
Artist: Stephen Gill
Designer: Melanie Mues
Editor: Stephen Gill
Imprint: Nobody
Printer: Push, London, UK
Publication date and place: 2006 / London, UK
Edition: 750
Format and binding: hardcover with C-type print in slipcase / sewn bound
Size: 5 3/8 x 7 1/2 in. (13.5 x 19 cm)
Number of pages and images: 32 pages / 29 images
Type of printing and paper: offset / uncoated
Retail price: 40 GBP / 62 USD
Cost per unit: $$$

Stephen Gill founded his imprint Nobody, through which he distributes his self-published titles, in 2005. He has published twenty-one books through his imprint, which he says gives him the freedom and independence to publish work in the way he chooses. For *Buried*, Gill took photographs he'd made in London's Hackney Wick and buried them underground, before digging them up again after varying periods of time. Swirling patterns caused by rain and soil acidity combined with the flowers, bushes, trees, and urban scenes in the images. Gill also buried the finished book, uniting the final work with the place and underlining his commitment to producing books where the hand of the artist is discernible.

I think there are no disadvantages to making your own books, and I would encourage people to continue to find ways to do it. Very often, key art and photography publishers will rely on the author to self-fund or raise the funds to make a book, with little to no financial return (as I experienced with my first non-self-published book). Plus, the book object itself could fail to align with your own feelings toward the subject. With this in mind, you may as well find ways of making your own books and create a book you are happy with. —Stephen Gill

BURIED

Stephen Gill

5

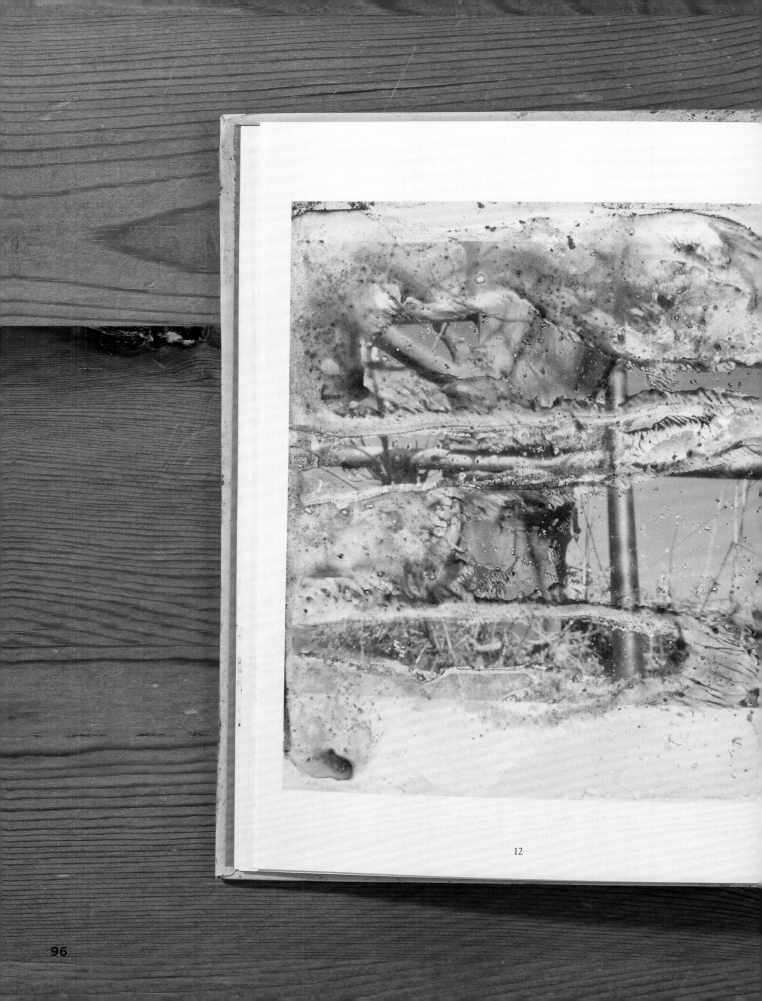

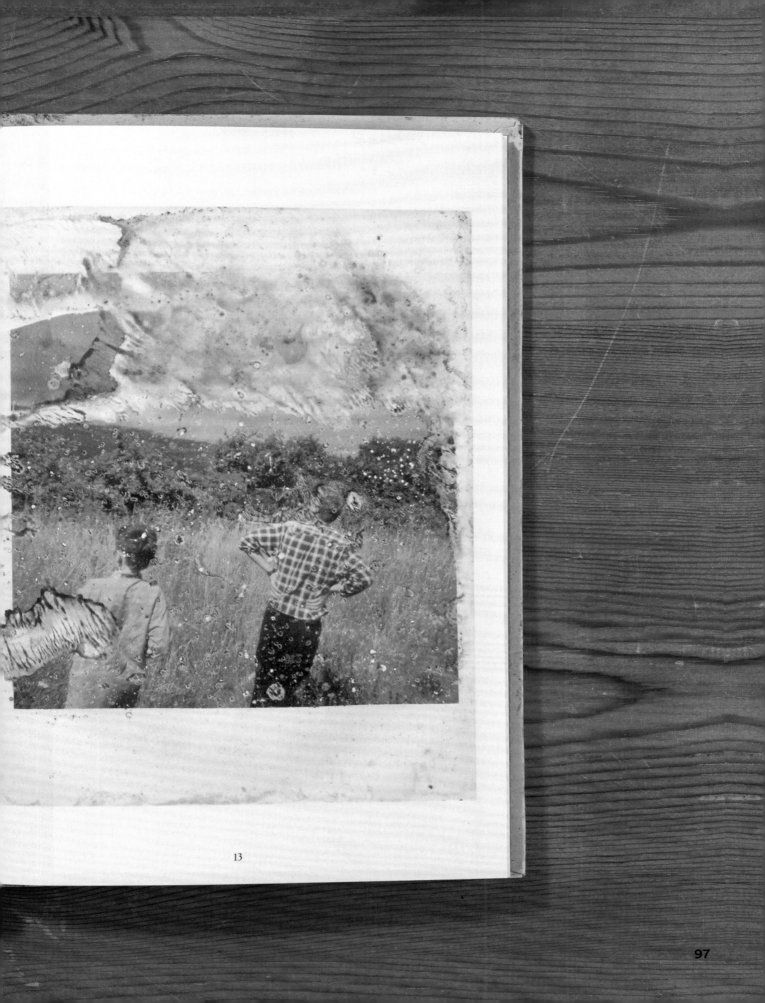

13

Bury your own

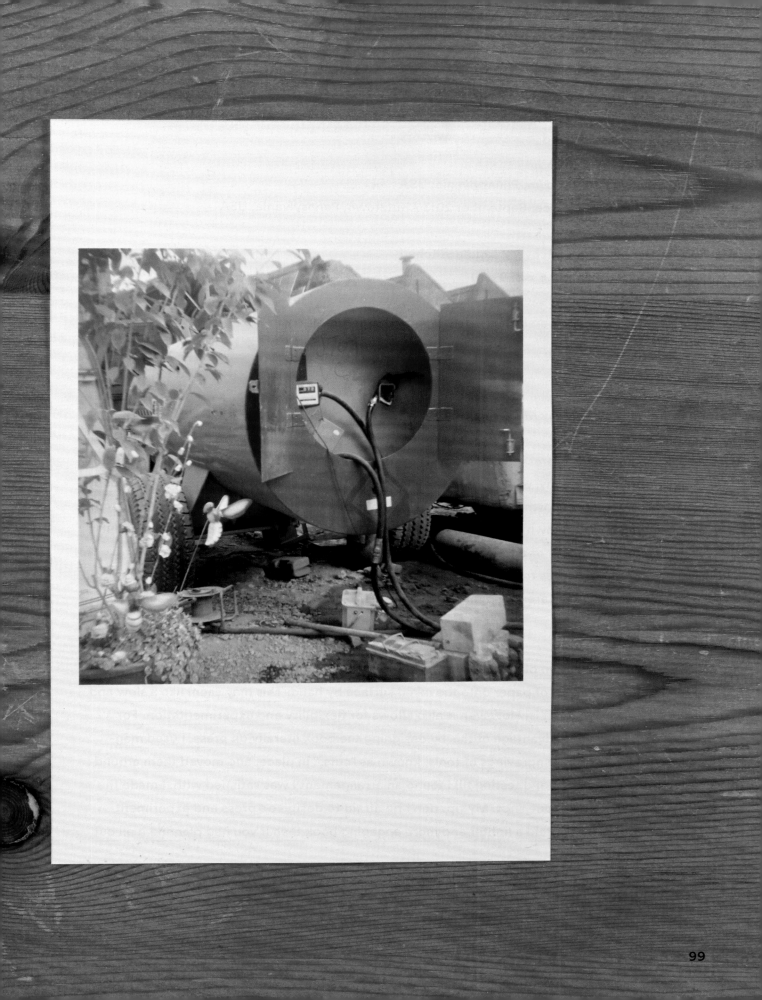

Title: Access to Tools

Artist: Nicholas Gottlund

Designer: Nicholas Gottlund

Editor: Nicholas Gottlund

Imprint: Gottlund Verlag

Printer: Gottlund, Kutztown, Pennsylvania, USA

Publication date and place: September 2013 / Kutztown, Pennsylvania, USA

Edition: 100

Format and binding: softcover / saddle stitched

Size: 5 3/4 x 8 5/8 in. (14.6 x 21.9 cm)

Number of pages and images: 32 pages / unknown number of images

Type of printing and paper: letterpress / Mohawk Superfine 104gsm

Retail price: 30 USD

Cost per unit: $$

Book soundtrack: *Dummy Mix 99* by Co La

Access to Tools is letterpressed with engravings of tools repurposed from Nicholas Gottlund's family's printing company, which printed catalogues for tool manufacturers. The book was published under Gottlund's own imprint, Gottlund Verlag, which publishes four to eight publications a year. Located in Kutztown, Pennsylvania, with a second studio space in Los Angeles, Gottlund Verlag employs a variety of approaches, including risograph, screenprinting, ink-jet printing, and letterpress. In *Access to Tools*, a series of arranged tools reveal letterpress's inherent tendency toward heavy ink areas, lap marks, and rubber roller textures, ensuring that each book is a unique object.

The letterpress I use is an old newspaper proofing press. I have to hand-ink everything and carefully drop the sheet of paper onto the inked surface by hand. This may seem like a slow and tedious process, which it is. However, it also allows for flexibility and experimentation. For *Access to Tools*, I took advantage of this by designing the book literally on press. I used magnets to hold the copper engravings of tools, known as "cuts," in place, and moved them around on the press bed, inking and testing till I found an arrangement I was satisfied with. I made the whole book this way in one shot. My tip: don't be afraid to design on press and experiment with your tools. It may yield a lighter and more engaging book than if you had planned it all out.
—Nicholas Gottlund

ACCESS TO TOOLS

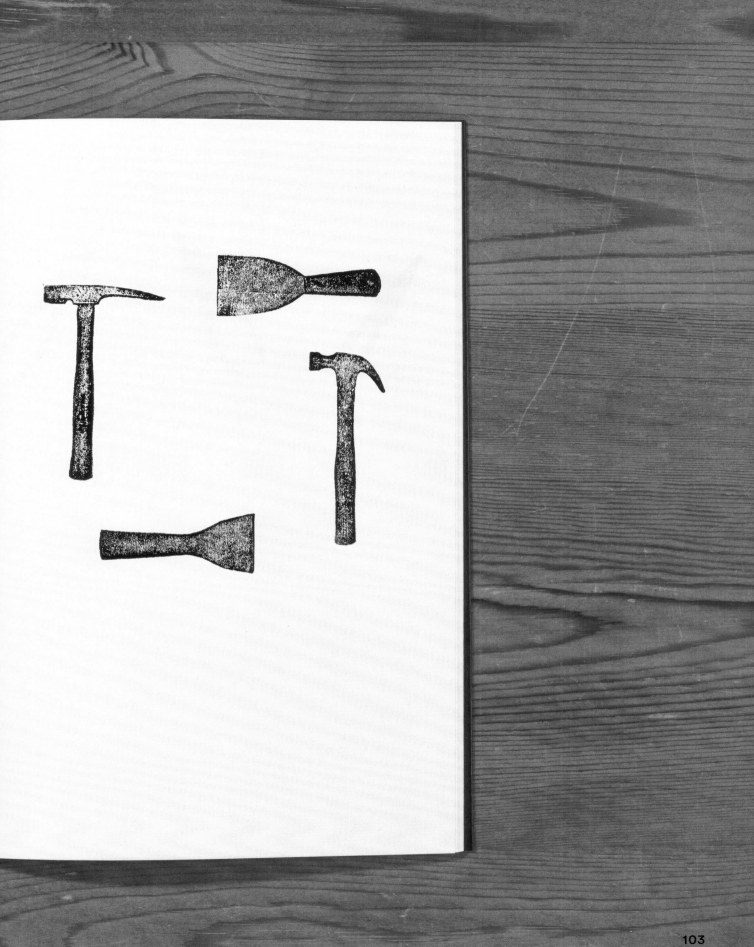

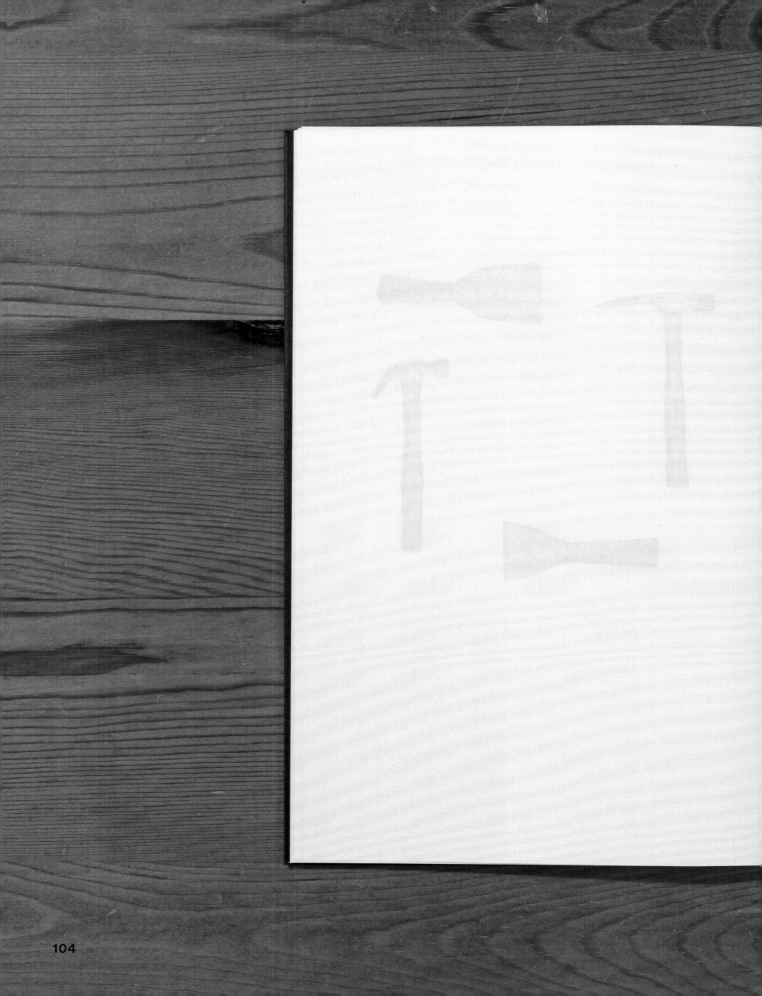

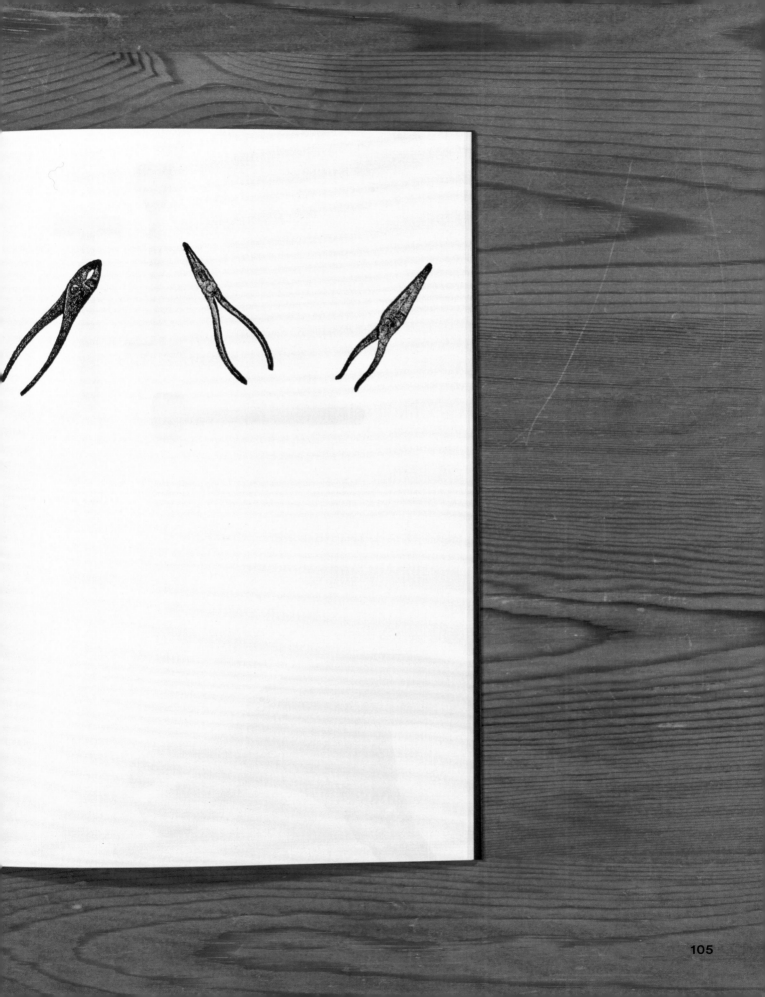

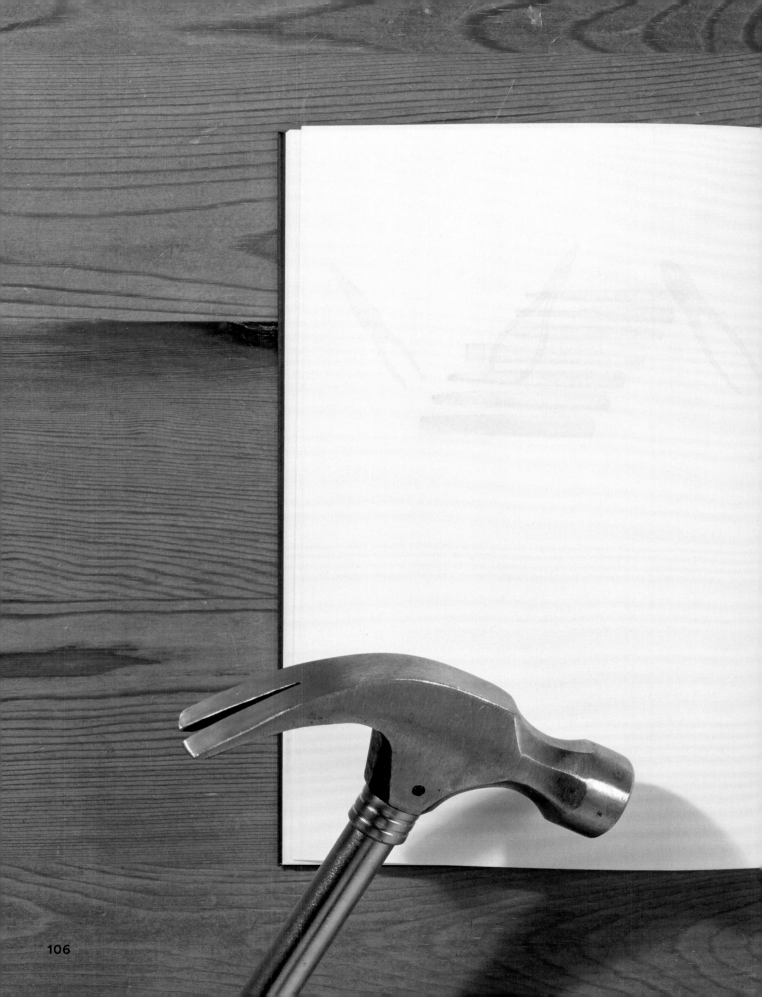

Self Publish, Be Yourself

Title: Lose Weight! Get Laid! Find God!

Artist: Jess Smith

Designer: Jess Smith

Editor: Jess Smith

Imprint: none

Printer: Magcloud

Publication date and place: September 2012 / London, UK

Edition: 25

Format and binding: softcover / perfect bound

Size: 8 1/4 x 11 6/8 in. (21 x 29.7 cm)

Number of pages and images: 154 pages / 112 images

Type of printing and paper: HP Indigo digital printing / unknown

Retail price: 24 GBP / 38 USD

Cost per unit: $$$$

Book soundtrack: "Deadweight" by Beck

The photographs in Jess Smith's *Lose Weight! Get Laid! Find God!* were shot over a seven-year period, beginning while he was still at university in Farnham, UK, and traveling back home to California for summer holidays. The photographs at the beginning of the publication feature people he encountered during this time and build up the fabric of an ongoing journey, while the later photographs tend toward objects and close-ups, with a more considered approach. In this way, the book becomes both a diary of his life at the time, and, simultaneously, a diary of his evolving relationship with photography. The book was an important transitional project for Smith, and represents a shift away from the concept of a photo story, and toward the idea of a photo collection. Smith used the print-on-demand service Magcloud to make his publication, championing the magazine format it offers to test formats, layouts, and edits before committing to larger print runs.

The title of the book was taken from the cover of a book I saw in a charity shop. I thought, *Wow, what a great title—click!*—and it was mine, added to the collection for later use. I like the humor and cynicism of the title and feel that it suits the editing and photo choices of the book.
—Jess Smith

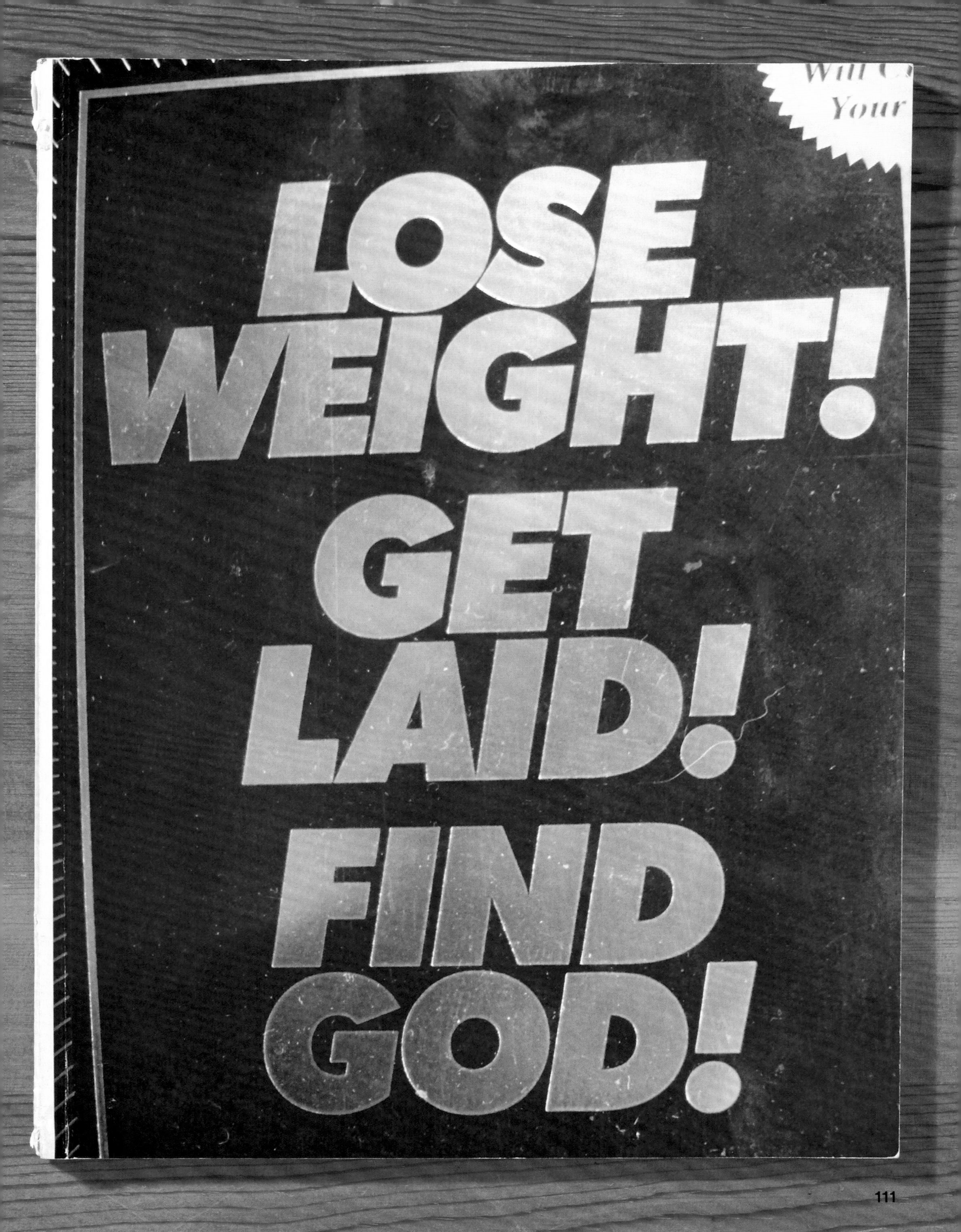
Will
Your
LOSE
WEIGHT!
GET
LAID!
FIND
GOD!

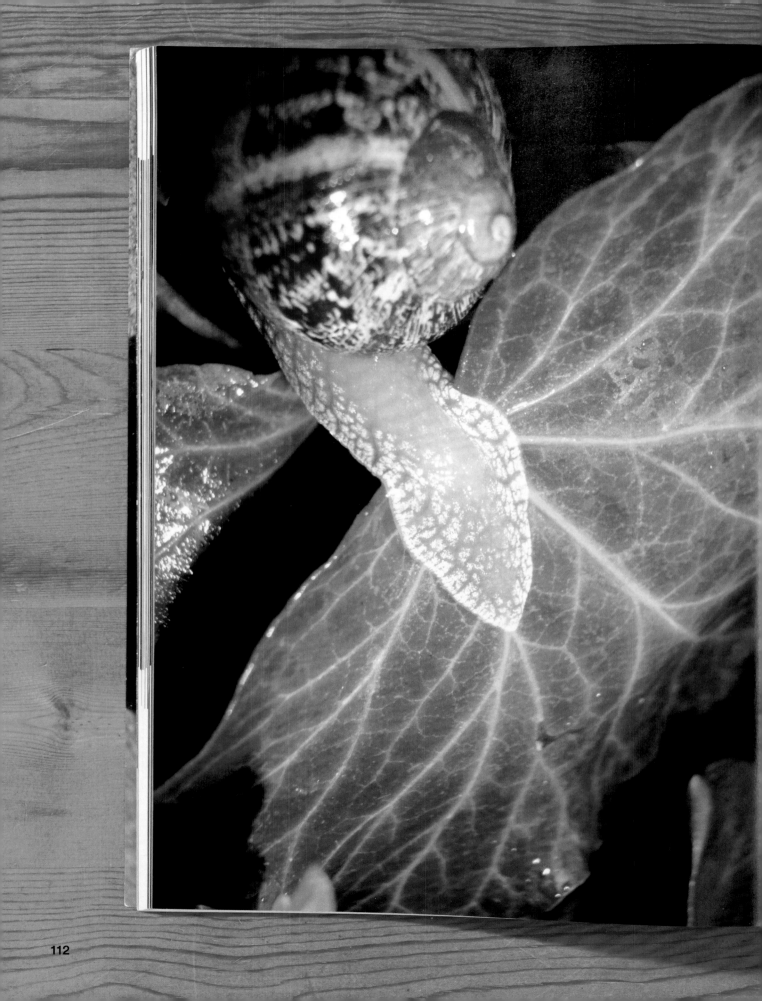

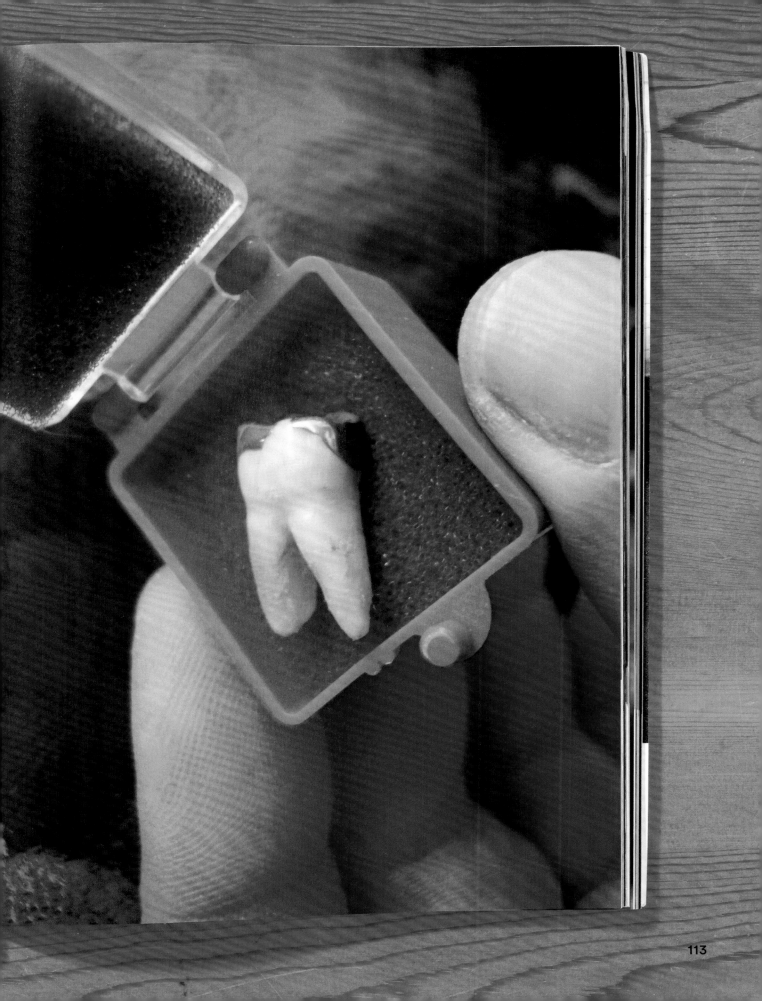

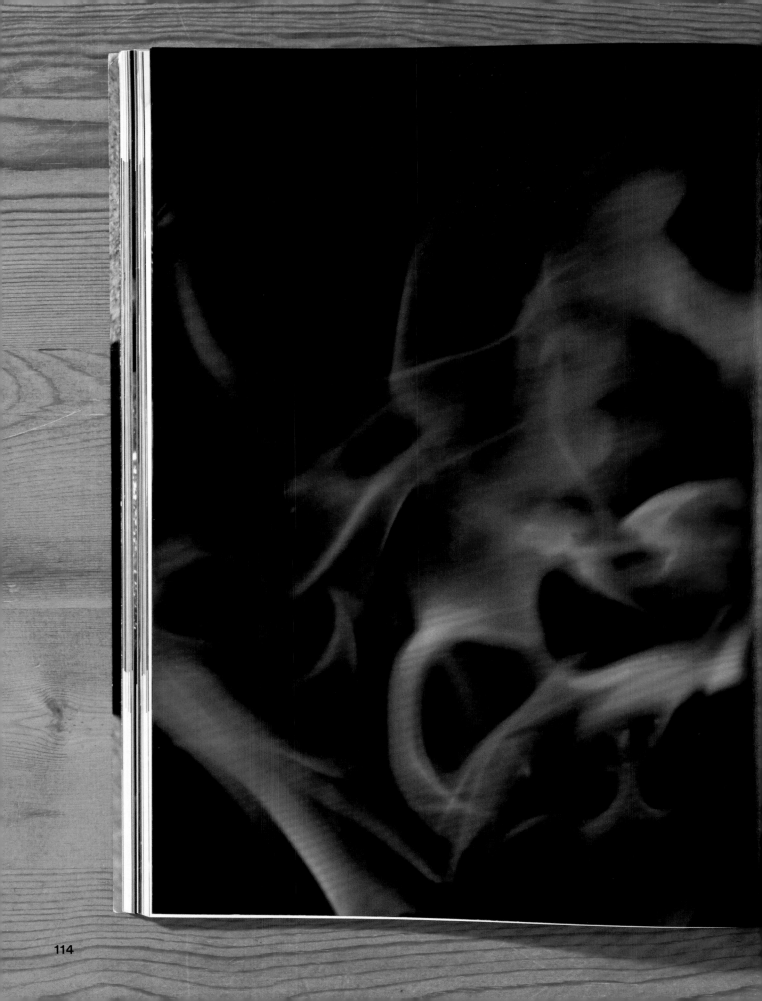

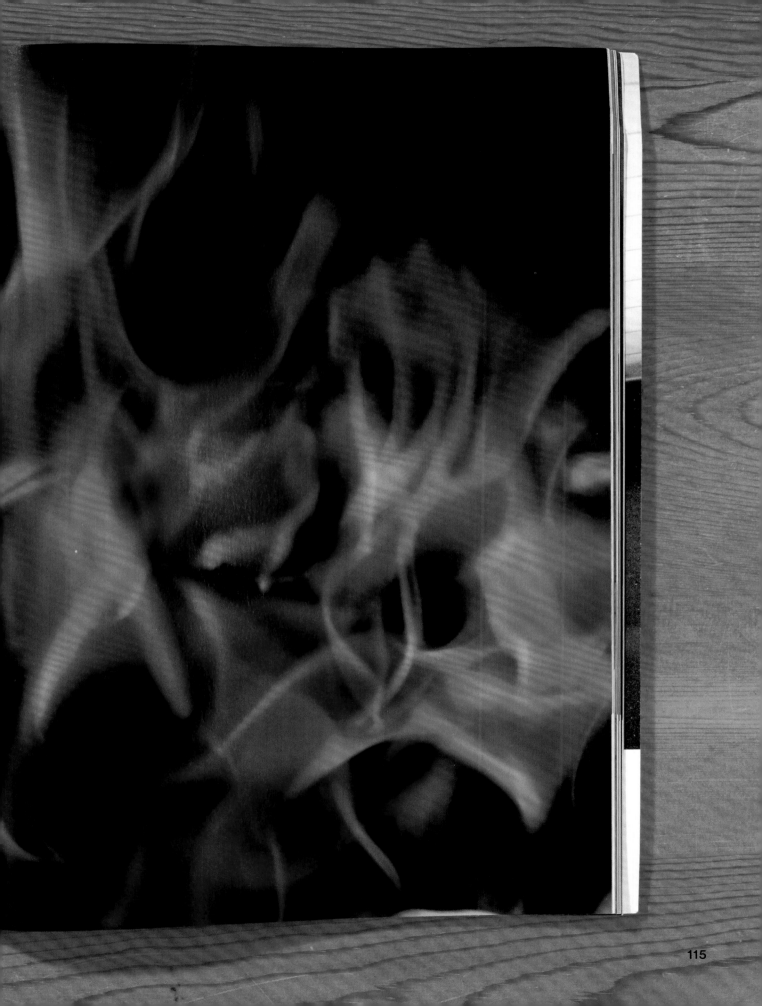

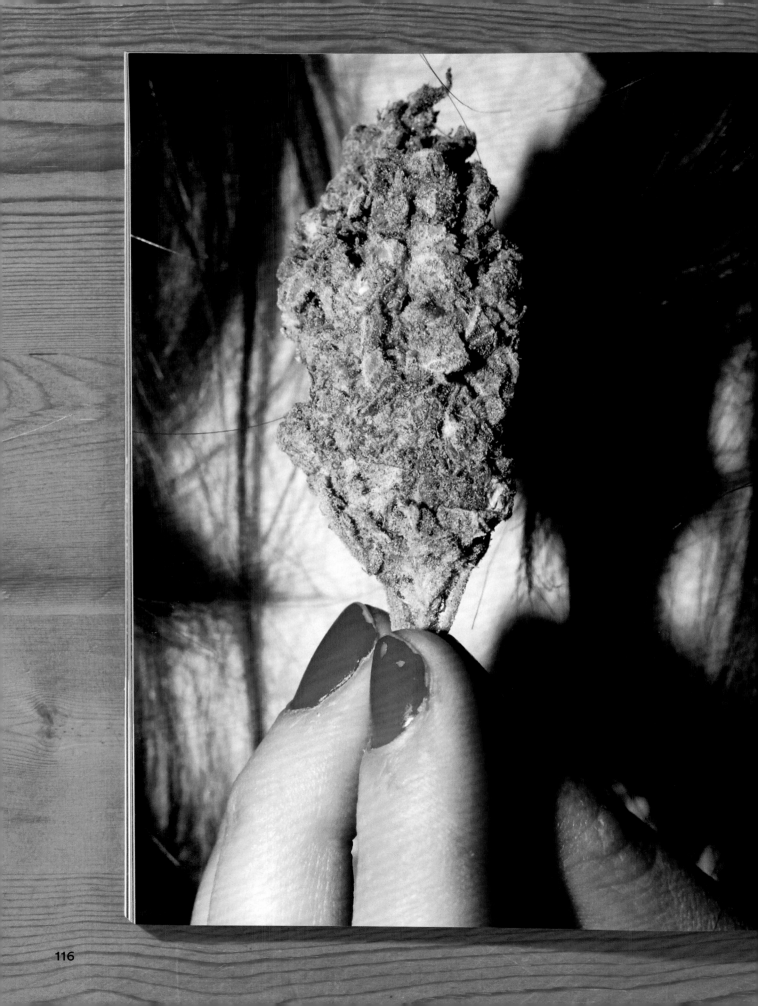

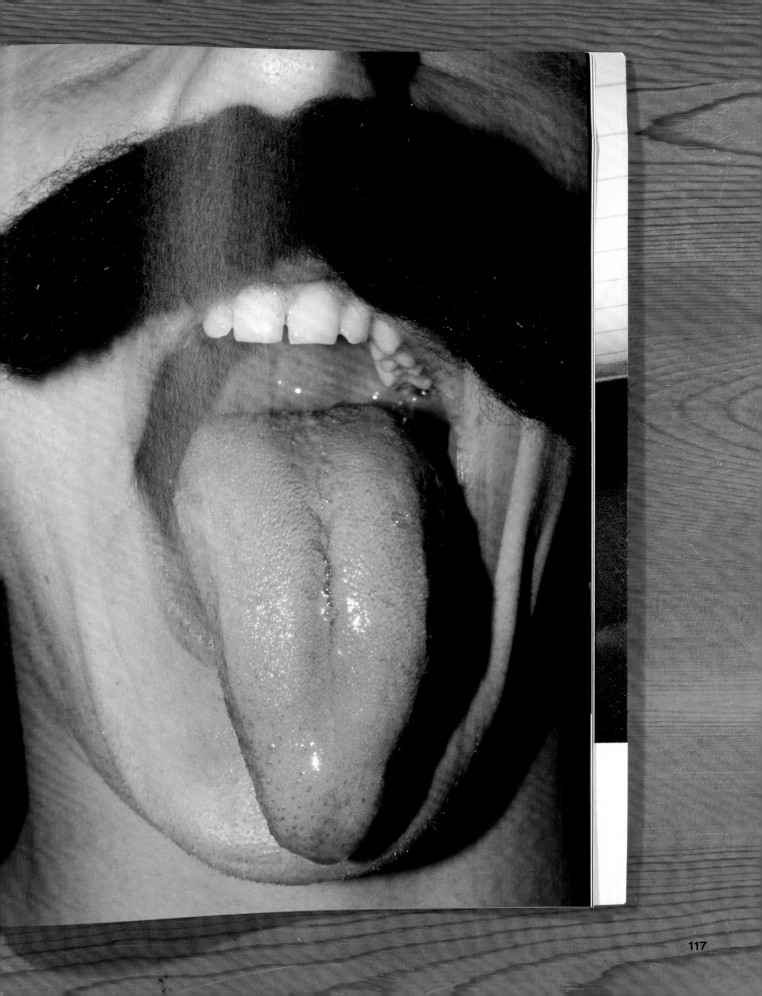

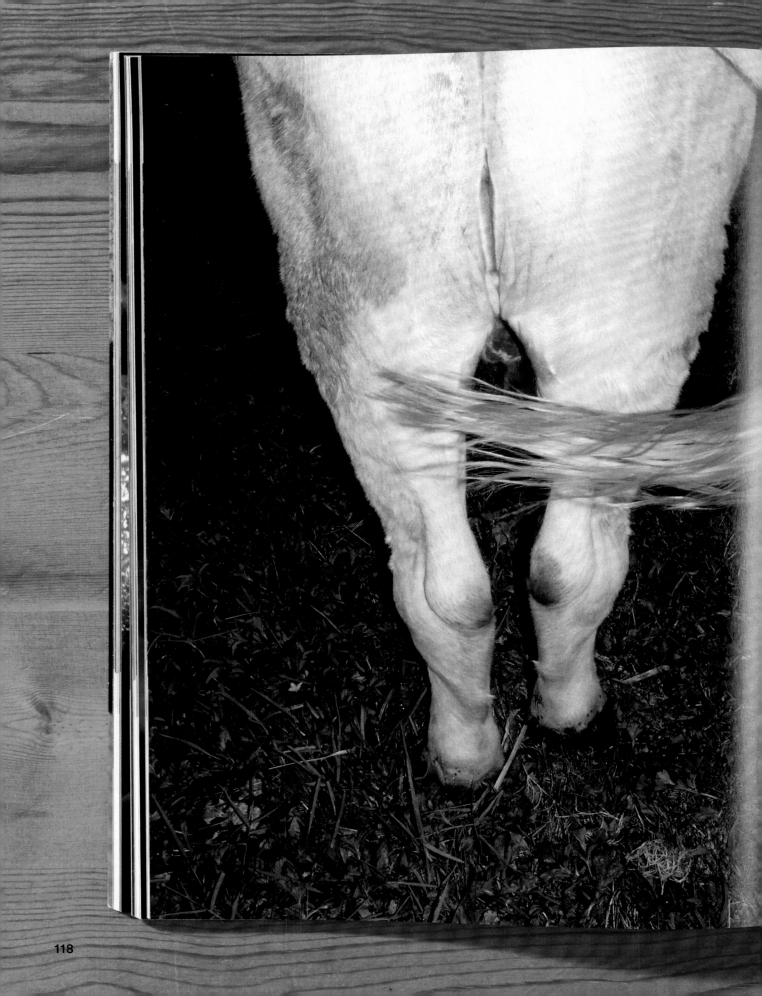

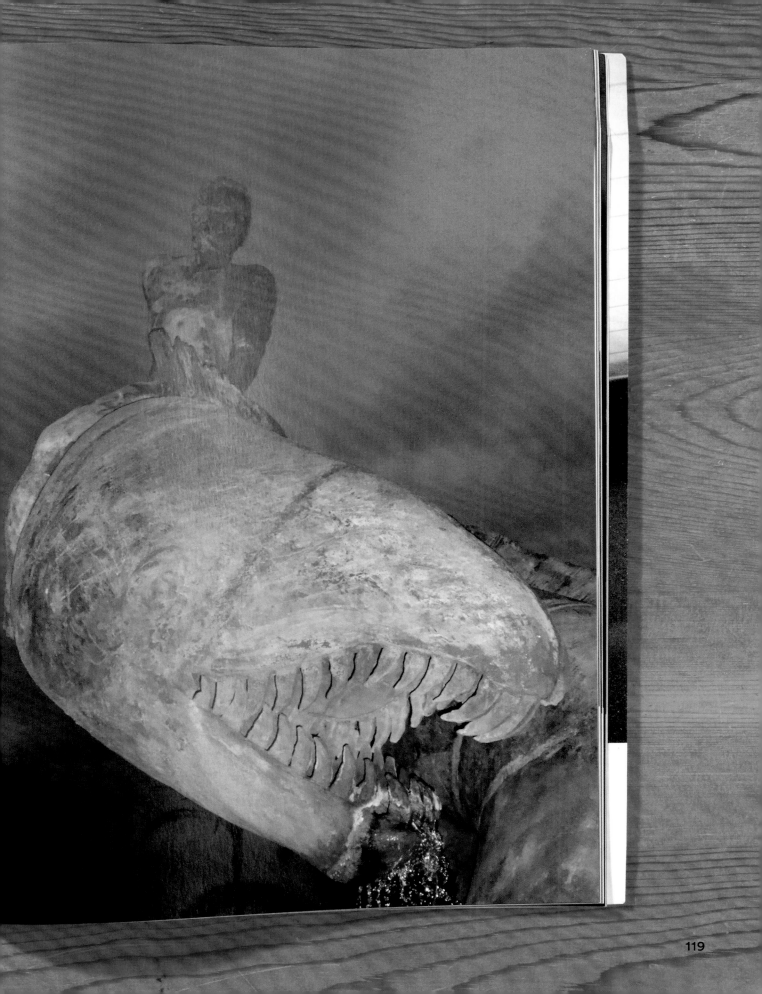

Title: 01–06

Artist: Lina Scheynius

Designer: Lina Scheynius

Editor: Lina Scheynius

Imprint: none

Printer: Aldgate Press, London, UK

Publication date and place: November 2012 / London, UK

Edition: 500

Format and binding: softcover, series of six volumes / perfect bound

Size: 5 7/8 x 8 1/4 in. (14.8 x 21 cm)

Number of pages and images: various / various

Type of printing and paper: digital / unknown

Retail price: 20 GBP / 31 USD

Cost per unit: $$

Book soundtrack: "Fifteen Feet of Pure White Snow" by Nick Cave and the Bad Seeds

Swedish photographer Lina Scheynius self-published her first book, titled *01*, in 2008. Since then, she has produced a book a year—each one as an intimate visual record of her life and experiences—and is currently working on *08*. (*07* is not pictured here.) The books feature many self-portraits, as well as photographs of her friends and ex-boyfriend in moments that she says meant a great deal to her. The outside of each book follows the same format, with a white cover and number on the spine. But inside, Scheynius experiments with different papers and layouts: sometimes an image fills an entire page, while other times the images are printed small. Inspired by her grandfather, who published a book of poems in the 1990s, Scheynius presents her images as a diary or scrapbook.

I have stuck to the same format and only experiment with layout and paper. After *03*, I was actually fed up with it and was about to give up and make something completely different, but a friend convinced me I should continue. The more of them I make, the nicer they look together on a book shelf, so I have fallen back in love with the format. It's nice to commit to something in that way—it's a marriage of sorts. —Lina Scheynius

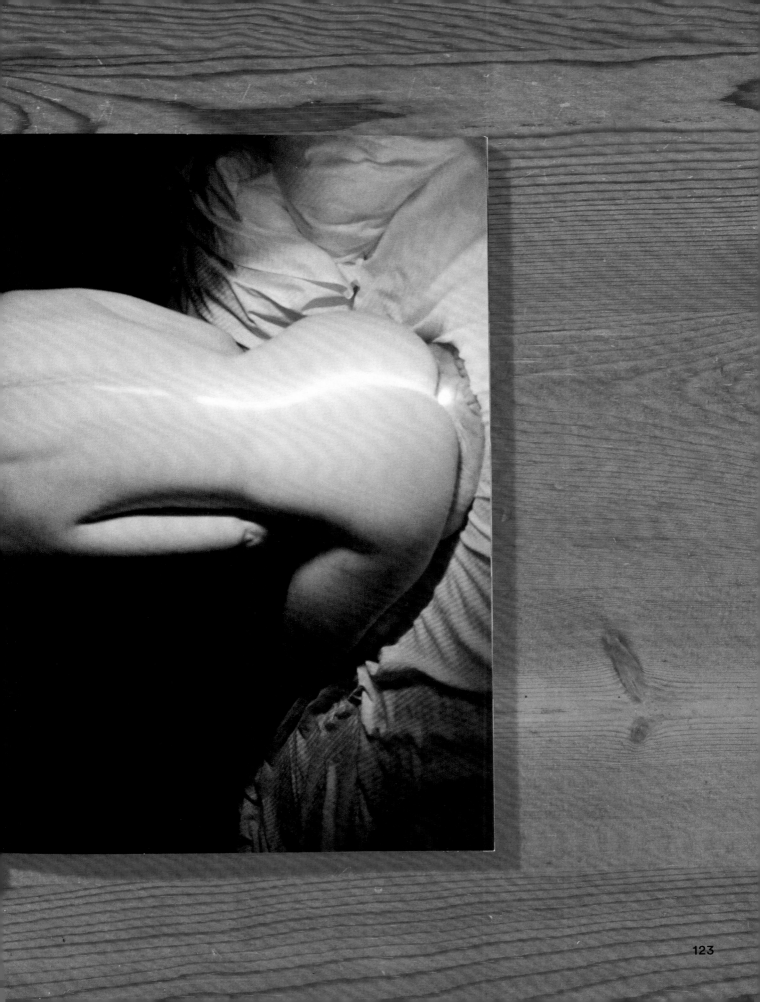

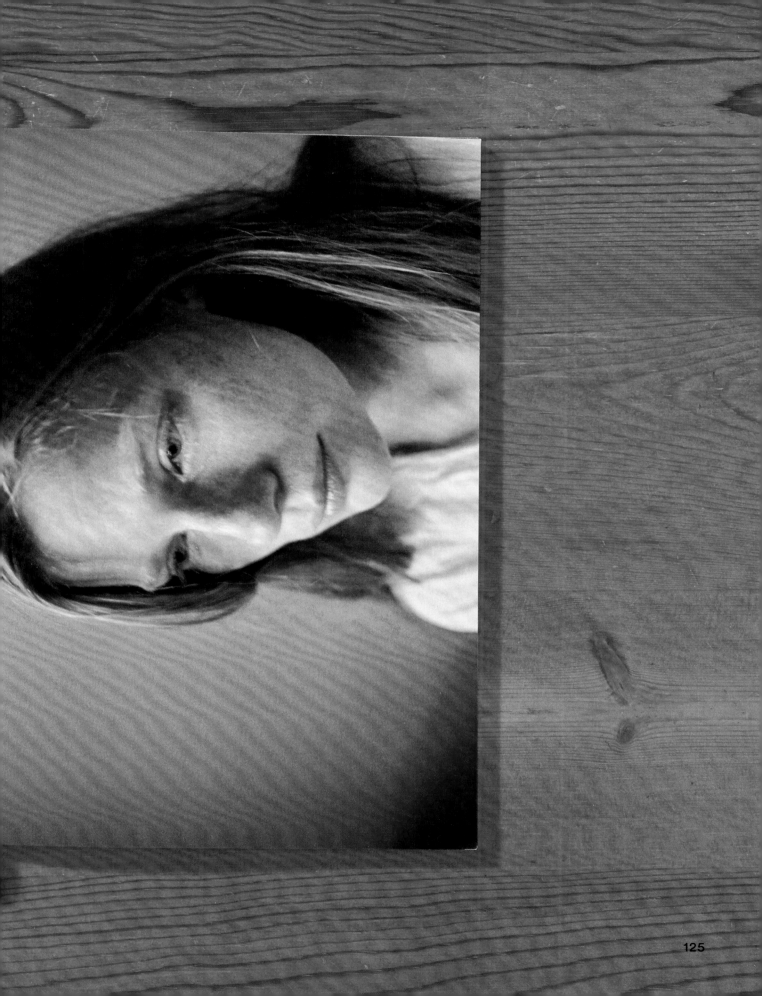

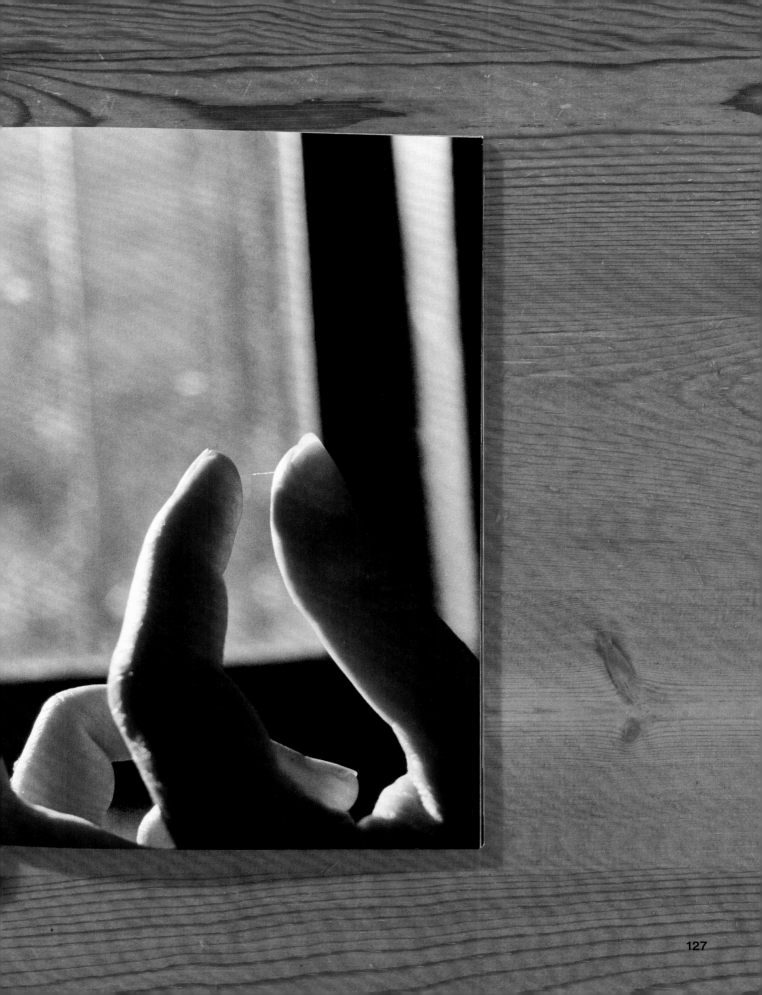

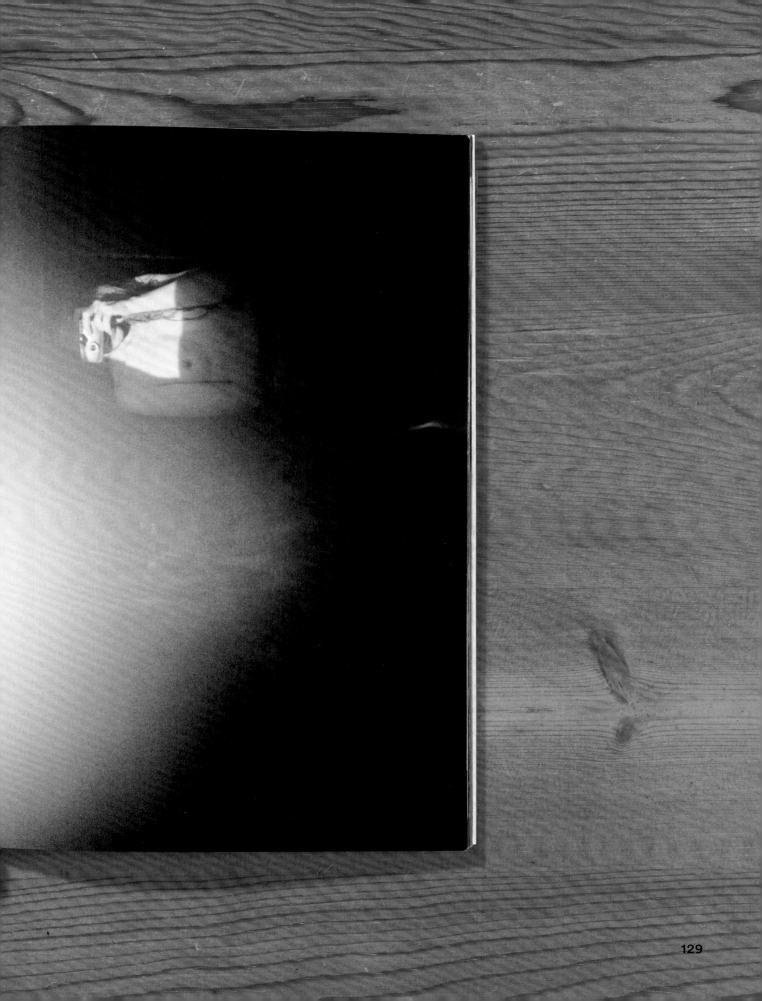

Title: Be Happy!

Artist: Igor Samolet

Designer: Igor Samolet

Editor: Igor Samolet

Imprint: none

Printer: unknown

Publication date and place: May 2013 / Berlin, Germany

Edition: 50

Format and binding: softcover in slipcase / saddle stitched

Size: 9 1/4 x 6 6/8 in. (23.5 x 17 cm)

Number of pages and images: 104 pages / 89 images

Type of printing and paper: digital / matte 170gsm

Retail price: 25 EUR / 28 USD

Cost per unit: $$$

Book soundtrack: "Rebenok i Zver" by Voditel dlya Vera

For three years, Igor Samolet photographed young people in a small town in northern Russia, where he had previously studied, as they experimented with sex, drugs, and alcohol. He got to know a group of friends, and spent time with them as they went about their debauched antics. The images he took during his time with these people form a kind of diary of his experiences. This is also a story of love and friendship, he says, and the struggle to find happiness. The book's title—which is not meant to be ironic—comes from the protagonists' insatiable desire to live in a permanent state of ecstasy. Presented full-bleed, the images are intimate and immediate, each tumbling into the next as they document the highs and lows of youth.

It was hard to create a story for the book—I didn't have an understanding of what to show during the shooting. I focused on everything at once. When choosing the material, I saw the characters moving in front of the camera all the time, with movement itself being the aim. Then there were relationships, and sex, and it became clear to me that looking for logic at this age is useless; it is the age of trial and error, which we've all gone through. There was a moment when negative shots came to dominate in the book, but the aim was to give the audience a chance to love the characters, so I had to remove those. They might have been good photos, though.
—Igor Samolet

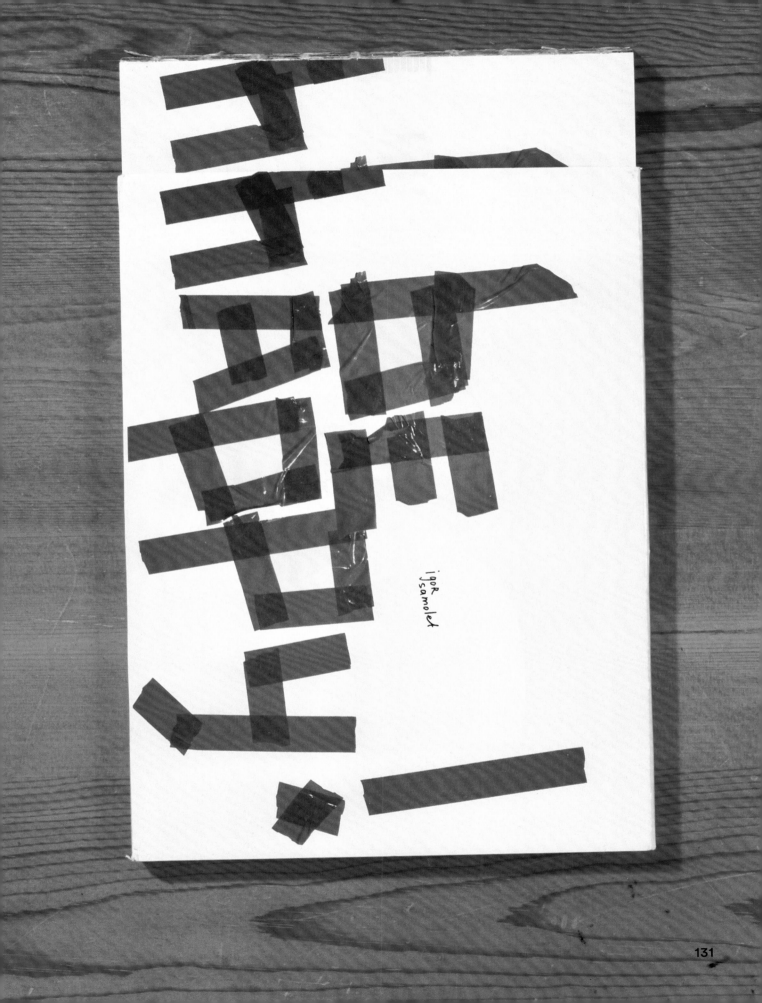

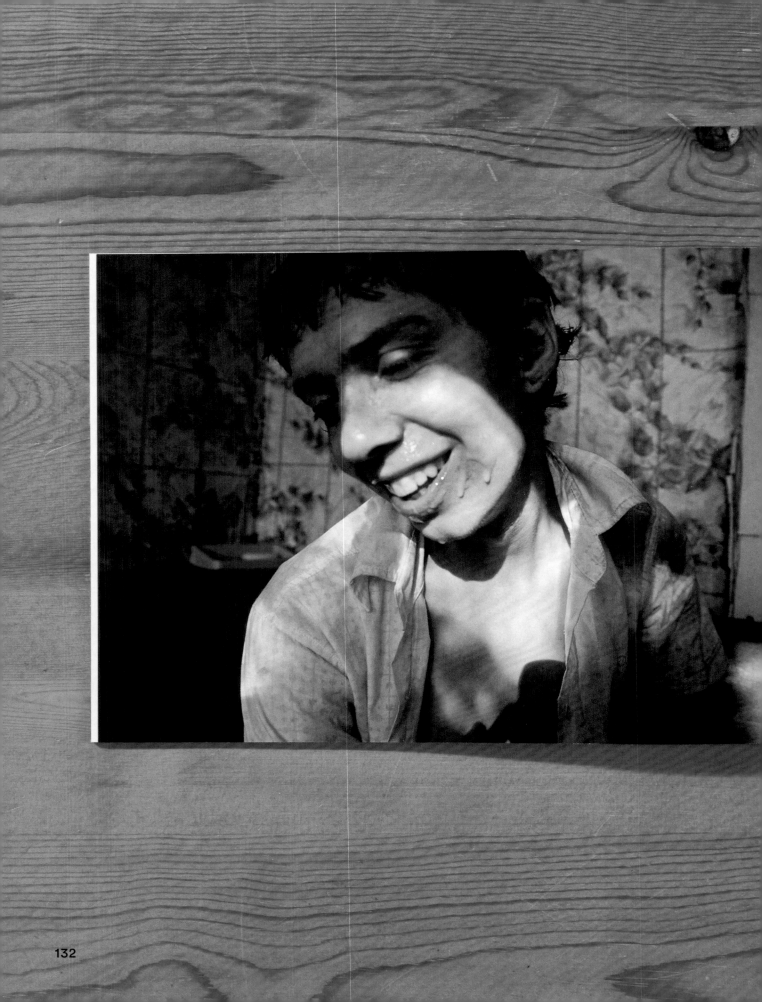

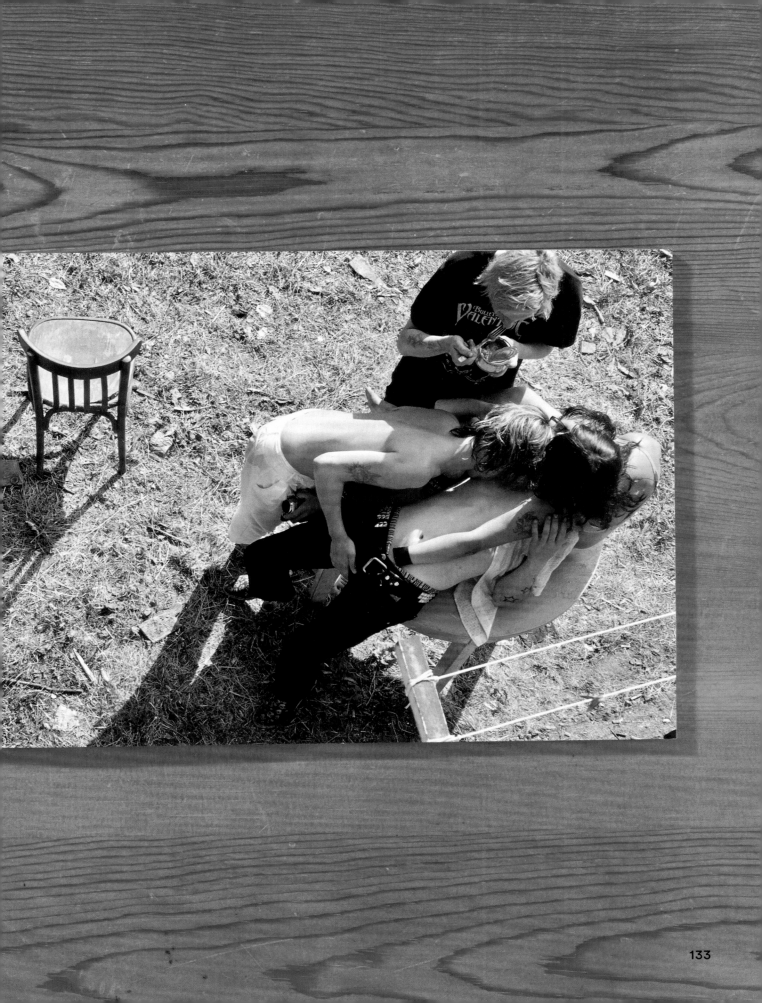

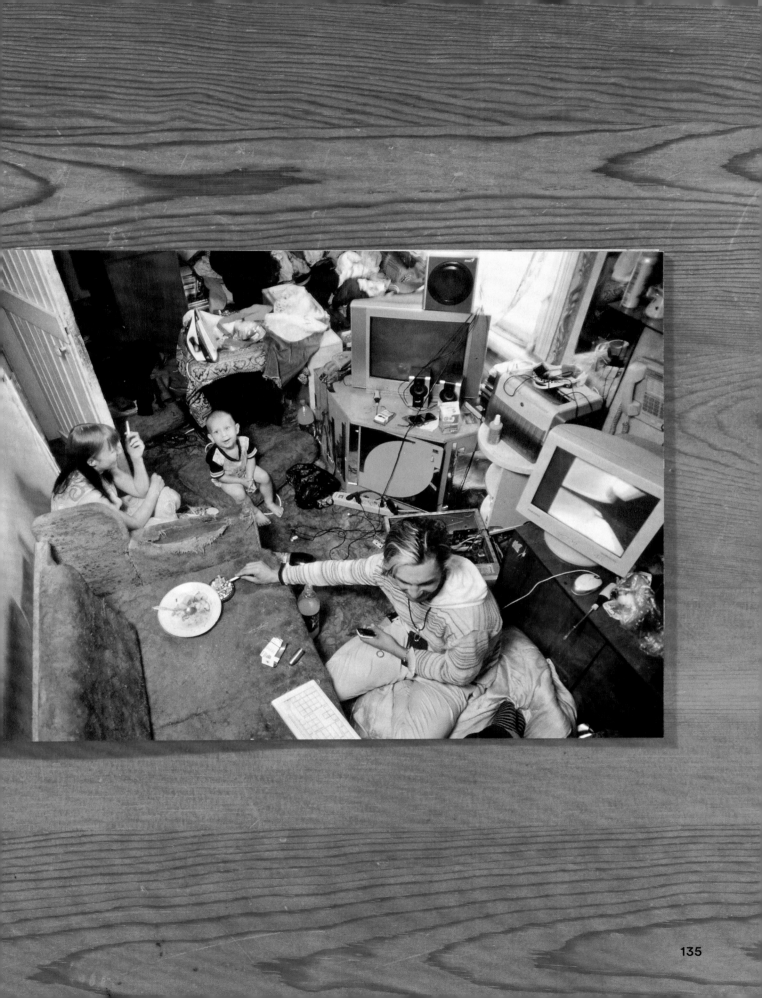

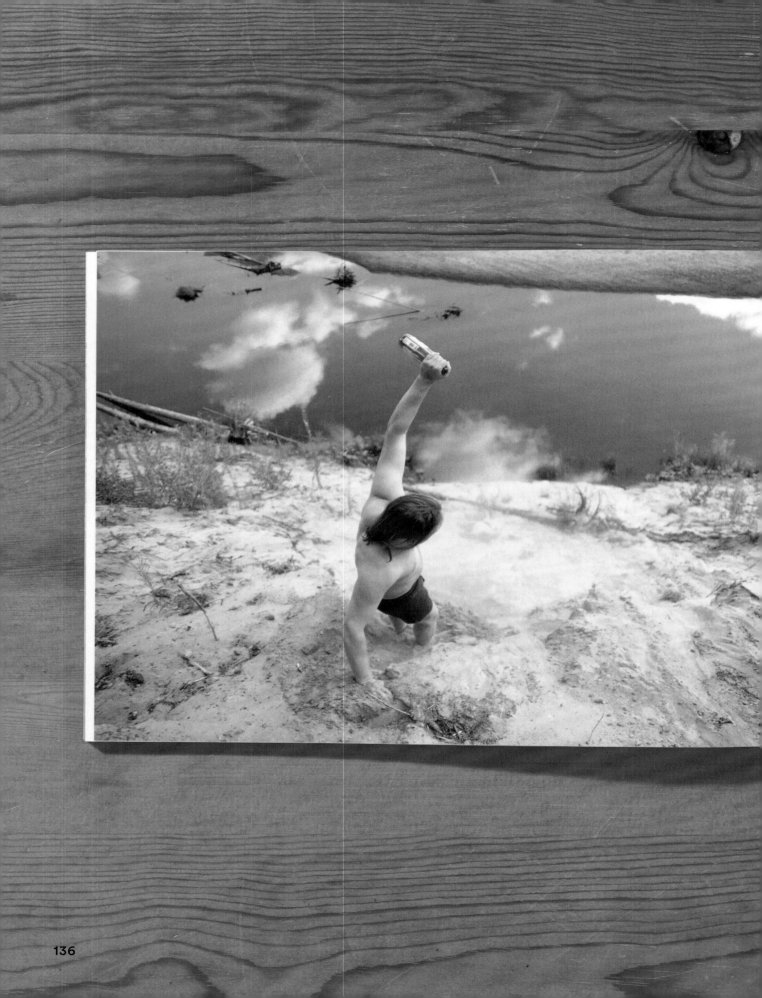

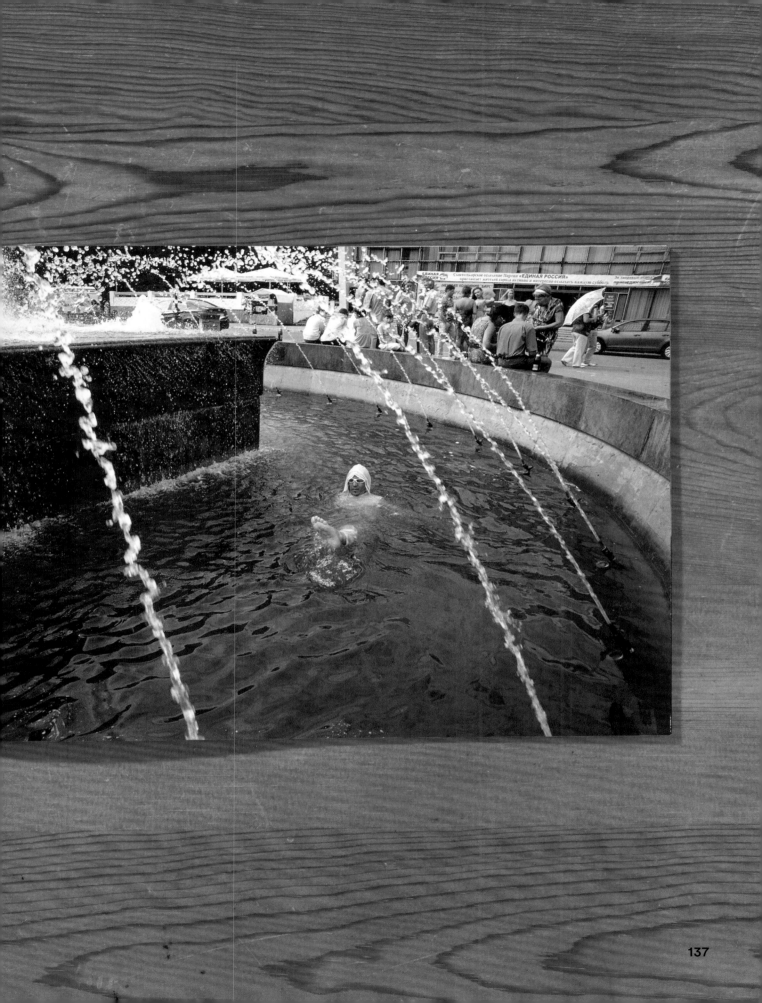

Title: <u>Good Mother and Father</u>

Artist: <u>Sacha Maric</u>

Designer: Jess Andersen

Editors: Sacha Maric and Jess Andersen

Printer: Cool Gray, Copenhagen, Denmark

Publication date and place: March 2012 / Copenhagen, Denmark

Edition: 250

Format and binding: hardcover / case bound

Size: 6 1/4 x 7 3/4 in. (15.7 x 20 cm)

Number of pages and images: 64 pages / 51 images

Type of printing and paper: four-color offset / Munken Lynx Rough 170gsm

Retail price: 35 EUR / 40 USD

Cost per unit: $$$$

Book soundtrack: "Black Balloon" by the Kills

After the birth of his first child, Sacha Maric took time off to look after his daughter Eleanor during the first few months of her life, while his wife went back to work. During this time he wandered extensively with her, taking trips to museums and the zoo as they got to know each other, and often took his camera with him. After a couple of years, Maric reflected upon the images he had accumulated and saw visual patterns and feelings that had emerged in this intensely emotional period of time. It was important for him that the book distilled the essence of what he had found: nuances of elation and joy, but also fear and vulnerability. Maric created the book as a poetic exploration of sex, life, and death, and as an honest depiction of a young couple feeling their way around parenthood for the first time.

<u>This project felt very true to myself as an artist and a father. I didn't have qualms about sharing such intimate pictures with the world. I see the book as a gift for my daughter; it's dedicated to her, and I hope that when she is older she will appreciate it.</u> —Sacha Maric

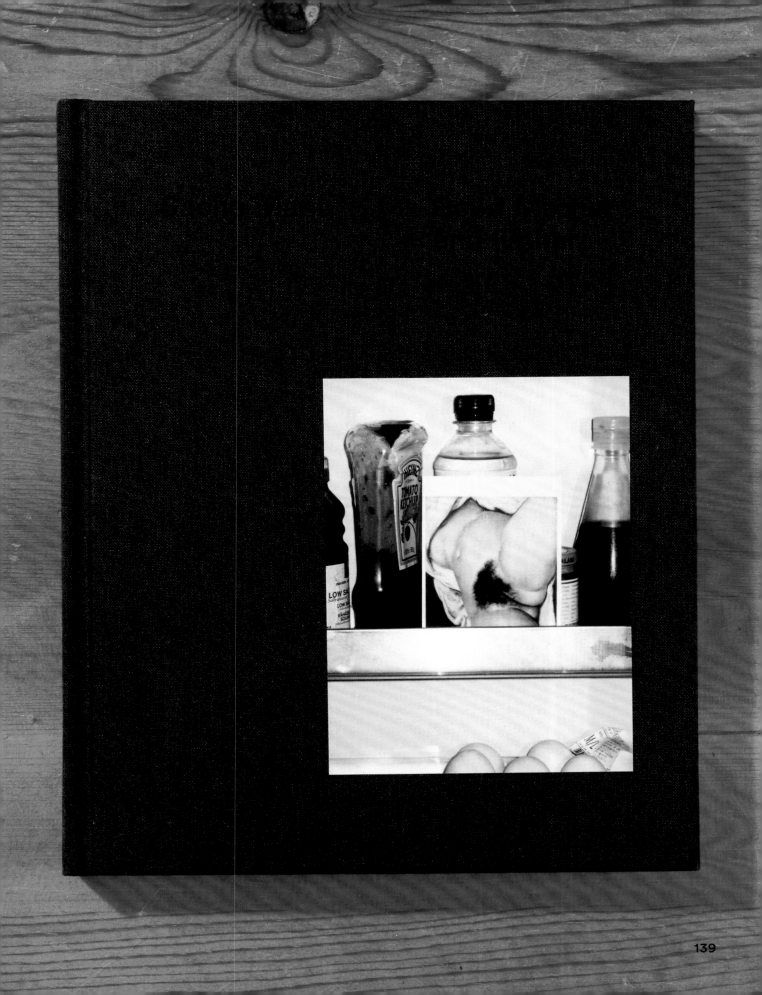

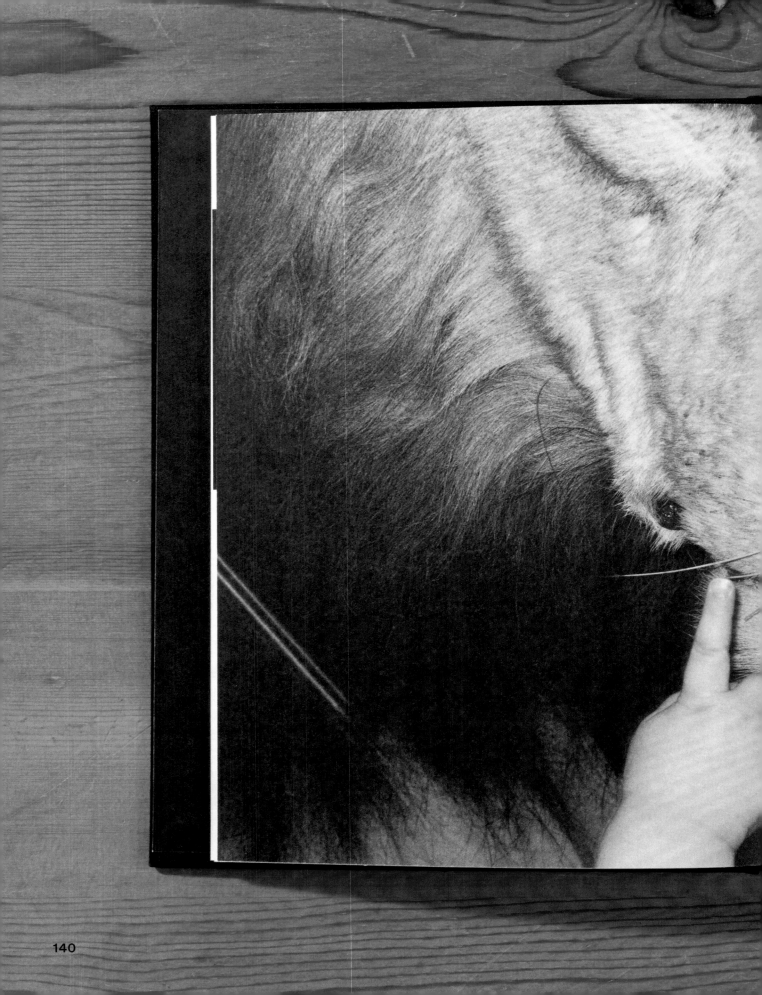

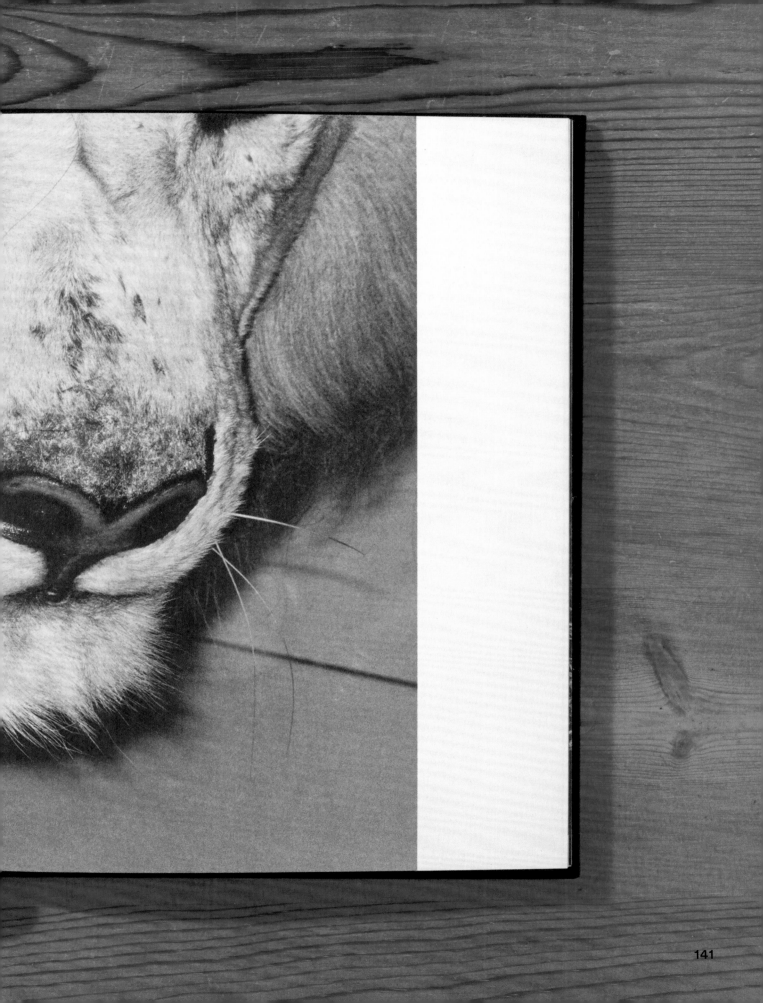

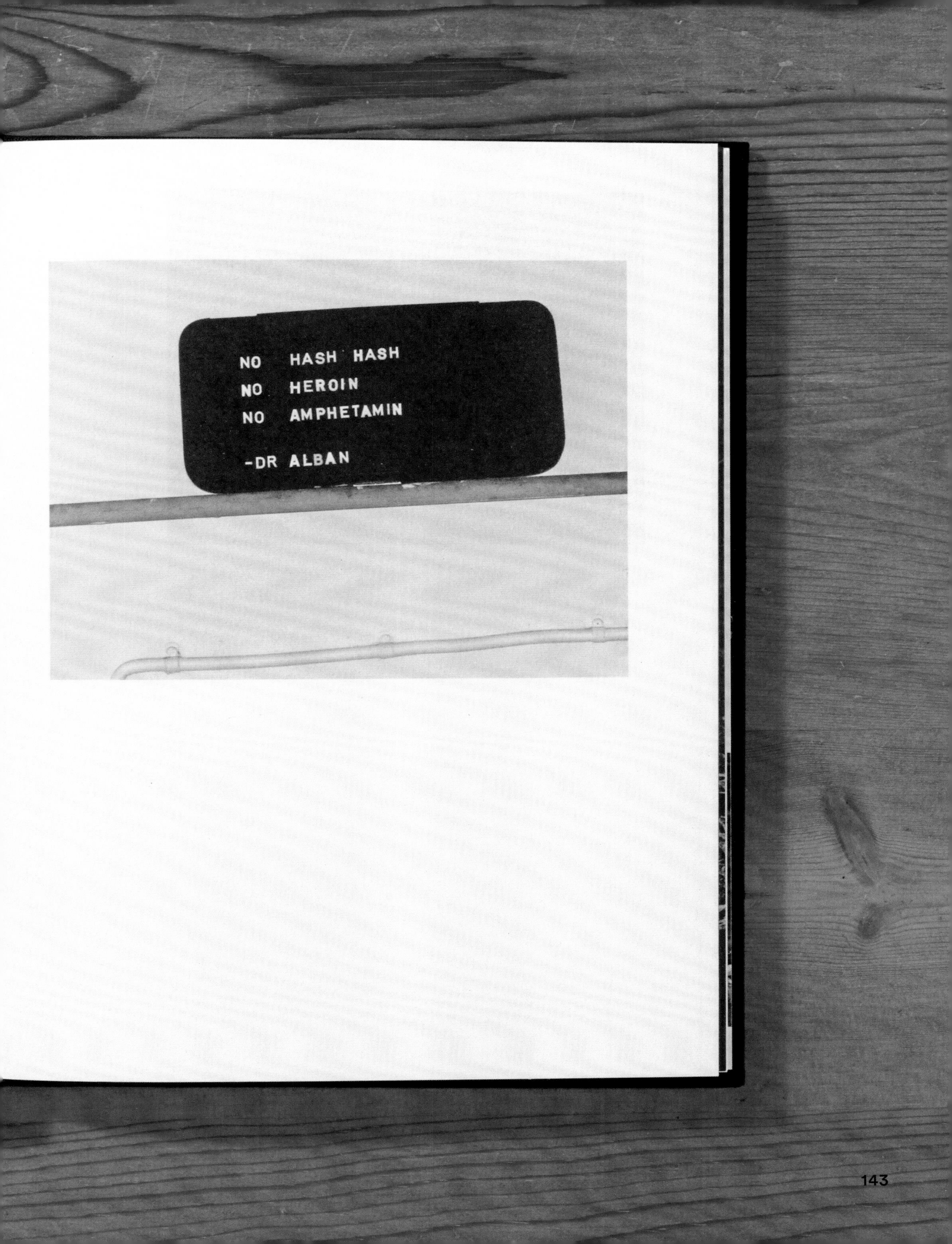
NO HASH HASH
NO HEROIN
NO AMPHETAMIN
-DR ALBAN

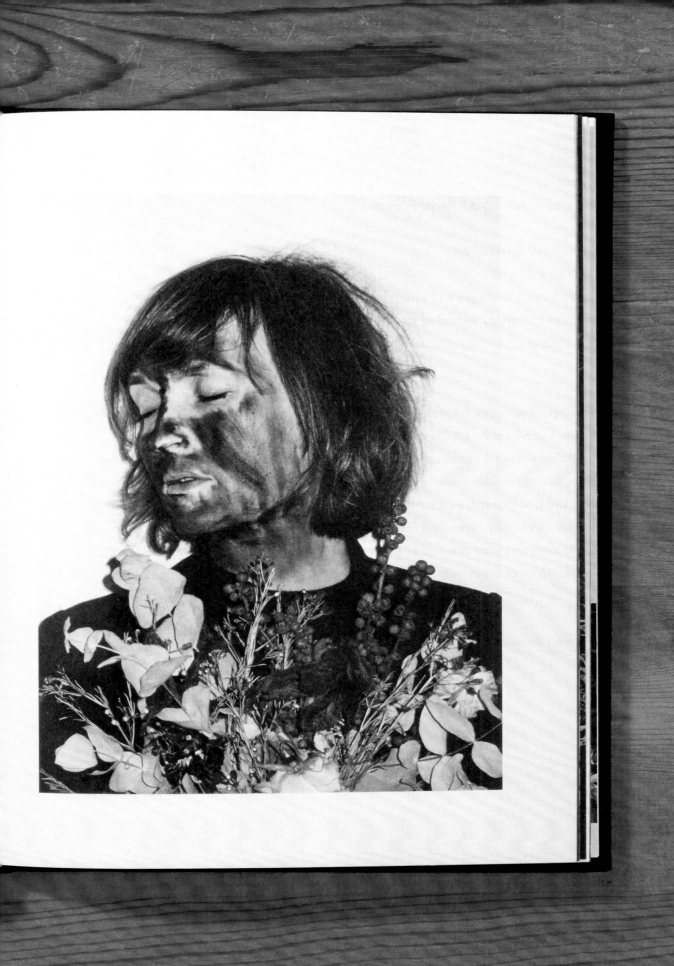

Title: Lucas

Artist: Eric Stephanian

Designer: Eric Stephanian

Editor: Eric Stephanian

Imprint: Stephanian

Printer: Xerox photocopier

Publication date and place: July 2013 / Paris, France

Edition: 150

Format and binding: softcover / stapled

Size: 7 7/8 x 11 6/8 in. (20 x 30 cm)

Number of pages and images: 16 pages / 15 images

Type of printing and paper: digital / recycled paper

Retail price: 15 EUR / 17 USD

Cost per unit: $$

Armenian artist Eric Stephanian's photocopied zine's sixteen pages feature just one photograph of a young boy: his son, Lucas, taken on the only opportunity he was given to meet him. The publication begins with an extreme close-up of Lucas's face, zooming out with each turn of the page. Frame by frame, Lucas recedes, slowly pulling away from Stephanian and the viewer until the final page depicts the photograph as a whole: Lucas playing in the garden with a friend. The book grapples with how to visually represent intangibles such as paternal loss, yearning, and empathy. Aside from the name *Lucas* printed at the front of the zine, there is no text; Stephanian did not print his own name or contact details. The object loses its tether to him as soon as it is sold.

One shot can bring a man down. —Eric Stephanian

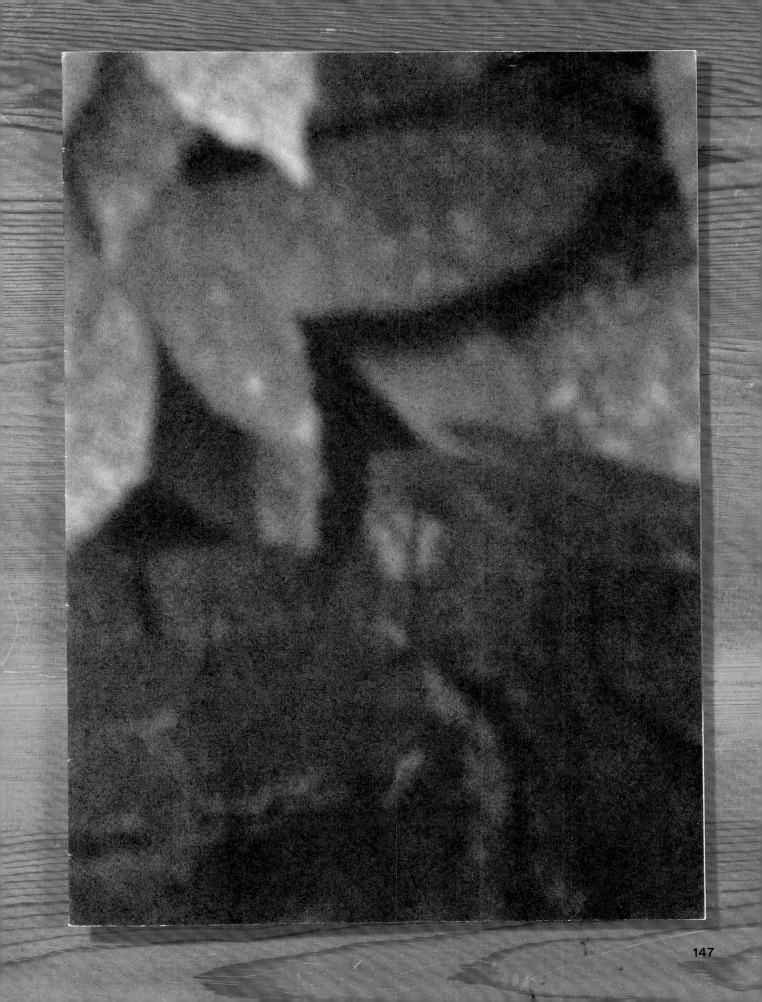

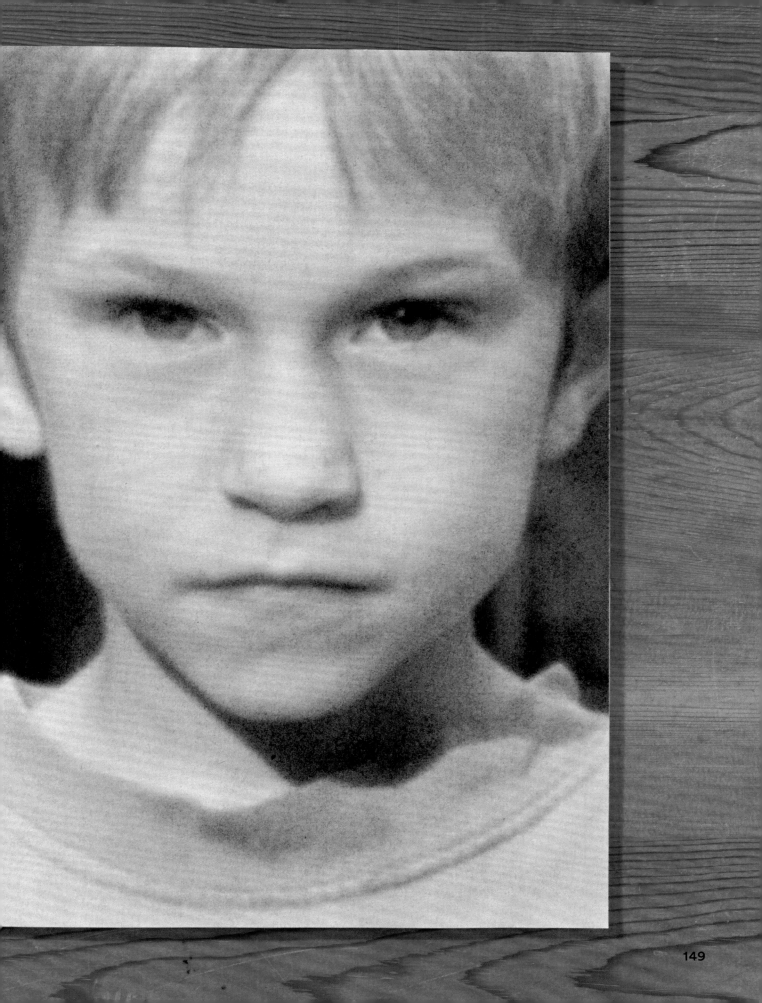

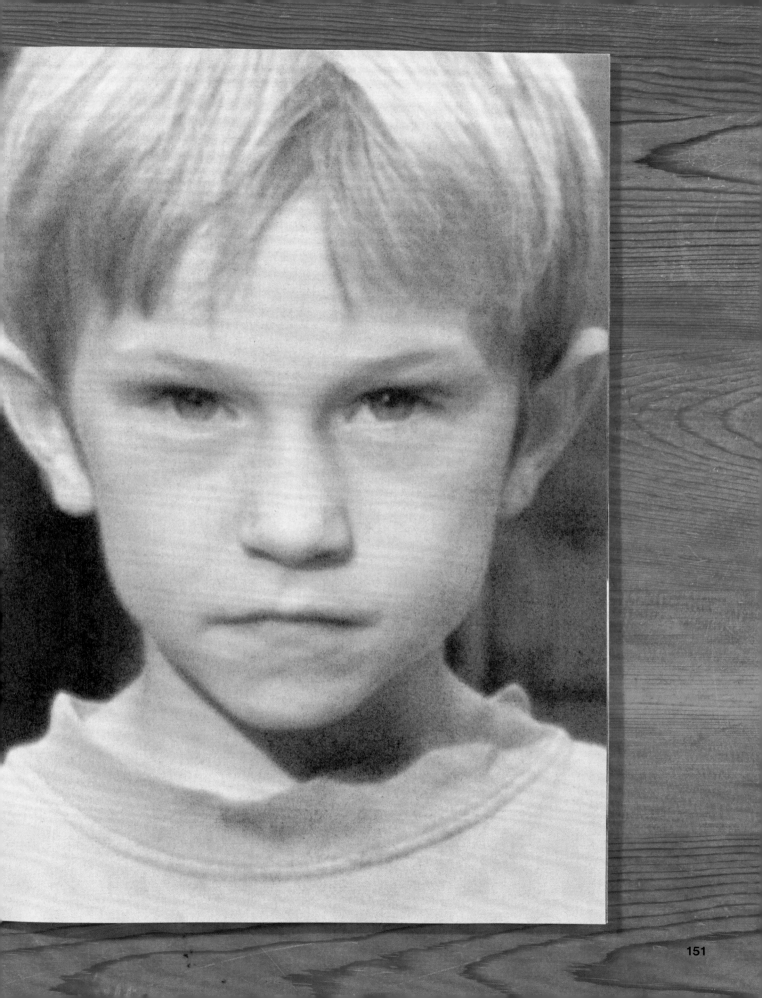

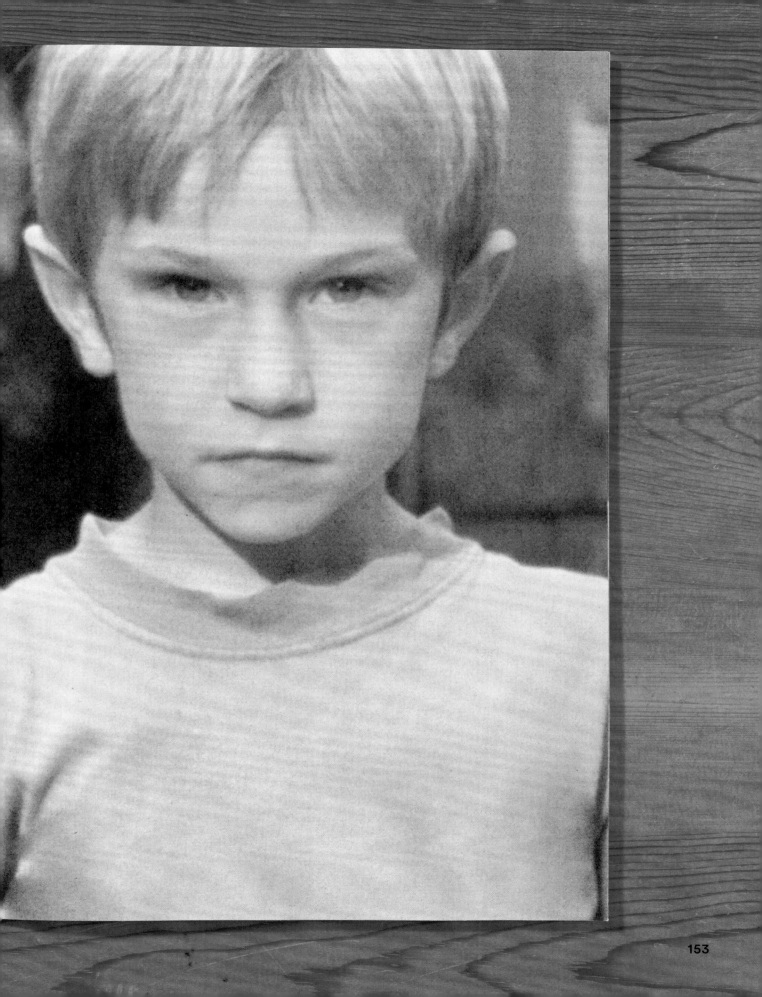

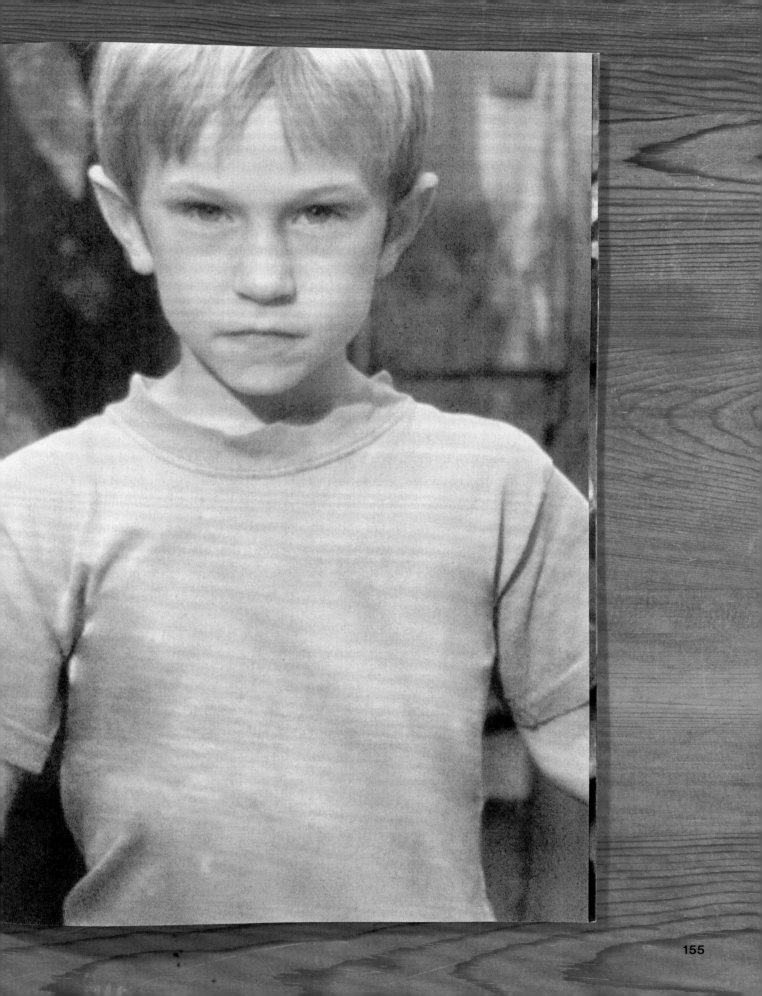

Title: Now Will Not Be With Us Forever

Artist: Maurice van Es

Designer: Charlotte Gilissen

Editor: Maurice van Es

Imprint: none

Printer: NDR, The Hague, the Netherlands

Publication date and place: June 2013 / The Hague, the Netherlands

Edition: 50

Format and binding: softcover, seven volumes in slipcase / saddle stitched

Size: 5 7/8 x 8 1/4 in. (14.8 x 21 cm)

Number of pages and images: various / various

Type of printing and paper: digital / unknown

Retail price: 50 EUR / 57 USD

Cost per unit: $$$$$

Book soundtrack: *A Red Score in Tile* by William Basinski

Maurice van Es's *Now Will Not Be With Us Forever* is an assessment of the things which make up a moment in the author's life. For this seven-volume series, Van Es documented fragments of his immediate surroundings—from his estranged brother leaving the house, to textures from childhood photographs. The urgency to document his life and its banal peculiarities stemmed from Van Es's first experience of loss. In the process, Van Es created a diary that contrasts with the usual off-the-cuff journal aesthetic, adopting a very composed typological approach to his environment in each book, which make up the whole publication.

I made this collection of books for my graduation project at the Royal Academy of Art in The Hague. It's about how everything you experience during a day, no matter how tiny, can be worth telling a story about. I started to produce a lot of books; I found so much joy in the making process—printing books at home, showing them to friends, and talking about the subject matter. However, it was really a struggle to graduate with seven different projects. My teachers tried to force me to present one "strong" final work, but in the end I was thankful because I learned the most important thing: listen to yourself. It's your work. —Maurice van Es

the past is a strange place

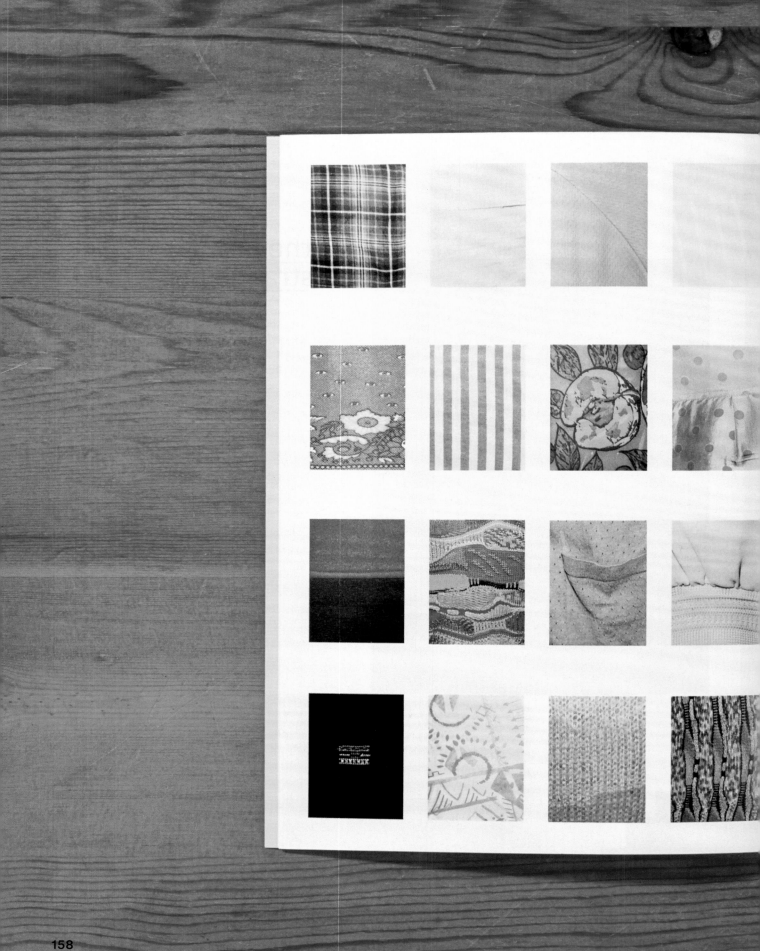

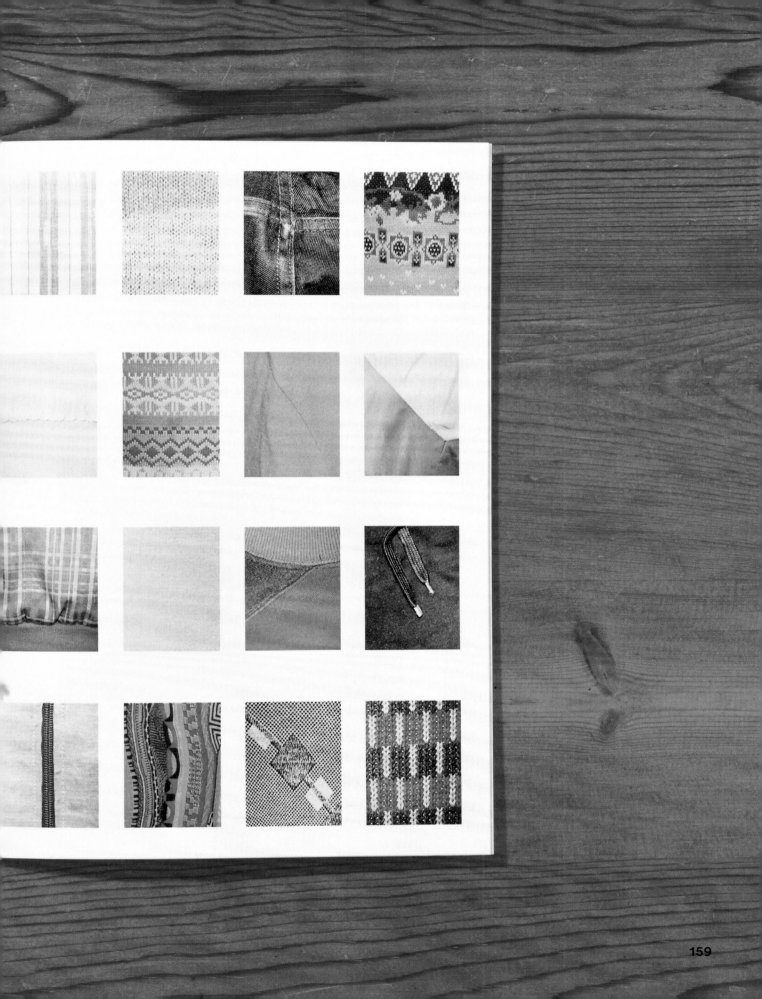

<u>to me you are a work of art</u>

Unintended installations made
by my mother. An ode to her
concentration.

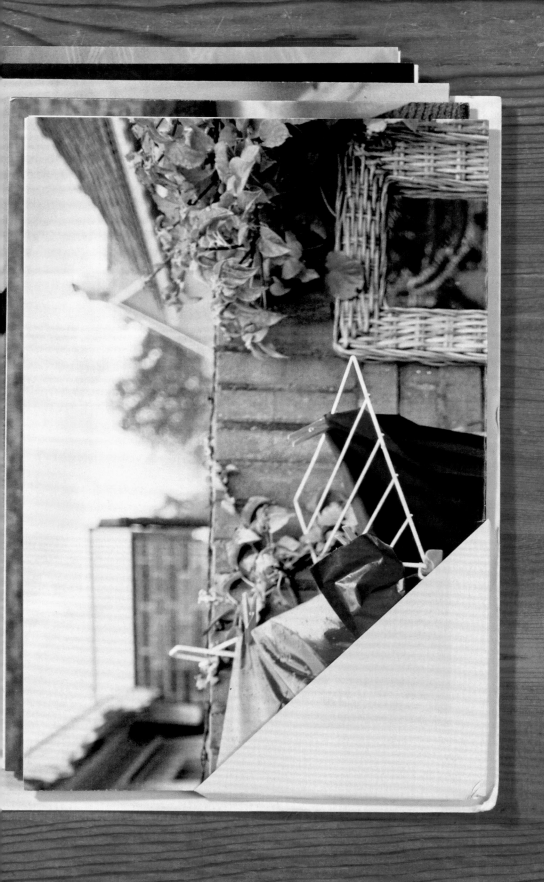

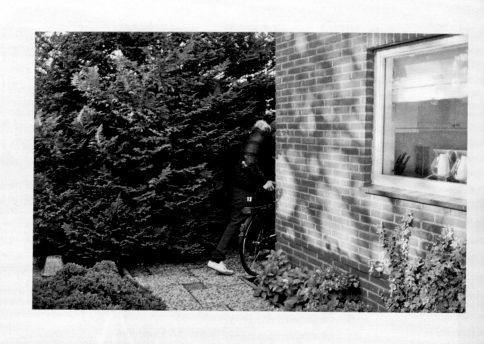

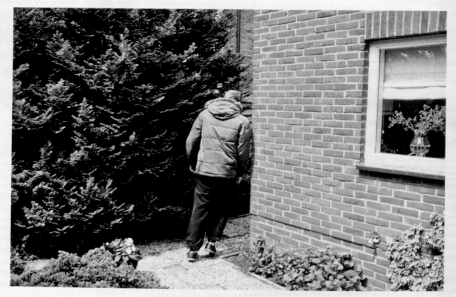

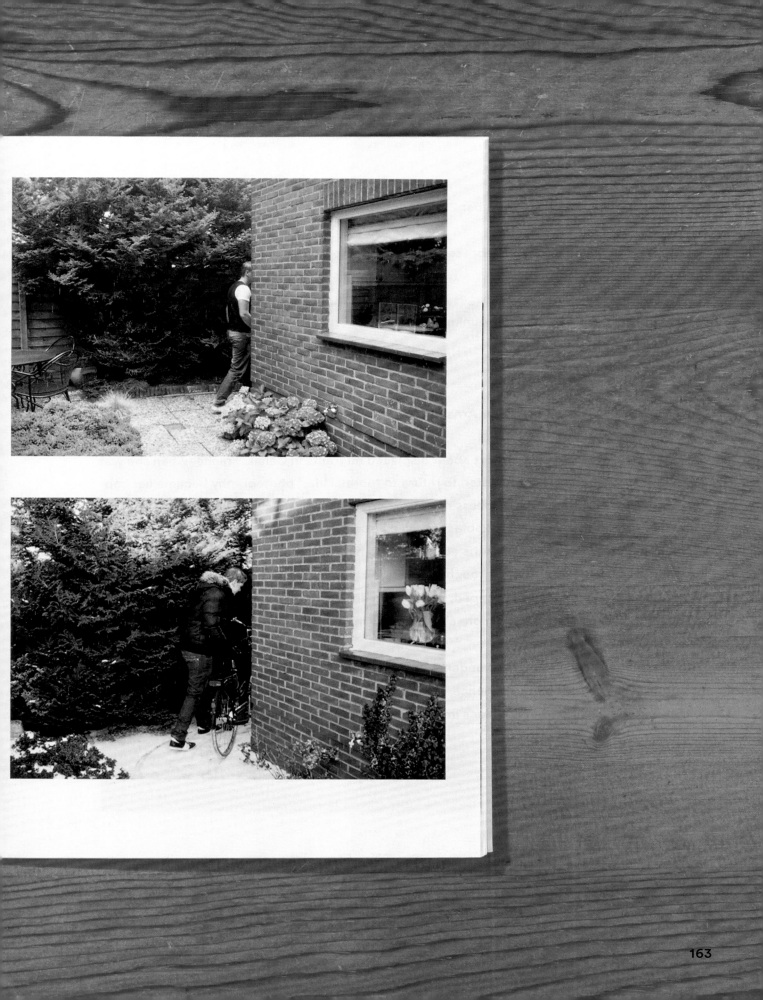

Title: Speaking of scars

Artist: Teresa Eng

Designer: Teresa Eng

Editor: Teresa Eng

Imprint: If / Then Books

Printer: Push, London, UK

Publication date and place: November 2012 / London, UK

Edition: 500

Format and binding: hardcover, debossed front cover / clothbound

Size: 6 6/8 x 9 in. (17 x 22.8 cm)

Number of pages and images: 68 pages / 50 images

Type of printing and paper: offset / unknown

Retail price: 31.95 GBP / 50 USD

Cost per unit: $$$$

Book soundtrack: "Raein" by Ólafur Arnalds

Teresa Eng was working on a project about displaced migrants in Calais, France, when she was physically assaulted. As she attempted to return to "normal life," photography became her coping mechanism and a means of processing the experience. Over the course of three years, Eng worked to give form to the unspeakable through a visual language, and *Speaking of scars* is the result. Using pictures made before the attack, during her slow process of recovery, and until the eventual trial, images repeat throughout the book to echo the lingering presence of trauma. Photographs are folded and overlapped, both hiding and revealing. The book becomes less about Eng's own experience, and more about trauma in general.

With *Speaking of scars*, I sought to understand the psychological condition of trauma to distance myself from my own violent experience. And I realized that through implying violence, the images lent themselves to the reader's imagination. —Teresa Eng

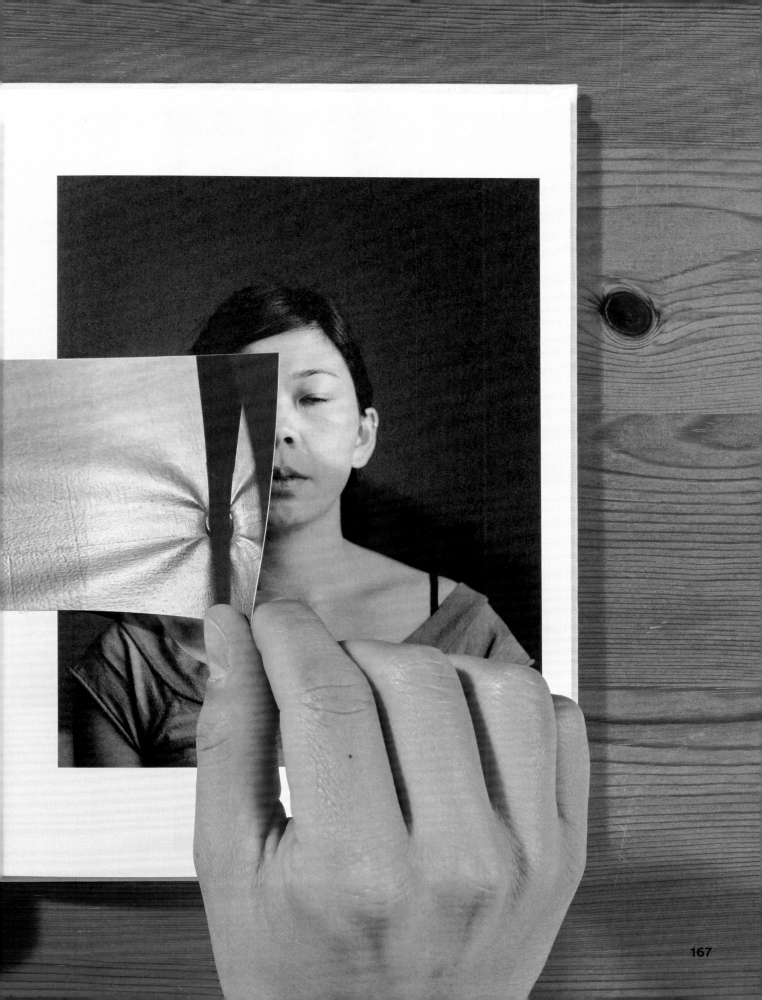

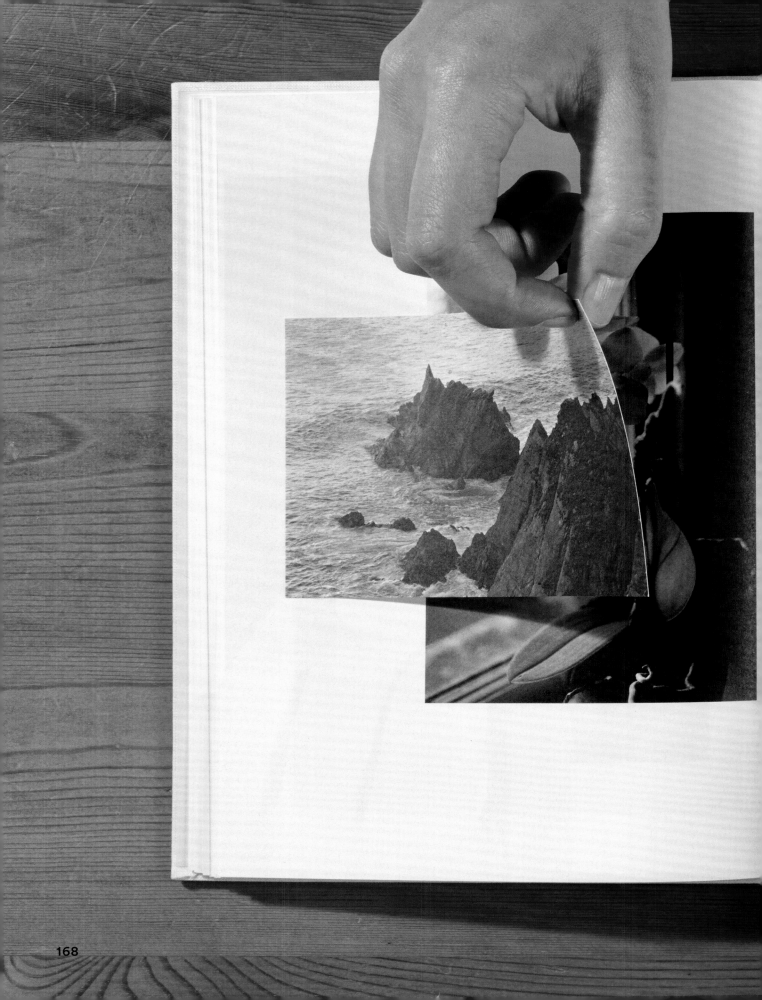

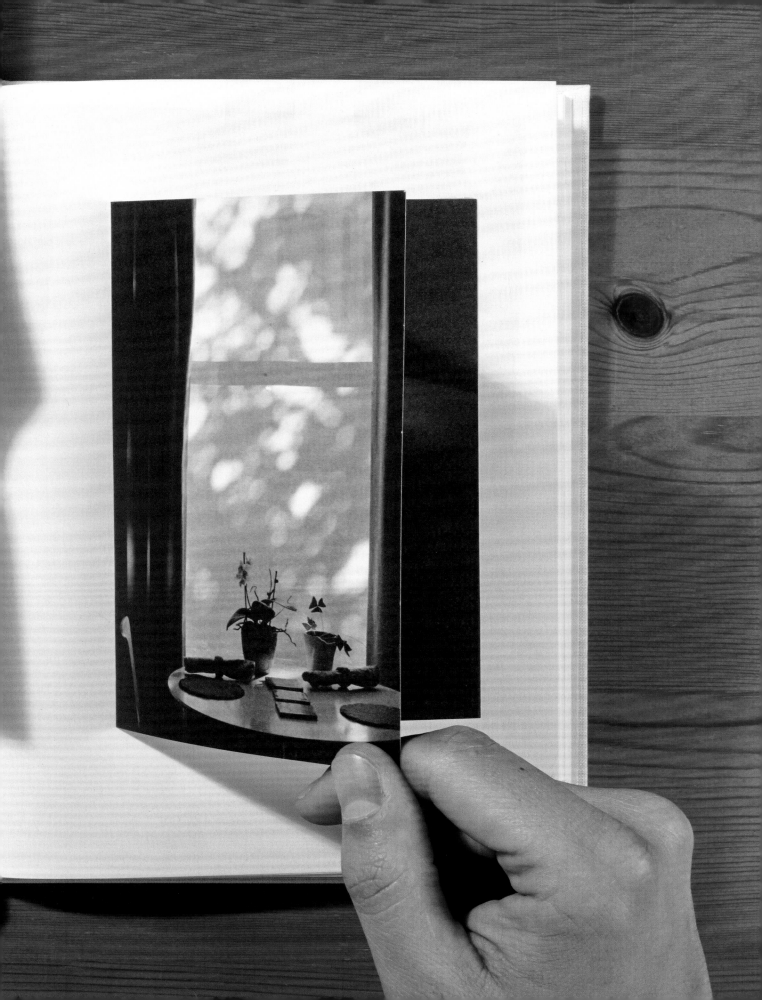

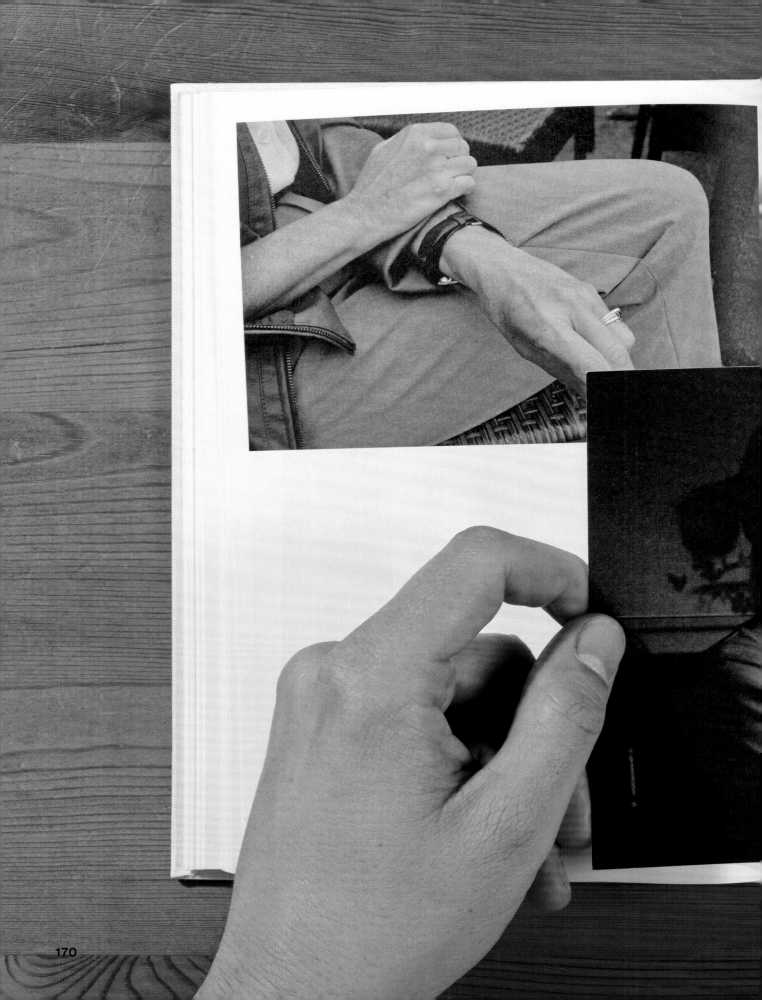

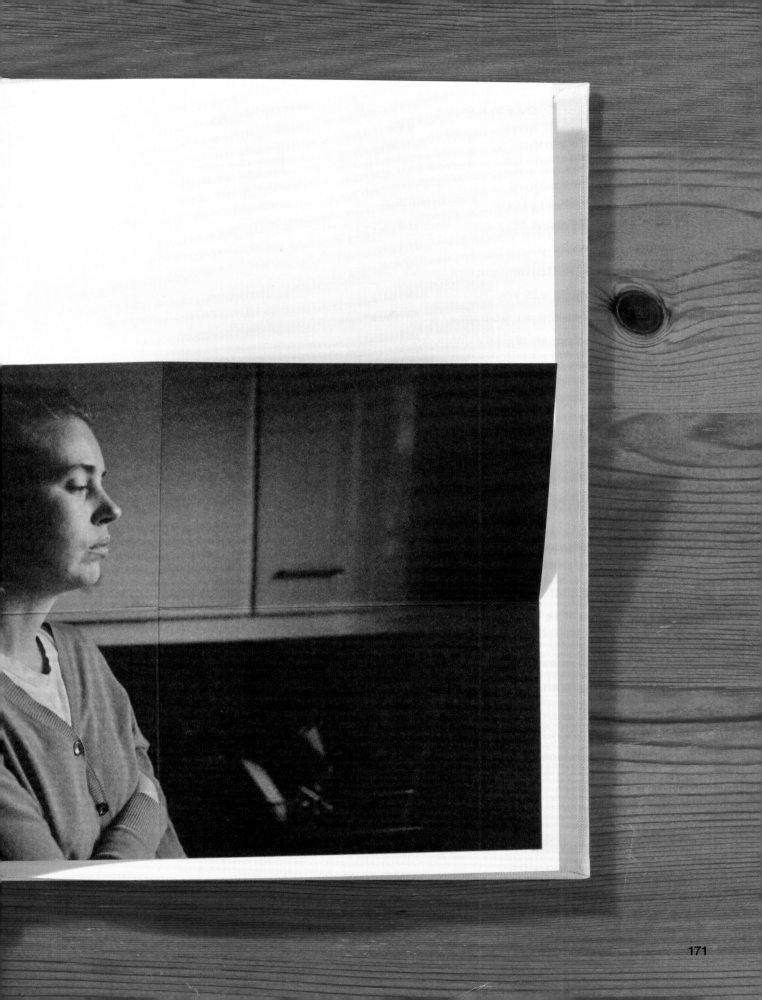

Title: Between Here and There

Artist: Delaney Allen

Additional contributor: Sydney S. Kim

Designer: Delaney Allen

Editor: Delaney Allen

Imprint: none

Printer: Publication Studio, Portland, Oregon, USA

Publication date and place: May 2010 / Portland, Oregon, USA

Edition: 20

Format and binding: softcover / perfect bound

Size: 8 1/4 x 9 3/4 in. (21 x 25 cm)

Number of pages and images: 96 pages / 80 images

Type of printing and paper: digital / unknown

Retail price: 65 USD

Cost per unit: $$$$$

Book soundtrack: "Rhythm of the Rain" by the Cascades

Between Here and There is an autobiographical account of a long-distance relationship and its eventual breakup. While attending school in Portland, Oregon, Delaney Allen and his then-girlfriend —who lived back home in Dallas—kept in touch via e-mail. As he tried to find his voice as a photographer, Allen took photographs of his surroundings and his travels back and forth and shared them with her, attaching them to their correspondence. After the relationship fell apart, he combed through these messages, searching for answers, and found that the text and images spoke to each other. This book is a diary reflecting their final year together.

For me, the process of making the book gave me a way of figuring out life at that moment. As I sat for a week with both the images and printed e-mails, I began to see a relationship between the two that ultimately led to *Between Here and There*. What had once been intended as simple imagery on gallery walls for a school thesis show ultimately transformed into an autobiographical book about life. —Delaney Allen

BETWEEN HERE AND THERE

DELANEY ALLEN

Subject: RE: ▨▨▨▨▨▨▨▨▨▨▨▨▨▨▨
From: Kelly ▨▨▨▨▨▨▨▨
To: Delaney Allen <delaneyallen@yahoo.com>
Date: Tuesday, April 14, 2009, 9:03AM (CST) Central Standard Time

So not that I necessarily want to do this here....but this could be a super cool place for us to get married. It is basically a studio with different rooms and it is actually made for weddings. $3500 to rent on a friday or saturday, which doesn't seem that bad to me.... I don't know. If for some reason we decided to go the more traditional route, then this would be really cool.

http://studios1019.com/index.html

May 1st we will start counting down til you're here officially, even though I already am. 33 days.

Friday, December 18, 2009 3:36 AM (PST) Pacific Standard Time
From: Delaney Allen <delaneyallen@yahoo.com>
To: Kelly ████████████████████

Really effin late bedtime for me but that's ok. I'm running on adrenaline now. But I have everything washed and laid out. My electronics bags are packed and ready. All I need to do tomorrow is get dressed and the put everything in the bag.

Ok. That's all from me. Time to shut it down. 12 hours from now I'll be on the runway and a little less than 16 hours from now I will be there for a month able to finally touch/see/hold/feel/smell you. I can't wait.

Love you.

RE: RE: RE:
From: Kelly ████████████████████████
To: Delaney Allen <delaneyallen@yahoo.com>
Date: Monday, April 5, 2010, 5:45 PM (CST) Central Standard Time

It can't happen now.

Title: Billie

Artist: Ofer Wolberger

Designer: Ofer Wolberger

Editor: Justin James Reed

Imprint: Horses Think Press

Printer: Sun Superior, Braintree, Massachusetts, USA

Publication date and place: September 2014 / New York, USA

Edition: 100

Format and binding: softcover / perfect bound

Size: 6 5/8 x 9 in. (16.7 x 23 cm)

Number of pages and images: 240 pages / 154 images

Type of printing and paper: digital offset, ink-jet cover / Mohawk Via Vellum Warm White 80lb

Retail price: 55 USD

Cost per unit: $$$$$

Book soundtrack: *Promenade* by the Divine Comedy

Comprised entirely of 35 mm half-frame photographs, *Billie* is both a moving portrait of the artist's wife and an evolving diary of collaboration between photographer and subject. Utilizing repetition and sequence, *Billie* presents one man's pursuit to capture a true image of the woman he loves, whose outfits and expressions shift and change throughout—although the sheer volume of pictures Wolberger offers seem to be an acknowledgment of photography's failure in this regard. His earlier titles *Visitor* and *Life With Maggie* also feature this recurring preoccupation with the idea of a portrait, as well as with questions of authorship and direction. Wolberger is cofounder of the Brooklyn-based publishing outfit Horses Think Press, alongside Justin James Reed.

The *Billie* pictures were shot over several years. When I returned to the archive of images, part of me felt they weren't my pictures any longer—they were different from anything I had shot before. Having that distance from the photographs gave me license to treat them as a "found" body of work. If I wasn't going to be the author, it seemed obvious that Billie herself would be. After that realization, the book came together quite easily. For the sequence of images, I relied heavily on the original sequence from the film I had shot. For the design, it felt natural to leave my name and all other text out, except for the title—and name of the author—*Billie*.
—Ofer Wolberger

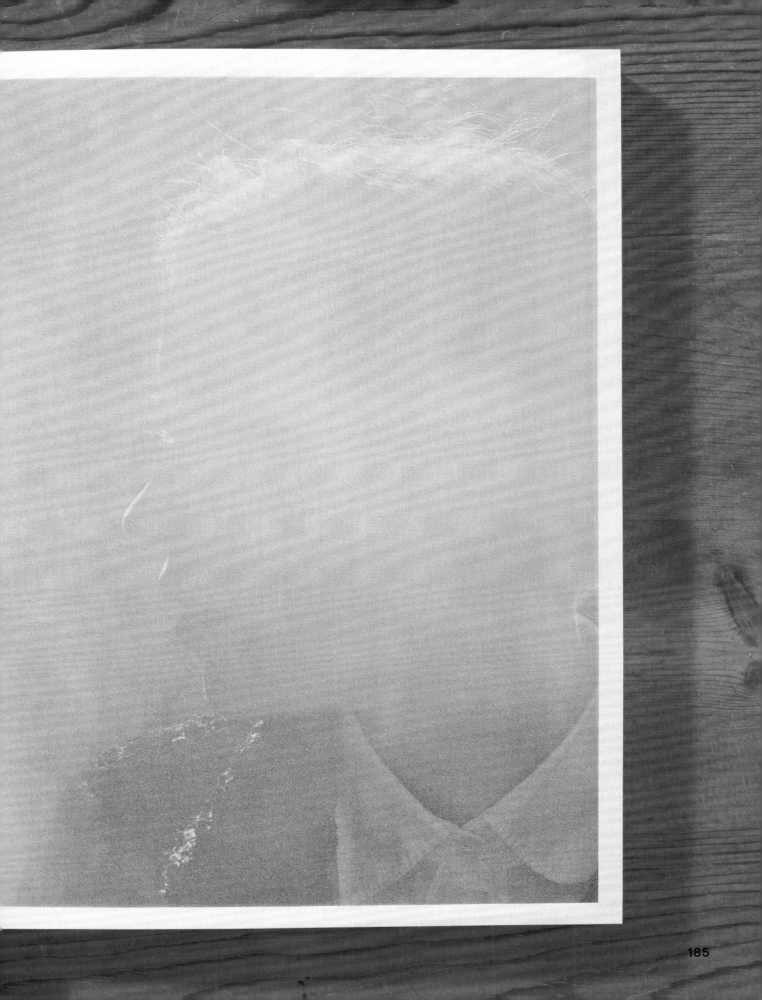

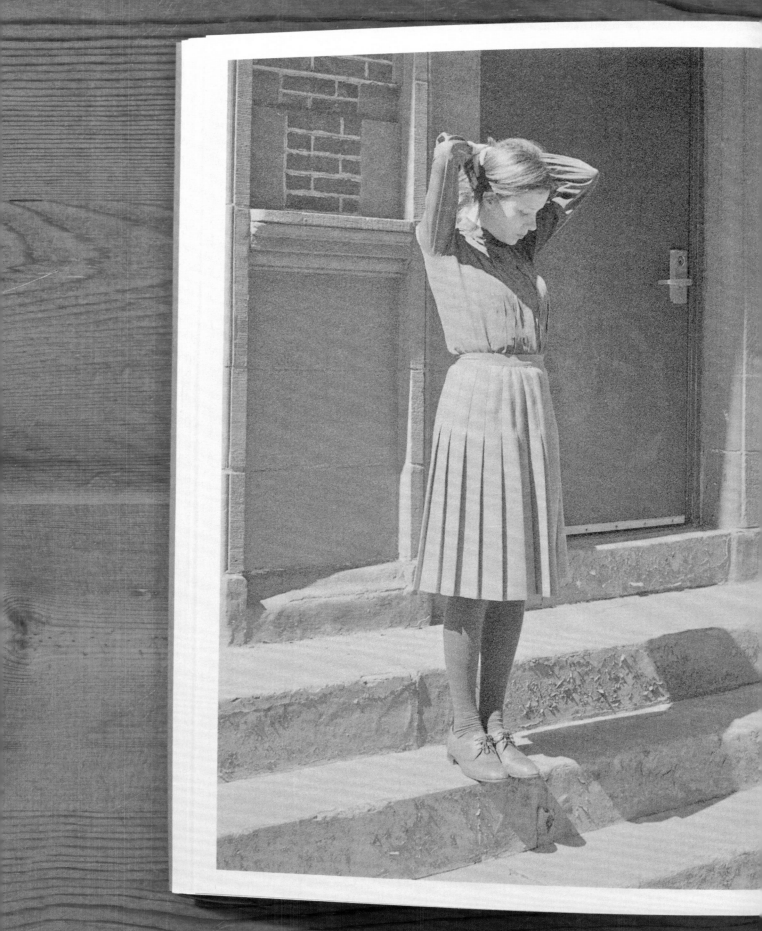

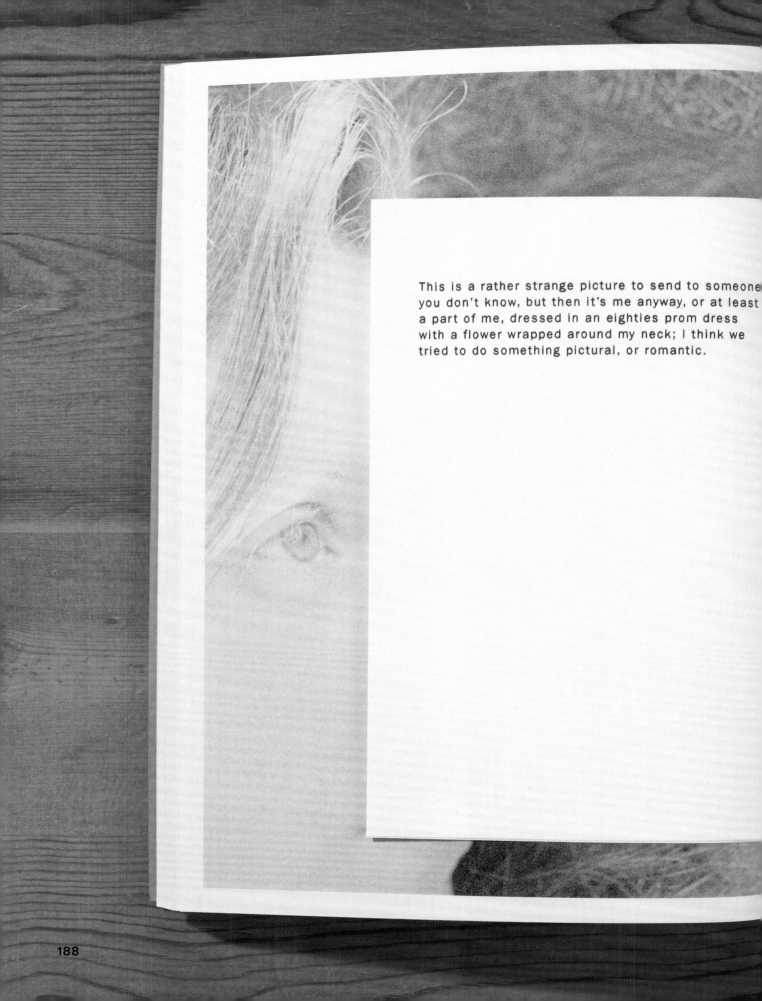

This is a rather strange picture to send to someone
you don't know, but then it's me anyway, or at least
a part of me, dressed in an eighties prom dress
with a flower wrapped around my neck; I think we
tried to do something pictural, or romantic.

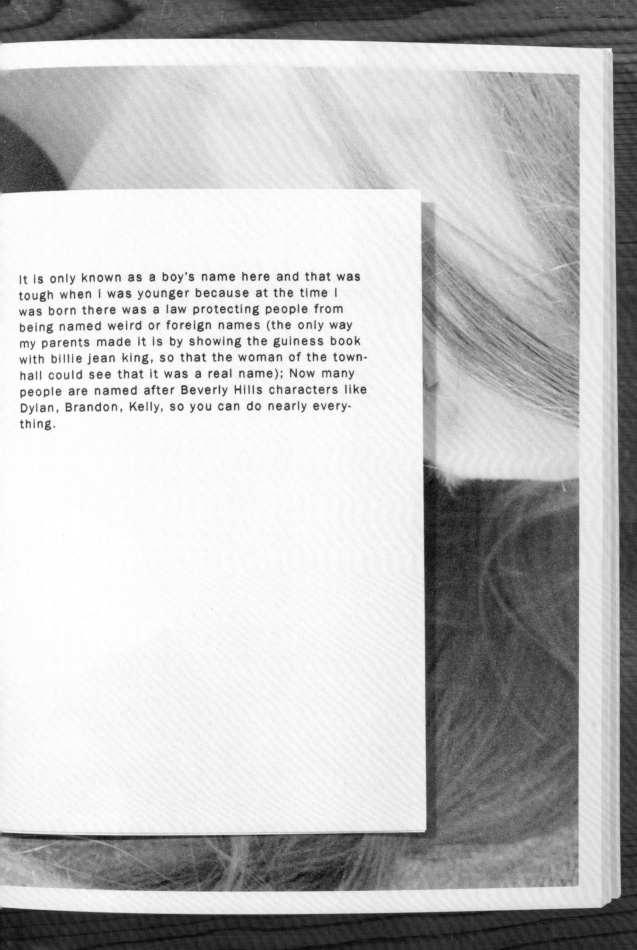

It is only known as a boy's name here and that was tough when I was younger because at the time I was born there was a law protecting people from being named weird or foreign names (the only way my parents made it is by showing the guiness book with billie jean king, so that the woman of the townhall could see that it was a real name); Now many people are named after Beverly Hills characters like Dylan, Brandon, Kelly, so you can do nearly everything.

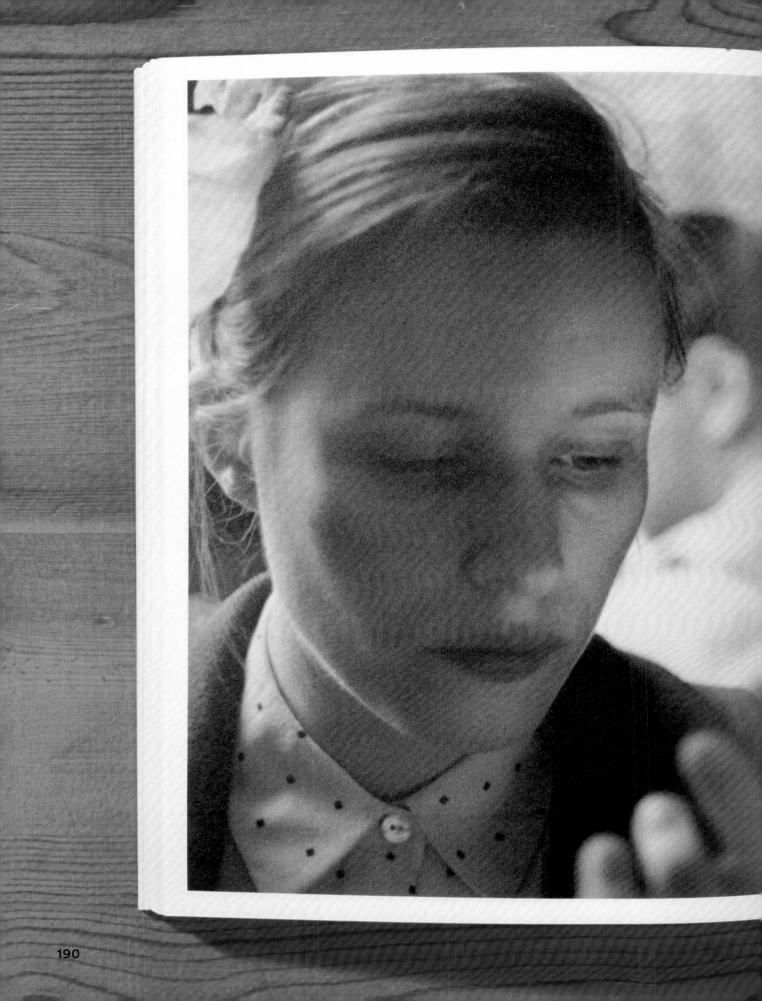

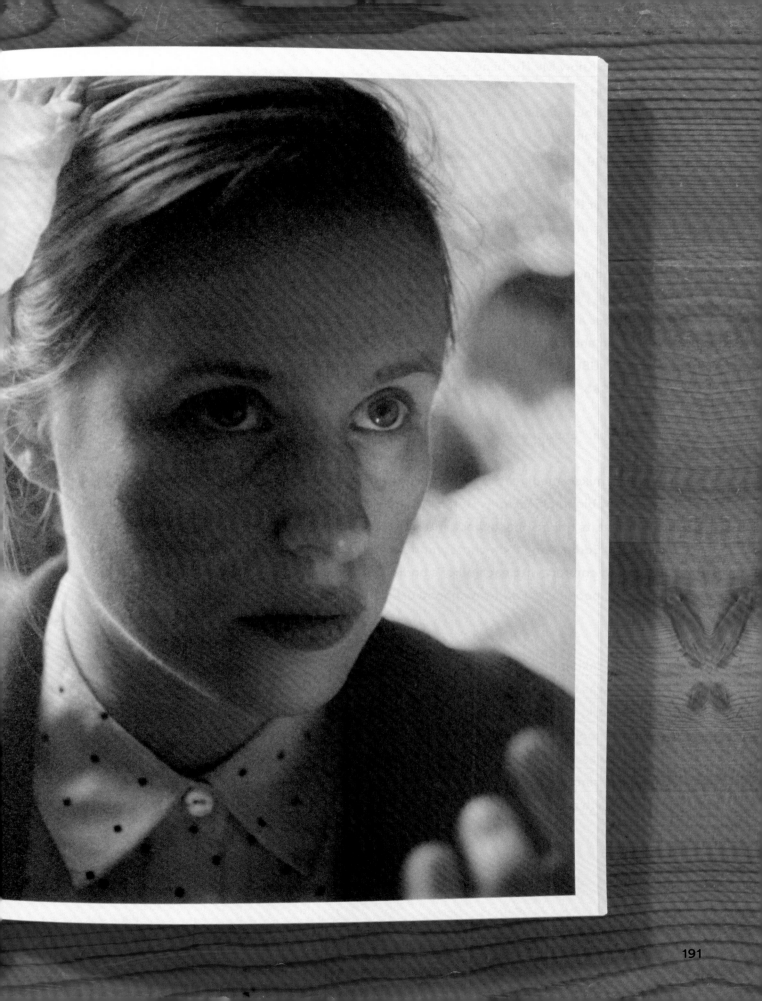

Title: Getting to Know My Husband's Cock

Artist: Ellen Jong

Additional contributor: Cindy Gallop

Designer: Ellen Jong

Editor: Ellen Jong

Imprint: none

Printer: Endeavor Printing, Long Island City, New York, USA

Publication date and place: May 2010 / New York, USA

Edition: 97

Format and binding: softcover / perfect bound

Size: 6 1/4 x 9 in. (15.8 x 22.8 cm)

Number of pages and images: 150 pages / 67 images

Type of printing and paper: digital / Mohawk Color Copy 120gsm

Retail price: 80 USD

Cost per unit: $$$

Book soundtrack: "Embraceable You" by Chet Baker

Ellen Jong is a mixed-media artist with a particular affinity for photography, and her work often takes on an autobiographical tone. *Getting to Know My Husband's Cock* is not the overtly graphic publication that its title might suggest, but rather a love story in photographs. Newly married to her husband Eddie, Jong took photographs as they got to know each other, and documented their increasing comfort with each other's bodies. Jong weaves nudes, still lifes, and landscapes throughout the book, with Eddie's manhood used more as a device to describe what it is to fall in love.

When I started taking these pictures, I always felt like we were taking them together. I didn't ever feel like I was taking pictures of him—I was taking pictures of us. In making the book and showing the work, it was important to me not to betray my subject, which happened to be my husband. It took a huge amount of trust from both of us to be vulnerable with the camera around, and it was super important for me to respect that. There is a fine line between intimacy and voyeurism, sincerity and mockery. The line shifts with every subject; I decide where I want to stand with each photo I take. —Ellen Jong

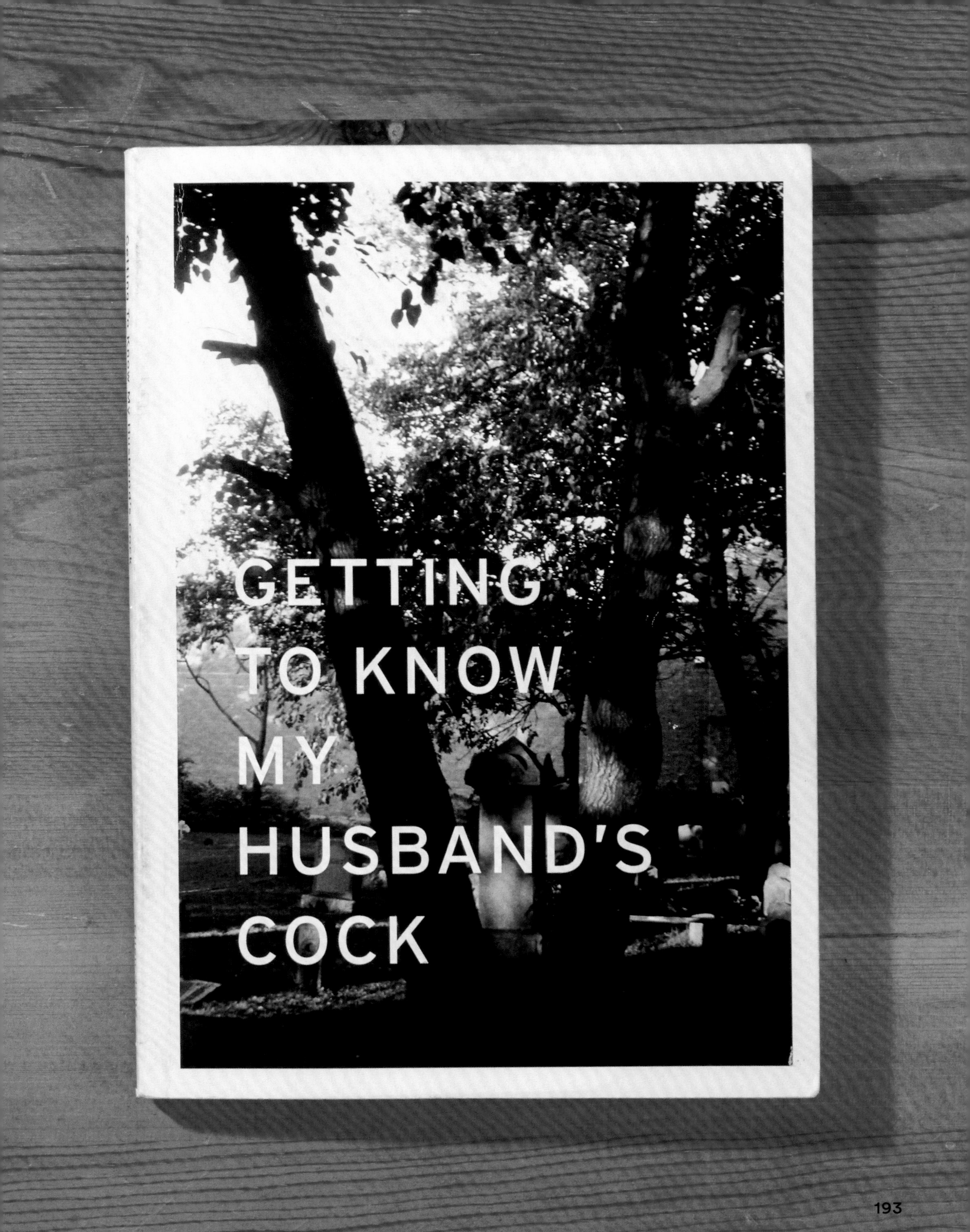

GETTING
TO KNOW
MY
HUSBAND'S
COCK

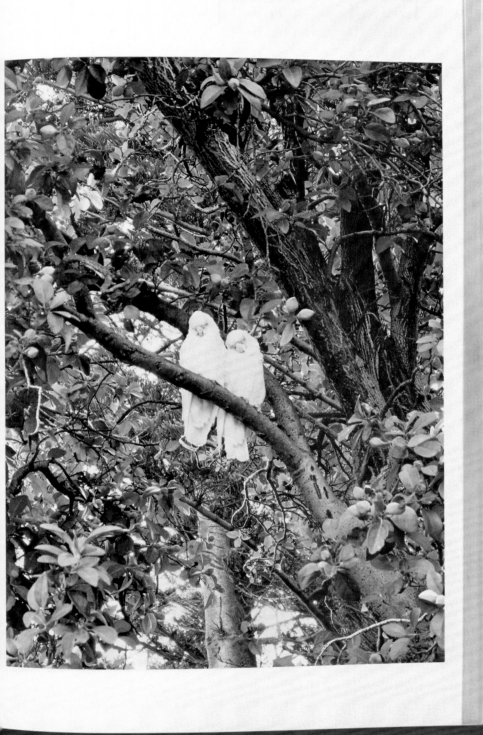

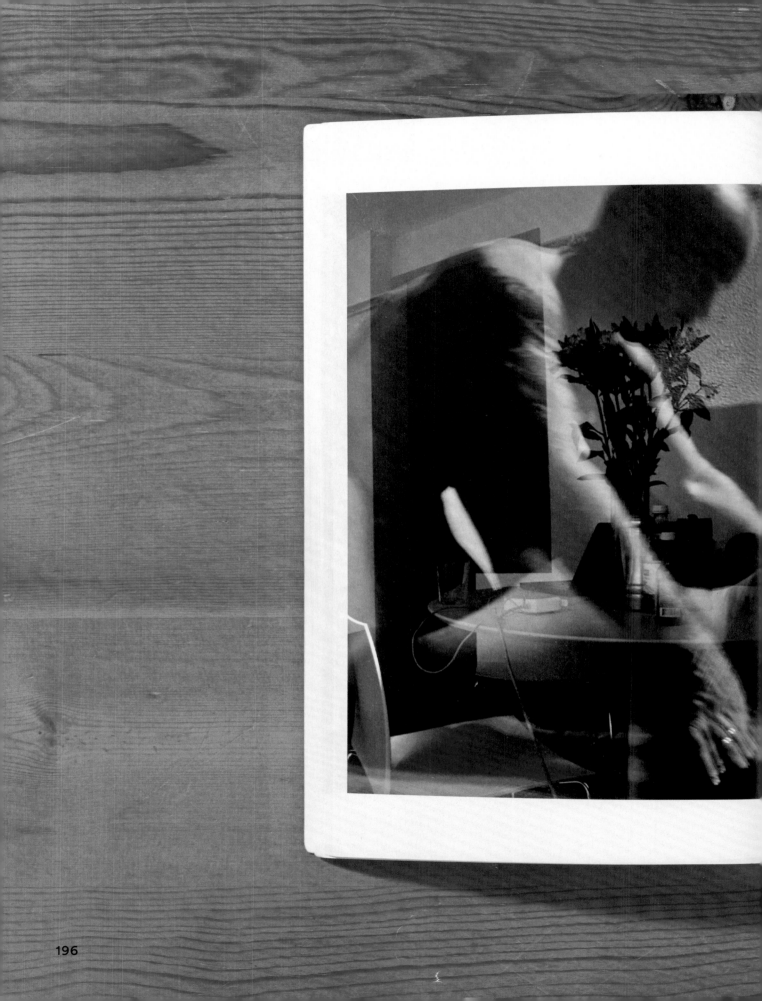

Smells Like Me
Smells Like You
-
Inside

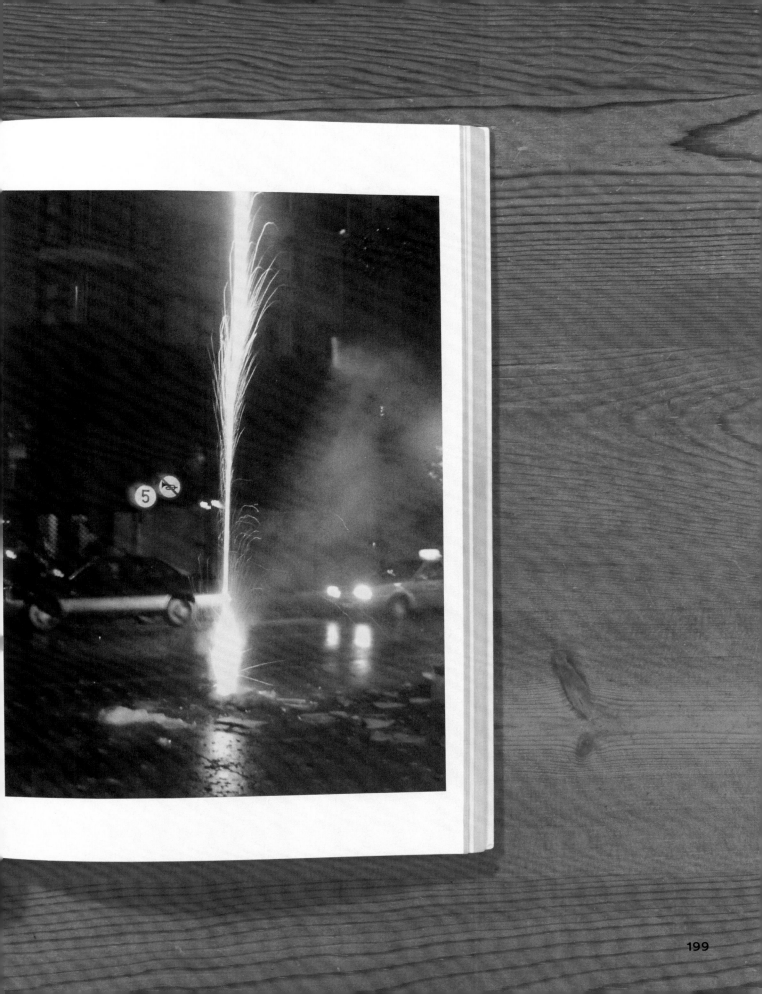

Self Publish, Be a Story- teller

Title: Thai Politics no. 2, vol. 1

Artist: Miti Ruangkritya

Designers: Jean Arunsirichok and Miti Ruangkritya

Editor: Miti Ruangkritya

Imprint: none

Printer: Rabbit, Bangkok, Thailand

Publication date and place: 2011 / Bangkok, Thailand

Edition: 500

Format and binding: softcover / saddle stitched

Size: 5 7/8 x 8 1/4 in. (14.8 x 21 cm)

Number of pages and images: 84 pages / 80 images

Type of printing and paper: laser / matte 80gsm

Retail price: 12 GBP / 19 USD

Cost per unit: $$

Book soundtrack: "J. Shivers Theme" by Zongamin

Miti Ruangkritya is a Thai image-maker whose series *Thai Politics* explores the differing ways in which images can be documentary. Each installment addresses a specific, controversial political event in Thailand. *Thai Politics no. 2, vol. 1* is a collection of appropriated images assembled from the "Thaksin where are you?" Facebook group in 2010. The images satirize former prime minister Thaksin Shinawatra, who fled the country in exile after facing criminal corruption charges, depicting him in impossible hiding places. The group's effort resisted censorship during a time of heightened political tension over Shinawatra's whereabouts.

I felt it was important to keep this series of manipulated images alive as part of a historical moment in Thai political history. To my knowledge, no one else collected these images; also, it could have been a difficult ordeal for a traditional publisher to print this kind of political content. Self-publishing thus became a natural outlet for preserving history in a physical form.
—Miti Ruangkritya

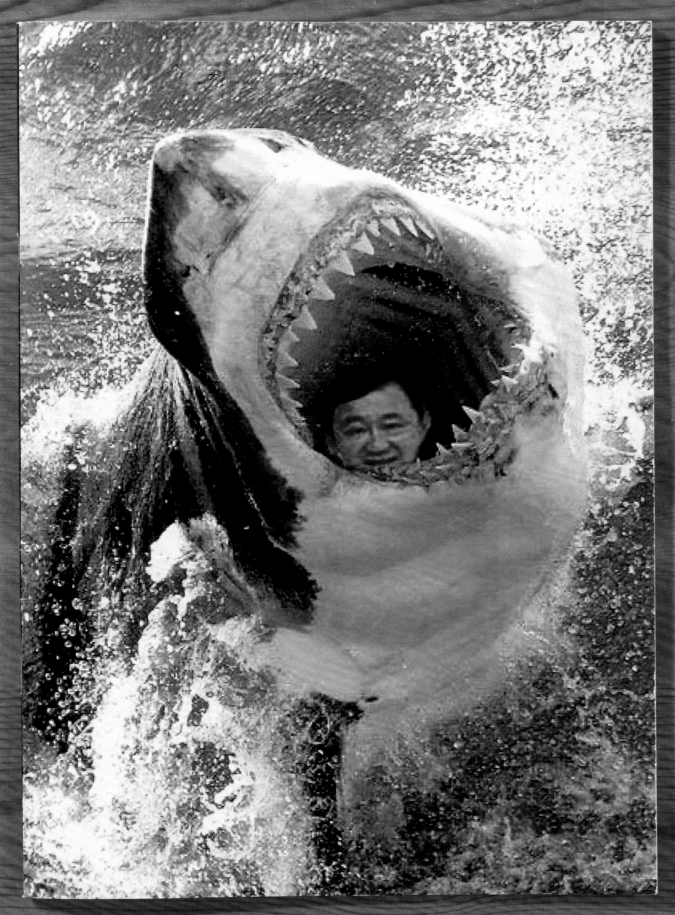

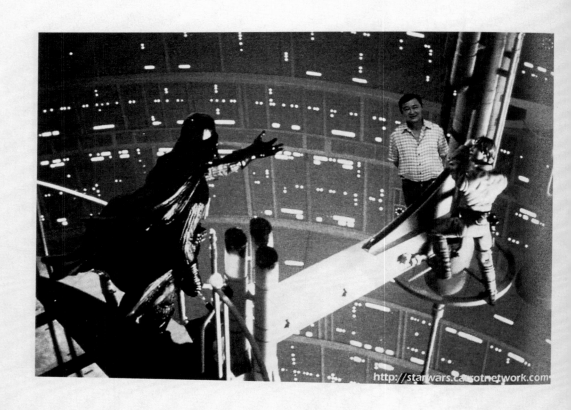

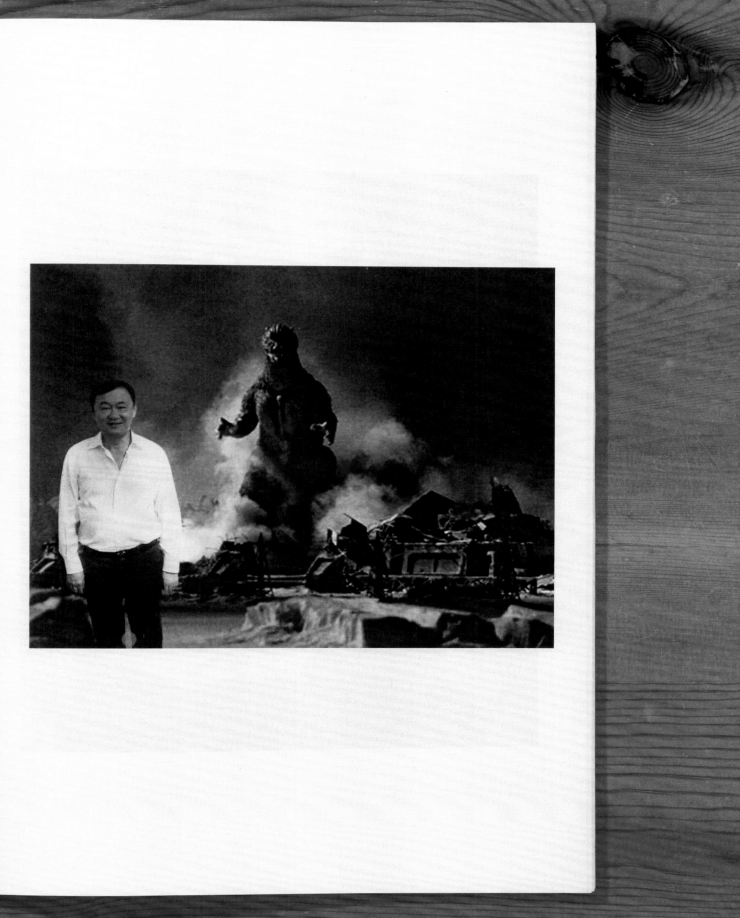

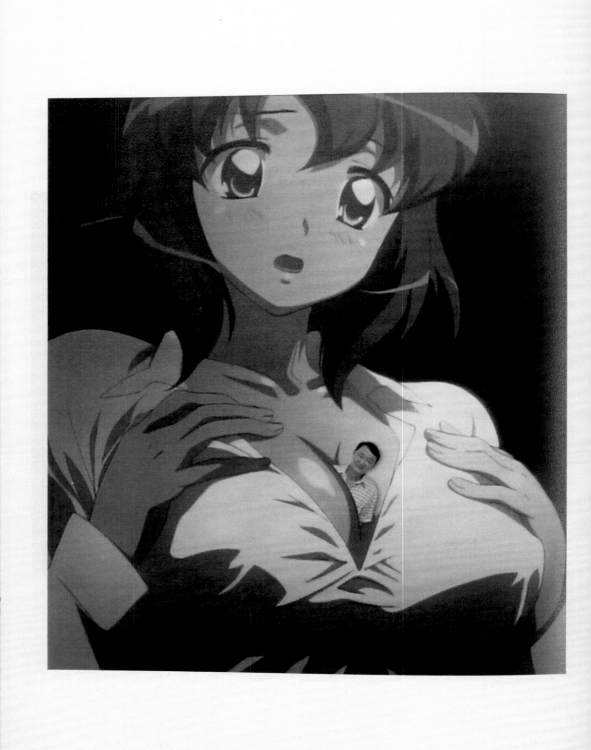

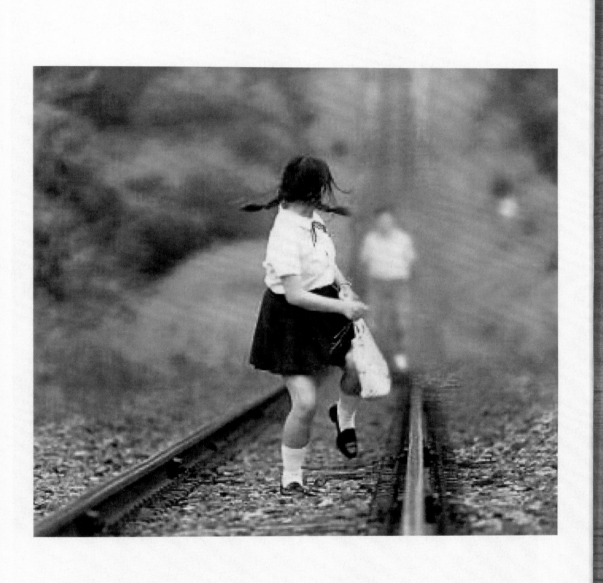

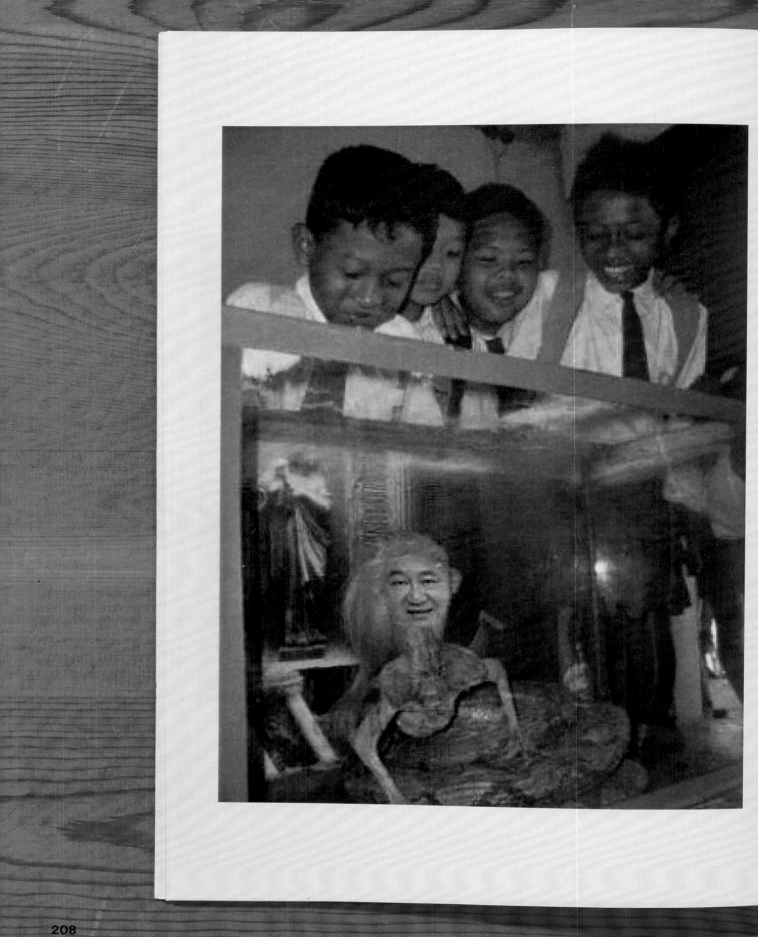

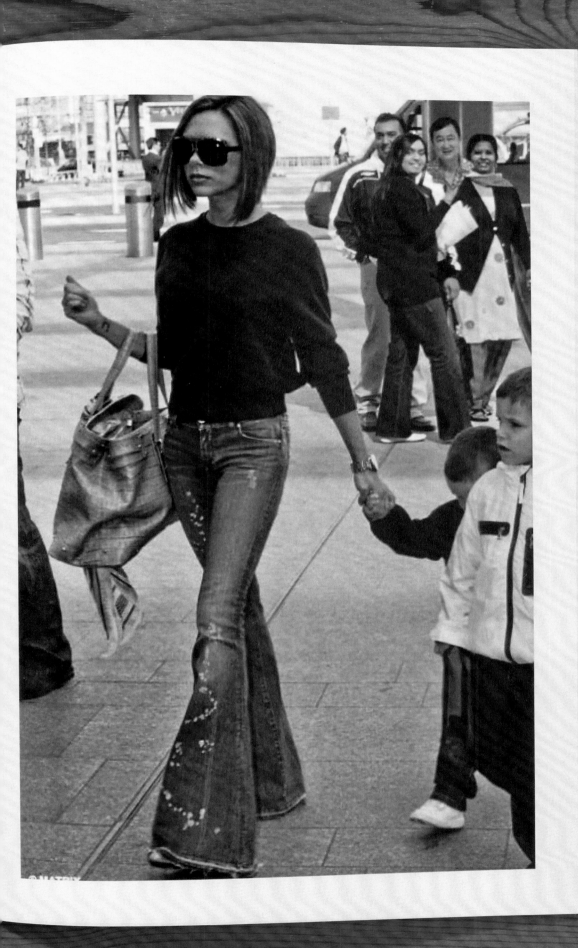

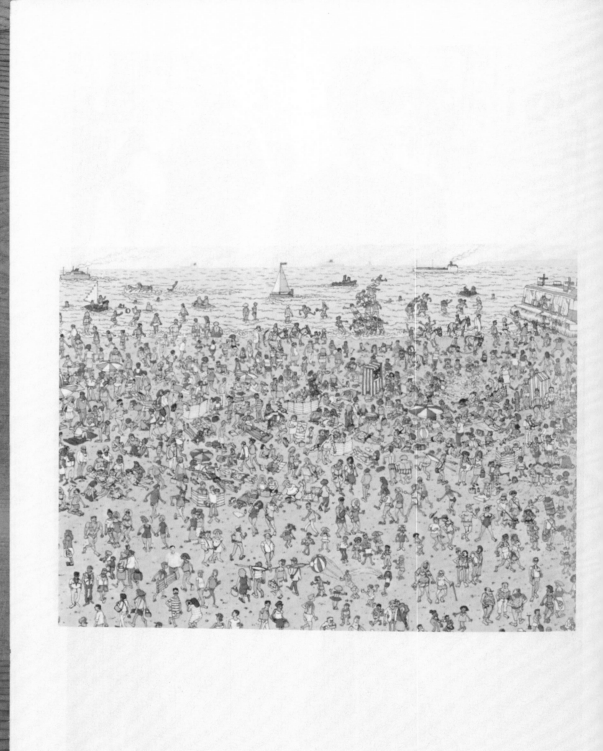

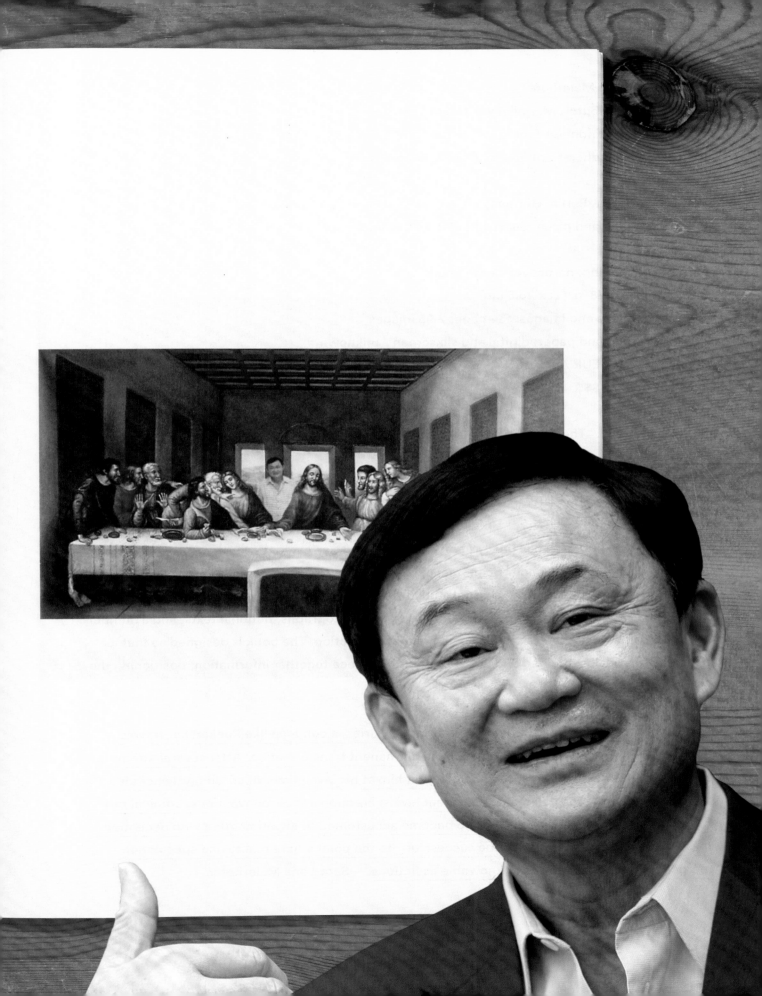

Title: Dear Clark,

Artist: Sara-Lena Maierhofer

Additional contributor: Marjolijn van Heemstra

Designer: Sven Lindhorst-Emme

Editors: Sven Lindhorst-Emme and Thanasis Kanakis

Imprint: none

Printer: Europrint, Berlin, Germany

Publication date and place: September 2013 / Berlin, Germany

Edition: 60

Format and binding: hardcover / case bound

Size: 8 1/4 x 10 3/8 in. (21 x 26.5 cm)

Number of pages and images: 134 pages / 95 images

Type of printing and paper: digital and silkscreen / unknown

Retail price: 240 EUR / 270 USD

Cost per unit: $$$$$

Book soundtrack: "The Great Pretender" by the Platters

Sara-Lena Maierhofer came across the story of Clark Rockefeller in a newspaper article. Born Christian Karl Gerhartsreiter in Germany in 1961, he traveled to America at age seventeen, took on different names, and, over the course of thirty years, became one of America's most illustrious con men. In 2008, his lies finally unraveled and he was arrested. With a background in portraiture and an interest in social phenomena, Maierhofer wrote to Rockefeller in prison. He never replied, so she decided to make a visual study from a distance. By gathering archival documents and found images, editing them together with staged photographs, fictional texts, and a number of "characters," Maierhofer creates a game of fact and fiction. The book is designed so that it has to be physically unfolded and worked through to piece together information, positioning the reader as jury.

As a time traveler can move between different centuries, a con man like Rockefeller travels between identities and lives, at home only in permanent transformation. After several attempts to pin down his persona, I realized I had to beat him at his own game. Accordingly, I encircled the phenomenon of the con man on different levels: his appearance, conventions, criminal profile, and pathologies. Above all, I had to become accustomed to experimenting with deception myself if I wanted my research to be successful—to the point where reality and speculation merged, and facts seemed as unknowable as fictions. —Sara-Lena Maierhofer

DEAR

CLARK

,

Portrait of a Con Man   Sara-Lena Maierhofer

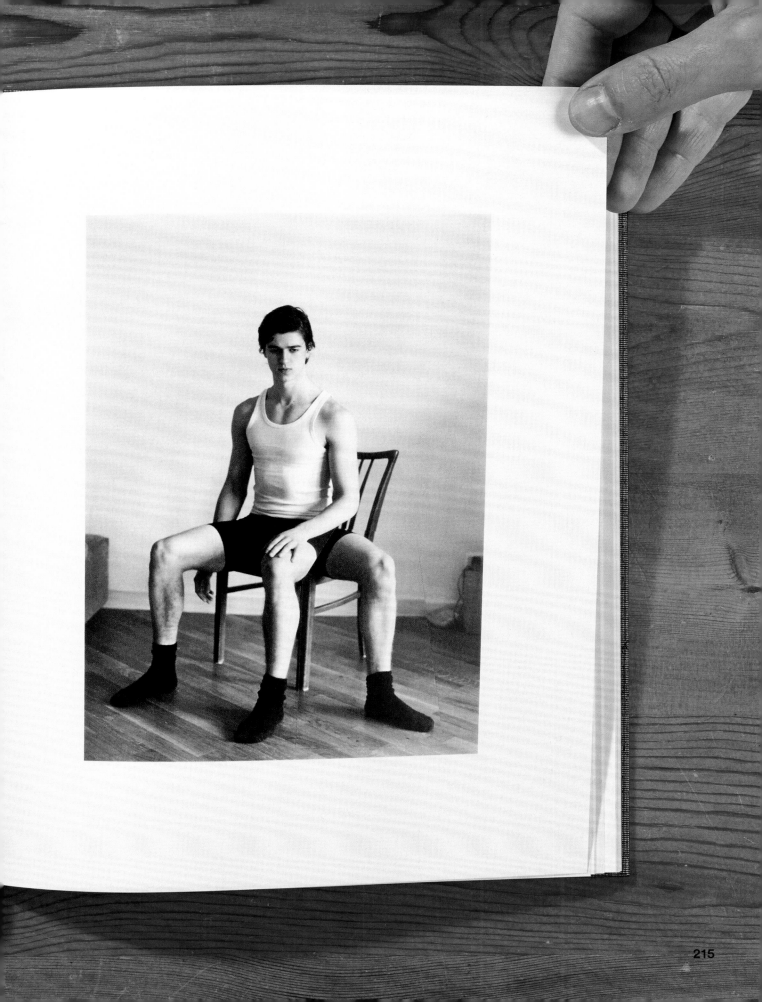

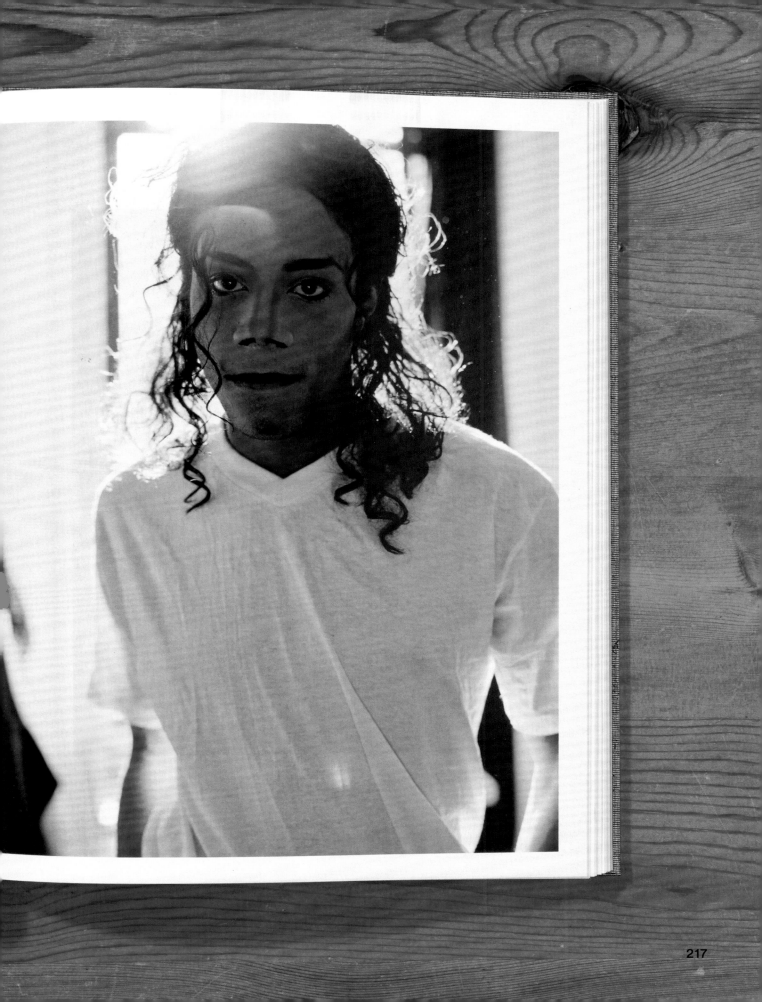

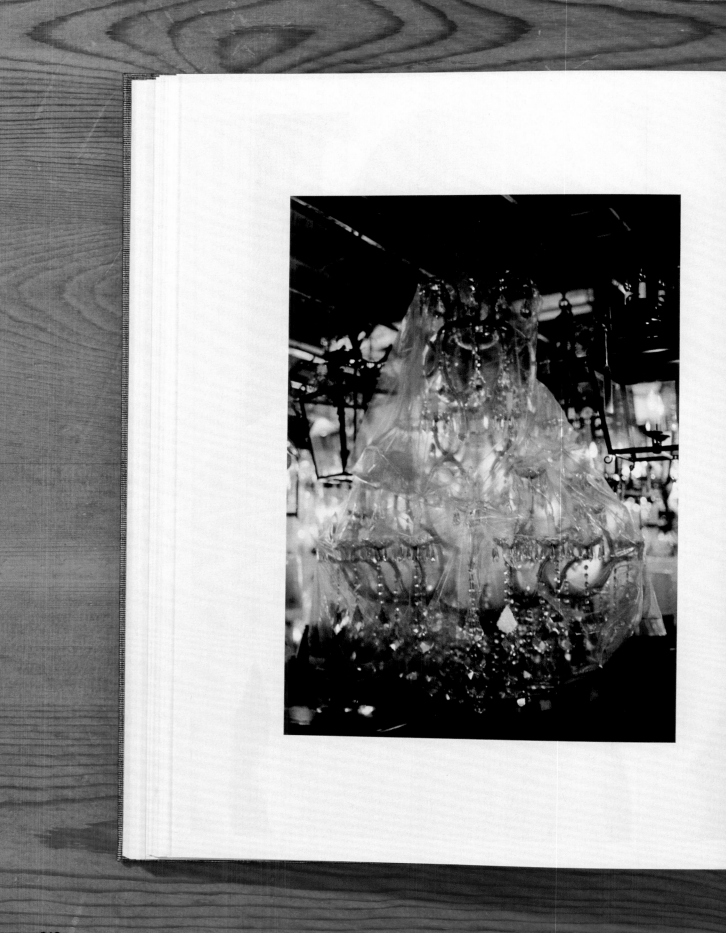

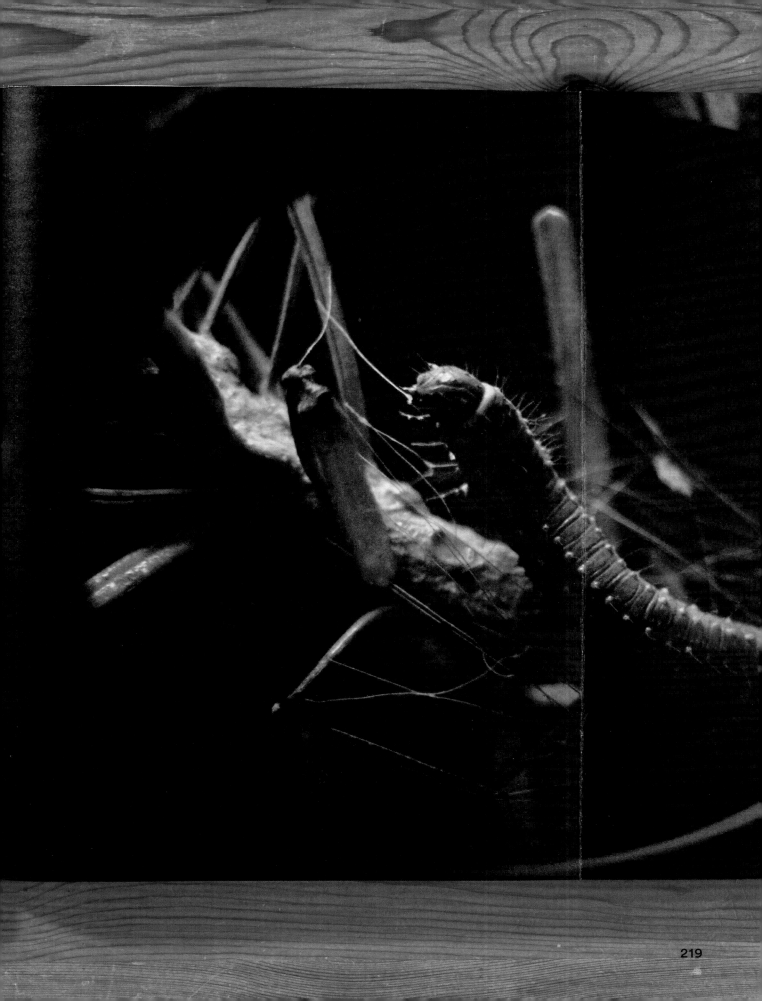

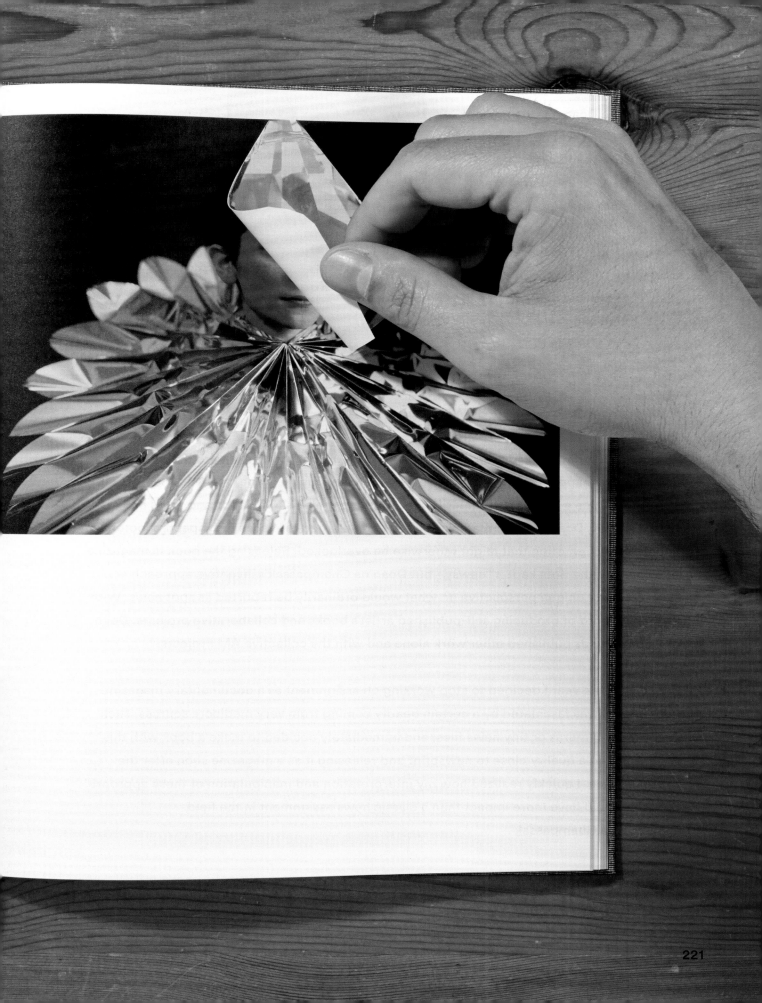

Title: Looters

Artist: Tiane Doan na Champassak

Designer: Tiane Doan na Champassak

Editor: Tiane Doan na Champassak

Imprint: Siam's Guy Books

Printer: Après Midi Lab, Paris, France

Publication date and place: September 2011 / Paris, France

Edition: 150

Format and binding: softcover / perfect bound

Size: 5 3/8 x 7 1/4 in. (13.5 x 18.5 cm)

Number of pages and images: 48 pages / 46 images

Type of printing and paper: risograph / Cyclus Offset

Retail price: 10 EUR / 12 USD

Cost per unit: $

Book soundtrack: *Cello Concerto* by Witold Lutoslawski

When the London riots kicked off in the summer of 2011, rather than rushing to the scene to record what was happening—as he would have done previously—Tiane Doan na Champassak decided to produce a response from his home. Sourcing grainy surveillance and news images from the Internet, Doan na Champassak isolated and enlarged the faces of suspected looters, revealing flickers of emotion that might otherwise be overlooked. Releasing the book in magazine format just after the riots kept it "newsy," but Doan na Champassak's inventive approach goes further, offering a unique perspective on what would ordinarily be reported as spot news. With a long track record of producing self-published artist's books and collaborative projects, Doan na Champassak has published other work alone and with the collective AM Projects.

I made *Looters* the year I decided to stop working on assignment as a documentary magazine photographer. I was fascinated by a certain beauty coming from very mediocre sources, such as surveillance cameras or tiny news files, and immediately decided to make a book with this material, keeping a quality close to newsprint and releasing it as a magazine soon after the events took place. I quickly realized how my interpretation and manipulation of these appropriated images could have more impact than a classic news assignment in the field.
—Tiane Doan na Champassak

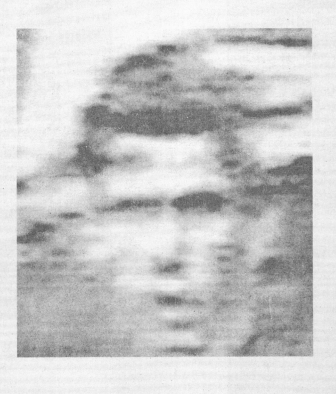

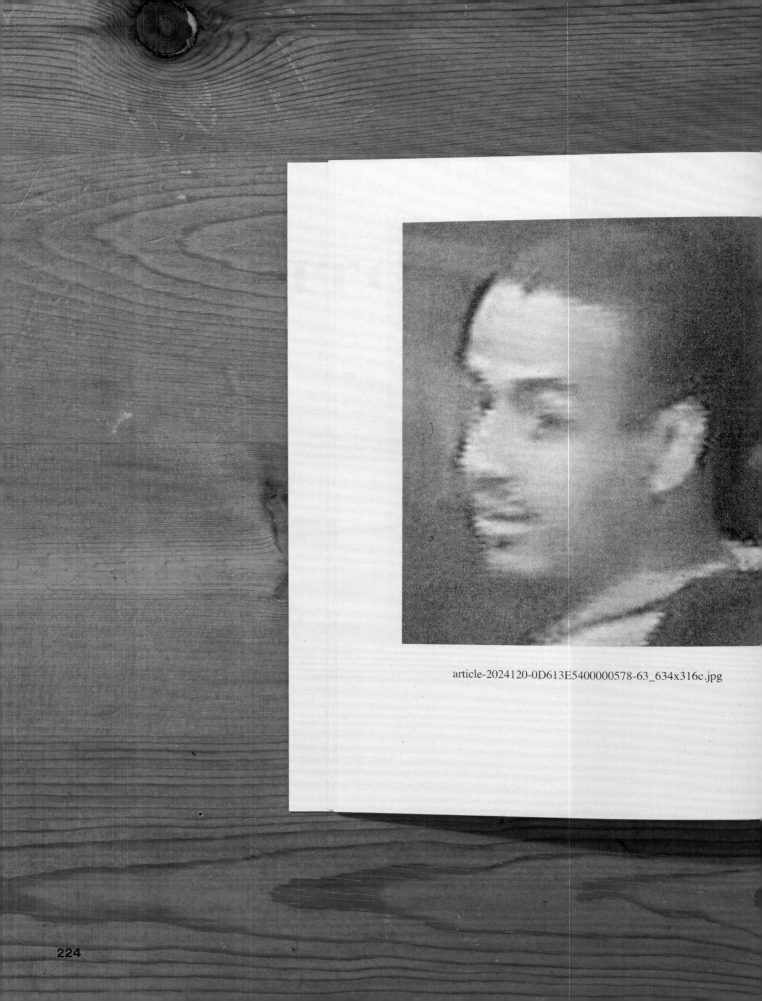

article-2024120-0D613E5400000578-63_634x316c.jpg

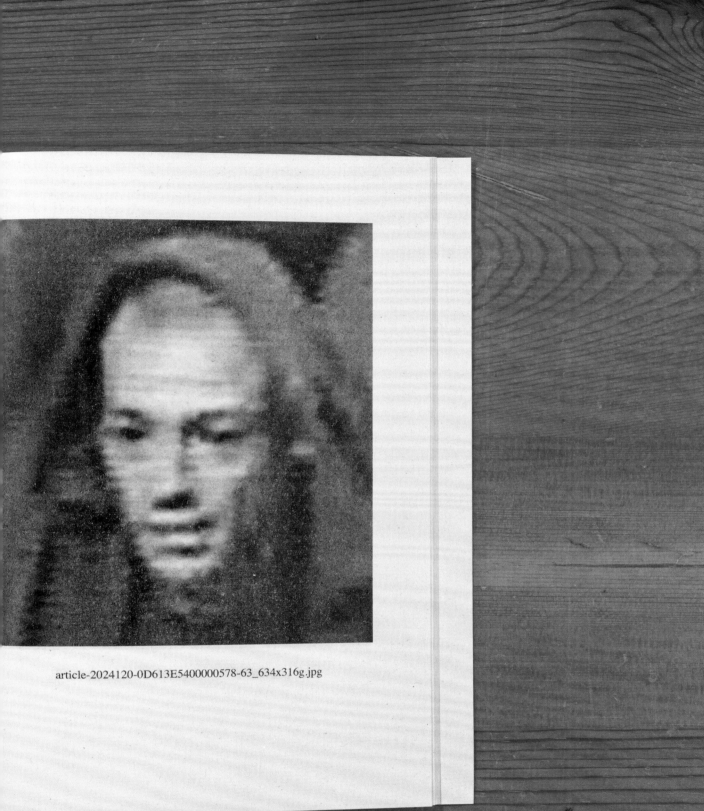

article-2024120-0D613E5400000578-63_634x316g.jpg

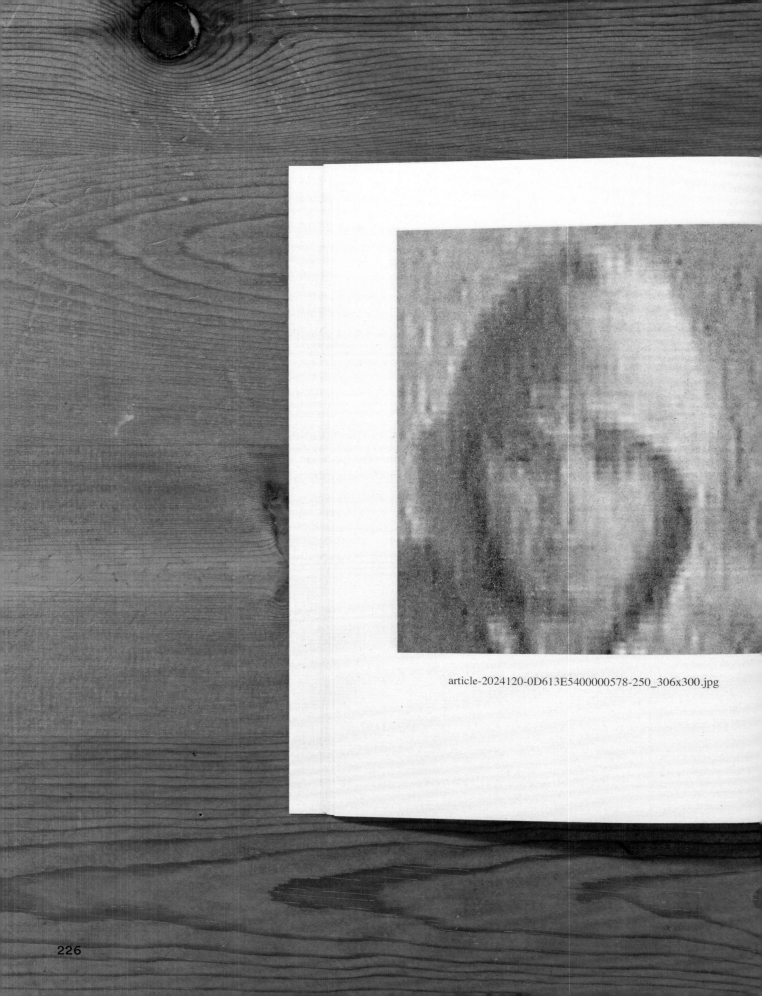

article-2024120-0D613E5400000578-250_306x300.jpg

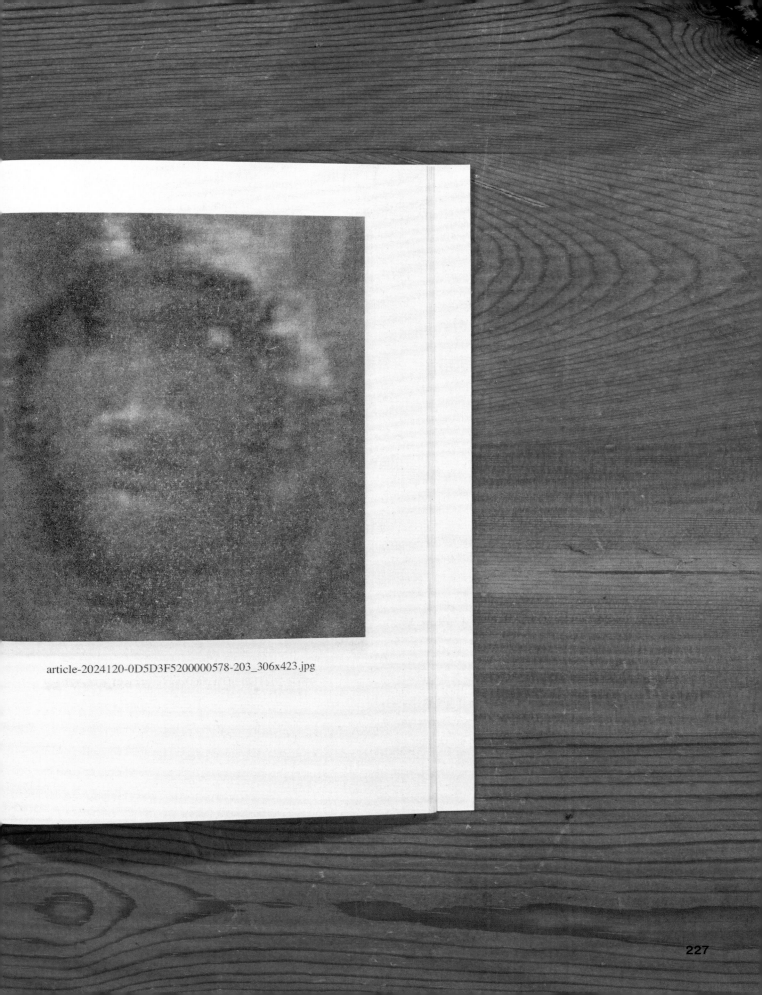

article-2024120-0D5D3F5200000578-203_306x423.jpg

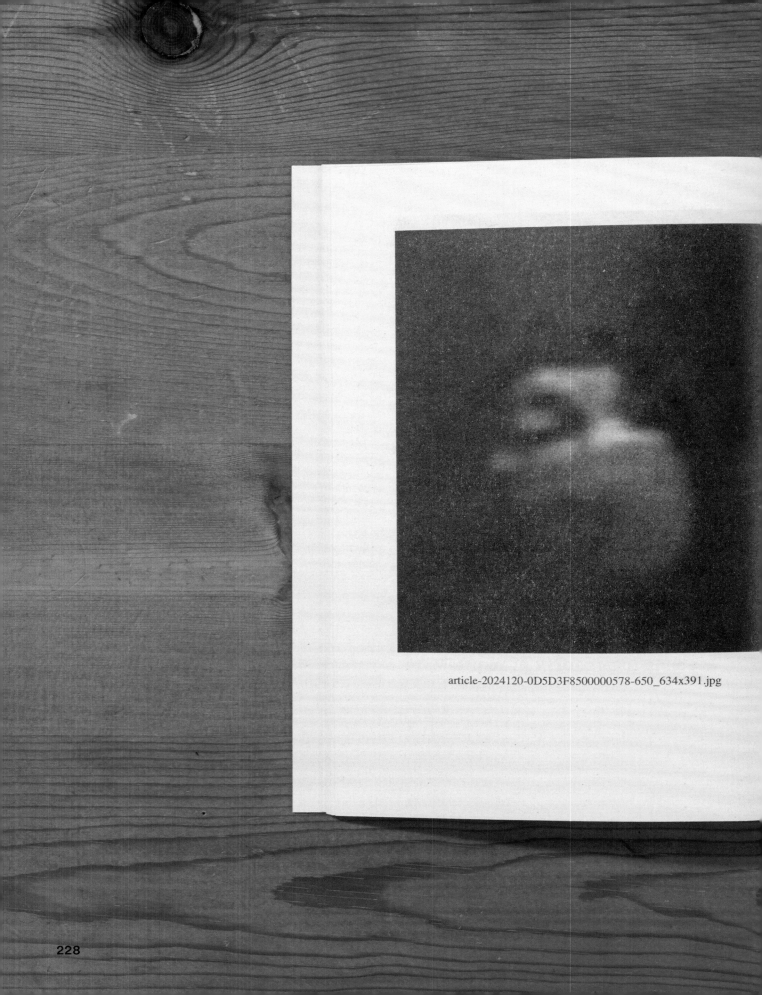

article-2024120-0D5D3F8500000578-650_634x391.jpg

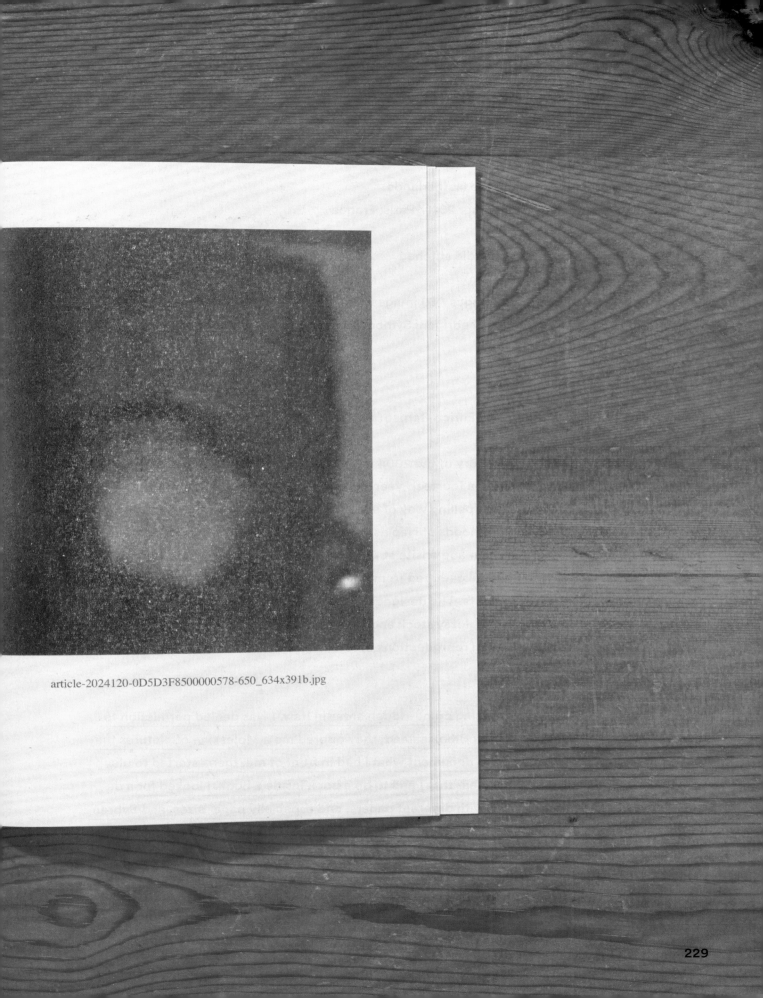

article-2024120-0D5D3F8500000578-650_634x391b.jpg

Title: Gomorrah Girl

Artist: Valerio Spada

Designers: Sybren Kuiper and Valerio Spada

Editor: Valerio Spada

Imprint: Cross Editions

Printer: KDR Marcom, Zaandam, the Netherlands

Publication date and place: November 2011 / Paris, France

Edition: 500

Format and binding: softcover / saddle stitched

Size: 8 7/8 x 13 1/8 in. (22.6 x 33.4 cm)

Number of pages and images: 80 pages / 59 images

Type of printing and paper: offset / Fedrigoni Symbol Tatami 150gsm; uncoated 100gsm

Retail price: 30 EUR / 34 USD

Cost per unit: $$$

Book soundtrack: "Core 'ngrato" by Enrico Caruso

Valerio Spada stumbled upon the story of the 2004 murders of three young women from Naples, including that of Annalisa Durante, a fourteen-year-old girl killed by crossfire during a mafia conflict. This struck Spada as a compelling way of exploring the larger story of mafia-driven violence in the impoverished neighborhoods of Naples, and violence against young women in particular. Combining photographs he made onsite at Annalisa's school, in her neighborhood, and at other sites in Naples, with material gathered from police dossiers, Gomorrah Girl reconstructs a portrait from evidentiary fragments. The designer Sybren Kuiper folded a suite of Spada's photos, printed at a smaller size on glossy stock and vertically bound, into the pages of a larger, newsprint-like notebook, containing reproductions of forensic evidence and pictures of the tools used to investigate the crime.

In one of my several trips documenting crime-ridden areas in Italy, I was denied permission to take pictures of the bullet used in a crime. Instead, they offered me a Moleskine of pictures they took at the crime scene. I started to document what I had in front of me, then I started to play with the elements, and it became clear that I had to do a book inside a book. I looked for a designer who would be able to work with different papers, and especially paper sizes, and Sybren Kuiper was the one. He had the brilliant idea of having all my portraits bound in vertically (which some may argue is very uncomfortable to look at, but was perfect for what I was thinking of as the book's form and respectful to the content), and printing the photos from the police Moleskine on thinner, larger paper. It was a perfect marriage of design and pictures. —Valerio Spada

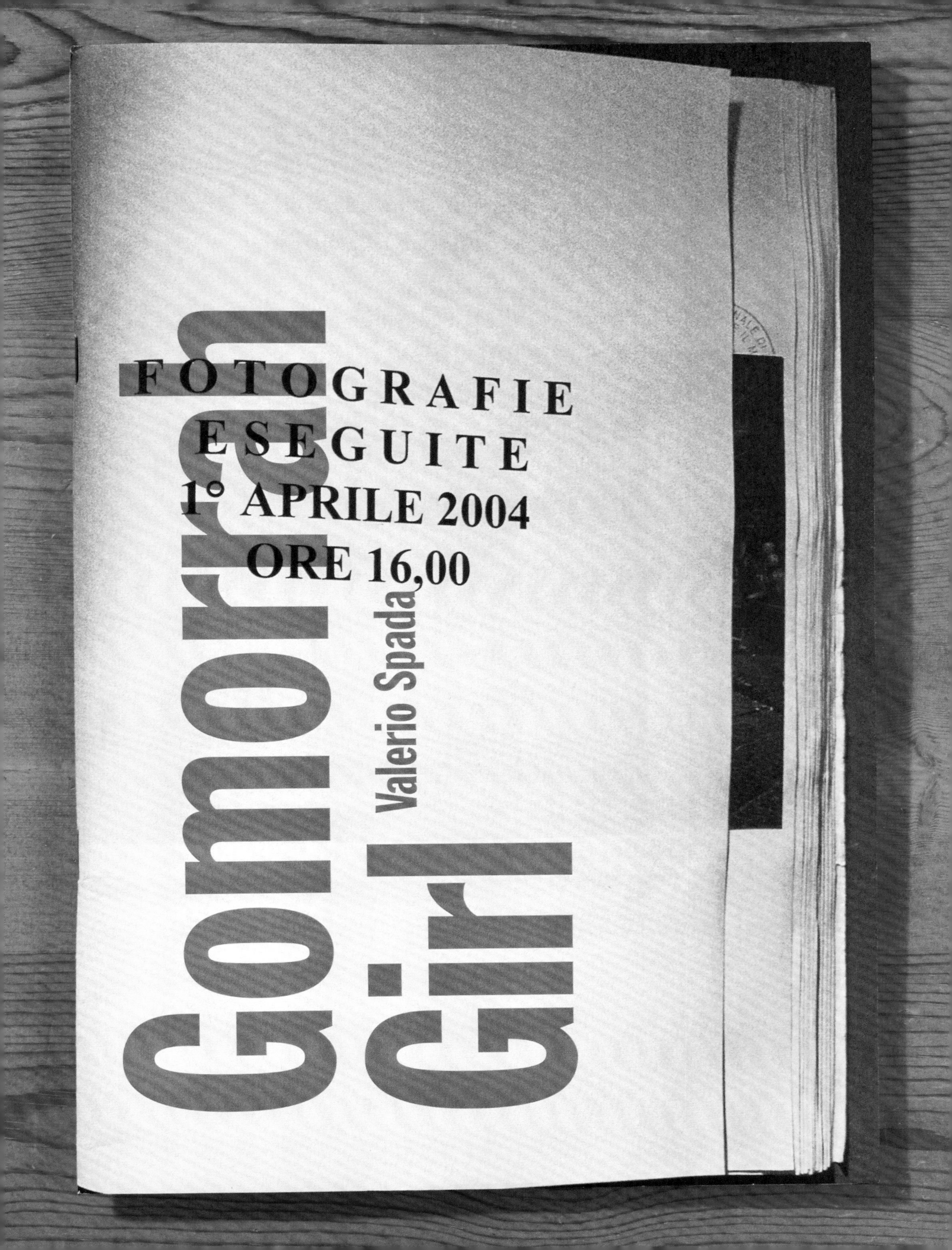

Gomorrah Girl

Valerio Spada

FOTOGRAFIE
ESEGUITE
1° APRILE 2004
ORE 16,00

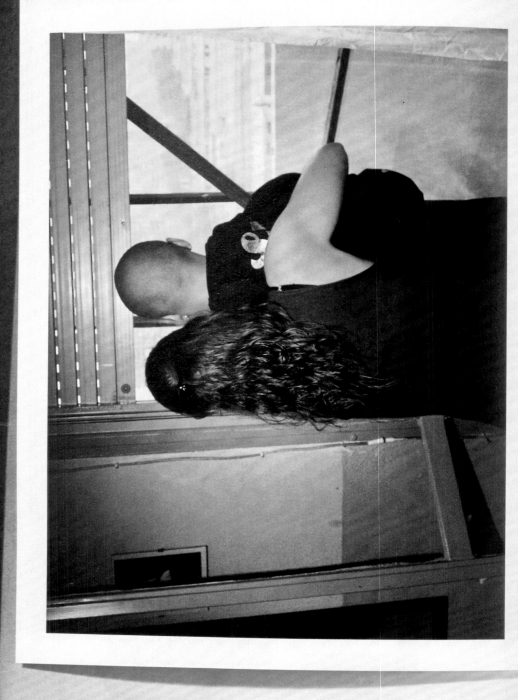

La Vela Rossa (The Red Sail), 11th floor, Scampia, Naples // Francesca and Pasquale.

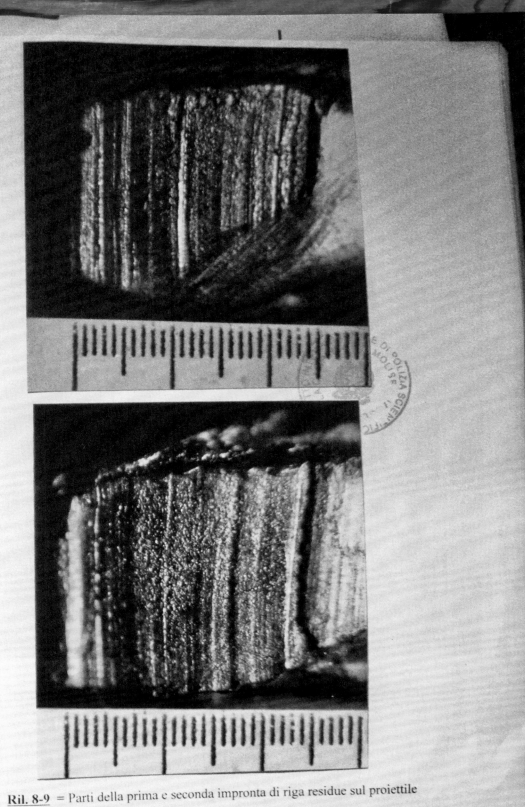

<u>**Ril. 8-9**</u> = Parti della prima e seconda impronta di riga residue sul proiettile "PR2".

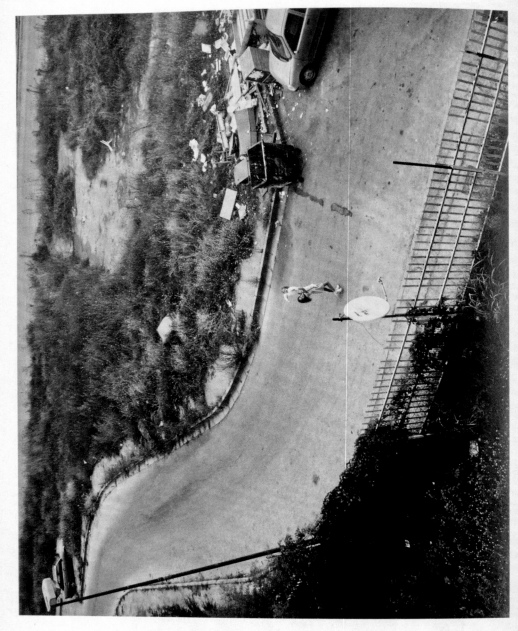

Main street between la Vela Rossa (Red Sail) and la Vela Gialla (Yellow Sail), Scampia, Naples // Anna, 9 years old

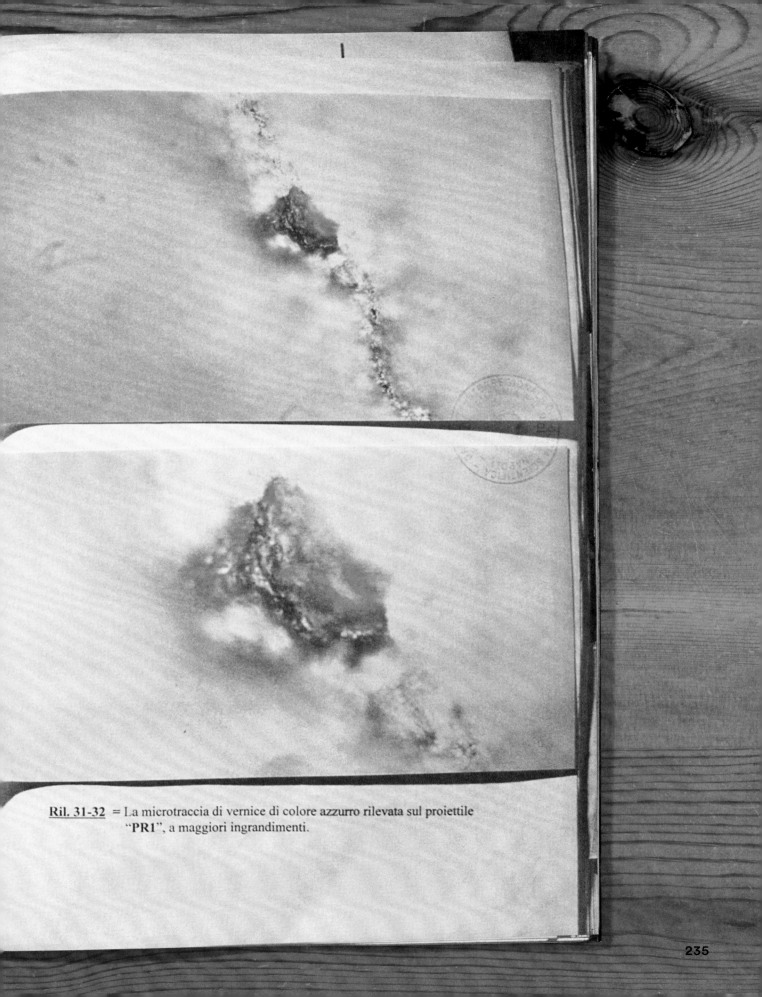

Ril. 31-32 = La microtraccia di vernice di colore azzurro rilevata sul proiettile
           "PR1", a maggiori ingrandimenti.

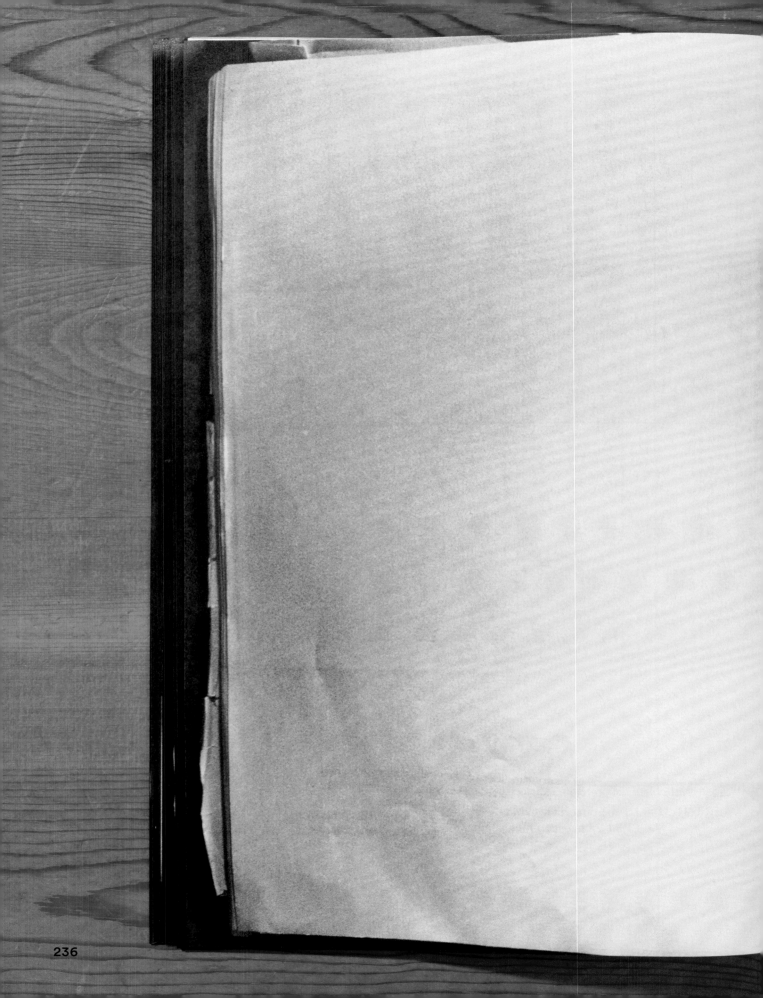

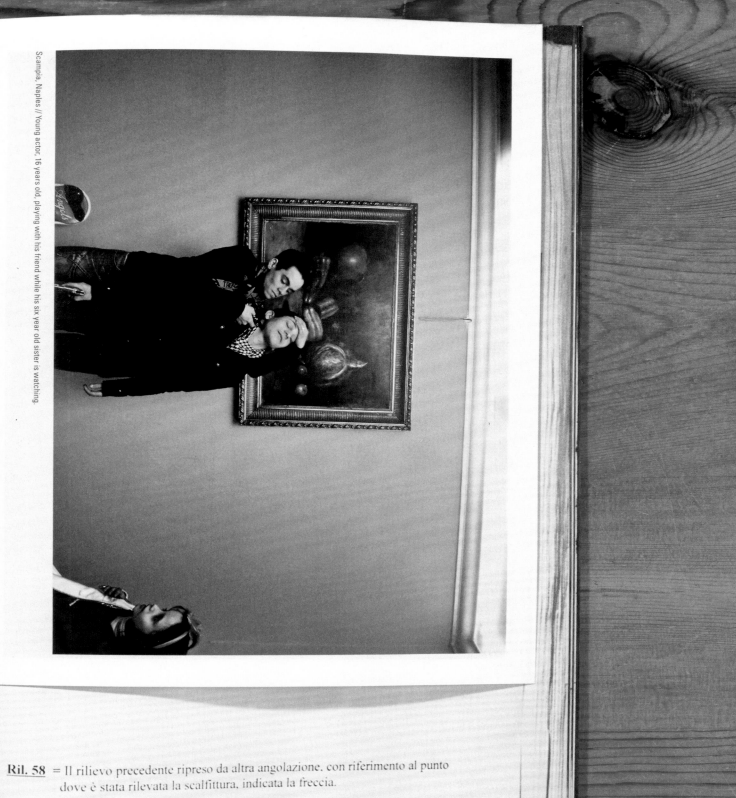

Scampia, Naples // Young actor, 16 years old, playing with his friend while his six year old sister is watching.

Ril. 58 = Il rilievo precedente ripreso da altra angolazione, con riferimento al punto
dove è stata rilevata la scalfittura, indicata la freccia.

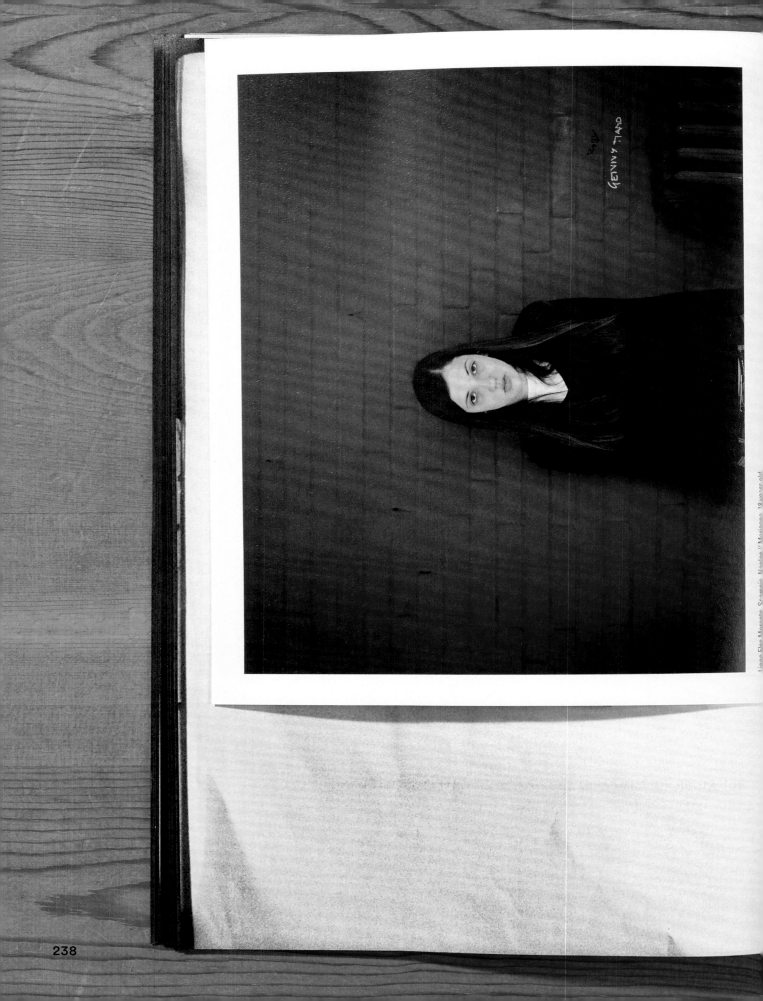

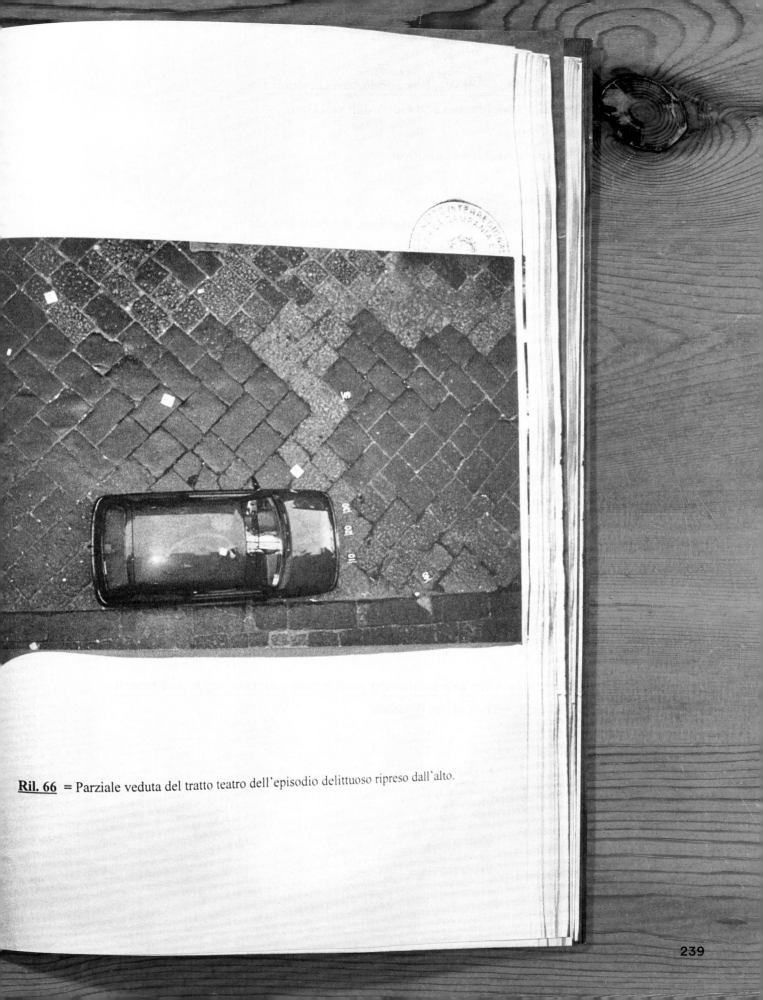

Ril. 66 = Parziale veduta del tratto teatro dell'episodio delittuoso ripreso dall'alto.

Title: Empty Bottles

Artists: WassinkLundgren (Thijs groot Wassink and Ruben Lundgren)

Additional contributors: Hans Molenman and Floris-Jan van Luyn

Designers: Kummer & Herrman

Editors: Thijs groot Wassink and Ruben Lundgren

Imprint: none

Printer: NPN Drukkers, Breda, the Netherlands

Publication date and place: March 2007 / Amsterdam, the Netherlands

Edition: 800

Format and binding: softcover / side stitched

Size: 9 1/2 x 12 3/8 in. (24 x 31.5 cm)

Number of pages and images: 64 pages / 24 images

Type of printing and paper: offset / Chromolux, coated on one side

Retail price: 15 EUR / 16 USD

Cost per unit: $$

Dutch photographers Thijs groot Wassink and Ruben Lundgren have made fifteen books together under the name WassinkLundgren, most of them self-published. *Empty Bottles* presents a series of twenty-four photographs, each depicting a Chinese refuse collector in the process of crouching down to pick up an empty bottle. (WassinkLundgren planted the bottles themselves, in hopes of luring in their subjects.) With each figure featured modestly in the frame, it's a simple, quasi-typological approach, further highlighted by the repetition of form and design; each full-bleed image is set against a light-blue page that echoes the tiny slice of sky seen peeking through the skyscrapers or landscape in the distance. This is a deceptively straightforward book that effectively describes an unofficial army of self-organized, individual recyclers, who scour Beijing and Shanghai in an effort to make a living.

There's no need to follow rules when self-publishing. Just follow your own logic, and have it tested by people you admire. —Thijs groot Wassink

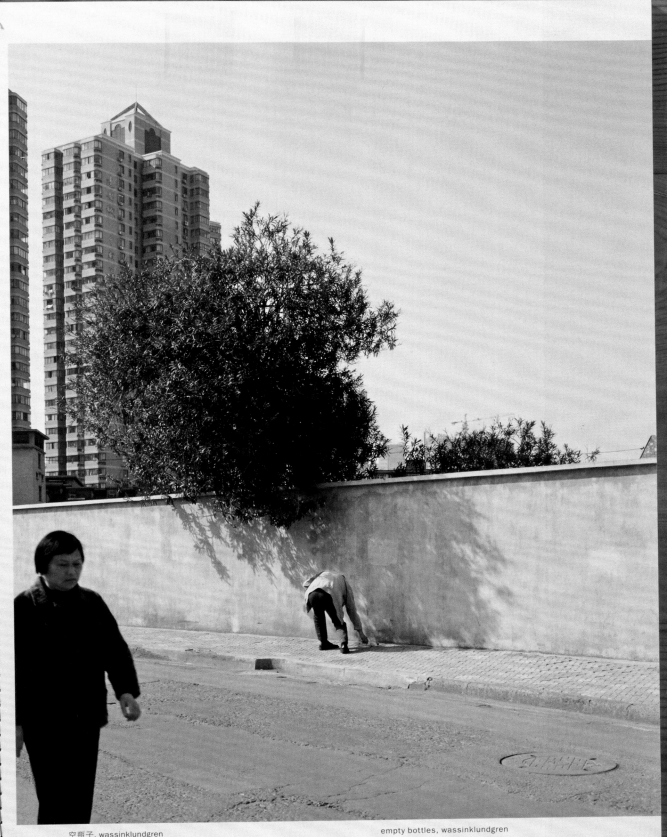

空瓶子, wassinklundgren   empty bottles, wassinklundgren

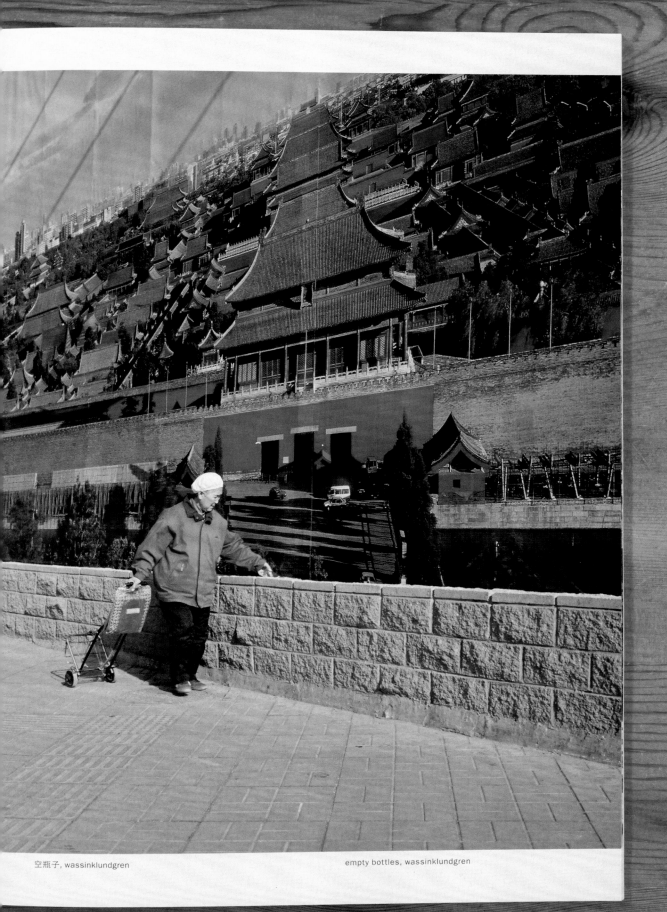

空瓶子, wassinklundgren
empty bottles, wassinklundgren

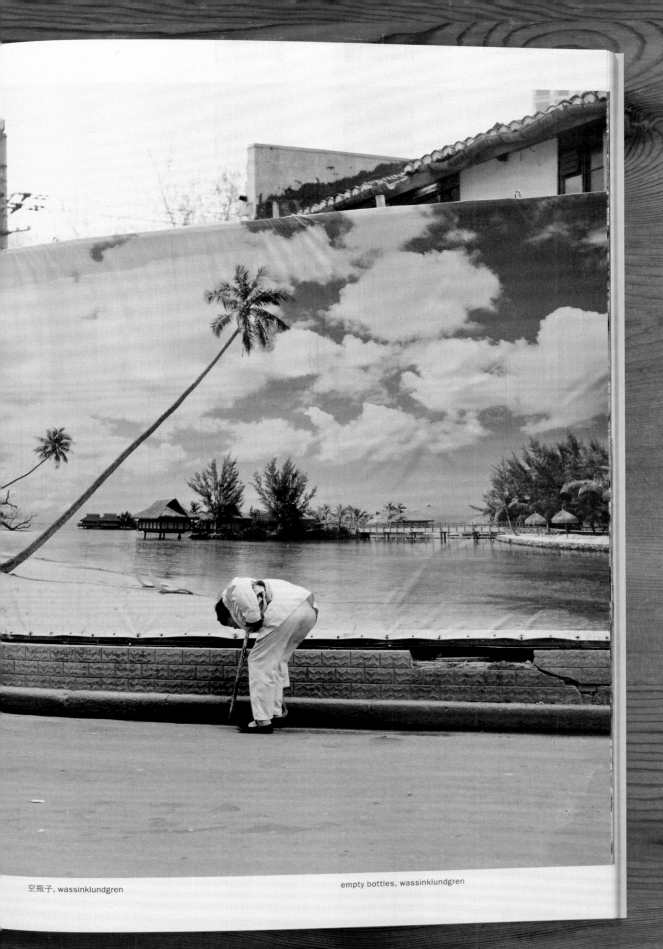

空瓶子, wassinklundgren

empty bottles, wassinklundgren

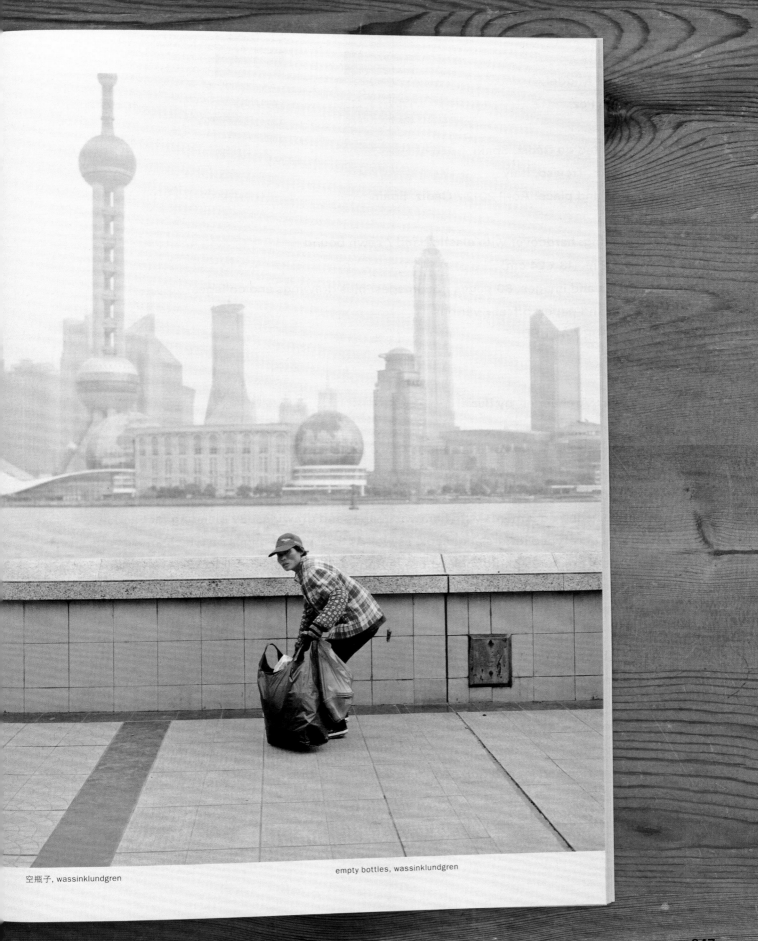

空瓶子, wassinklundgren

empty bottles, wassinklundgren

Title: The Afronauts

Artist: Cristina de Middel

Designer: Ramon Pez

Editor: Laia Abril

Imprint: Universidad de Cádiz, Spain

Printer: Tintoretto, Treviso, Italy

Publication date and place: April 2012 / Cádiz, Spain

Edition: 1,000

Format and binding: hardcover with elastic band / sewn bound

Size: 7 1/8 x 9 1/2 in. (18 x 24 cm)

Number of pages and images: 80 pages / 36 images, plus drawings and collages

Type of printing and paper: offset / various

Retail price: 35 EUR / 40 USD

Cost per unit: $$

Book soundtrack: "Archangel" by Burial

The Afronauts tells the story of Zambia's 1960s space project, which sought to send astronauts to Mars. The project, led by Edward Makuka Nkoloso, never came to fruition, but the story caught Cristina de Middel's attention. She decided to tell her own version of it by manipulating and combining existing documents with her own images and drawings. By blending fact and fiction, via foldouts of retyped letters and maps, as well as transparent pages on which images are printed, De Middel created a photobook whose multilayered form echoes the carefully woven narrative contained inside. De Middel went on to devise an exhibition of the work, which traveled internationally.

I didn't know publishing *The Afronauts* would become such a life-changing experience. After its success, it has taken some time and some mistakes to learn how to recognize real friends among the crowd of people who just want to ask for some kind of help. I like helping people, but I do not have a magic formula that I can share, as I don't know how the books became so desirable! I've had people waiting at my door and even received hate mail, but I've also had the chance to meet really interesting and stimulating people to collaborate with and rely on.
—Cristina de Middel

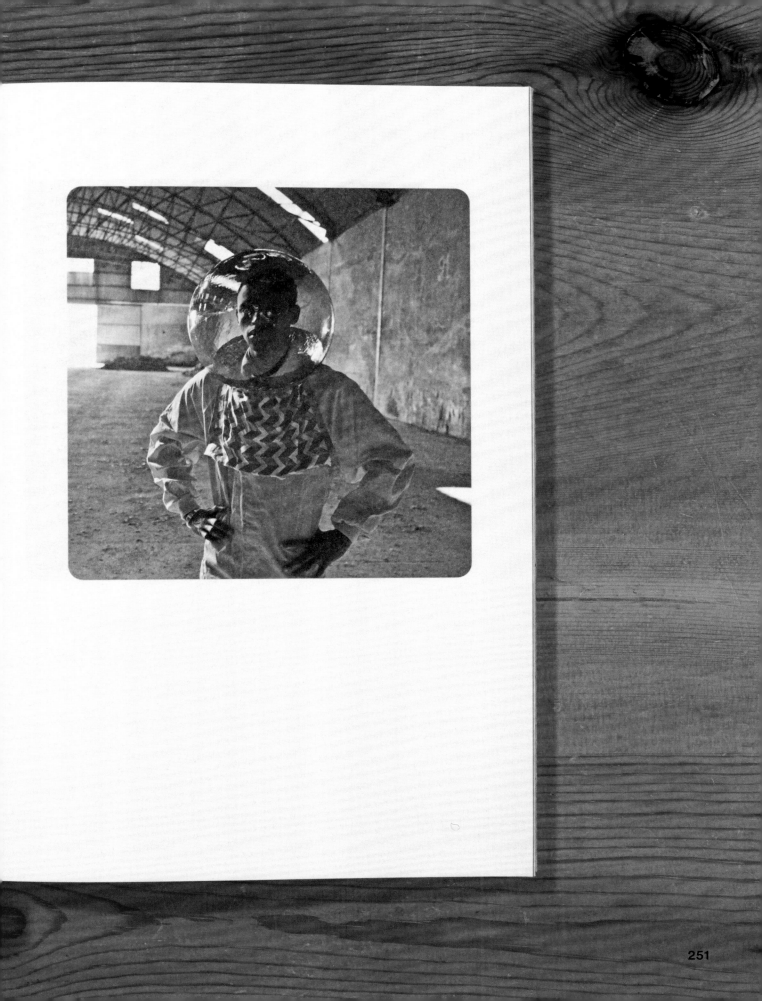

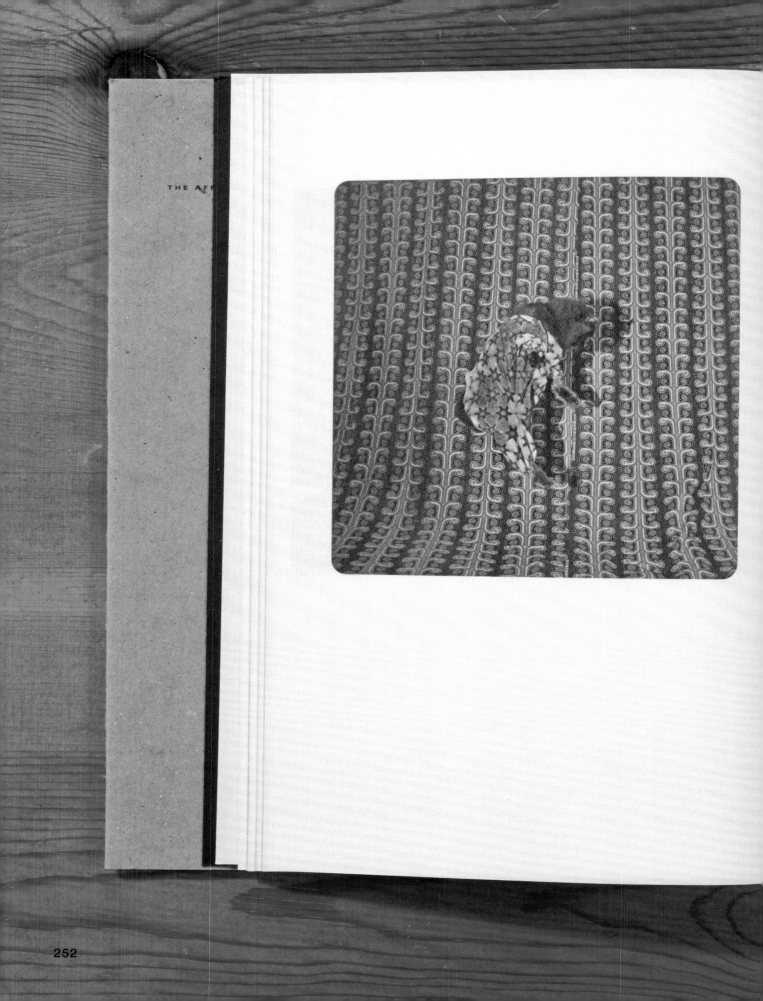

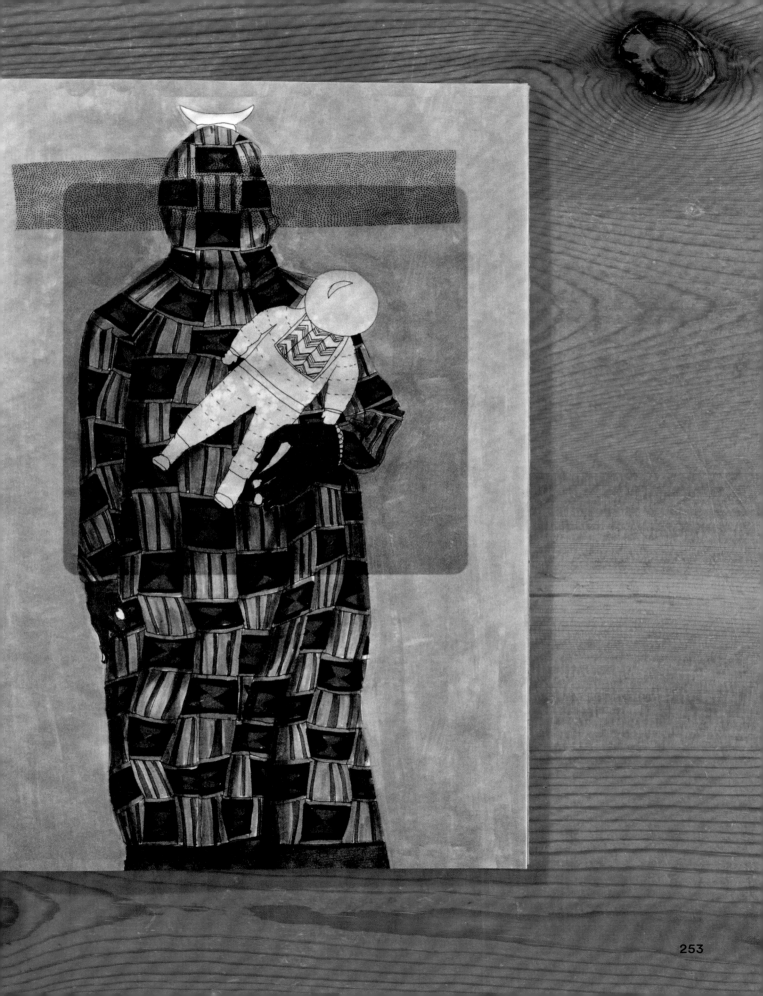

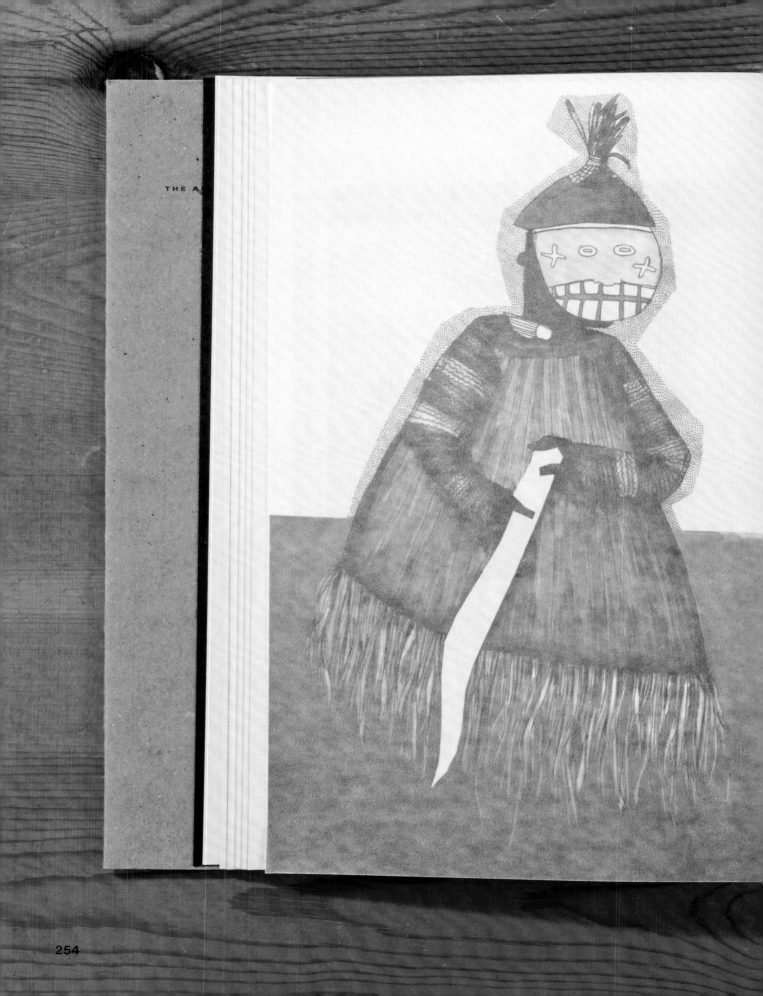

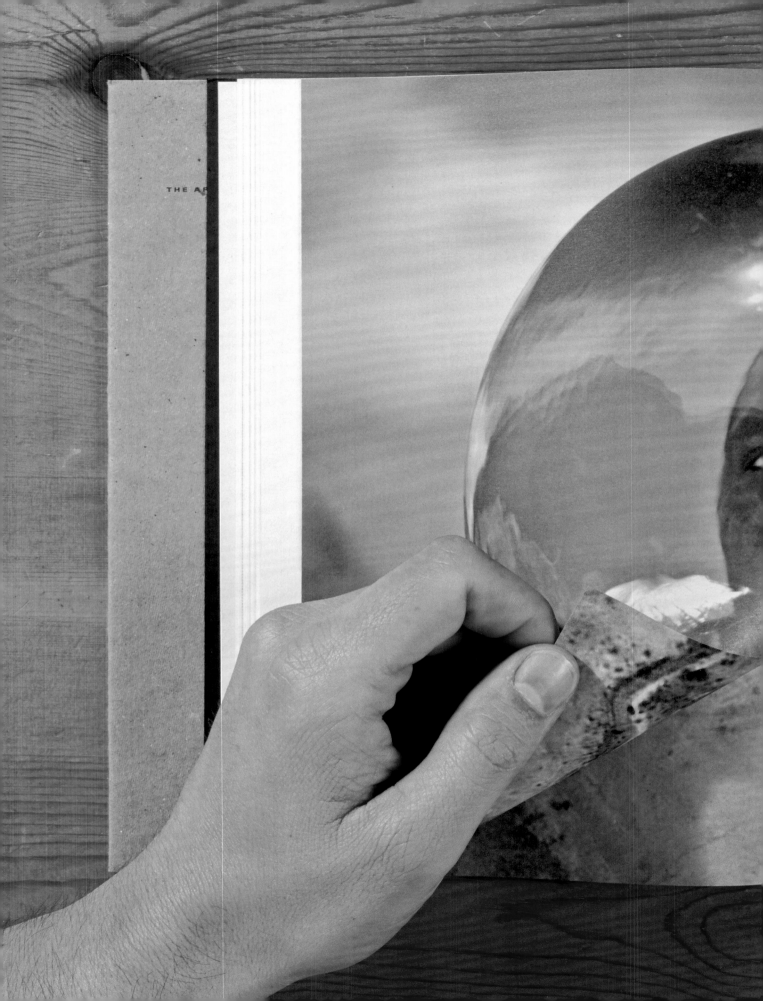

THE AR

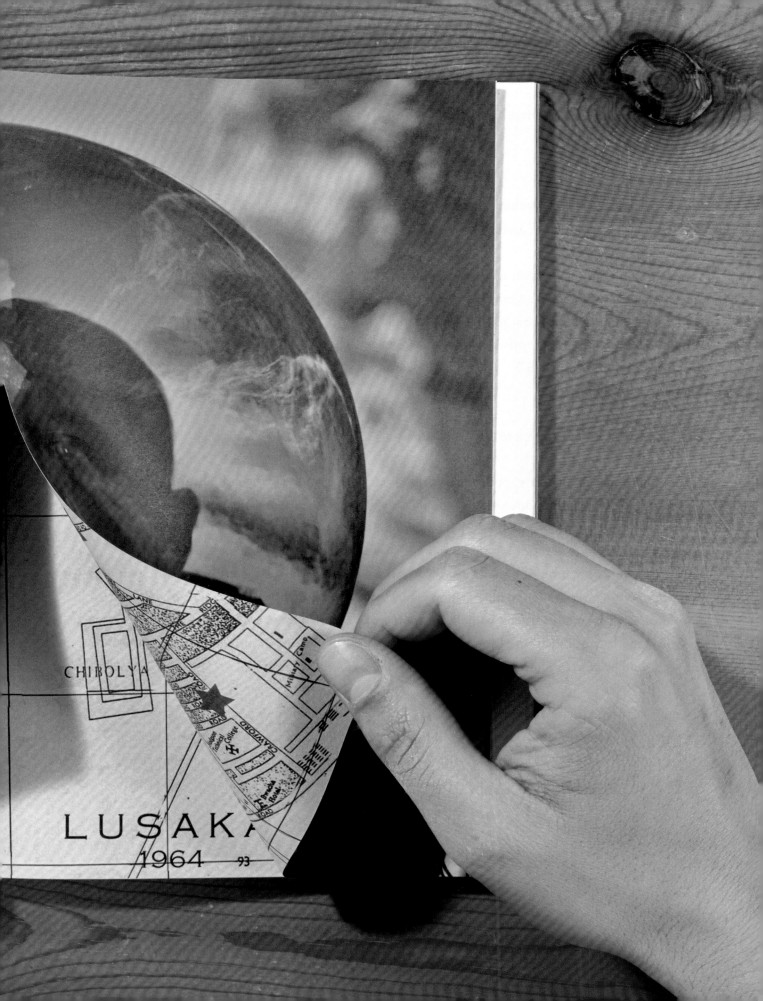

Title: J_Subs

Artist: Oliver Sieber

Additional contributor: Christoph Schaden

Designer: Oliver Sieber

Editor: Oliver Sieber

Imprint: BöhmKobayashi

Printer: Baecker + Häbel, Willich, Germany

Publication date and place: June 2009 / Düsseldorf, Germany

Edition: 50

Format and binding: softcover in plastic sleeve / stab stitched

Size: 8 1/4 x 10 1/4 in. (21 x 26 cm)

Number of pages and images: 160 pages / 78 images

Type of printing and paper: offset / Munken Lynx 80gsm

Retail price: 48 EUR / 54 USD

Cost per unit: $$$$

Book soundtrack: "Stranglehold" by U.K. Subs

J_Subs functions as part zine, part documentary catalogue of Japanese subcultures—from mohawked punks to pompadoured rockabilly chicks and dreadlocked surfer boys. A series of classic portraits set against a white backdrop are interspersed with fliers from a variety of clubs, all of which are stapled together and packaged in a clear plastic sleeve, like a record. Oliver Sieber began his documentation of the various flavors of Japanese subculture in 2006, working in tandem with and paralleling his partner, the artist and designer Katja Stuke, as one half of BöhmKobayashi, an imprint and vehicle for their work as individuals and as collaborators. *J_Subs* is the first publication of the work, the first salvo in a series of publications from the project, culminating in Sieber's book *Imaginary Club,* published in 2013.

In London, there is a shop where you can buy old music magazines which are all stocked with cardboard backing, in sleeves similar to those that cover comic books. From the beginning, I have really liked to play with the idea of the book as a collectible, so I did the same for this book. The staple binding reminds me of the first three issues of *i-D* magazine. —Oliver Sieber

i Publishing Project

Title: Oliver Sieber; J_Subs
Special Interest: Youth Culture/Japan/Punk/Music
Date: 2010
Price: € 55,-
Condition: 2nd Edition   Excellent ⊘   Good ○   Fair ○

OLIVER SIEBER
J_SUBS

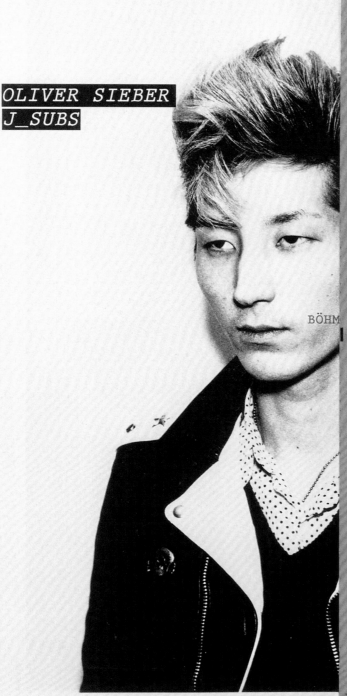

BÖHM

JAPANESE PUNK / HARDCORE RARE 7"/EPs

⑦ あぶらだこ-S.T. (ADK/'83 Orig. 6-Track Flexi) Very Rare 1ST Flexi ¥12800
■ ADDICTION-Voice Of Bristle Punk (Discrete/'95 Orig.6-Track 7") ¥3500
-Blind Soldier Kids (NAT/'98 Ltd. Yellow Vinyl 3-Track 7"+Insert) ¥2800
■ ANTI AUTHORIZE-S.T. (MCR/'94 Orig.7-Track 7") ¥3500
■ ASPHYXIA-Wardrugs (Crust War/Orig. 7-Track 7"+Insert) ¥2800
■ BAD VULTURES-Gang Up(Human/ '87 Orig.3-Track 7") ¥7800
■ BALZAC-Lord Of The Light And Of The Darkness (Evilegend 13/ '93 Orig.3-Track 7"+ Insert) Very Rare 1ST Single ¥9800
-Atom Age Vampire In 308 (MCR/'95 Orig.4-Track 7"+Insert, Pink Logo PS) ... ¥4800
-Isolation From No, 13 (HG-fact/ '96 Ltd.3-Track Picture 7"+Insert, Sticker) .. ¥4800
上記Picture 7"の4 x Sticker, 布パッチ,Insert付きバージョンもあります ¥4800
-Isolation From No, 13 (HG-fact/ '96 Ltd.Pink Vinyl 3-Track 7"+Inser, PS) ¥3800
上記のPurple Vinyl バージョン, 別PS付きもあります ¥3800
-Neat Neat Neat / The End Of Century (Phalanx/ '99 非売品Flexi) ¥2800
-Hands Of 9 Evils-It's Only Fear- (Diwphalanx/ '00 Orig. 7") ¥1800
-When The Fiendish Ghouls Night (Evilegend 13 / '96 Ltd.308 Copies Green Vinyl 1 Sided 7"+新聞PS)大阪、東京でのライブ会場限定 激レア・シングル! ¥5800
-(V.A)Safe Rock And Roll Sucks (HG-fact/ '95 Orig.6-Track 7")Inc.Balzac.. ¥3500
■ BLUE HEARTS-人にやさしく/ハンマー (Juggler/ '87 Orig. 7")1ST Single ¥4800
■ CANNONS-Guts & Truth (US/Vulture Rock/'94 Orig.3-Track 7")EX/M- ¥5800
■ C.F.D.L.-Atrocity Exhibition (S.O.R./ '90 Orig.6-Track 7") ¥6800
■ CONFUSE-Contempt For The Authority (Confuse/ '85 Orig.4-Track 7") ¥4800
■ CORRUPTED-Horrible:El Tren (Japan Overseas/ '95 Orig.4-Track 7"+Insert) ¥3800
-La Victim Es Tu Mismo (Czech Republic / View Beyond /Orig. 7")q ¥2800
■ CROCODILE SKINK-S.T. (Asia/ Orig.4-Track 7") ¥4800
■ DEAD COPS-Kill The Cops (ADK / '84 Orig.3-Track 1 Sided Flexi) ¥8800
■ DEATH SIDE-Satisfy The Instinct EP (Selfish/ '87 Orig. 6-Track 7"+Insert) ¥4800
■ EASTERN YOUTH-For Skins And Punks (自主/ Orig.3-Track 7") ¥7800
■ EXECUTE-Driminal Flowers (Hit Parade/ '84 Orig.3-Track 7") ¥4800
■ FEROCIOUS X-Vaga Tanka Sjav EP (US/Distort/ Orig.10-Track 7"+insert) ¥3800
■ FRAMTID-8 Track EP (Crust War / Orig.8-Track 7") ¥3800
-Chainsawsplit'04 (男道 / '04 Orig. Split 6-Track 7" w/ Disclose) ¥2800
■ GAS-The Day After (自殺 / '84 Orig.6-Track Flexi) ¥4800
■ GHOUL-Jerusalm (Hold Up / '85 Orig.4-Track 7") ¥6800
■ GLOOM-Speed Noise Hardcore Rags (Crust War /'93 Orig.8-Track 7") ¥4800
■ GRIFFIN-資金源強奪EP (H.O.L/ '93 Orig. 3-Track 7") ¥3800
-Rockers Daylight (H.O.L/ '94 Orig.7")B面Shangri-Lasのカバー収録 ¥3800
-Sons Of The Dr. Streets (H.O.L/ Orig. 1 Sided 7")ライブ会場限定7" NO/PS ¥3800
-No Call (MCR / '98 Orig.7"+Insert) ¥2800
-France '98 issue (MCR/ '98 Orig.7") ¥2800
■ GRUESOME-Throw Light On (Ger / DIM /再発6-Track White Vinyl 7") ¥4800
■ G-SPOT-Radical & Shout (Deadlock / '83 Orig.4-Track Flexi) ¥6800
■ GUDON-Howling Communication (Selfish/ '87 Orig.6-Track 7") ¥4800
■ Hi-STANDARD-1995 Special EP (Pizza Of Death / '95 Promo Only 7") ... ¥12800
-Split (HG-fact/ '94 Orig.Split 4-Track 7" w/ Legitime Defence) ¥6800
■ JERRY BERRY-Girl's On My Mind (Spice Of Life / 再発4-Track 7")EX/EX .. ¥4800
■ JUDGEMENT-Process (HG-fact / Orig.7"+insert)ライブ会場限定7" ¥5800
■ K.G.G.M.-Fight Back Do It (Wild West / '88 Orig.4-Track 7"+Insert) ¥3500
-D.D+5 (Loose Nut / Orig. 6-Track Flexi) ¥6800
■ 奇形児-Plastic Scandal (ADK / '83 Orig. 4-Track 7"+Inner, Insert) ¥12800
-Pressure (ADK / '84 Orig. 4-Track Flexi+Insert) ¥6800
■ LAUGHIN' NOSE-When The L, Nose Go Marchin' Inn (AA? / '85 Orig.1 Sided Flexi)新宿アルタ前とアメ村三角公園で配布された Rare Flexi ¥3800
■ LIFE-Freedom And Liberation (Punk Bastard / Orig.10-Track 7")VG/M .. ¥5800
-The Master Of Darkness (Punk Bastard / Orig. 6-Track 7") ¥1800
■ MASTER BATION-死躰 (Abnormal / Orig.2-Track 1 Sided Flexi) ¥5800
■ MIRRORS-Out Of Order (Gozira / '79 Orig.7") ¥7800
■ MOBS-Diabolism (Noise Room / Orig. 5-Track 7") ¥6800
-Projection Of Astral Body (Advance / Orig.4-Track 7"+メンバー写真PS) ¥6800
■ 南海ボークウインド-S.T. (Underground /'87 Orig. 7"+髪の毛) ¥18000
■ NIGHTMARE-S.T. (Selfish / Orig. 7-Track 7"+Insert) ¥6800
Split (MCR / Orig. Split 5-Track 7" w/ Concrete Sox) ¥4800
■ 日本脳炎-Hard Hit Virus EP (Mangrove / '04 Orig.7"+Video, Insert, パッチ) .. ¥3800
■ OUTO-Many Question Poison Answer (AA / '84 Orig.6-Track 7"+Poster PS) ... ¥8800
-Hair Wit Life (Hold Up / Orig. 4-Track 7") ¥5800
■ RESULT-I Can Go Die (MCR / Orig.5-Track 7"+Insert) ¥3800
■ RUSTLER / SO WHAT-Split (Axxe /'90 Orig.Split 7-Track 7") ¥5800
■ ROOSTERS-Let's Rock(日本コロムビア /'82 Orig.7")爆裂都市のO.S.T. ¥5800
■ SA-I Get Possion (Club The Star / '85 Orig. 5-Track 8" Flexi)Rare! ¥12800
■ SIC-Get Up And Do It EP (Dogma/'89 Orig.7") ¥5800
■ SLEDGE HAMMER-Anthem E.P(US / Vulture Rock/'94 Orig.3-Track 7") ¥5800
■ S.O.B-Leave Me Alone (Selfish /'86 Orig.9-Track 7") ¥4800
-Suck Up Brain Or Fuck Ya Brain (S.O.B/'89 Orig.1 Sided Flexi)NO/PS ¥3800
-Thrahs Night (UK / Rise Above /'89 Orig.9-Track Black Vinyl 7") ¥4800
-UK'Euro Tour June '89 (S.O.B/'89 Orig.9-Track 7"+ Numbered Sleeve) ¥5800
-Split (S.O.B/'89 Orig.Split 10-Track Flexi w/ Napalm Death+白黒PS+Inser) . ¥1800

2nd_Edition

■ TWEEZERS-Favourite (Target Earth /'98 Orig.3-Track 7") ¥3800
■ WANDERERS-Charming All Those Changes (AA /'86 Orig.2 x 7"+GS) ¥4800
■ WARHEAD-Drive It In Your Head (Fast Nail/ '99 Orig 7"+Poster Sleeve) ¥3800
■ W.P. CITY INDIAN-W.P.C.I Warning (AA /'95 Orig.4-Track 7") ¥6800
■ V.A.-Neo Punk Disordery (ADK/Orig. 15-Track 7"+Insert)EX/EX Gabelift ¥3800
■ V.A.-Not-superstitious (Snuffy Smile /'94 Orig.4-Track 7") Blew佐 ¥5800
■ V.A.-Shizuoka City Hard Core (MCR /Orig 8-Track Flexi)Mental佐 ¥4800
■ V.A.-Too Late To Kiss The Truth A Tribute To Snuff (Snuffy Smile /'93 Orig. 4-Track 7") Samntha's Favourite, Coke Head Hipsters, Not Enough佐 ¥6800

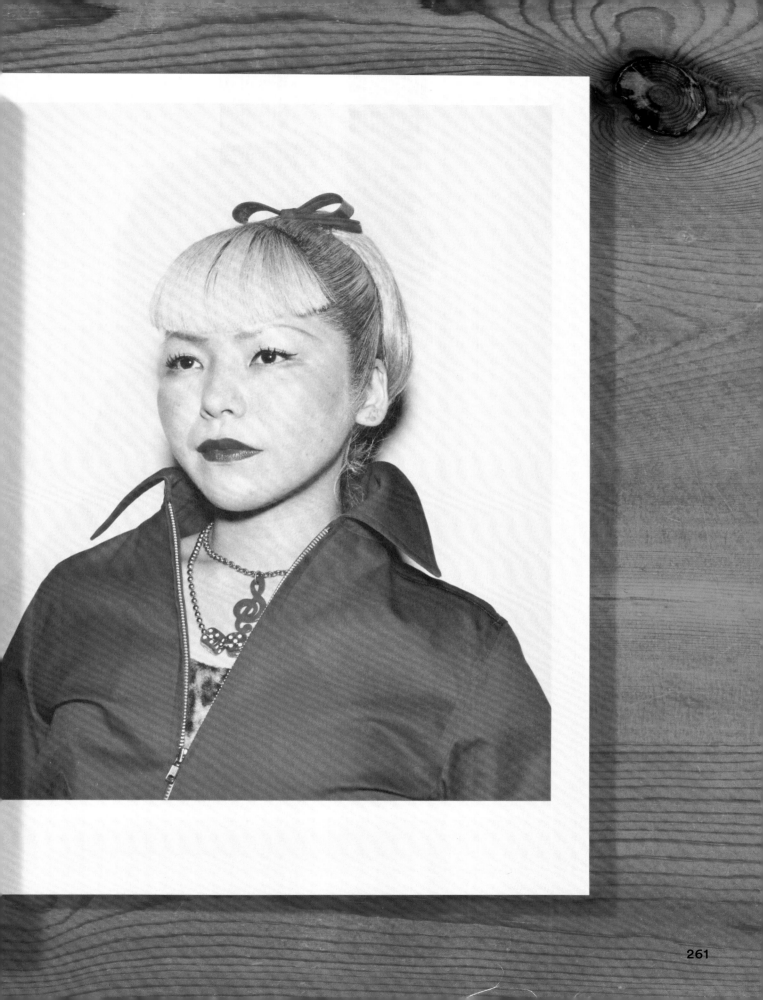

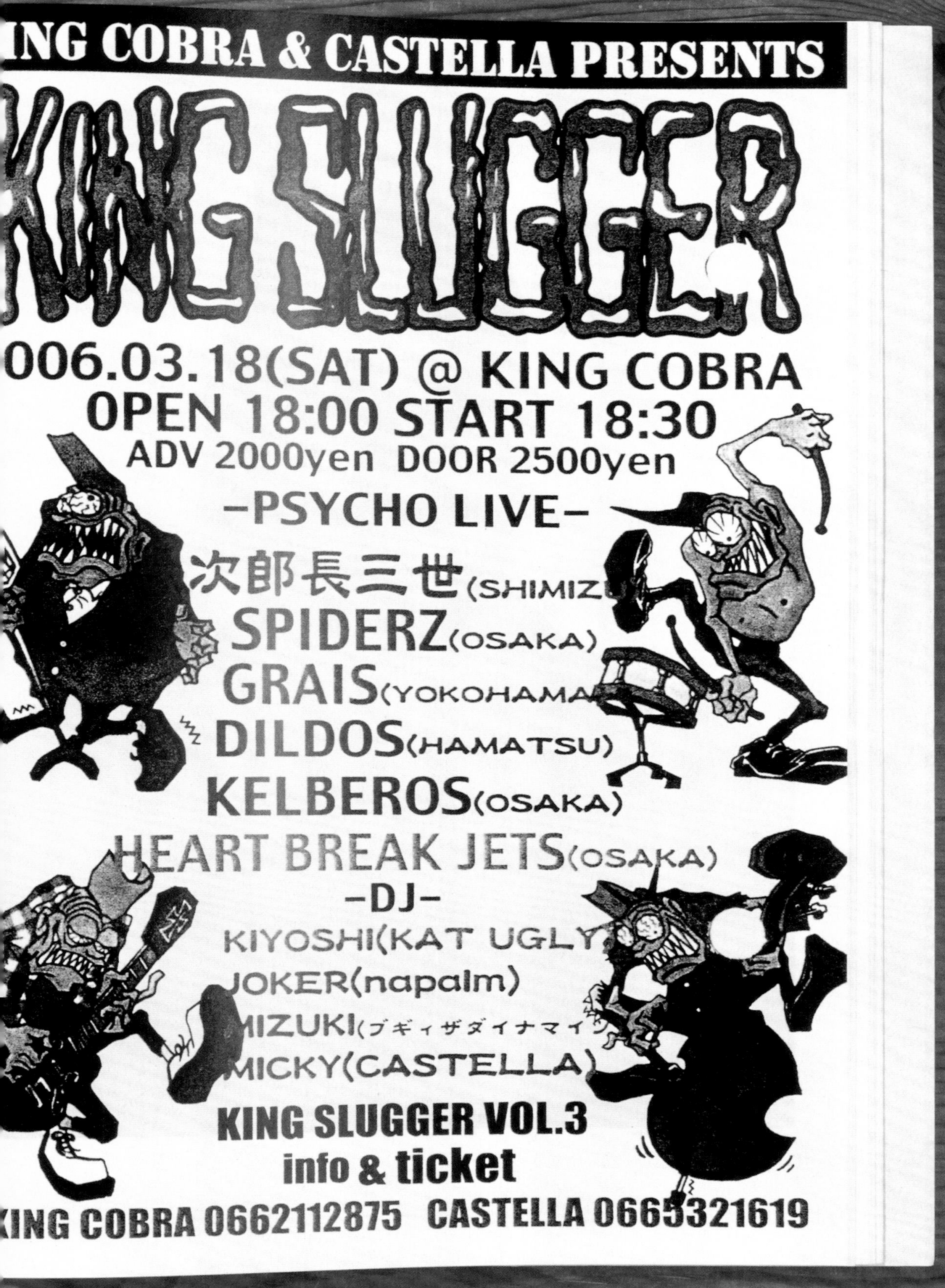

KING COBRA & CASTELLA PRESENTS

KING SLUGGER

2006.03.18(SAT) @ KING COBRA
OPEN 18:00 START 18:30
ADV 2000yen DOOR 2500yen
-PSYCHO LIVE-
次郎長三世(SHIMIZU)
SPIDERZ(OSAKA)
GRAIS(YOKOHAMA)
DILDOS(HAMATSU)
KELBEROS(OSAKA)
HEART BREAK JETS(OSAKA)
-DJ-
KIYOSHI(KAT UGLY)
JOKER(napalm)
MIZUKI(ブギィザダイナマイ)
MICKY(CASTELLA)
KING SLUGGER VOL.3
info & ticket
KING COBRA 0662112875   CASTELLA 0665321619

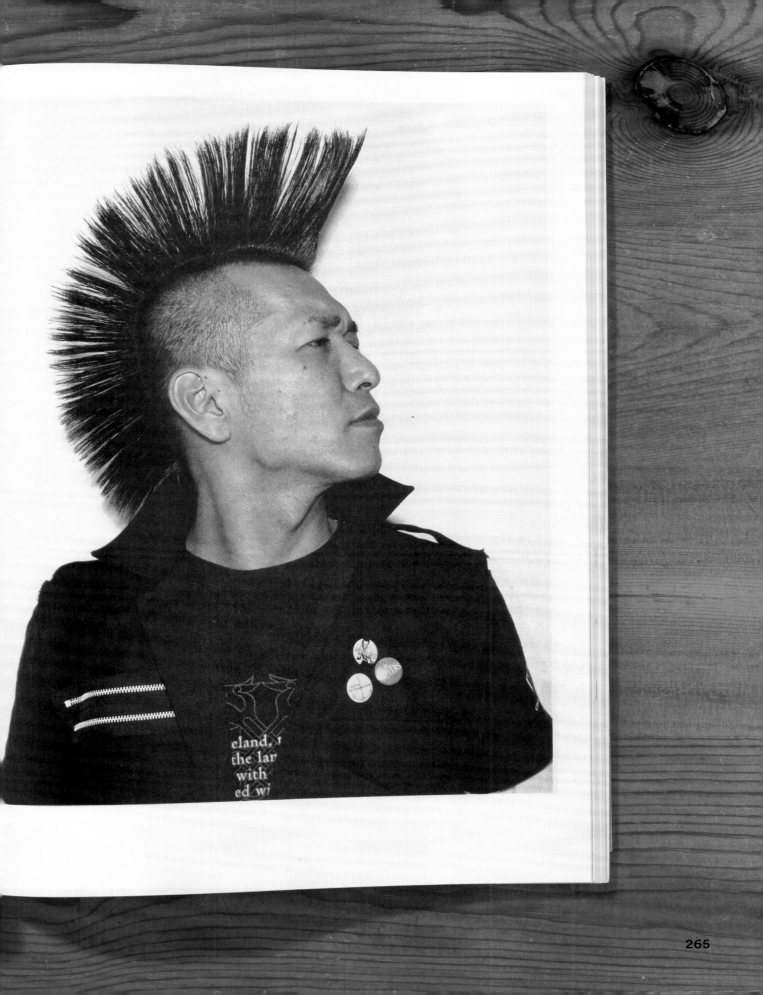

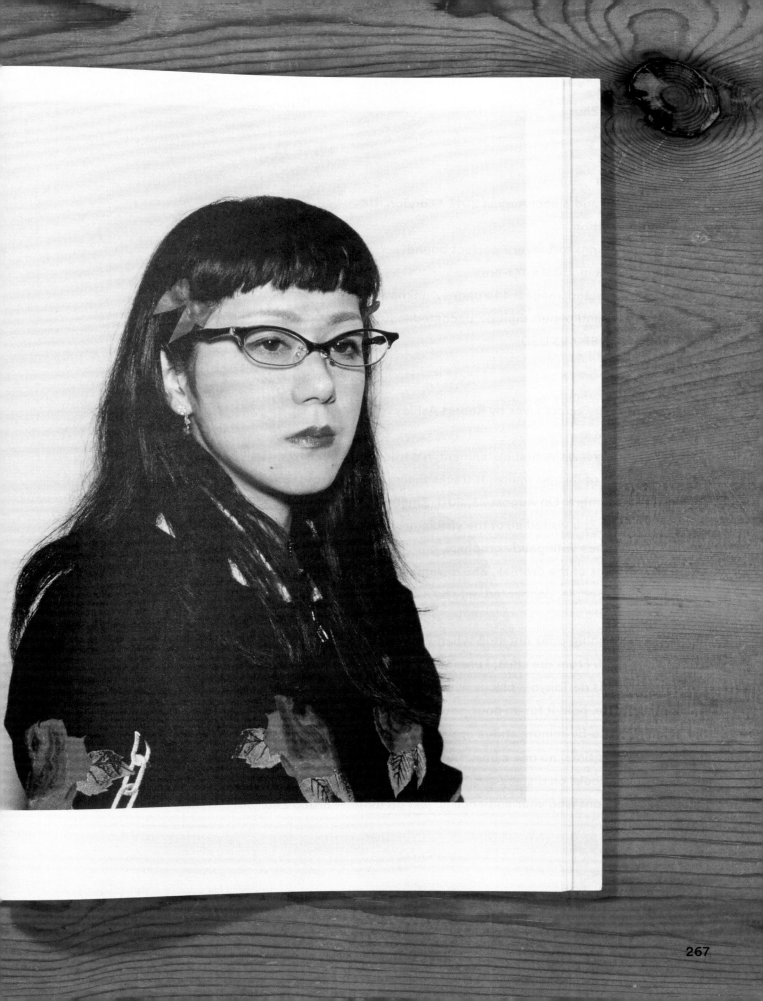

Title: Facsimile I: A Novel

Artist: Bruno Zhu

Designer: Bruno Zhu

Editor: Bruno Zhu

Imprint: bzbooks

Printer: Lulu.com

Publication date and place: August 2013 / London, UK

Edition: open edition

Format and binding: softcover / perfect bound

Size: 4 1/4 x 6 7/8 in. (10.8 x 17.5 cm)

Number of pages and images: 444 pages / unknown

Type of printing and paper: digital / uncoated matte 89gsm

Retail price: 15 GBP / 23 USD

Cost per unit: $$

Book soundtrack: *Perfect Lives* by Robert Ashley

Facsimile I: A Novel is the first installment in a trilogy of books by artist Bruno Zhu, designed to explore the lives of images online. It tracks the virtual journey of a single photograph, by Zhu, of a surveillance camera. On August 23, 2011, Zhu uploaded the image to Tumblr; by May 22, 2013, it had 677 notes. Zhu visited all of the visible profiles that had reblogged the image and found that it shared space with gaudy graphics, one-liners, and slices of autobiographical text. Collating screenshots of the profiles, Zhu designed a coming-of-age novel that brings together the stories of these people, connected only by a CCTV camera.

The act of publishing does not stop when you publish your book—it is also about how you "publish" yourself. From the start, I created "book launches" in venues such as the book store Foyles or at Palais de Tokyo—places which have café areas with free wi-fi. All I did was hustle a four-person table, hold it for an hour, and broadcast the hell out of it: Facebook events, installation shots, minute-by-minute status updates. No permission asked. Only two people came to the first one; another time, no one came. The staff looked at me suspiciously—what is he doing here alone, with ten books on display and business cards? The online crowd was there for me, though. Once you figure out who your audience is, just go for it. —Bruno Zhu

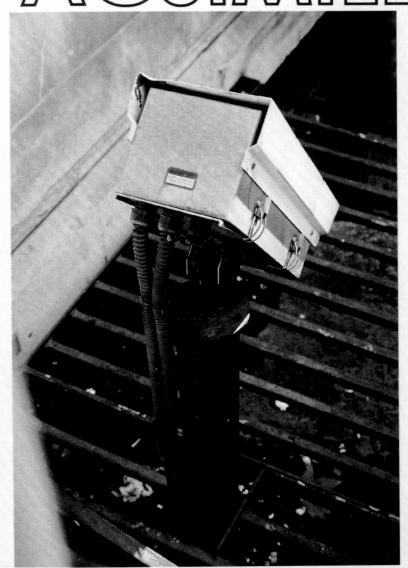

FACSIMILE

BRUNOZHU

talk to me, i don't bite.

LINKS:

skype- mynameisjanie

my face.

22

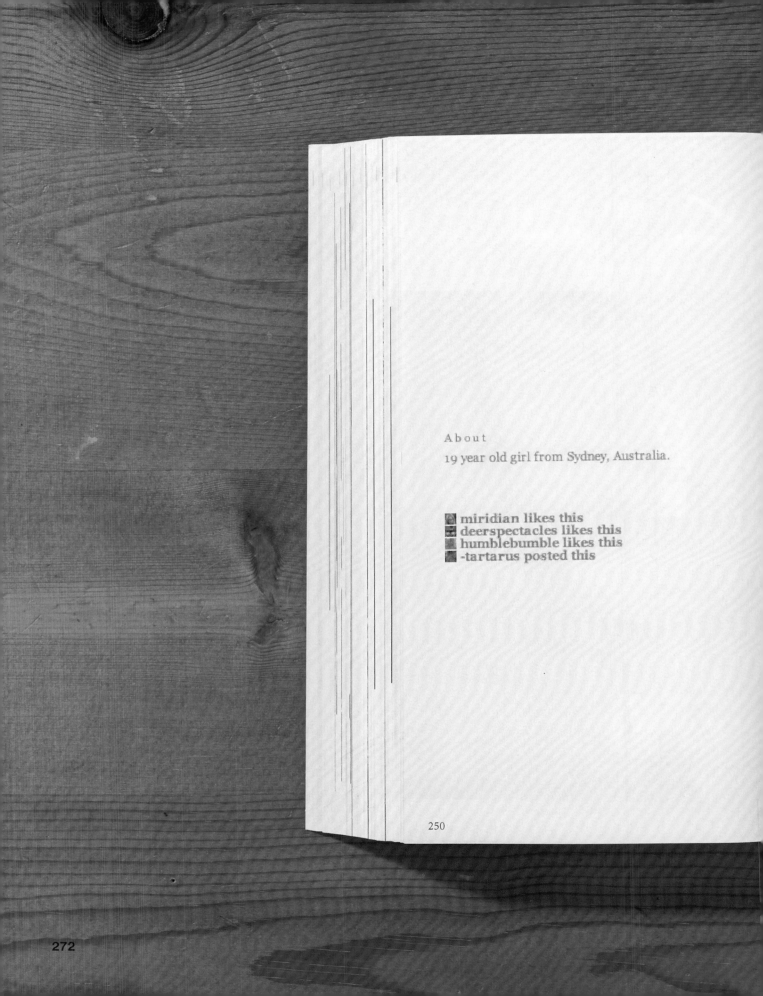

About

19 year old girl from Sydney, Australia.

miridian likes this
deerspectacles likes this
humblebumble likes this
-tartarus posted this

$$$

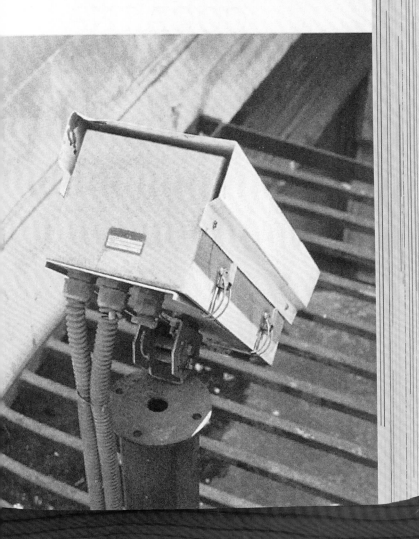

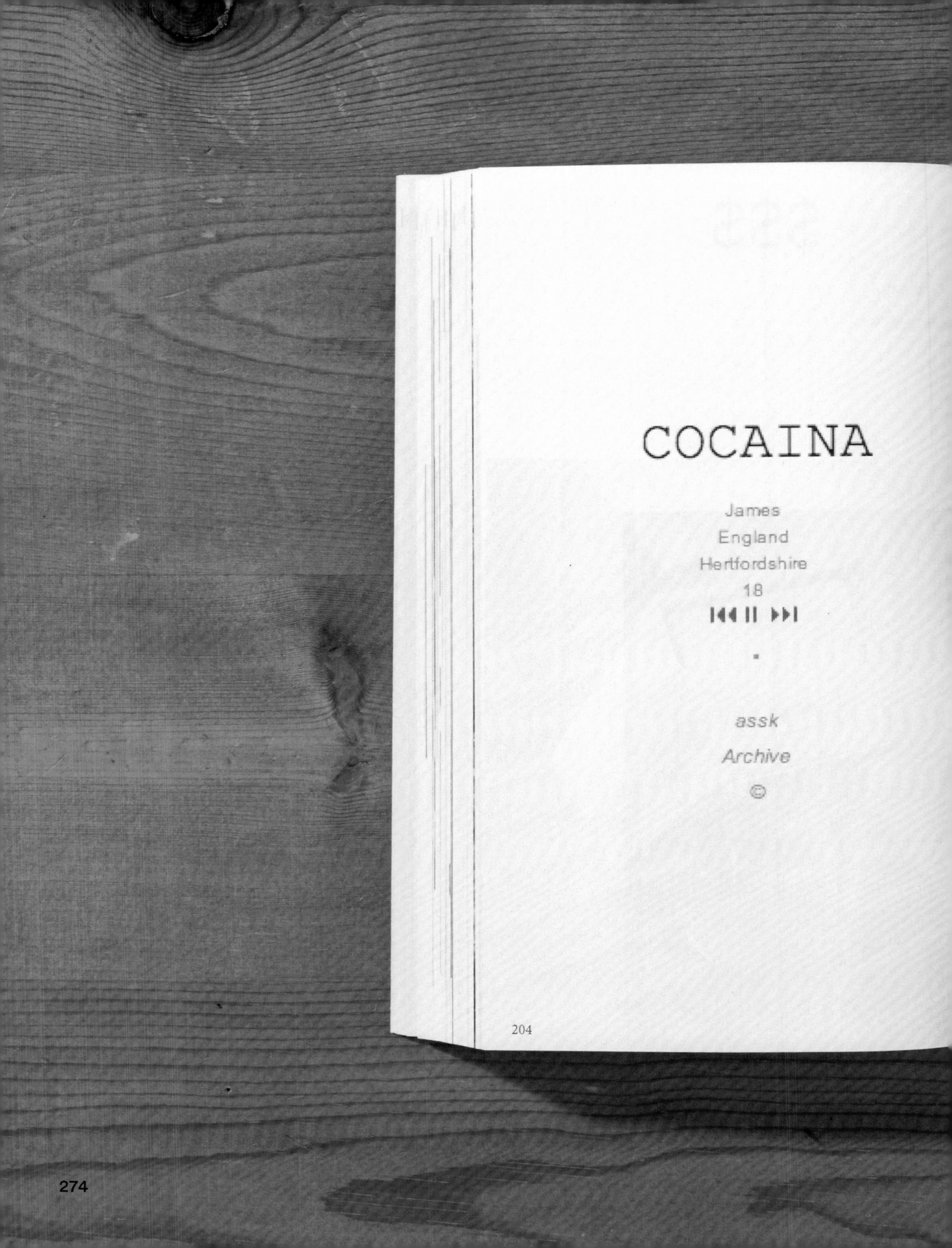

COCAINA

James
England
Hertfordshire
18
|◀◀ ❚❚ ▶▶|

▪

assk

Archive

☺

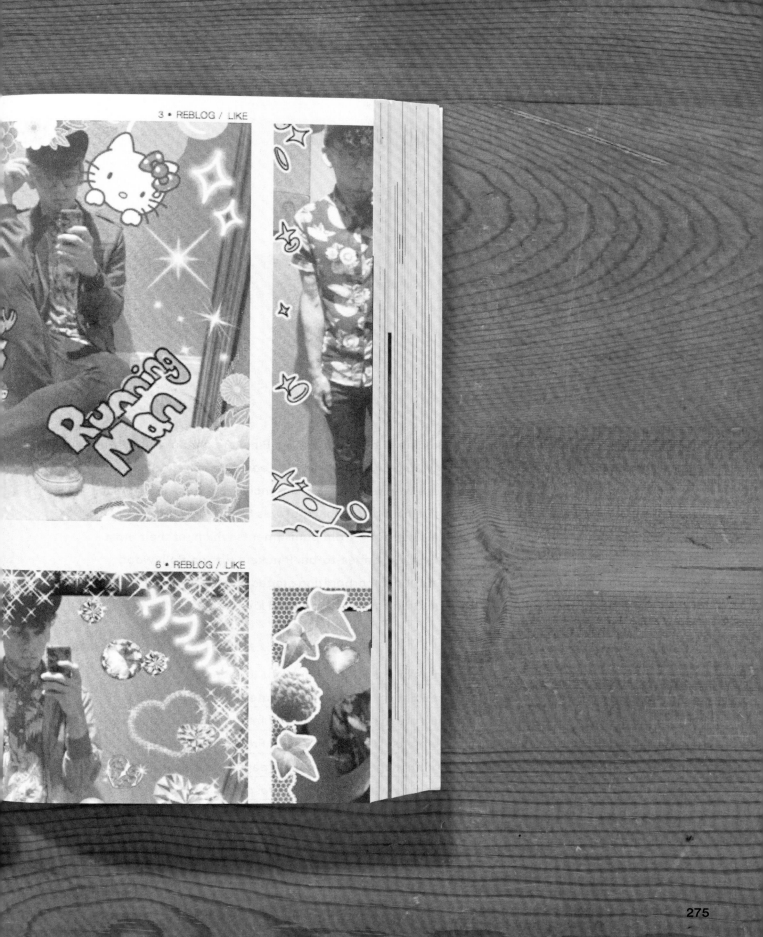

Title: Will They Sing Like Raindrops or Leave Me Thirsty

Artist: Max Pinckers

Additional contributor: Hans Theys

Designer: Jurgen Maelfeyt

Editor: Max Pinckers

Imprint: none

Printer: Die Keure, Bruges, Belgium

Publication date and place: May 2014 / Brussels, Belgium

Edition: 1,000

Format and binding: softcover with flaps / Otabind

Size: 8 1/4 x 11 1/2 in. (21 x 29 cm)

Number of pages and images: 232 pages / 140 images

Type of printing and paper: four-color offset / various

Retail price: 50 EUR / 56 USD

Cost per unit: $$$$

Book soundtrack: *Floral Shoppe* by Macintosh Plus

This is the fourth self-published book by Belgian photographer Max Pinckers on the subject of love and gender relations in India. *Will They Sing Like Raindrops or Leave Me Thirsty* focuses specifically on arranged marriages and those who resist them. This includes the Love Commandos, a group with several chapters in New Delhi and Mumbai that was formed to protect couples who wish to marry against their families' wishes—from punishments which, at their most extreme, can include honor killings of disobedient brides-to-be. Pinckers riffs on Bollywood aesthetics of romance and melds fact and fiction, incorporating staged scenes from real-life stories, newspaper clippings, and e-mail petitions from star-crossed lovers seeking the help of the Love Commandos.

In my documentary approach, different types of imagery are brought together as a book. Every kind of image has its own distinct visual aesthetic; the redefined context establishes the way they are read and consequently defines their meaning. Every type of image is given its own presentation through several subtle design elements, such as the use of French binding, glossy or colored paper, repetitive image sequencing, full page bleeds, double page spreads, or differences in image size. This creates a hierarchal system to which the images respond, each gaining a certain value and importance within the narrative threads that form the story as a whole.

—Max Pinckers

est
nen'

Study

nong
n in India, 2010

| f deaths (% of |
| al deaths) |

| 8,200 (9.6) |
| 1,700 (0.2) |
| — |
| 700 (8.5) |
| 500 (7.8) |
| — |
| 00 (2.3) |
| 500 (5.5) |
| 000 (100) |

ue about
one of

INDIA DIGEST

Bro beheads sister

In a bizarre incident, a 20-year-old girl was killed by her brother, who went to a police station with the severed head after a suspected case of honour killing on Sunday in UP's Bahraich district. Objecting to her desire to marry a 50-year-old person, her brother Nanke chopped off her head on Saturday.

Curfew in Kudankulam: Clamping down on the anti-nuclear protesters, the Tirunelveli district administration on Sunday imposed curfew in the villages falling within a seven-km radius around Kudankulam nuclear power plant.

Tibetan attempts suicide: A Tibetan youth attempted self-immolation in Dharamshala's McLeodganj town on Sunday.

JUST LIKE THAT   AJIT NINAN

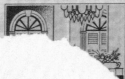

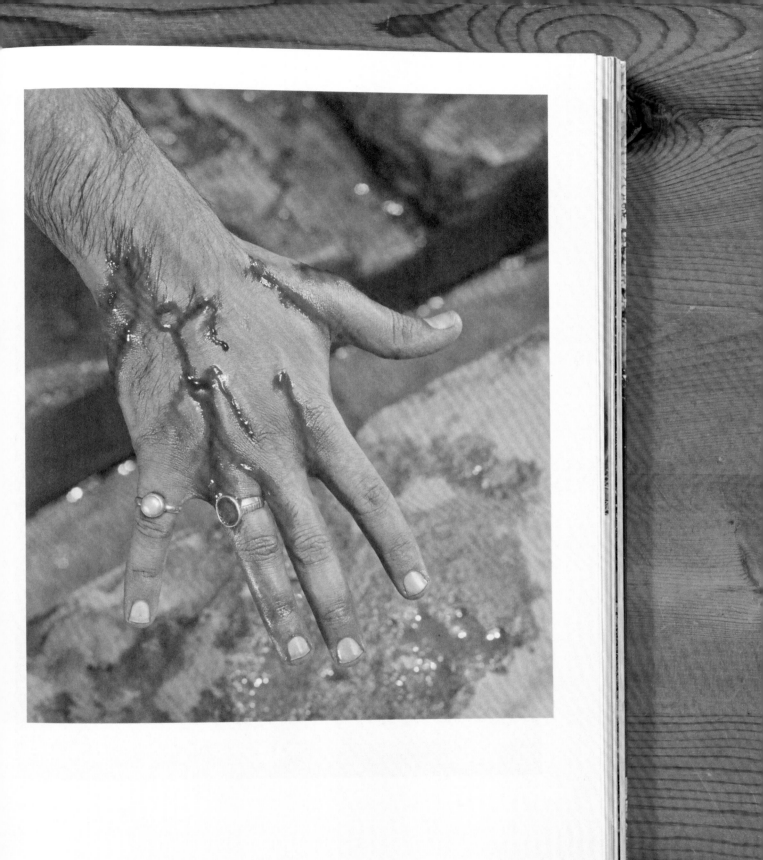

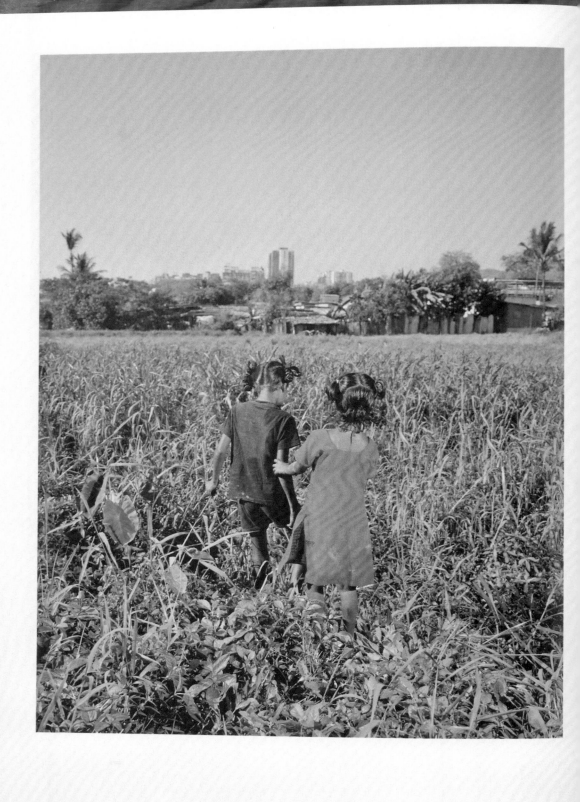

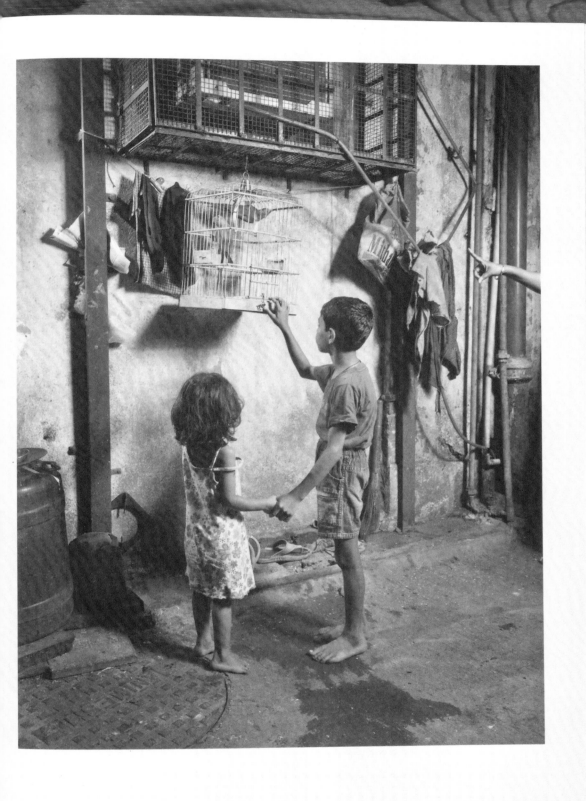

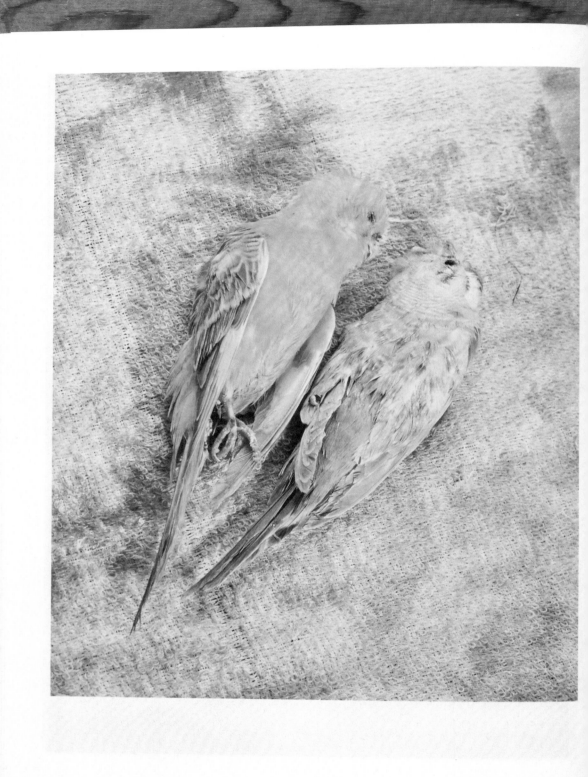

MP village home to 16th C tale of Tota Maina love birds

Amarjeet Singh | TNN

Burhanpur: The famous Kishore Kumar song "Tota Maina Ki Kahani" from the '70s film, 'Fakira', has always epitomized eternal love. What is little known is that the story originated in Burhanpur, a nondescript district in Madhya Pradesh. Now, 40 years after 'Fakira', Suraj Nagar, a sub-divisional magistrate, is making a movie which has a scene dedicated to this love story.

Quamaruddin Falak, a historian, claims that this love story is not a myth but a forgotten history. When Abdul Rahim Khan-i-Khana, one of Akbar's navratnas, ruled this city in the 16th century, the region suffered a severe drought. Rahim then got a reservoir constructed on the top of a hill from where water was later brought to the city. It still exists.

But few know the role Tota and Maina played in getting water to the city. They belonged

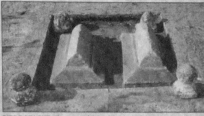

BIRDS OF LOVE: The grave of Tota Maina in Burhanpur

to a seer called Hazrat Shah Mustaqbil and fell in love while being kept in different cages.

It was said that whoever went to the seer seeking water never returned empty-handed. During the drought, Rahim went to him and the seer said he would set his birds free and they would guide him to water. "The birds went to a hill and sat on a stone which suddenly caved in to reveal a hollow, full of water," adds Falak. But the

birds could not be found. Later, they were found dead, wrapped in each other's wings.

When they were brought to the seer, he said that they preferred dying together than living in seperate cages. Impressed, Rahim got their graves built next to each another. Falak claims that this is a fact recorded by books, including one written by Sir Thomas Roe, a British ambassador who visited Burhanpur.

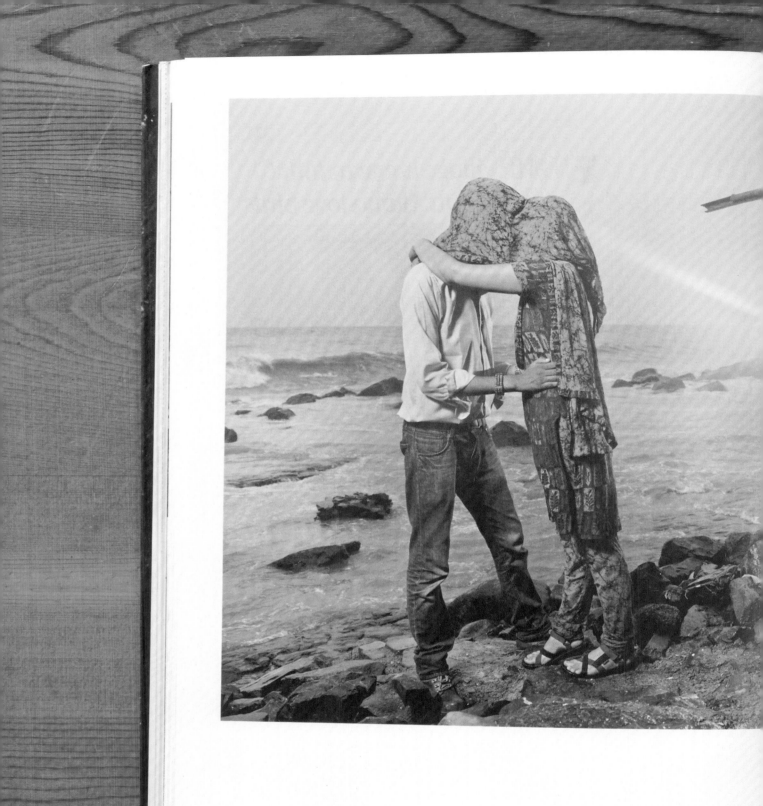

Title: Lang Zal Ze Leven (Happy Birthday to You)

Artist: Anouk Kruithof

Additional contributors: Armand Hoppener and Sascha Landshoff

Designer: Anouk Kruithof

Editor: Anouk Kruithof

Imprint: Stresspress

Printer: Bergdrukkerij, Amersfoort, the Netherlands

Publication date and place: March 2011 / Amsterdam, the Netherlands

Edition: 500

Format and binding: softcover, wrapped with white ribbon / saddle stitched

Size: 11 6/8 x 16 1/2 in. (29.7 x 42 cm)

Number of pages and images: 80 pages / unknown

Type of printing and paper: offset / various

Retail price: 25 EUR / 30 USD

Cost per unit: $$$$$

Book soundtrack: "Lang Zal Ze Leven" (Dutch birthday song)

In 2011, Anouk Kruithof took part in an artist residency during which she resided at a psychiatric institution in Den Dolder, the Netherlands. Taking a social-practice approach to documentary, she interviewed ten residents over the course of her stay—about what their birthday meant to them, how they would like to celebrate, and their favorite color. She organized parties for each, including baking a cake decorated with an edible portrait of the patient. She photographed throughout the process, and the final book, which includes texts from the interviews and photographs of the interactions, was assembled with the help of the patients, who tied each book with a bow once complete. Kruithof has frequently described her publications as central to her practice, viewing the book as the final form for many of her projects. All of her publications are self-published under her own imprint, Stresspress.

Do you have ideas too wild for someone else to understand or digest? Do you have the urgency to get your book out there, know exactly what you want to do, and have the feeling your book is ready the way you want it? Just do it. Self-publishing is liberating. Self-publishing is only for people who love to work hard. Make sure you have the financial support to produce it, and that you're prepared for what you have to do once you're sitting next to ten boxes full of books.
—Anouk Kruithof

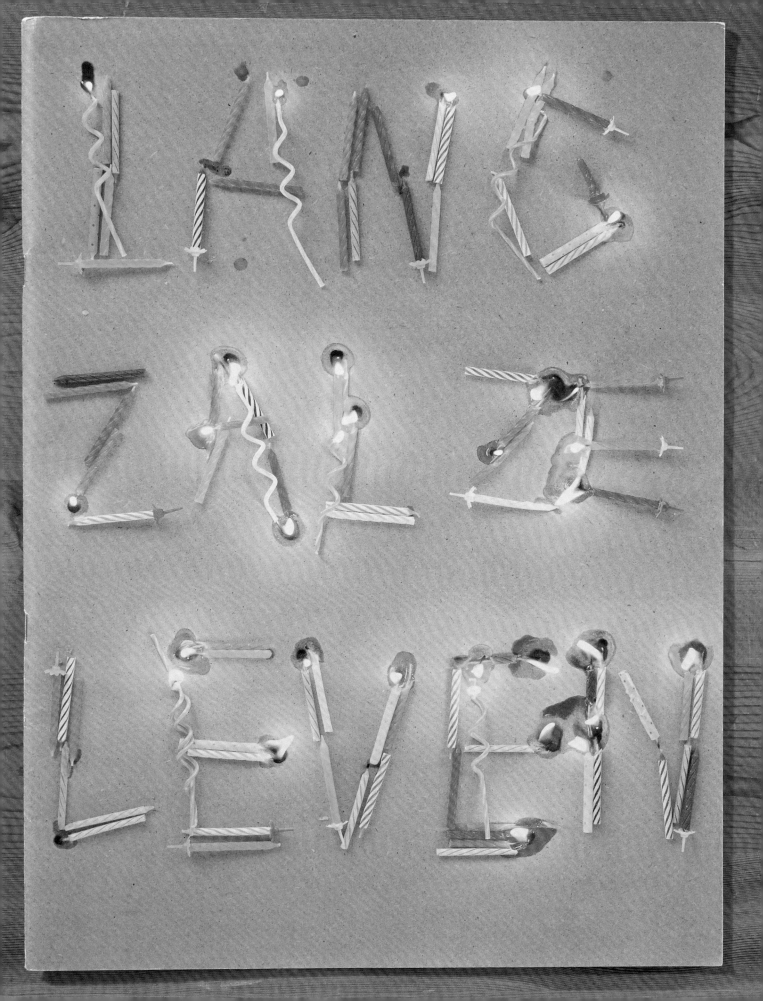

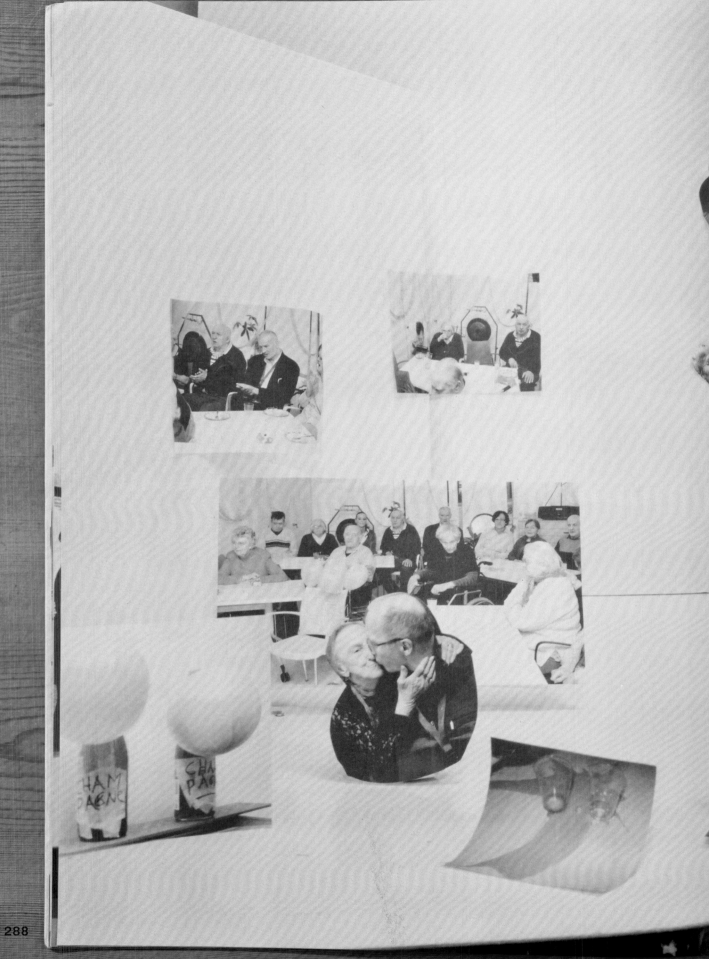

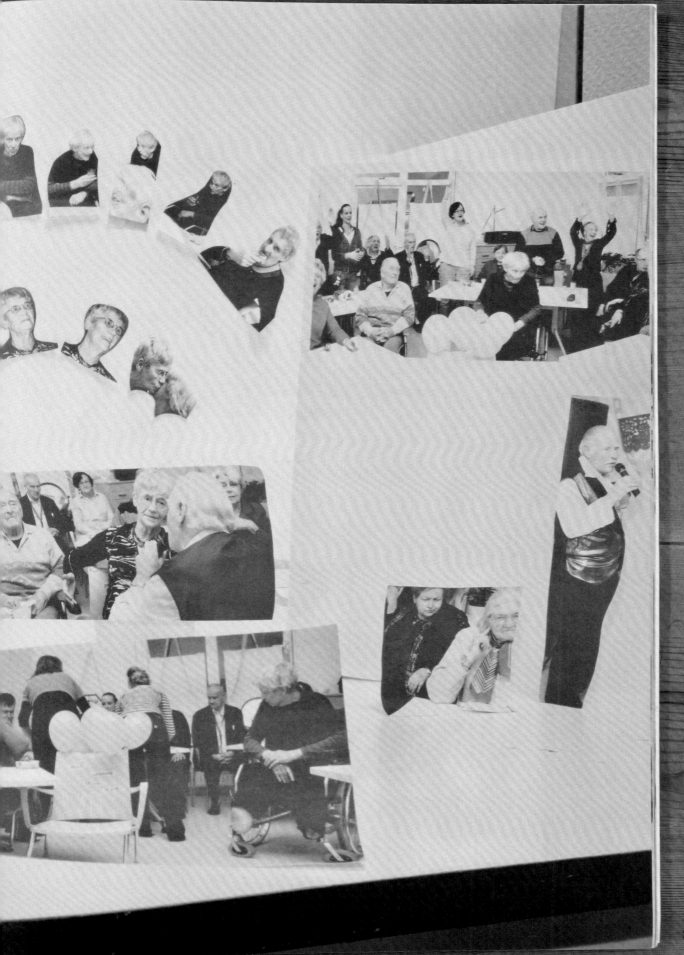

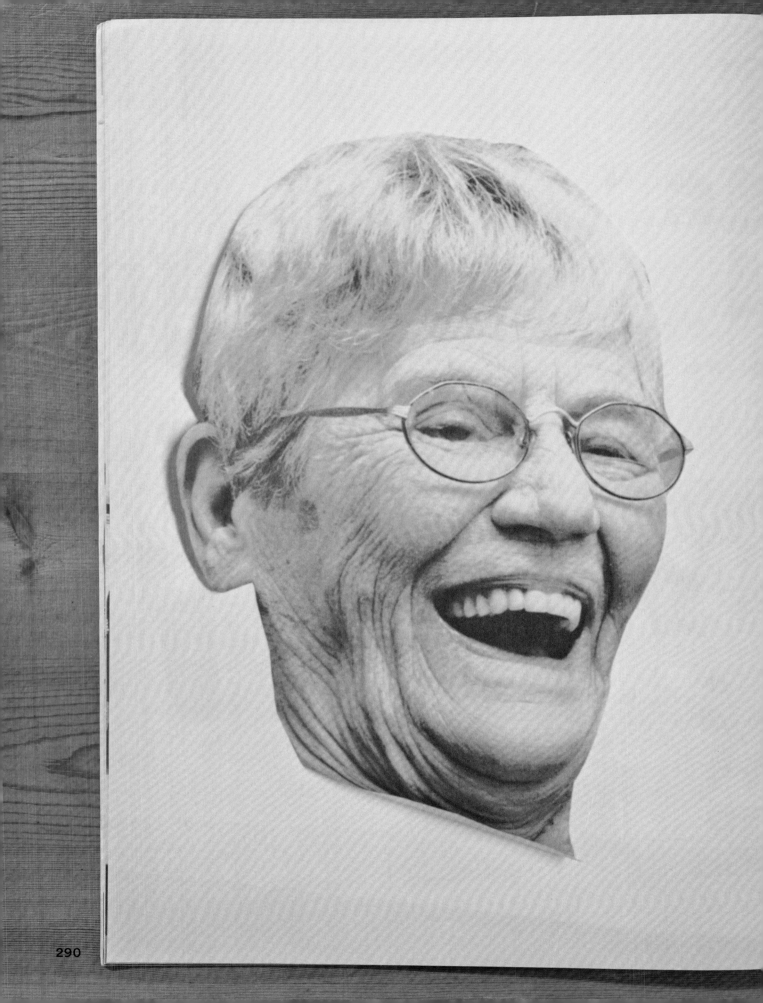

W I L   D I E T E R M A N

23-02-1935

76

lievelingskleur = GRASGROEN

de Linde, afdeling Korenveld, Heide 2

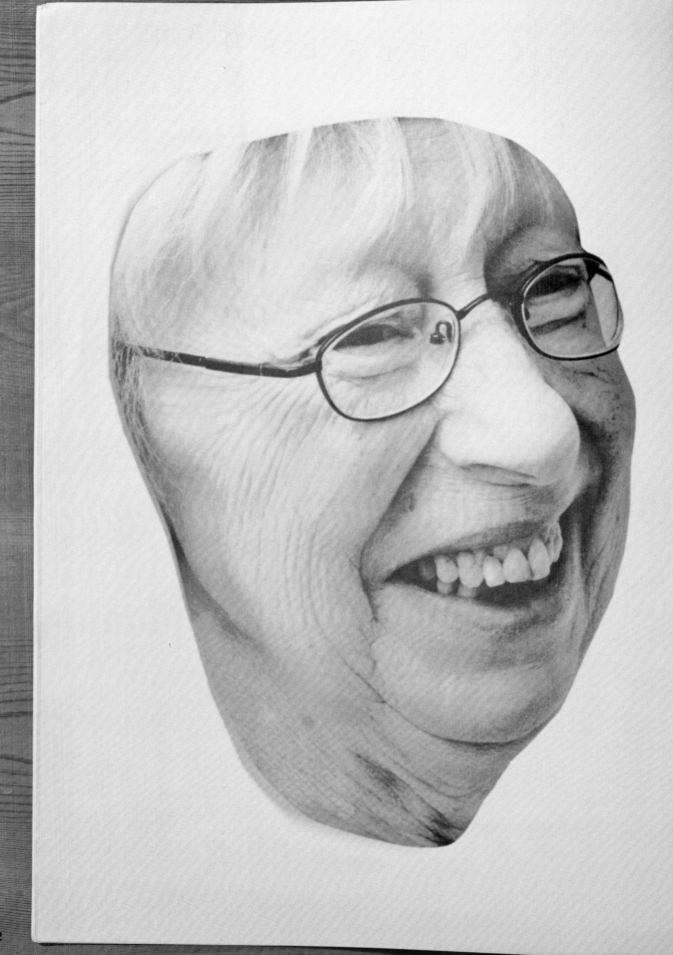

MAARTJE SPEK

11-02-1946

65

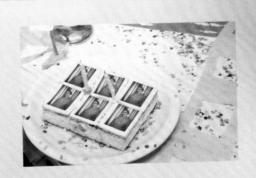

lievelingskleur = ROZE

de Linde, afdeling Erasmus, groep 4

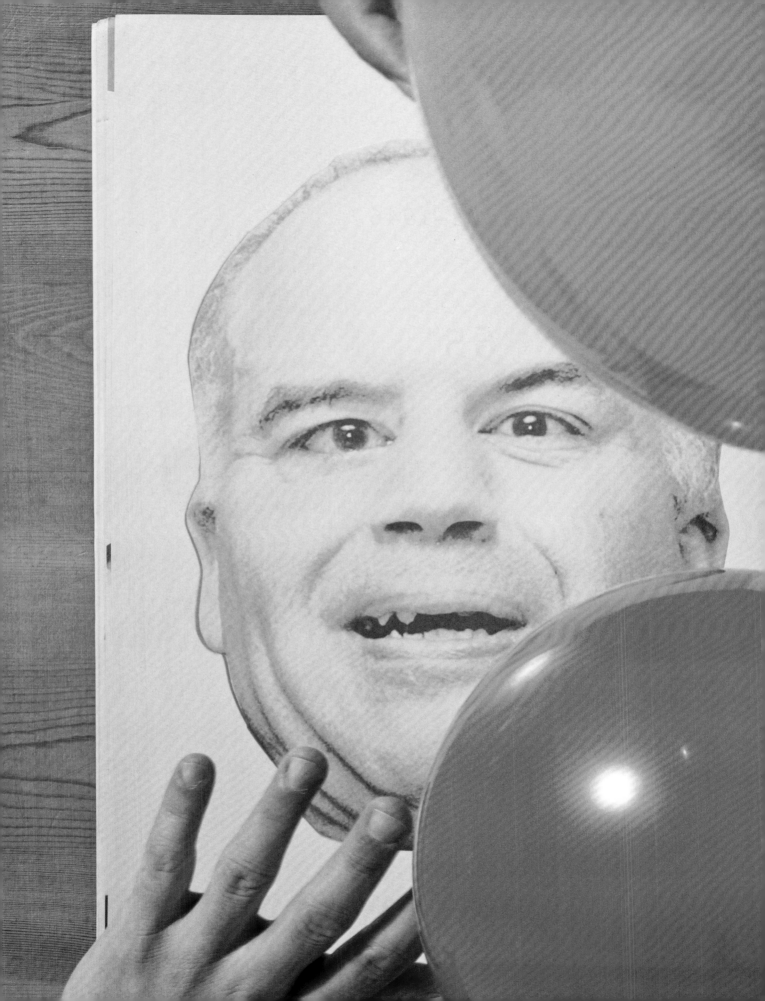

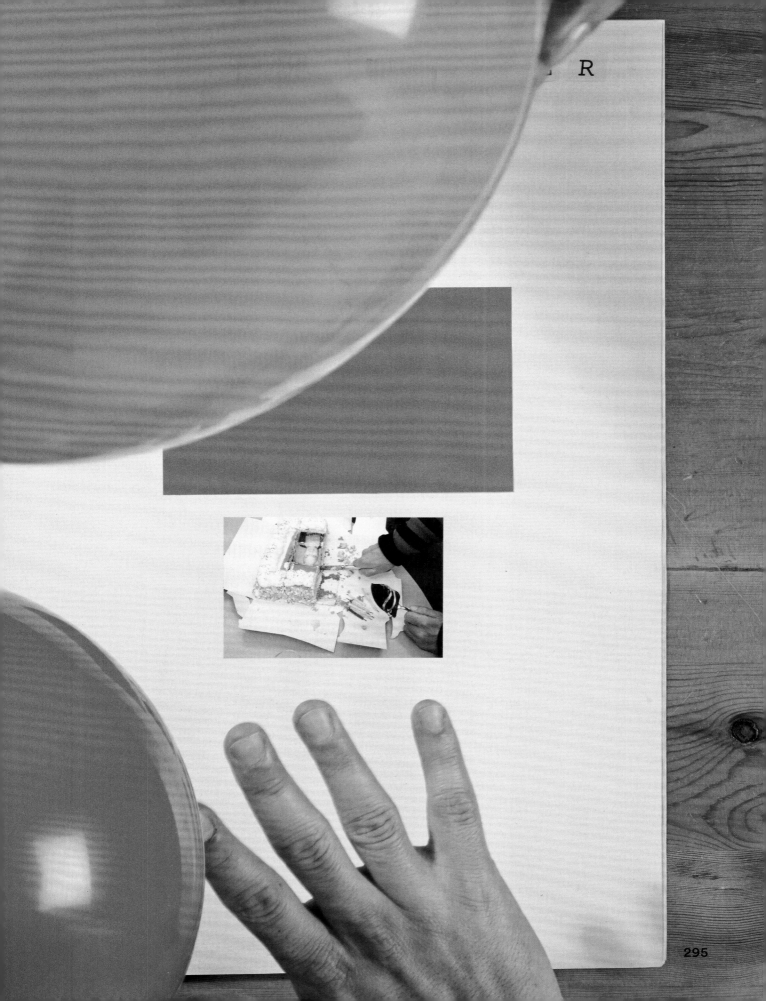

Self Publish, Be a Team

Title: *Hired Hand*

Artists: Stuart Bailes, Bea Fremderman, Ingo Mittelstaedt, and Athena Torri

Additional contributors: Flemming Ove Bech and Johan Rosenmunthe

Designers: Flemming Ove Bech, Johan Rosenmunthe, and Rasmus Michaëlis

Editors: Flemming Ove Bech and Johan Rosenmunthe

Imprint: Vandret Publications

Printer: Narayana Press, Odder, Denmark

Publication date and place: June 2012 / Copenhagen, Denmark

Edition: 350

Format and binding: softcover with die-cut cover / perfect bound

Size: 7 7/8 x 10 1/4 in. (20 x 26 cm)

Number of pages and images: 64 pages / 32 images

Type of printing and paper: four-color offset / Munken Polar Rough 170gsm

Price: 35 EUR / 40 USD

Cost per unit: $$$$

Book soundtrack: "Syv Cirkler" by Else Marie Pade

The Danish artists Johan Rosenmunthe and Flemming Ove Bech cofounded the publishing project Lodret Vandret in their hometown of Copenhagen. For *Hired Hand*, Rosenmunthe and Ove Bech drew together the photographic work of four young artists—Stuart Bailes, Bea Fremderman, Ingo Mittelstaedt, and Athena Torri—and asked for free reign over the artists' raw material. Playfully reappropriating their landscape and still-life works, they set about experimenting with the idea of collaboration, placing one artist's work on top of another's to form new collages, and finding Internet stock images to work into the edit. In this publication, Rosenmunthe and Ove Bech strike a balance between facilitating and participating in a collaborative journey through photographic juxtaposition.

We started Lodret Vandret as a reaction to what was essentially a feeling of lack of community. We wanted to join in the fun we were seeing online: young artists taking agency to publish and show each other's work, generously sharing and endorsing the projects of their peers and colleagues. At the time we had not yet identified people around us in Copenhagen who we felt shared our taste and interests, so we looked abroad—or rather, we looked at our bookmarks folder—for people whose work we liked. The next step was sending an e-mail saying just that, and asking if each person would want to do a project. It was an enormously energizing experience getting positive replies! —Flemming Ove Bech

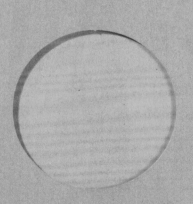

HIRED HAND

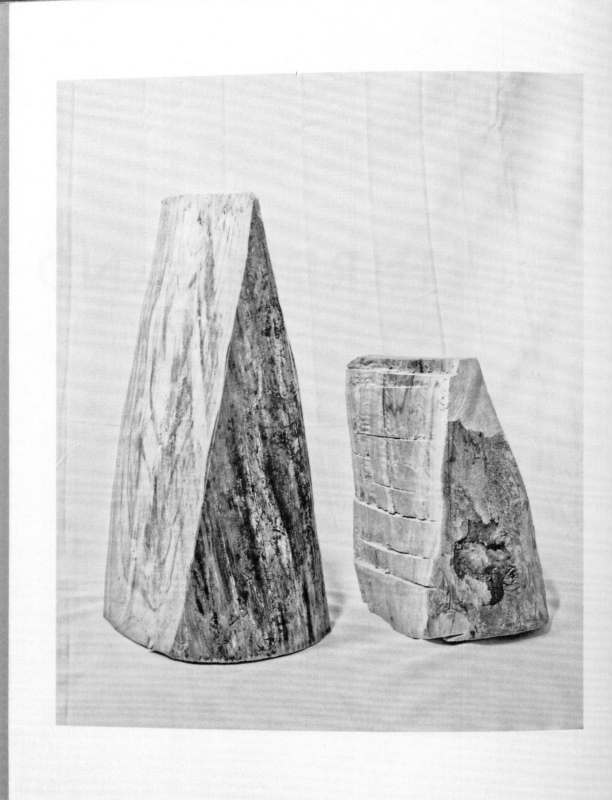

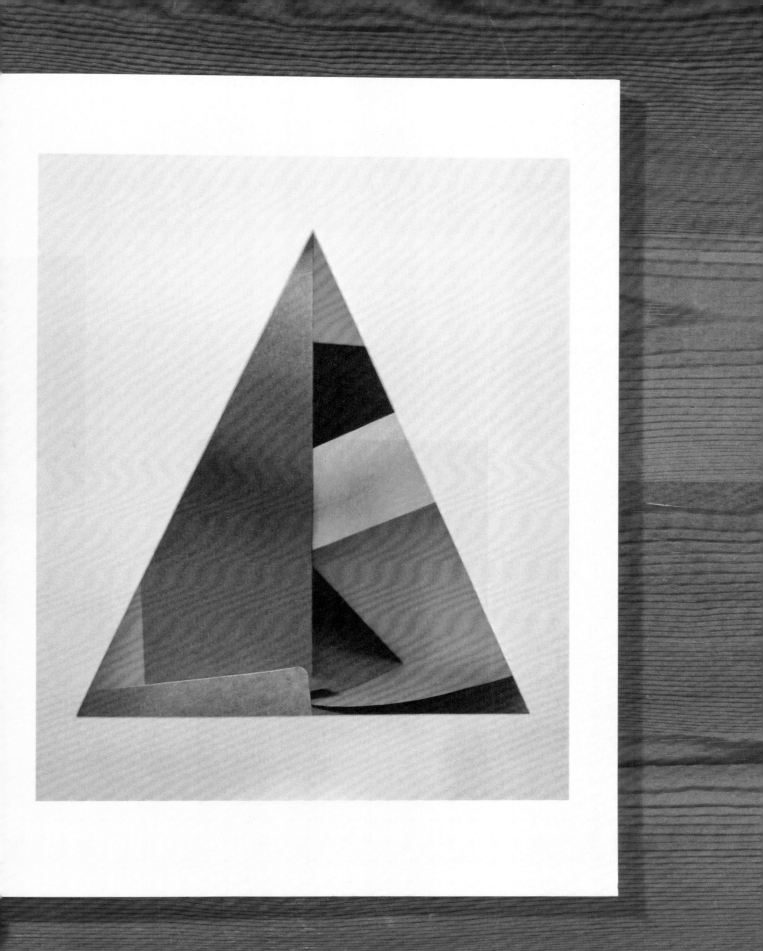

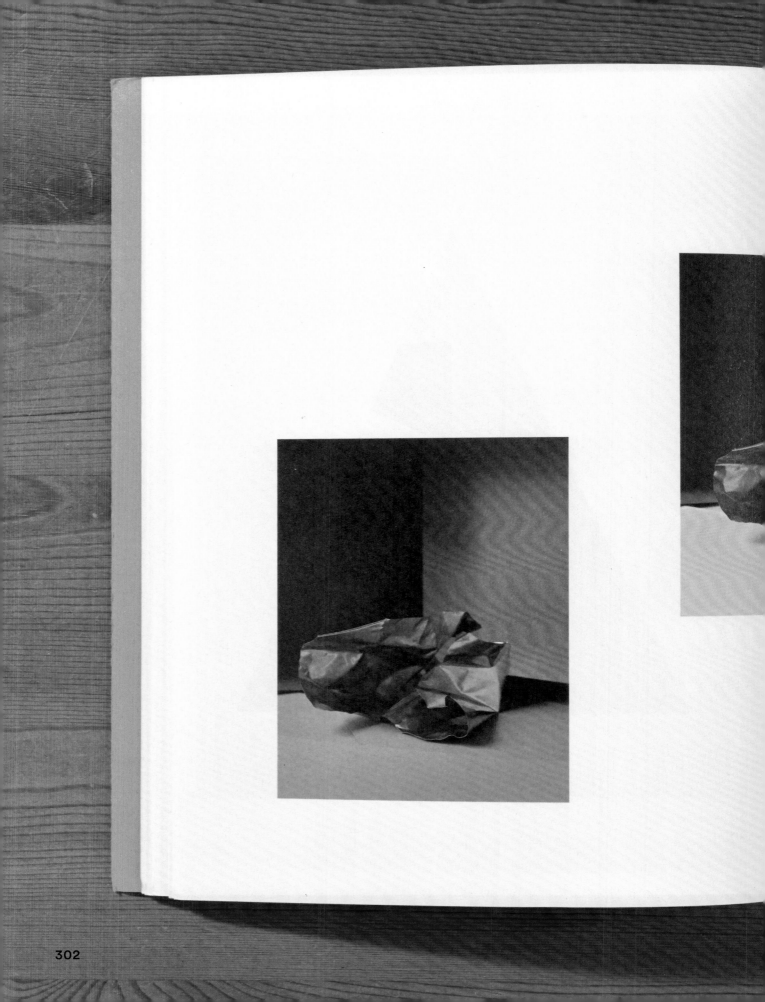

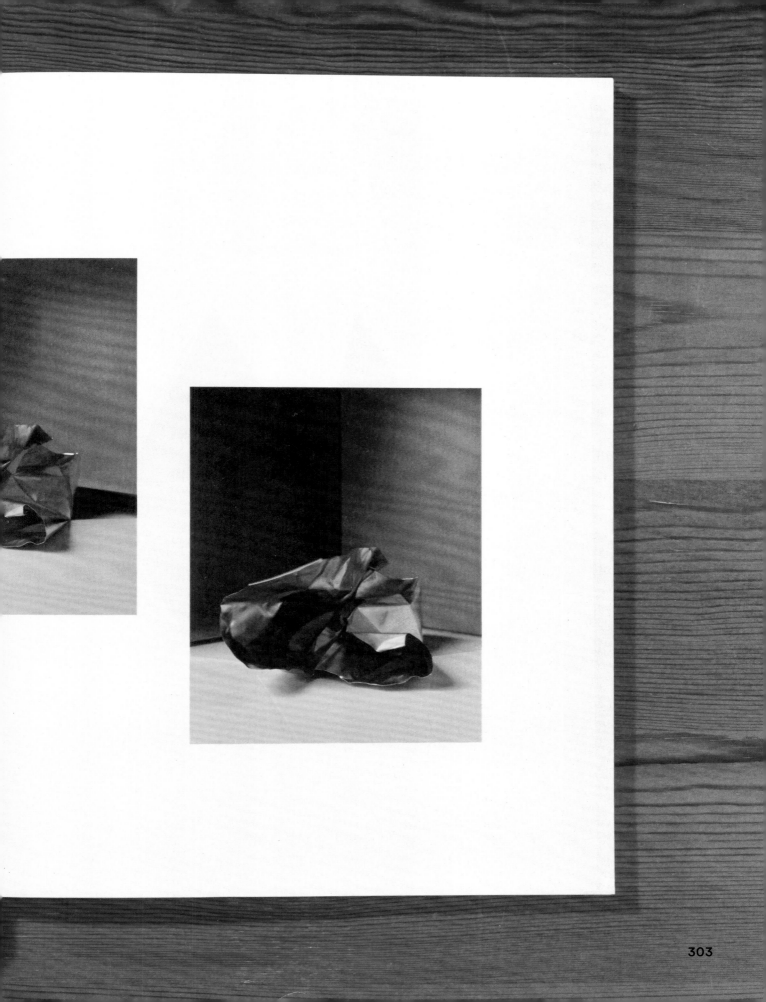

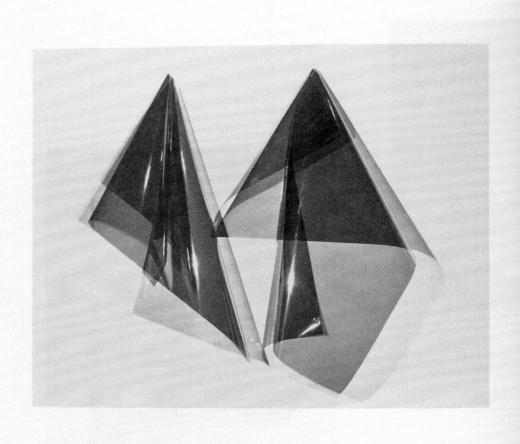

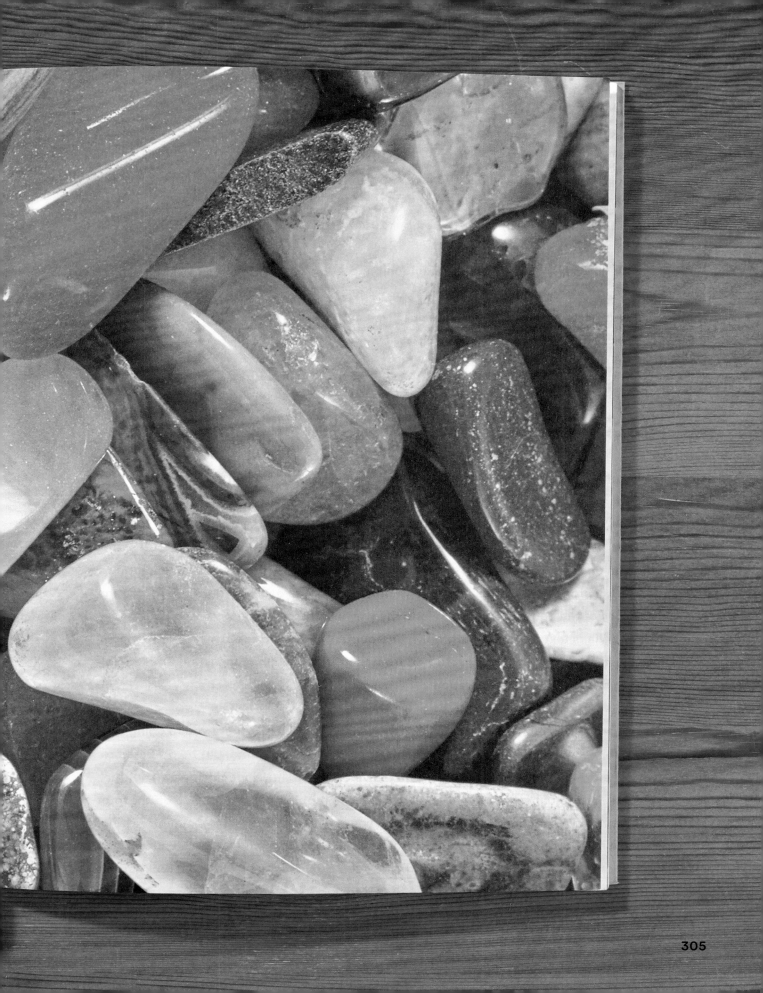

Title: The LBM Dispatch 1–7

Artists: Alec Soth and Brad Zellar

Designers: Meredith Oberg and Jenny Tondera

Editor: Brad Zellar

Imprint: Little Brown Mushroom

Printers: Linco Printing, Long Island City, New York, USA (*LBM Dispatch* 1–2); Shapco Printing, Minneapolis, Minnesota, USA (*LBM Dispatch* 3–7)

Publication date and place: May 2012–November 2014 / St. Paul, Minnesota, USA

Edition: 2,000

Format and binding: newspaper / unbound folded pages

Size: 11 1/4 x 15 in. (28.6 x 38.1 cm)

Number of pages and images: various / various

Type of printing and paper: offset / newsprint 50lb

Retail price: 18 USD

Cost per unit: $

Book soundtrack: "This Land Is Your Land" by Woody Guthrie

The *LBM Dispatch* is a series of newspapers documenting the periodic journeys that photographer Alec Soth and writer Brad Zellar take together across the United States. Beginning in May 2012 with a road trip to Ohio, the pair have taken seven trips to date, covering upstate New York, Michigan, California, Colorado, Texas, and Georgia. Following vaguely preplanned routes, they have formed an ongoing collaborative investigation into community life in the U.S., exploring the landscapes, histories, narratives, mythology, and literature of each region. They record the faces and voices of the people they meet along the way using their respective mediums, and edit together Zellar's text, Soth's photographs, and quotes from literature. The first newspaper was printed just a week after the pair returned from their trip, making it an instant and tangible way of making sense of their collaboration.

Do lots of research and planning so you have some general idea about where you're going and what sorts of things you're looking for. Have some general themes in mind, but be prepared to throw every one of them out as things do or don't develop. Try to have specific destinations in mind every day, but don't hesitate to go down a promising rabbit hole. Get the hell off the interstate. Don't be afraid of people or situations. When you see someone or something interesting, stop the van. When you sense an emerging theme, zero in on it. Eat good food, listen to good music, and be enthusiastic. Stay open, go hard, and keep shoveling gravel into the rock tumbler. Expect surprises, and try to do them justice. —Brad Zellar

TEXAS TRIANGLE

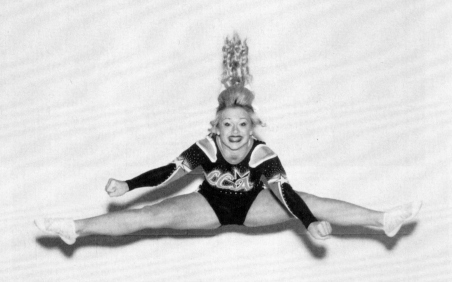

Alec Soth & Brad Zellar   November 19 – December 3, 2013

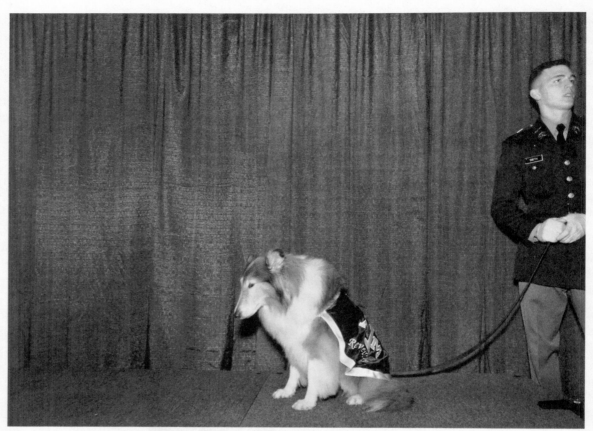

Reveille VIII, Texas A&M mascot. College Station.

Reveille VIII is the latest in a line of Texas A&M Mascots that stretches back to 1931. Her predecessors are buried in a cemetery near the north end zone of Kyle Field, A&M's massive football stadium. Reveille is the highest-ranking member of the University's Corps of Cadets, and she has her own cell phone and student I.D. card. A Mascot Corporal —who is required to be with her 24 hours a day, seven days a week— shares a dorm room with her and accompanies her to University sporting events and Corps functions. Reveille's Mascot Corporal is chosen every year after an arduous two-month tryout.

Sophomore Parker Smith, who is handling the Reveille duties this year, said, "The tryouts are quite the ordeal, but this is a huge honor. She's obviously a big deal in our outfit. The rules are that I can't leave her alone for even one minute, so she goes everywhere with me —class, dates, and home for the holidays."

Cadets are required to address Reveille as "Ma'am," and tradition holds that if she barks while in a classroom the class must be immediately adjourned.

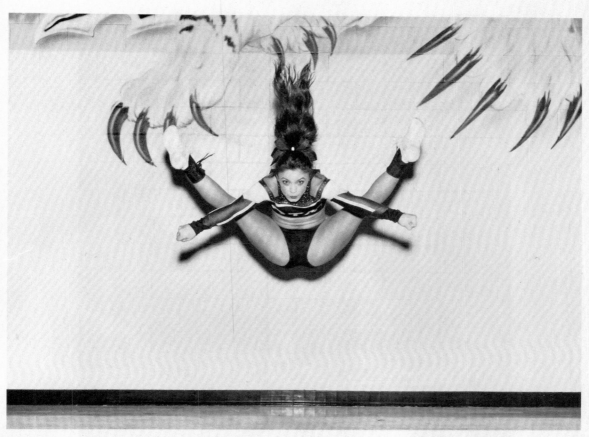

McKenna. Corsicana Tumbling Academy. Corsicana.

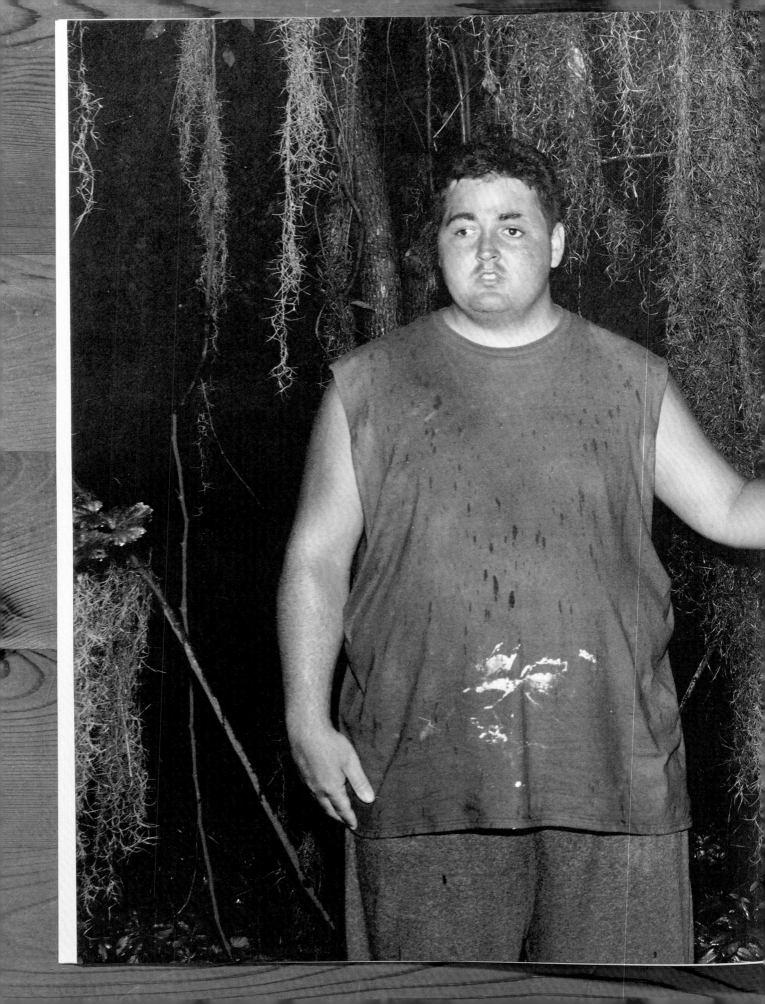

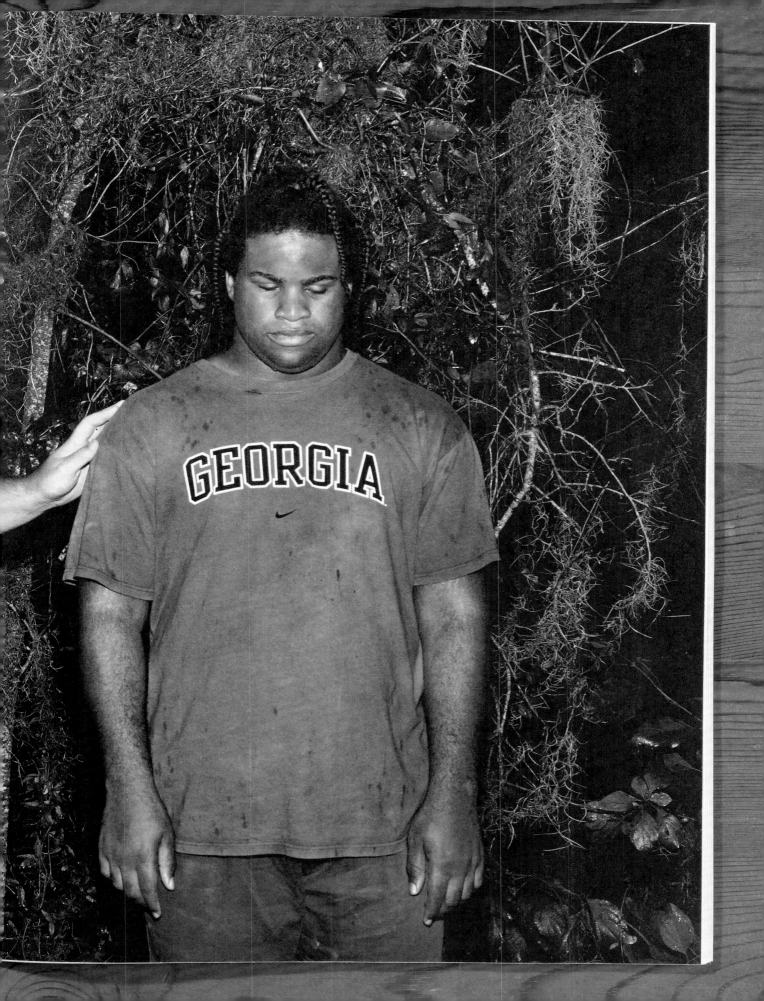

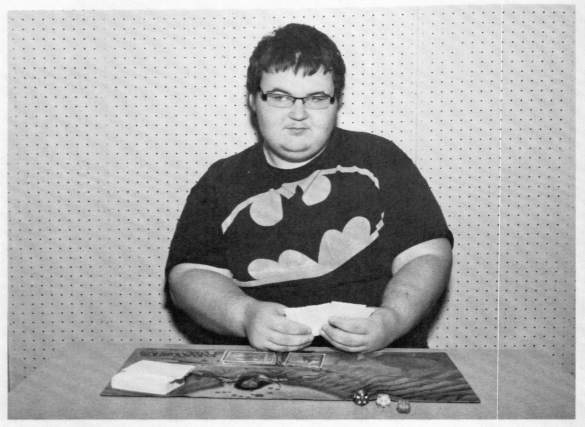

Patrick. Rookie's Den, Clyde, Ohio

———

This is a way to get out of the house, meet new people, and use different parts of my brain. It's easy to get stuck at home on the computer, but when you're interacting with people face-to-face there's a whole different dynamic. We do this every Friday, and mostly play Standard Magic. Everybody down here sort of has their own style. I guess I'd say I'm a pretty conservative player, but I try to mix up my deck so that I can also introduce the element of surprise. I also play the tuba in the band at school.

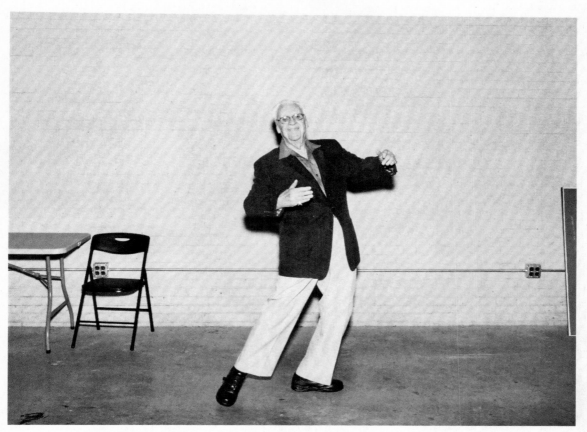

88-year-old Bil ("My mother said she couldn't pronounce the other L"). Dance N Swing. Sandusky, Ohio

My people were Baptists, so we never went to dances. I also never smoked or drank. When I was overseas during World War II I used to trade my cigarettes for chocolate bars. Though I didn't dance, I was always infatuated with Latin music. One night in the late '40s I went out to see a band and this girl came over and asked me to dance. I told her I didn't know how, and she handed me a card for an Arthur Murray studio. I stopped into the place the next week, took my first dance steps at the age of 28, and have been dancing ever since. I'm also a photographer, and have traveled all over the country taking photos of ballroom dancers.

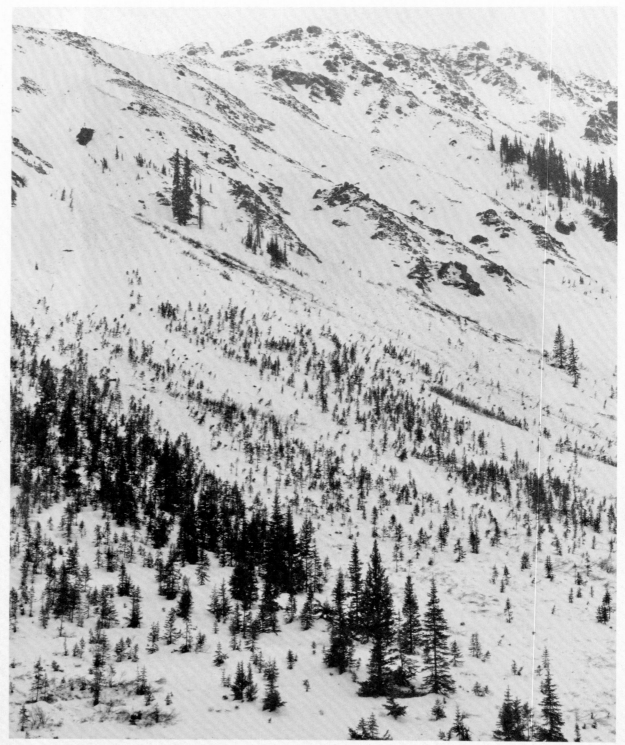

Along Colorado State Highway 550, near Silverton.

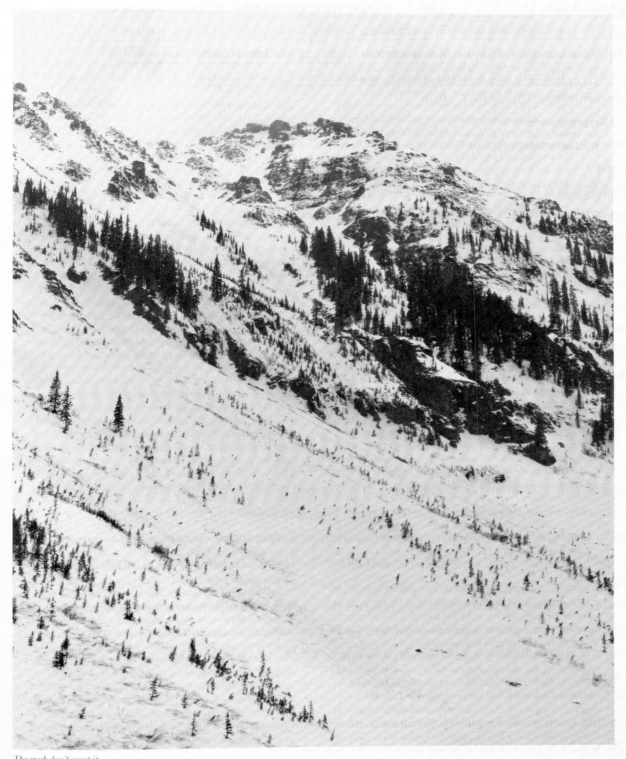

The meek don't want it.
—James Galvin, from "Avatar"

Title: As Dark As the Inside of a Needle.

Artists: Carolin Bollig, Selin Bourquin, Michael Etzensperger, Fabian Flückiger, Douglas Gil, Léa Girardin, Pascal Grob, Johanna Grünenfelder, Tamara Janes, Sami El Kasm, Helvetia Leal, Elena Linke, Nora Longatti, Etienne Messikommer, Johanna Muther, Angelo Ressegatti, Aljoscha Thomas, Claudia Sofia Torres, Martin Walther, and Dominik Zietlow

Additional contributor: Charlotte Cotton

Designer: Tamara Janes

Editors: Adam Broomberg, Oliver Chanarin, and Marianne Mueller

Imprint: none

Printer: Buchbinderei Burkhardt, Zurich, Switzerland

Publication date and place: March 2013 / Zurich, Switzerland

Edition size: 90

Format and binding: softcover / coptic stitch

Size: 7 1/2 x 10 1/4 in. (19 x 26 cm)

Number of pages and images: 192 pages / 137 images

Type of printing and paper: digital / Munken Lynx and Kaskad Colour

Retail: 30 GBP / 40 USD

Cost per unit: $$$

Book soundtrack: "Too Much" by Bonaparte

As Dark As the Inside of a Needle. is a collaborative publication made by artist duo Adam Broomberg and Oliver Chanarin, and students at the Zurich University of the Arts. The London-based artists were invited to teach a class for a term, and each week they would supply a set of readings to the students. These texts were a mix of theory, philosophy, religious, and scientific texts, both related and unrelated to photography. Simultaneously, they sent the students a weekly brief to follow when making photographs. At the end of the module, the group employed the Dadaist "cut-up" literary technique, chopping up the supplied texts to rearrange the words. In a similar manner, the students gave up ownership of their own photographs and a pool of material was created. Editing the publication became a communal task, and they printed a small run using the university's facilities.

I've learned that people will forget what you said, people will forget what you did, but people will never forget how you made them feel. —Maya Angelou

AS   DARK AS THE

INSIDE OF   A NEEDLE.

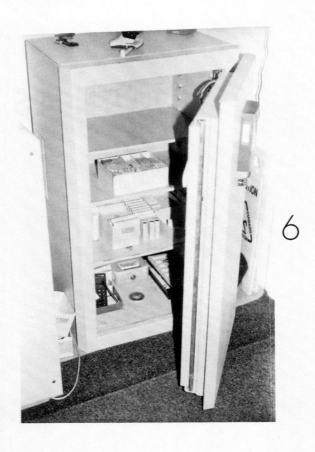

6

An average human body contains enough
iron to make a nail, enough sugar for
one cup of coffee, magnesium sufficient
to take one photograph.

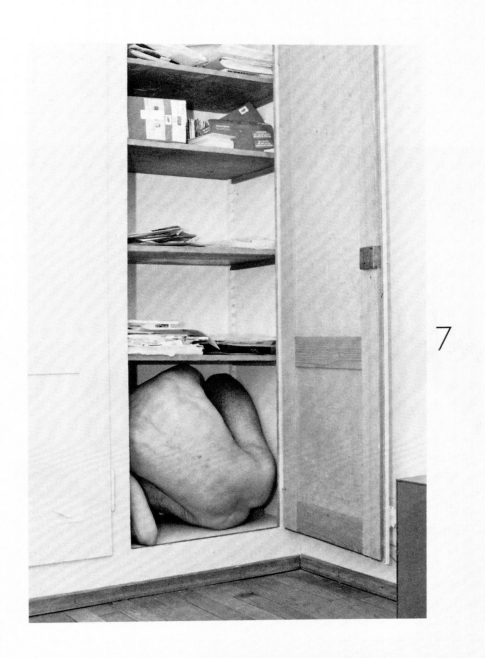

7

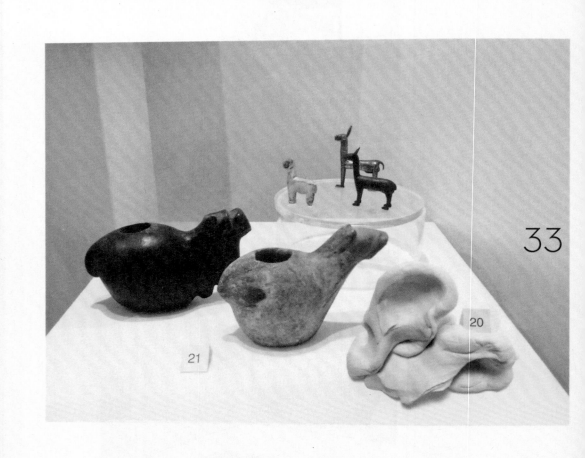

33

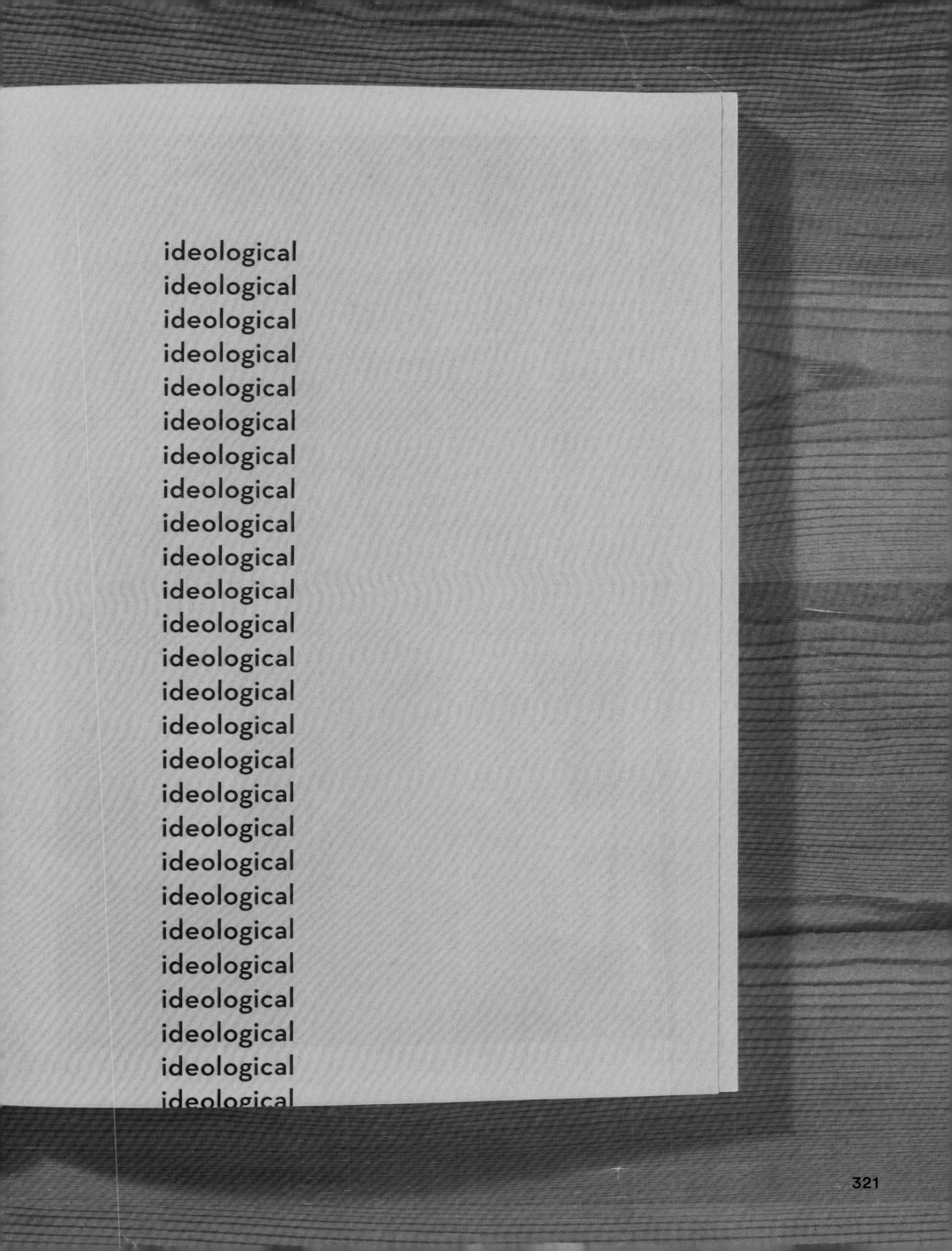

ideological
ideological
ideological
ideological
ideological
ideological
ideological
ideological
ideological
ideological
ideological
ideological
ideological
ideological
ideological
ideological
ideological
ideological
ideological
ideological
ideological
ideological
ideological
ideological

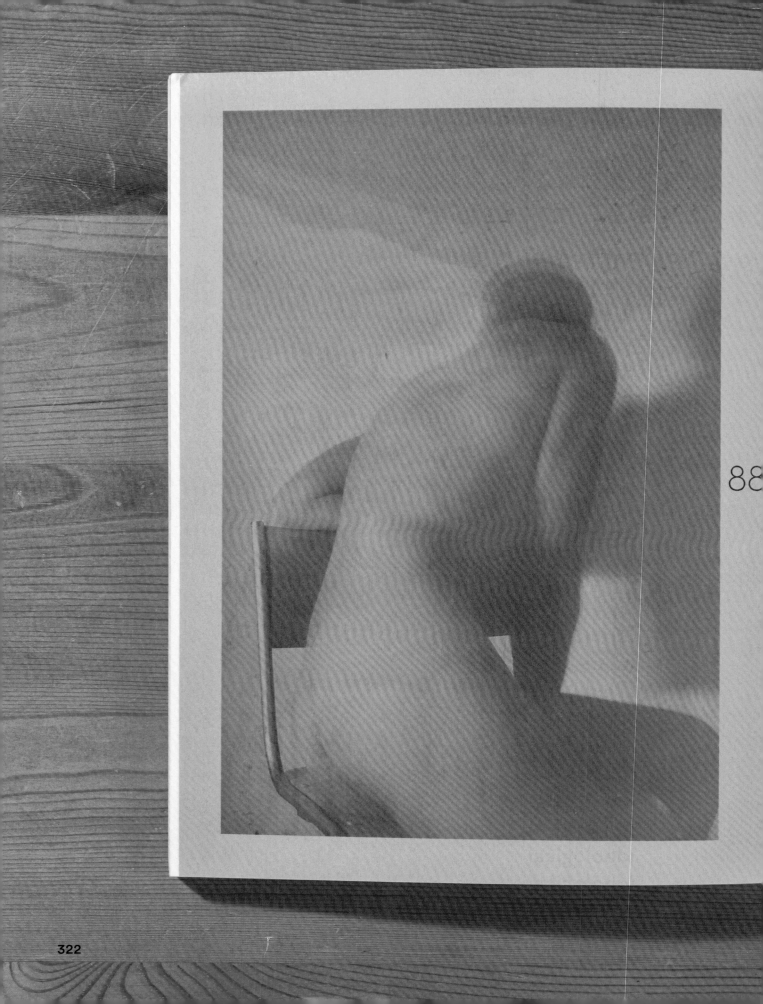

88

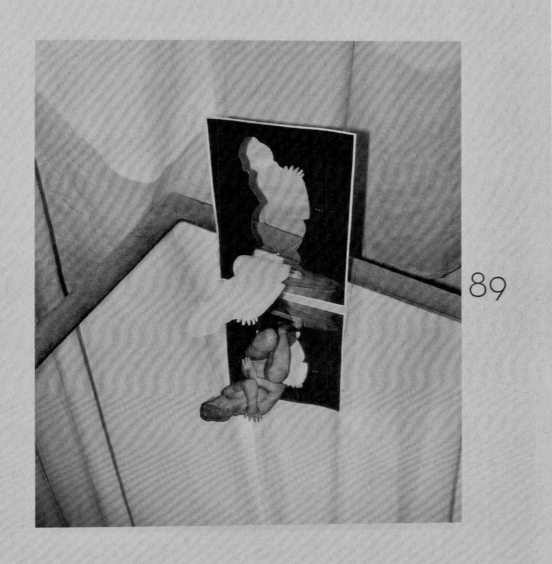

89

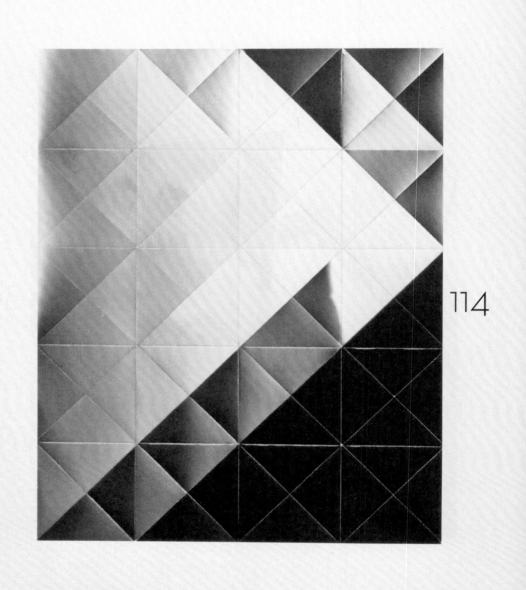

114

Nazism was a cinematic project.

Title: This Is My Driver's License
Artists: Valerie Phillips and Arvida Byström
Designer: Valerie Phillips
Editors: Valerie Phillips and Arvida Byström
Printer: Push, London, UK
Publication date and place: August 2013 / London, UK
Edition: 400
Format and binding: softcover / saddle stitched
Size: 5 7/8 x 8 1/4 in. (14.8 x 21 cm)
Number of pages and images: 48 pages / 43 images
Type of printing and paper: offset / coated 150gsm
Retail price: 15 GBP / 27 USD

Book soundtrack: anything by the Twilight Singers

Swedish blogger and artist Arvida Byström has been posting images of herself online since she was sixteen, and is part of a generation of young people who have become Internet famous. Fashion photographer Valerie Phillips is known for her depictions of youth culture—particularly young girls in their transition to adulthood—and was first introduced to Byström through a friend. After meeting via Skype, Phillips flew her out to London for a photo shoot and an unplanned, organic collaboration unfolded from there, resulting in Phillips printing a series of five zines with pictures of Byström. For *This Is My Driver's License*, the model-photographer collaboration evolved a step further, as Phillips's photographs are juxtaposed with Byström's own artworks, and held together by fragments of their online conversations chronicling the story of their relationship to date.

I think it's really important to put work out into the world without the content being determined by someone else's agenda. Publishing zines (and books) is the best way I know to get my work out 100 percent on my terms, undiluted. And the nature of zines being limited-run, inexpensive, and easy to make means I can put out as many projects as I like, as often as I like.
—Valerie Phillips

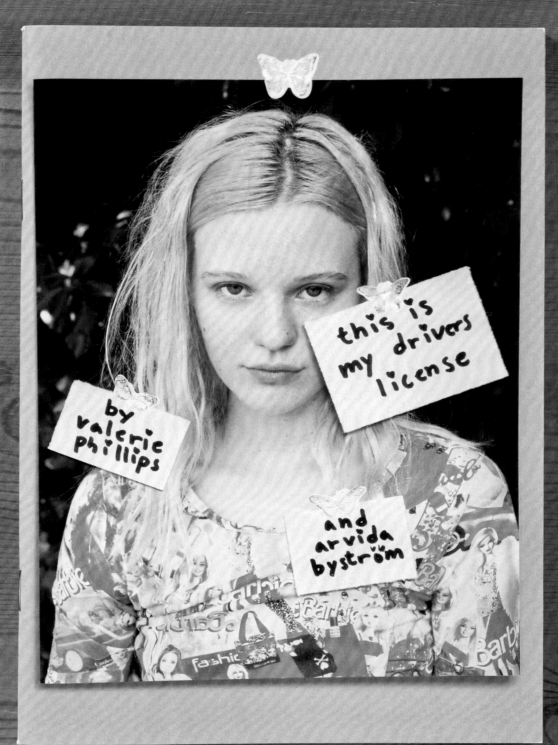

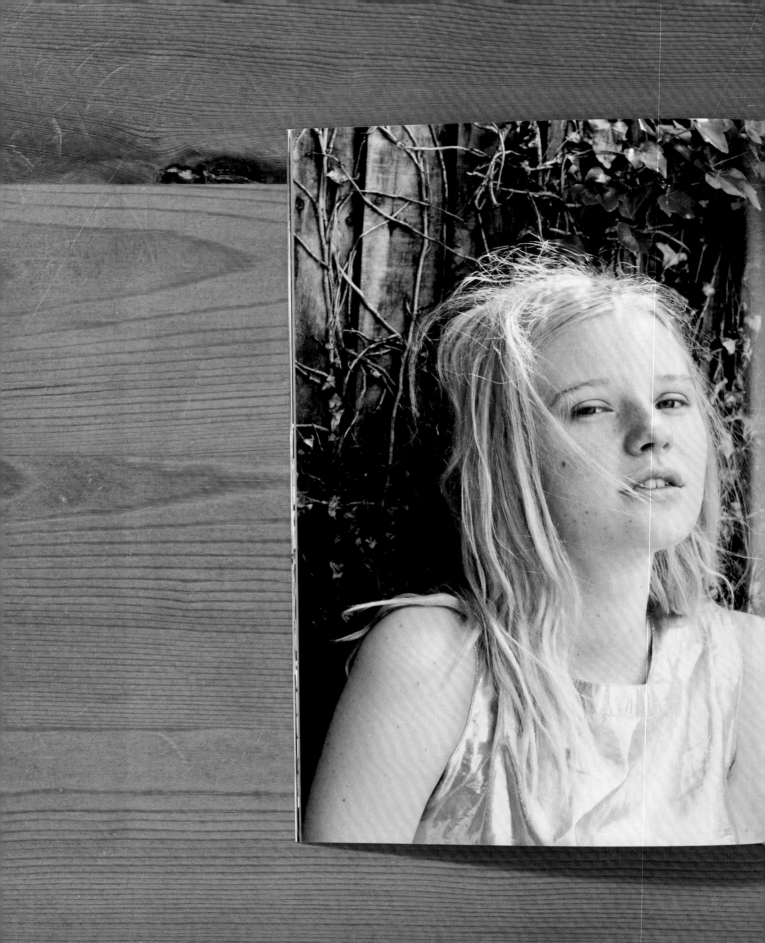

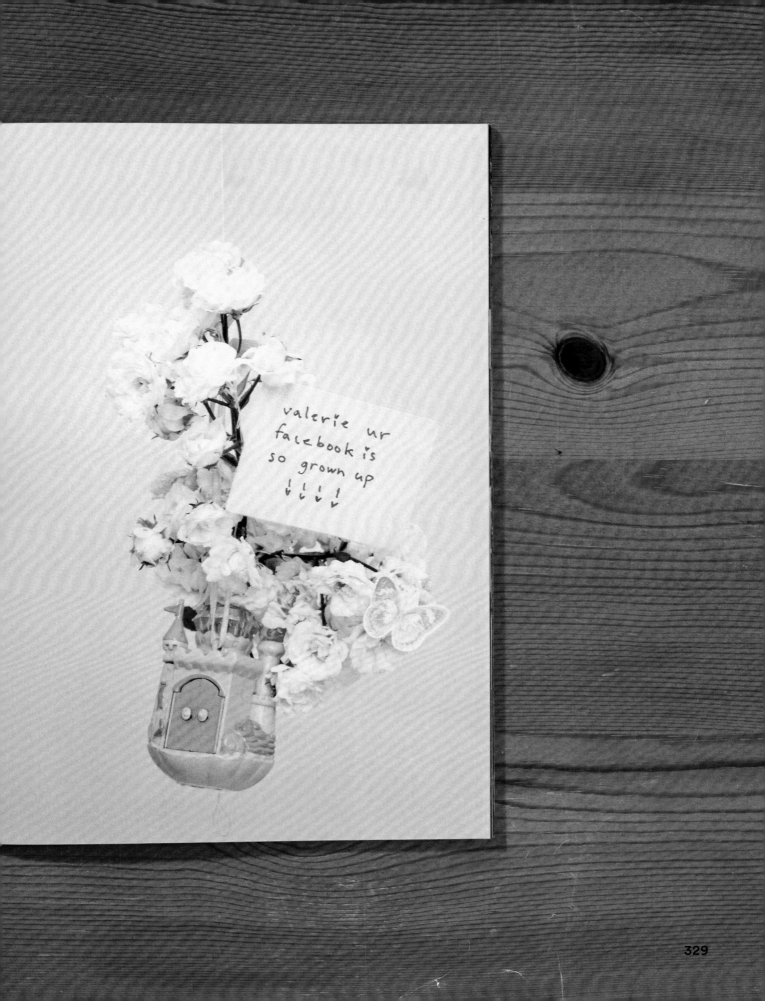

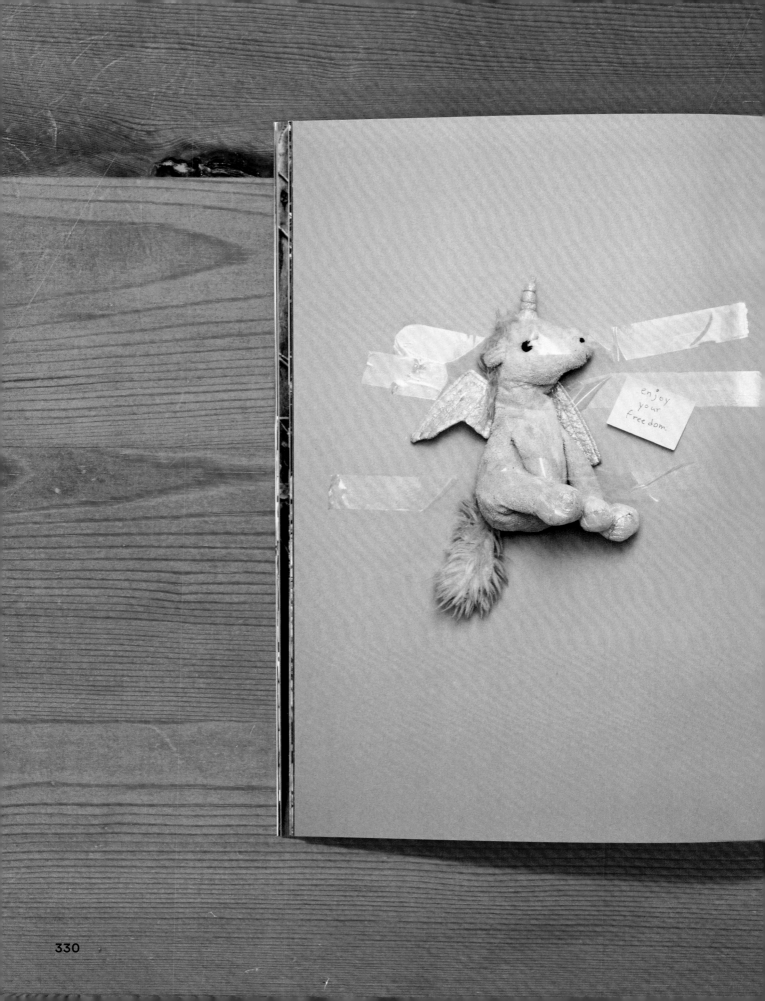

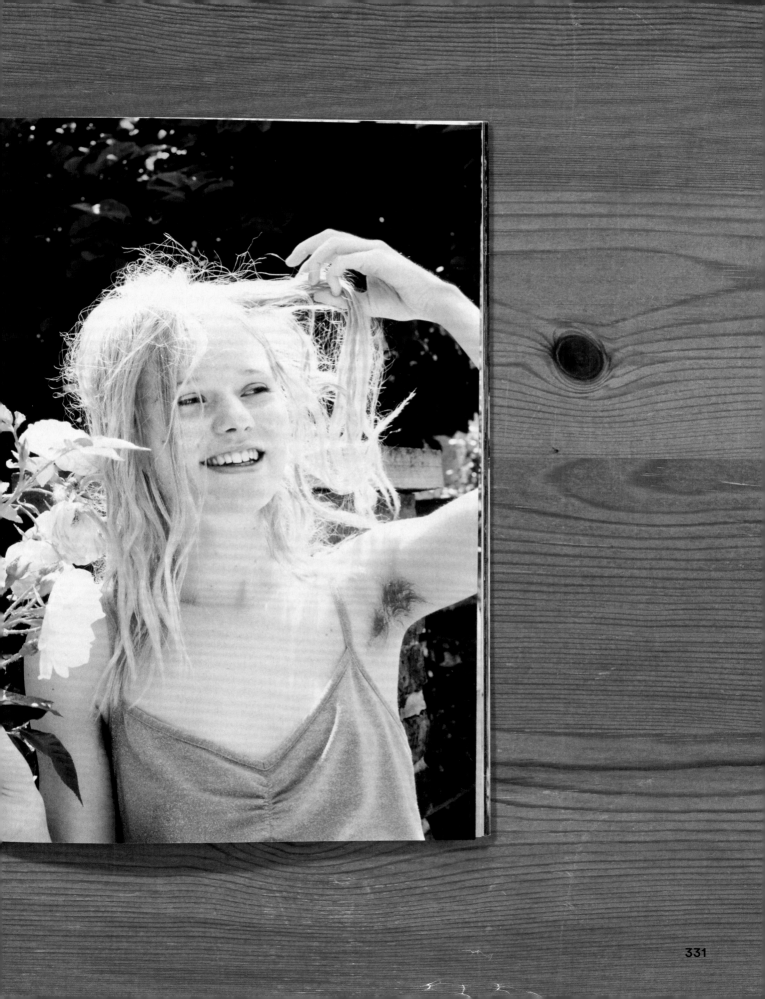

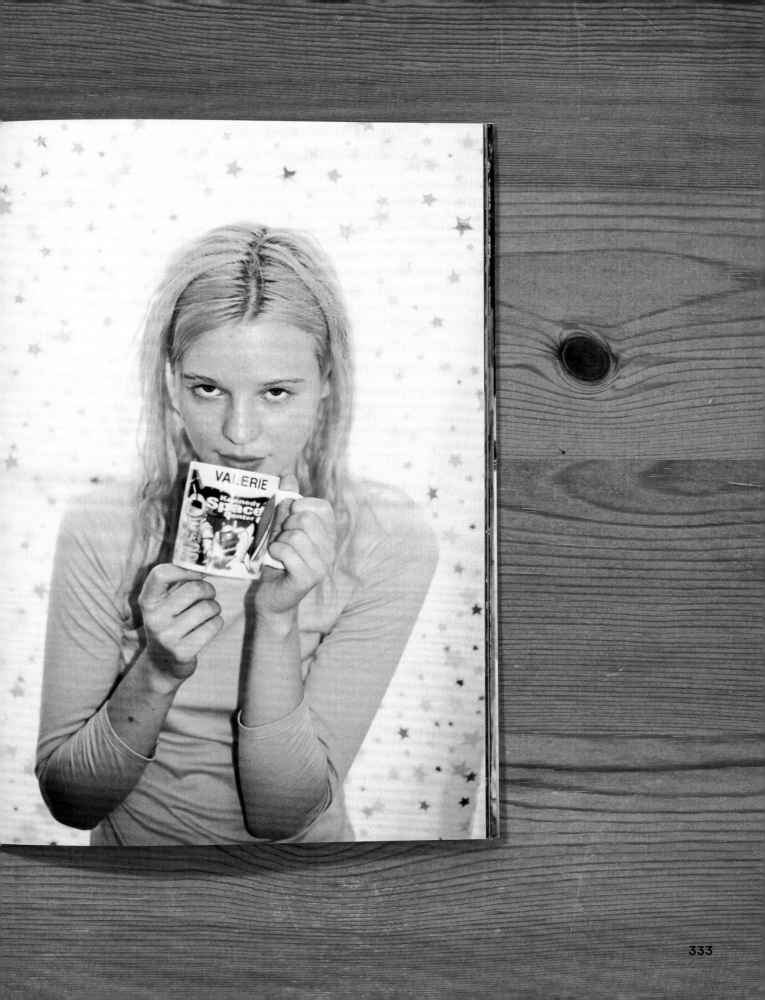

Title: Preston Bus Station

Artists: Adam Murray, Robert Parkinson, and Jamie Hawkesworth

Additional contributor: Aidan Turner-Bishop

Designers: Adam Murray, Robert Parkinson, and Jamie Hawkesworth

Editors: Adam Murray, Robert Parkinson, and Jamie Hawkesworth

Imprint: Preston is my Paris Publishing

Printer: Newspaper Club, Glasgow, UK

Publication date and place: October 2010 / Preston, UK

Edition: 500

Format and binding: tabloid / folded and unstapled

Size: 11 3/8 x 15 in. (29 x 38 cm)

Number of pages and images: 12 pages / 17 images

Type of printing and paper: web offset / newsprint

Retail price: 4 GBP / 6 USD

Cost per unit: $

Book soundtrack: "Public Transport Soundscape" by Rob Griffiths

Adam Murray and Robert Parkinson set up the photography project Preston is my Paris in 2009 with the aim of focusing attention on their English city, and exploring it as both a hub and a subject for creative practice. In 2010, Murray and Parkinson collaborated on *Preston Bus Station* with fellow photographer Jamie Hawkesworth after hearing the city's iconic bus station was scheduled for demolition. Over a single weekend, the group set up a temporary studio in the station's disused ticket office and engaged the people that passed through, making portraits and creating a document of the building. Their chosen format was based on the free newspapers given out on public transit, and allowed the group to make something free and accessible to the community, which could inspire interest in the cause. The publication became an important tool in the successful campaign to save the bus station.

1. Get on with it: Whatever idea you've been thinking about, that you've been putting off for whatever reason, just make it happen.
2. Collaborate: Many projects would not exist without this. Identify your own strengths and those in other people. Develop close working relationships with people who want to collaborate with you. Know your limitations and what you have to offer.
3. Awareness of people: It's important to keep things in perspective. Photography and photo publishing is still small in the greater scheme of things. Keep in mind that there is a much bigger audience out there who would probably enjoy engaging with the work, but find the output formats and channels quite intimidating. —Adam Murray

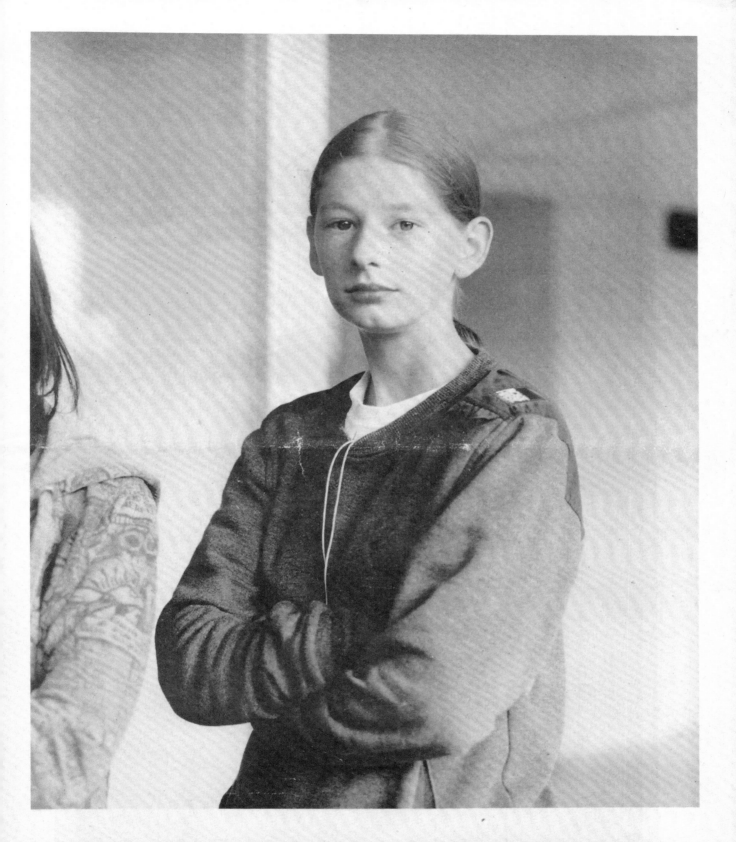

PRESTON BUS STATION

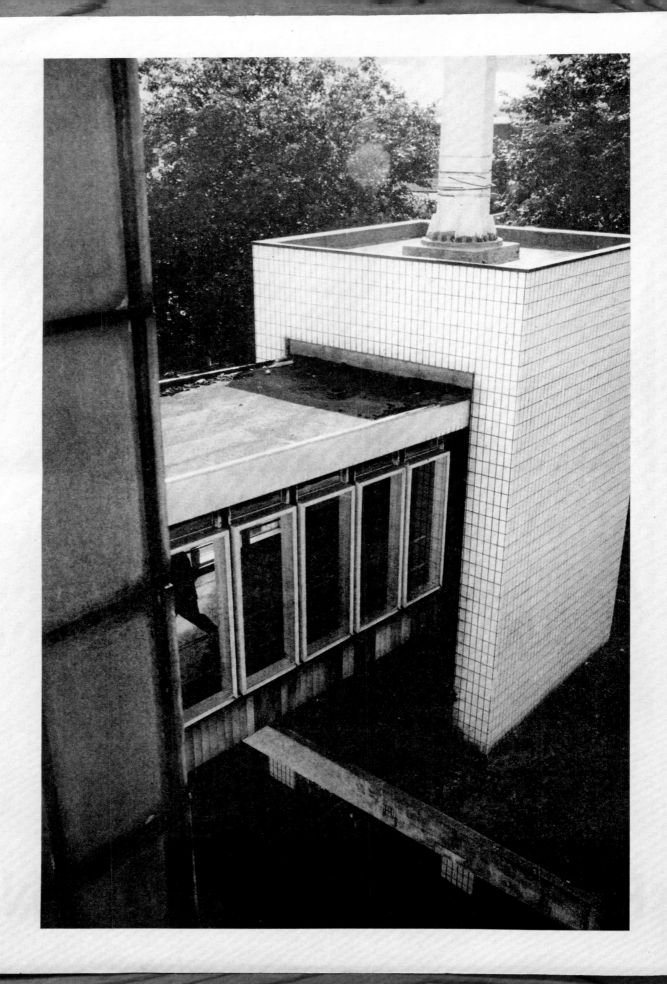

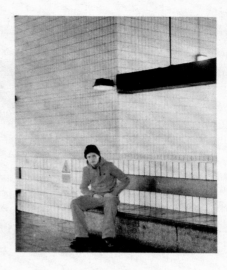

Bus station reflections

They say that if you want to find something you should stay still and it will eventually find you. These images of Preston Bus Station are like that. Trying to understand the building's character they reveal deeper truths in the eyes and faces of those photographed.

The bus station was designed with ambitious hope for the future. Only the best architects and materials were used. Its scale befitted a regional centre, a hub on the national coach network. Look at the curving roof panels, springboarding into a prosperous future for industrial Lancashire. Consider the elemental confidence of the yellow arrows and the fastidious modernist design. Each tile is placed exactly where it should be. The finest tropical timber was used. Every detail was chosen with care. But look at it now...

Details tell stories too. Pay phones from pre-mobile times needed a clunking coin to connect you to your mum.

A building is more than its design and aspirations. Thousands pass through every day.It's an interchange of hopes, triumphs, worries, desires and anxieties. True, for many it's just somewhere on the way to work, school or the shops. But pause a while and examine the faces in the crowd. Sometimes a face of great beauty, worthy of Vogue magazine, shines through, like the Pre-Raphaelite auburn haired young woman who looks directly at us. She has both the confidence of youth and its underlying vulnerability.

But what is the young man in the hoodie thinking? He too looks at us. He penetrates our concerns and anxieties. The young people pass us: cocky, cheeky, tender and anxious. Where are they going?

The architectural critic Jonathan Glancey called Preston Bus Station a 'baroque cathedral for buses'. But it's more: an interchange of circling emotions, worries and confidences: life rolling on.

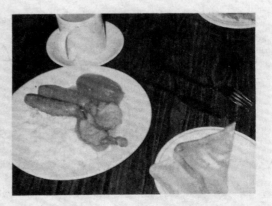

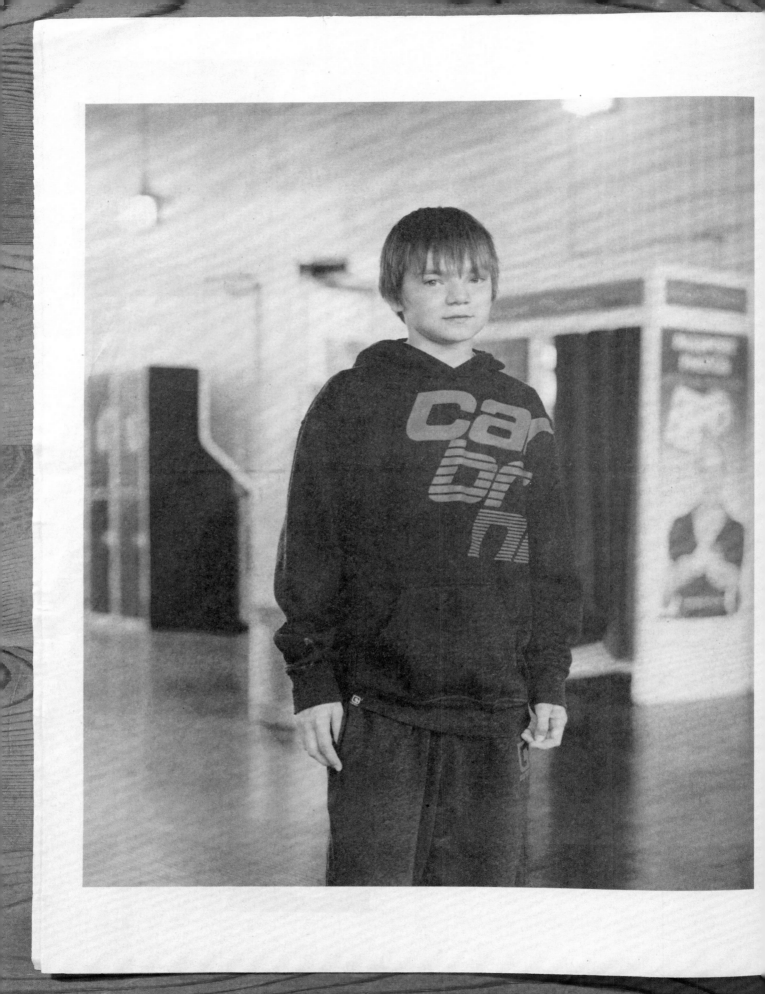

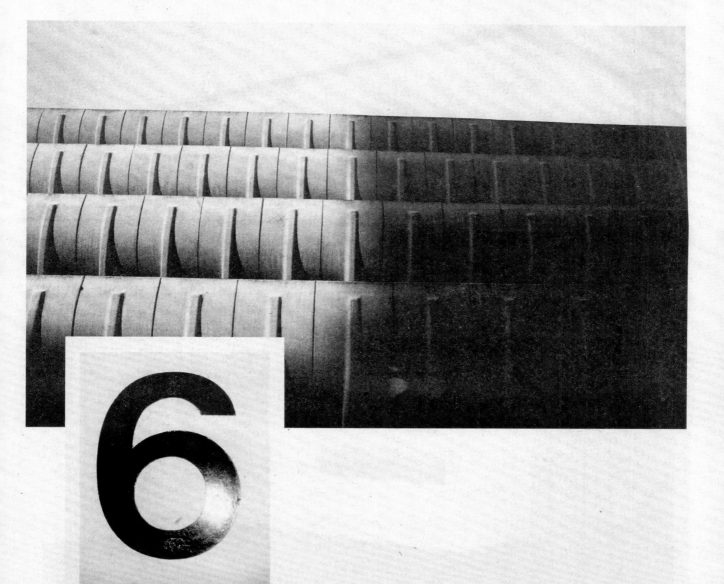

6

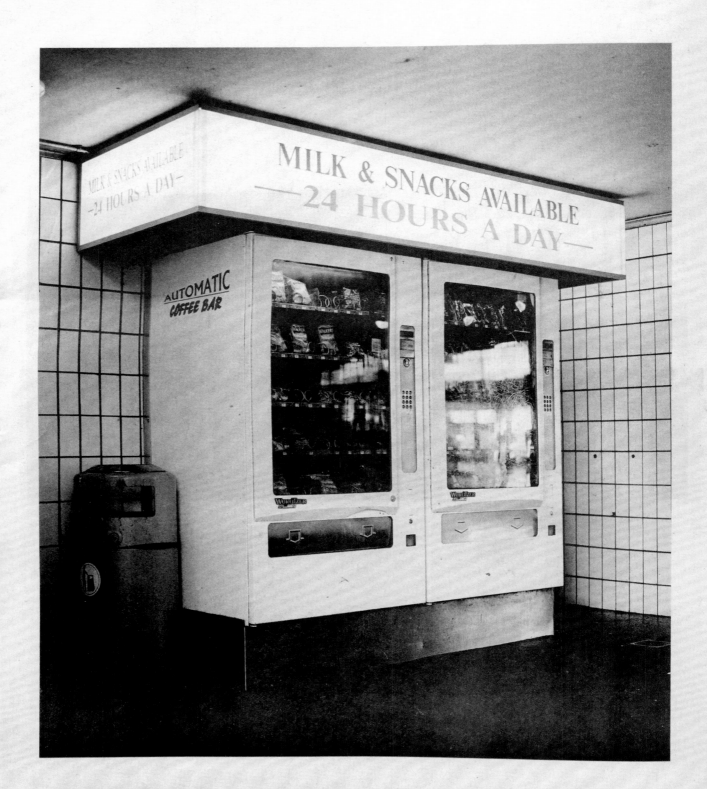

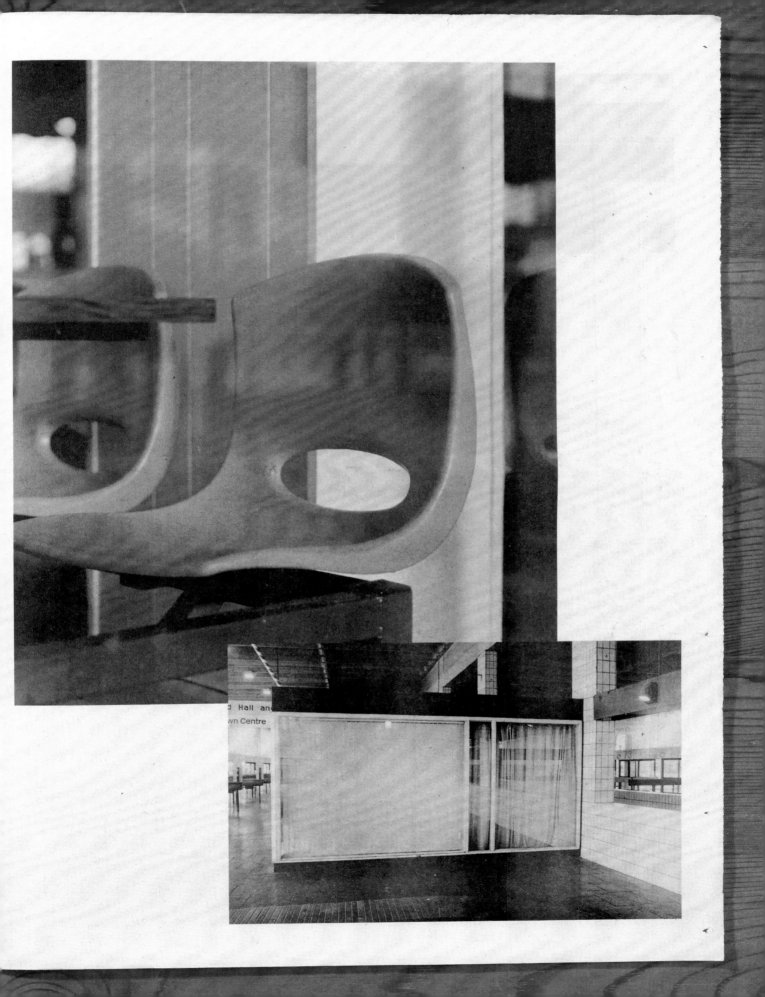

Hall and
wn Centre

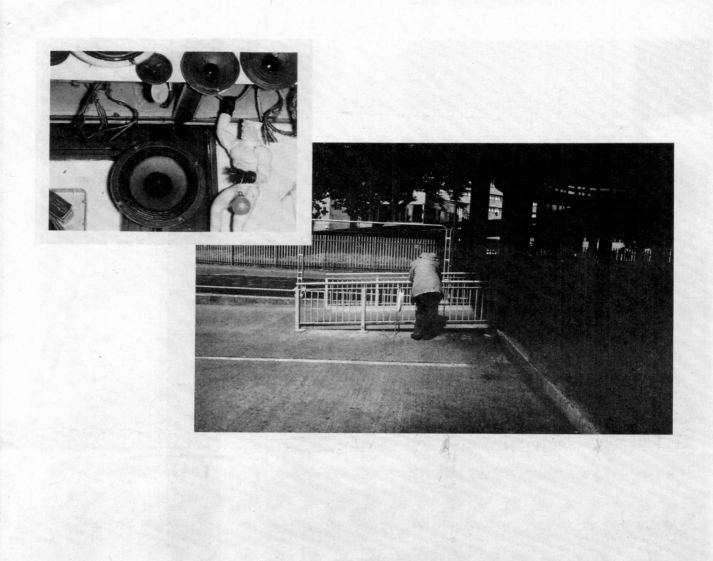

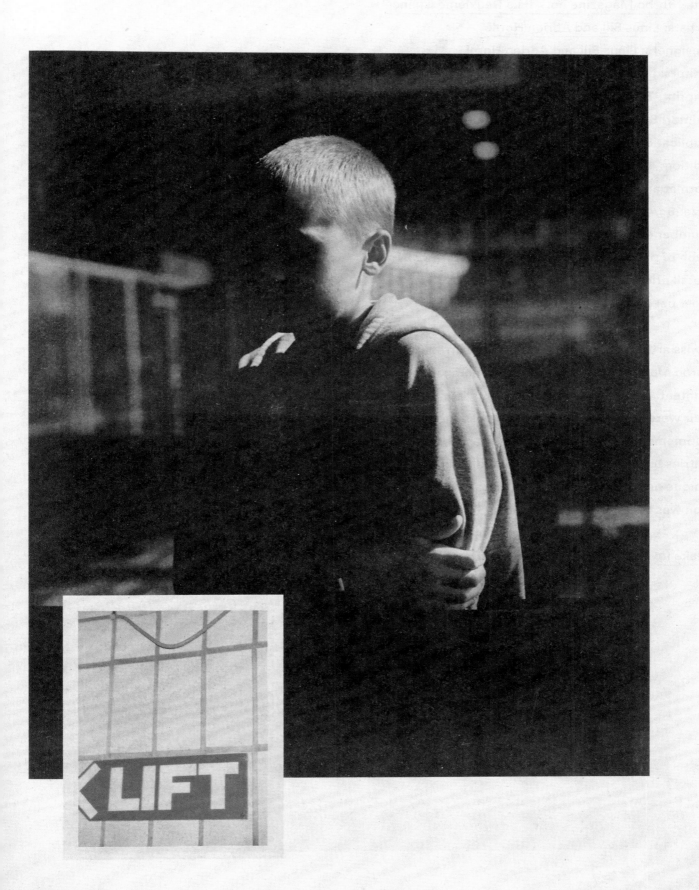

Title: Turbo Magazine no. 41: La Deuxième Chance

Artists: Linus Bill and Adrien Horni

Designers: Linus Bill and Adrien Horni

Editors: Linus Bill and Adrien Horni

Imprint: *Turbo Magazine*

Printer: Siggset Print & Media AG, Albbruck, Germany

Publication date and place: June 2011 / Bienne, Switzerland

Edition: 400

Format and binding: softcover / perfect bound

Size: 8 1/4 x 11 3/4 (21 x 29.7 cm)

Number of pages and images: 432 pages / 432 images

Type of printing and paper: offset / Lettura 72 80gsm

Retail price: 30 CHF / 30 USD

Cost per unit: $$

Swiss artist Adrien Horni publishes his irregular collaborations with other artists under the title *Turbo Magazine*. The magazine has no fixed format and changes every time, depending on its content. After a collaboration with fellow Swiss artist Linus Bill on an early issue of *Turbo*, the pair were commissioned by the Swiss Advertising Commission in 2011 to create an artistic supplement to the organization's yearbook. The artists sought inspiration from the unsuccessful entries to the yearbook, and worked with a black-and-white photocopier to make a total of 432 unique new collages out of the discarded entries—one for each page of the book. The publication was simultaneously printed as *Turbo Magazine* no. 41.

Make up rules. Give yourself tasks to fulfill. Build obstacles and limit yourself. —Linus Bill

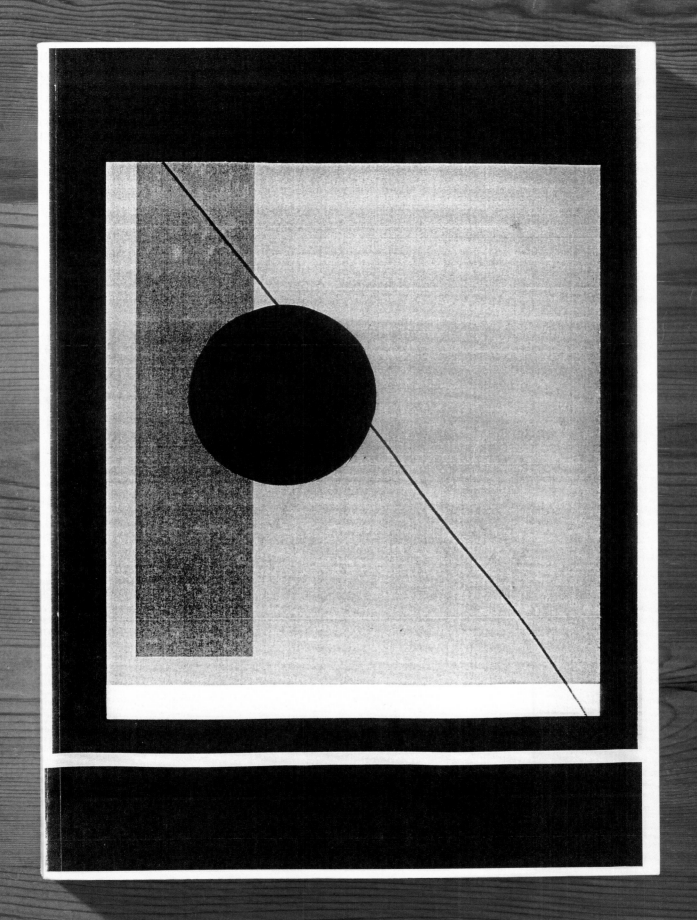

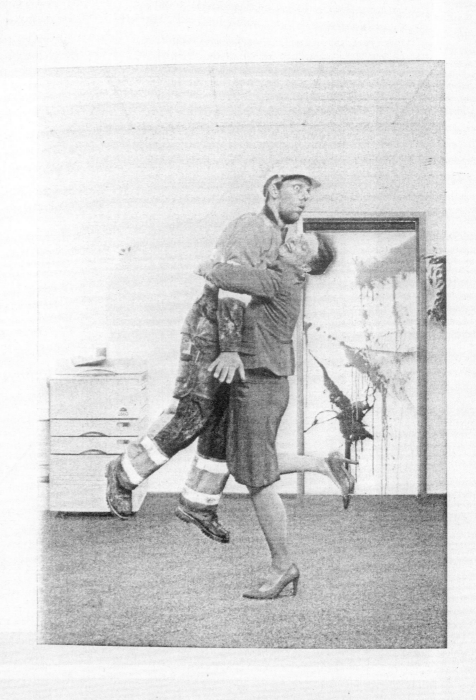

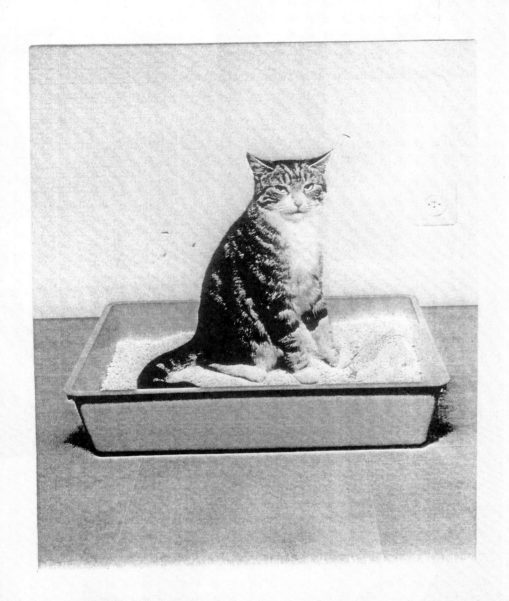

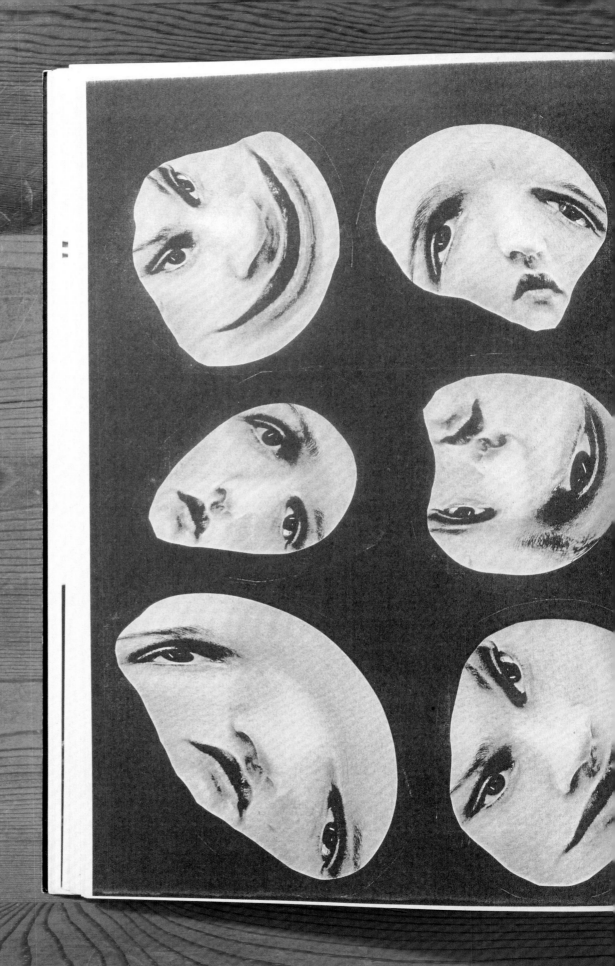

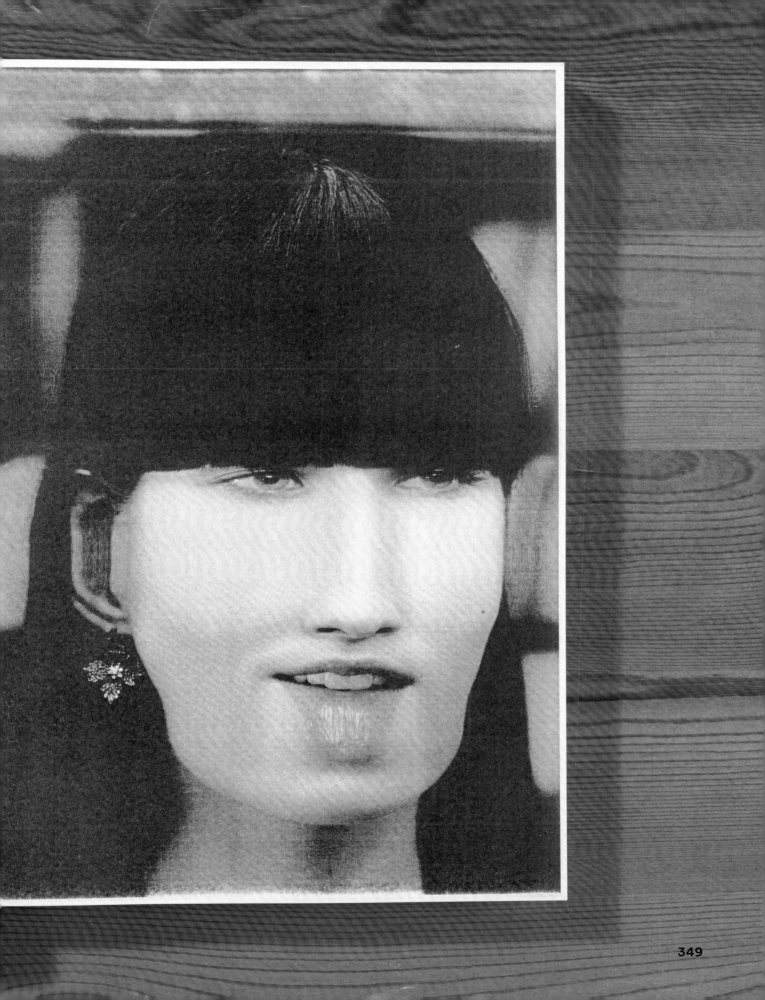

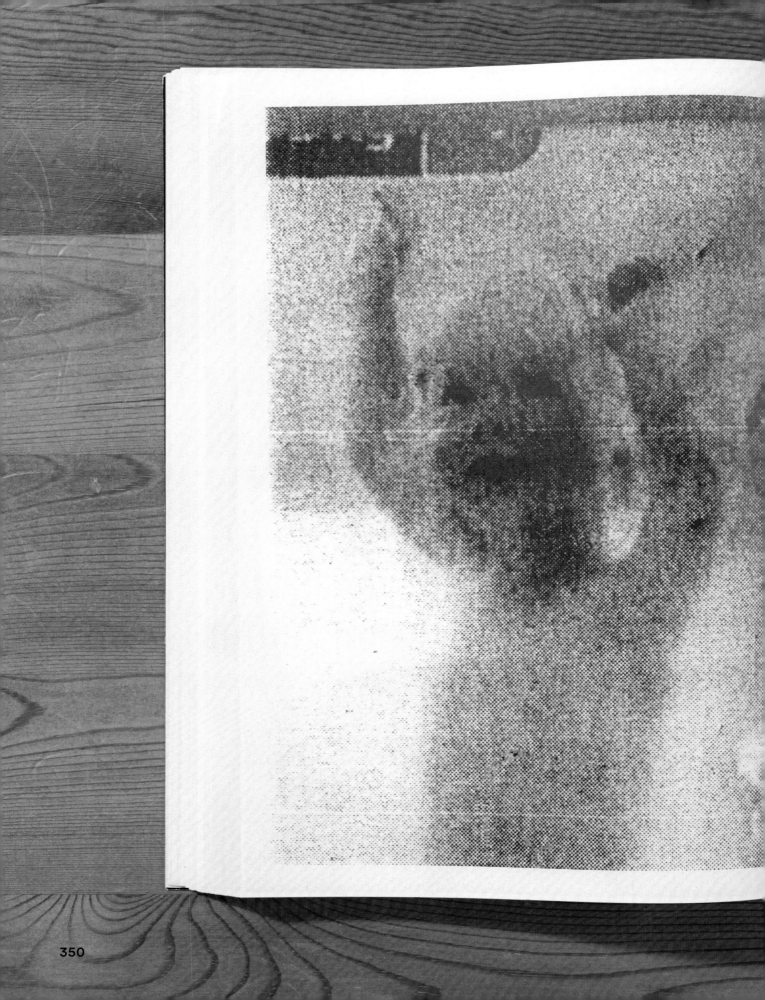

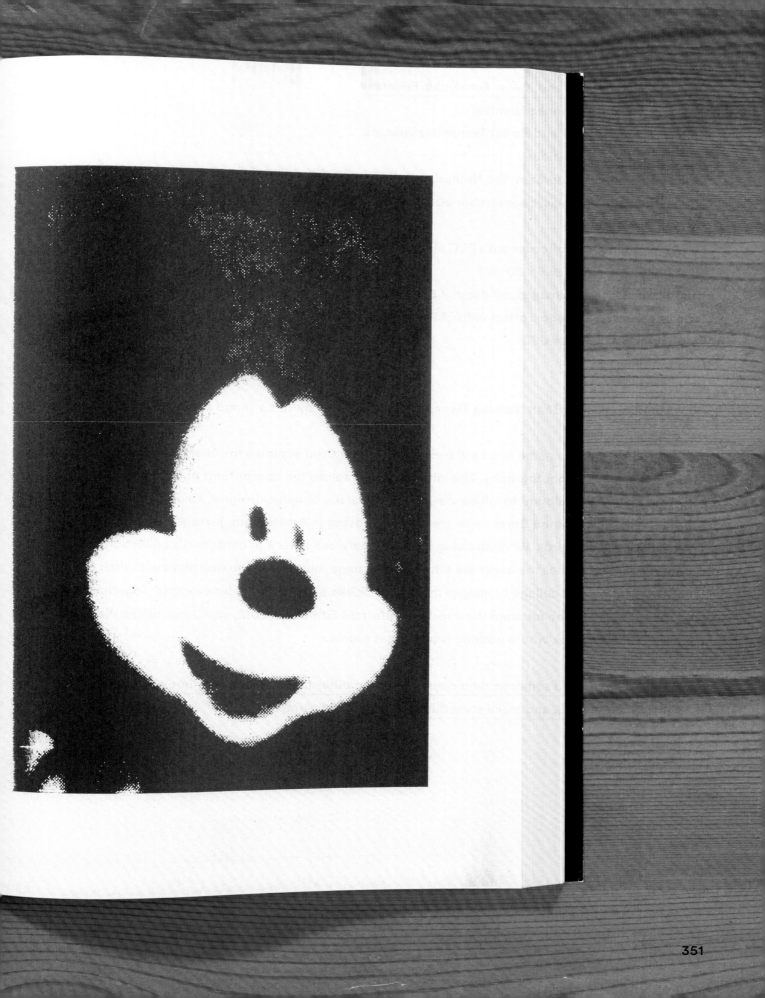

Title: Everybody's Card

Artists: Martine Derks and Xavier Fernández Fuentes

Designer: Xavier Fernández Fuentes

Editors: Martine Derks and Xavier Fernández Fuentes

Imprint: Centerfold Editions

Printer: Robstolk, Amsterdam, the Netherlands

Publication date and place: September 2011 / Amsterdam, the Netherlands

Edition: 700

Format and binding: softcover with PVC sleeve / Singer sewn

Size: 7 5/8 x 11 3/4 in. (19.5 x 30 cm)

Number of pages and images: 60 pages / 50 images

Type of printing and paper: offset with FM screening / Munken Lynx 120gsm

Retail price: 21 EUR / 24 USD

Cost per unit: $$$

Book soundtrack: *And Then Nothing Turned Itself Inside-Out* by Yo La Tengo

Taking its title from the name of a card trick, *Everybody's Card* explores the everydayness and universality of album photography. The initial goal was to use the conventions of photo albums to create "a universal album" to which viewers could relate. Graphic designer Xavier Fernández Fuentes and artist Martine Derks, who met while studying in Amsterdam, juxtapose found images with playing cards, wryly drawing a parallel between a deck of cards and a collection of photographs. Sometimes the cards are affixed to the page, but mostly the duo plays with their motif—a hand holds a collage of images made to look like a fan of cards, for example. Together, Fernández Fuentes, who founded the imprint Centerfold Editions in 2012, and Derks utilize their talents to create a book where nothing is quite as it seems.

Work with people. Find someone who does something other than what you do, but who lives on the same planet as you, and make something together. —Martine Derks

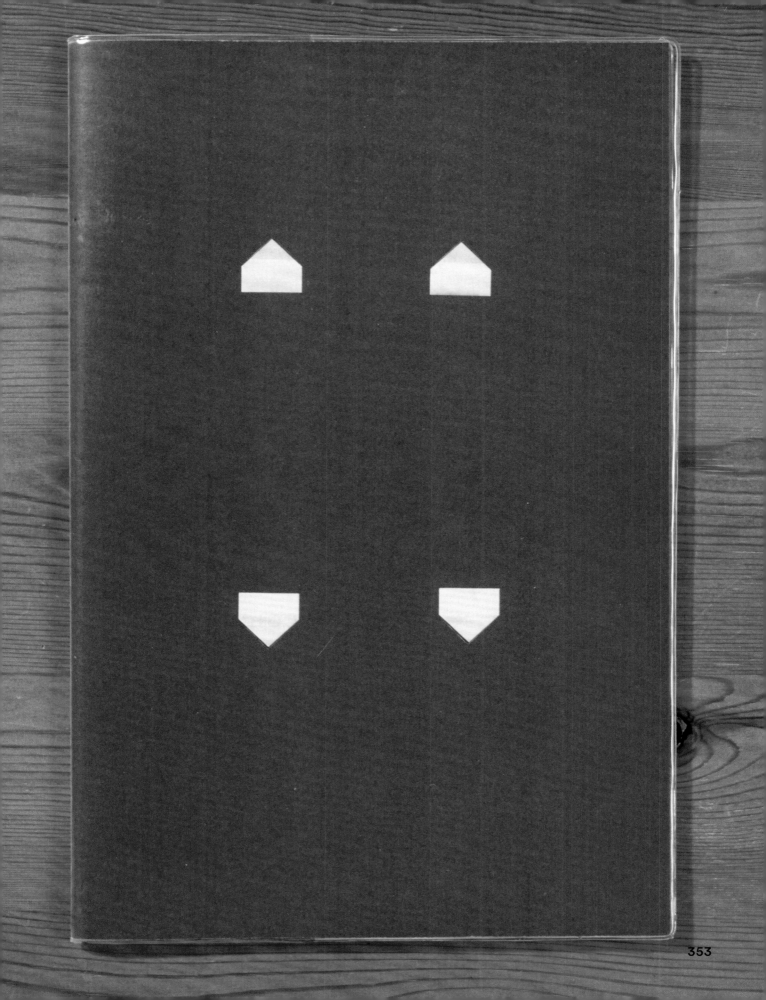

353

'The plot is simple. Four cards are drawn by as many persons. One of them is shown to each in turn, and it changes successively, the one card becoming everybody's card.' [1]

10 x 15cm

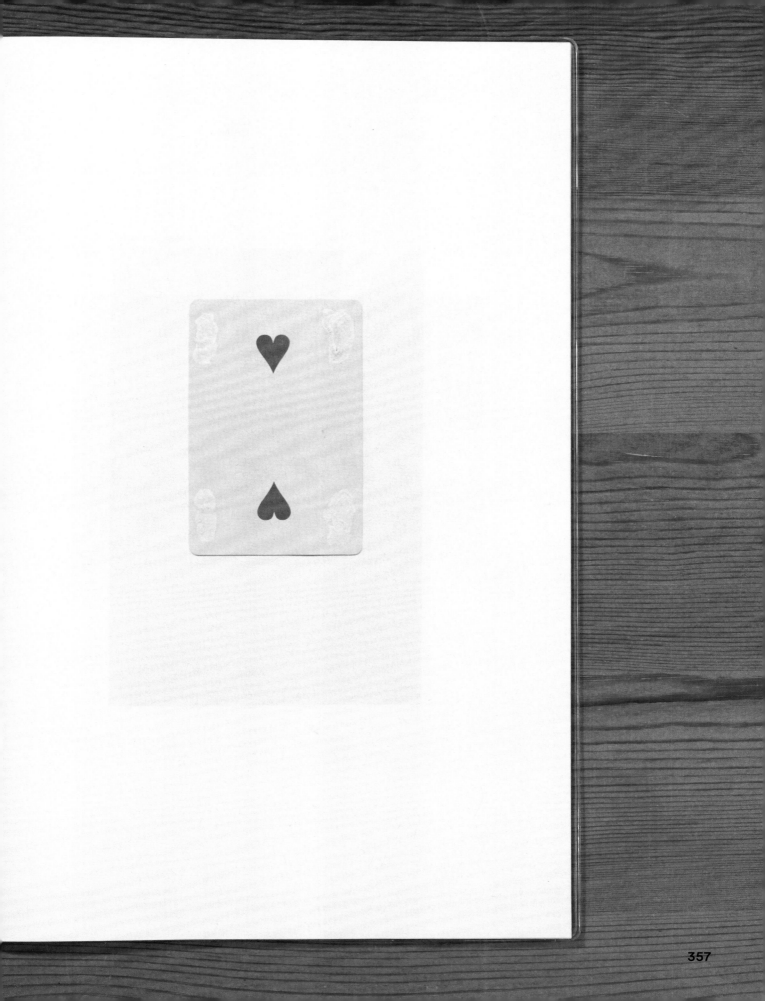

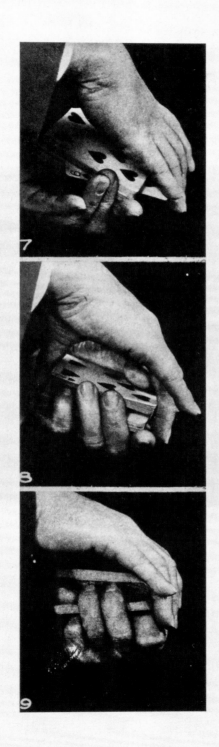

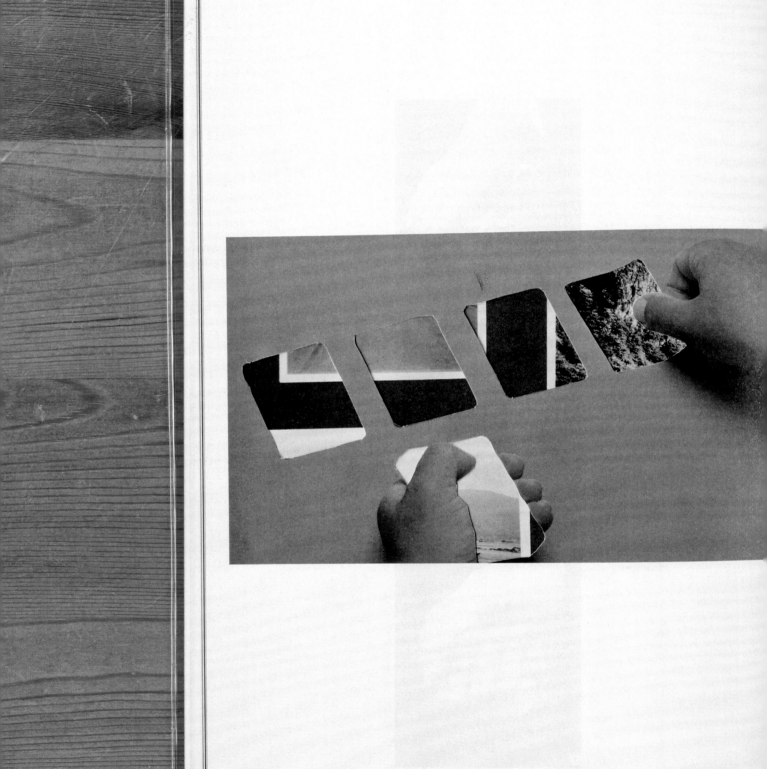

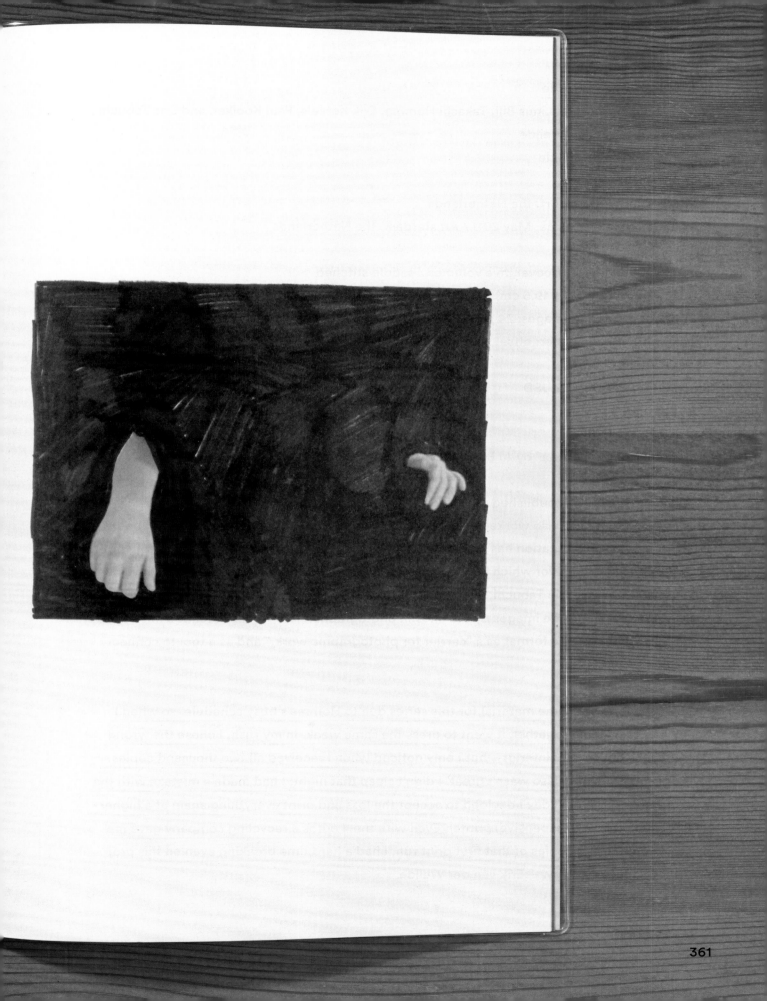

Title: Foto.zine nr.4

Artist: Erik van der Weijde

Additional contributors: Linus Bill, Takashi Homma, Erik Kessels, Paul Kooiker, and Eric Tabuchi

Designer: Erik van der Weijde

Editor: Erik van der Weijde

Imprint: 4478zine

Printer: Wilco, Amersfoort, the Netherlands

Publication date and place: May 2011 / Amsterdam, the Netherlands

Edition: 500

Format and binding: softcover, five volumes / saddle stitched

Size: 5 1/2 x 7 5/8 in (14 x 19.5 cm)

Number of pages and images: 24 pages per book (120 pages total) / 101 images

Type of printing and paper: offset / Munken Pure Rough 170gsm (cover) and Munken Print 90gsm (interior)

Retail price: 28 EUR / 32 USD

Cost per unit: $$

Book soundtrack: "Felicità" by Al Bano and Romina Power

Erik van der Weijde has published more than fifty books and zines, mostly through his own imprint, 4478zine. He has also worked with other publishers, and since 2014 has published books by other artists. Collaboration has long been an important part of what he does, not least with his *Foto.zine nr.4* series, for which he worked with five other photographers: Erik Kessels, Linus Bill, Takashi Homma, Eric Tabuchi, and Paul Kooiker. Each zine features a selection of work by Van der Weijde, alongside images by the chosen photographer. It is Van der Weijde's mission to experiment with the zine format as a "carrier for photographic work," and as a tool to connect with others.

It took a while to get some material for this series due to Homma's busy schedule, so when I finally had everything together, it went to press the same week. In my rush, I chose the wrong paper for the covers and interior—but I only noticed when I received all two thousand copies. Overall printing quality also wasn't great. I didn't sleep that night; I had made a mistake with the work of others. The next day I decided to accept the loss and print everything again at a higher-quality (and way more expensive) printer. Even with the 4 euros a recycling company gave me for the two thousand copies of that first print run, I had a hard time breaking even on this project. But I slept like a baby. —Erik van der Weijde

362

FOTO.ZINE NR.4 #1

ERIK KESSELS / ERIK VAN DER WEIJDE

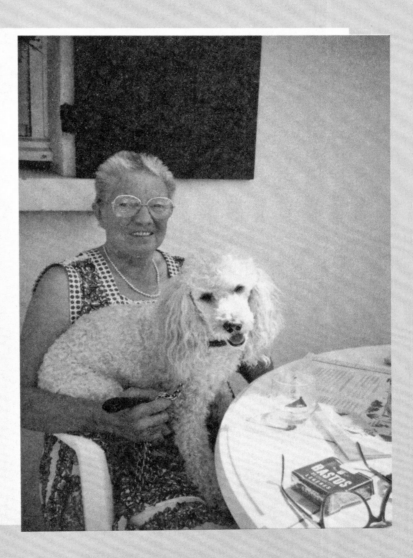

4478zine

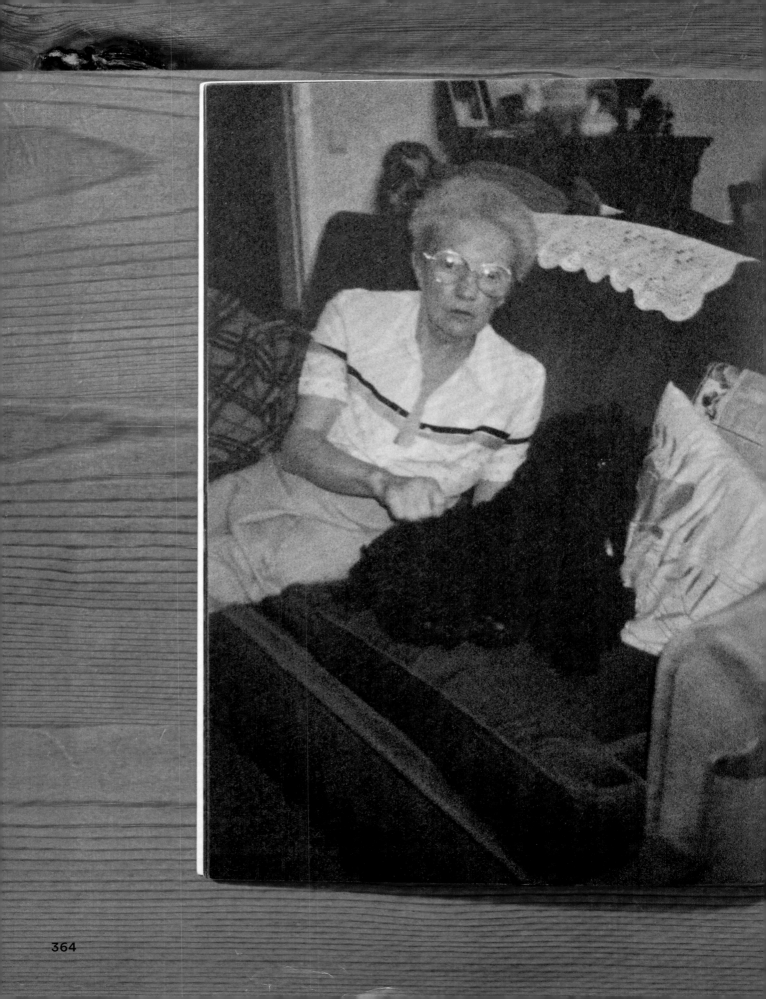

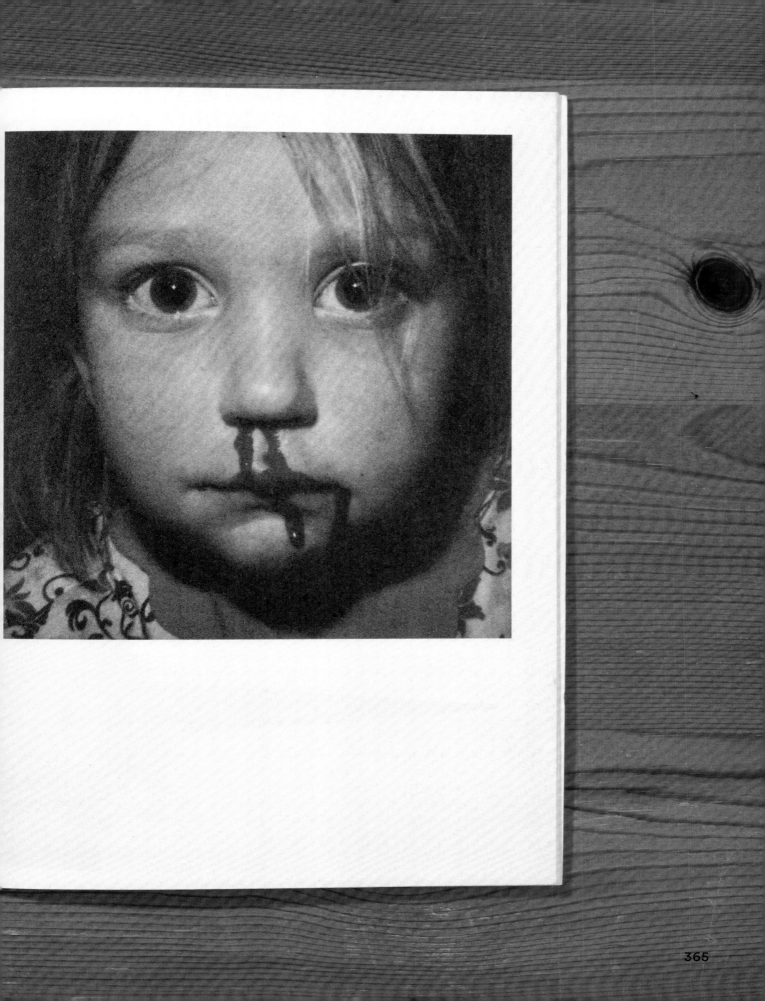

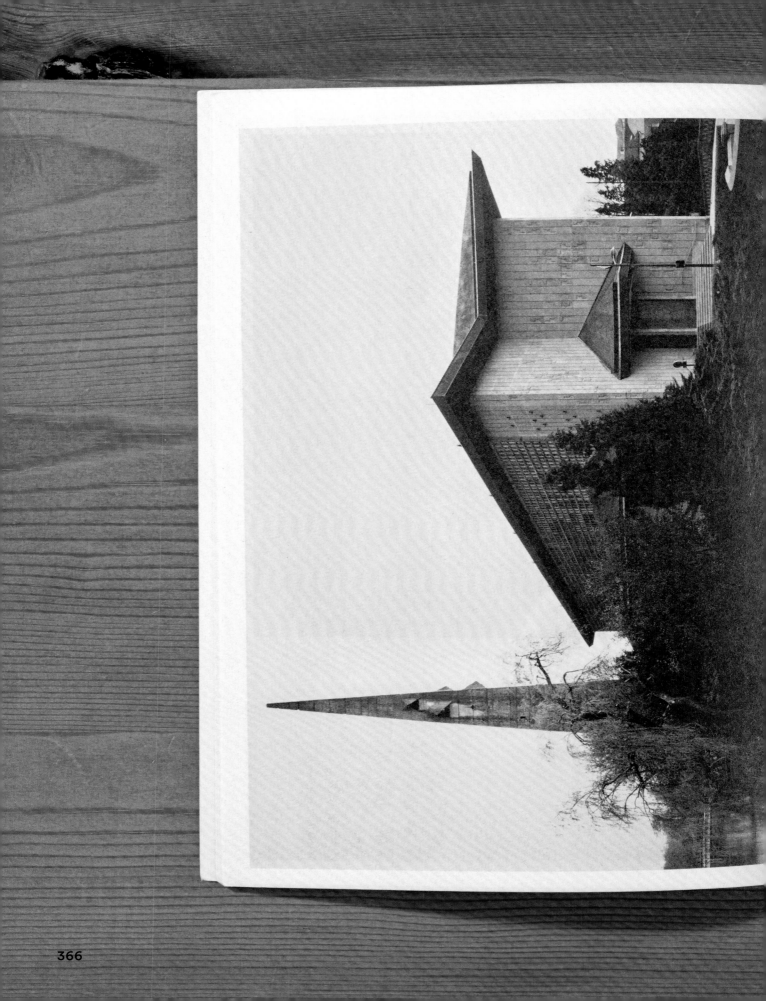

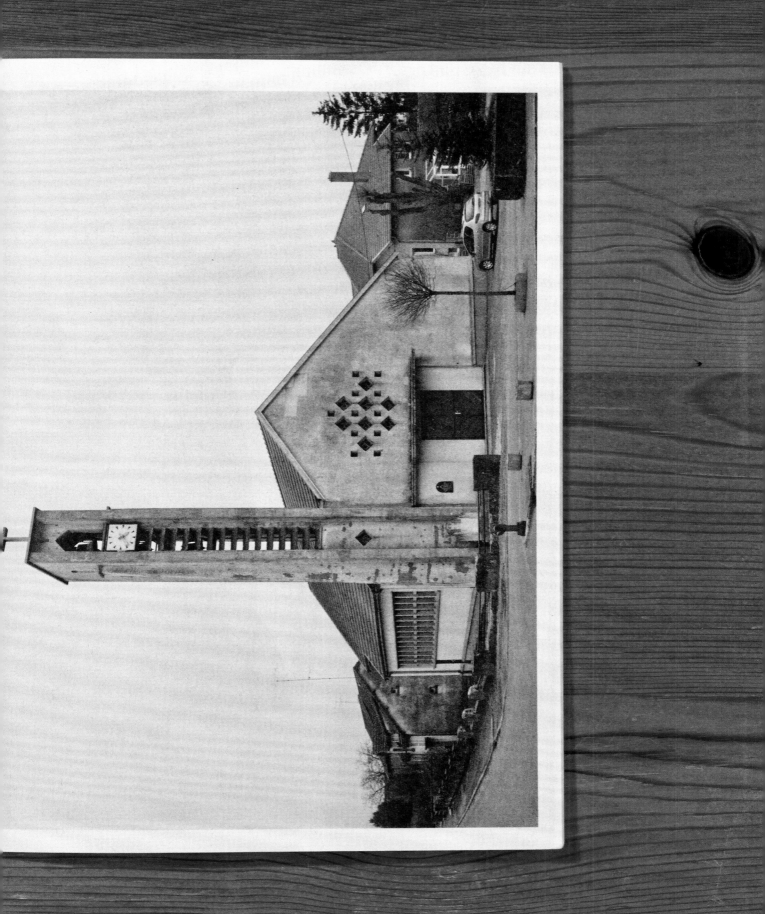

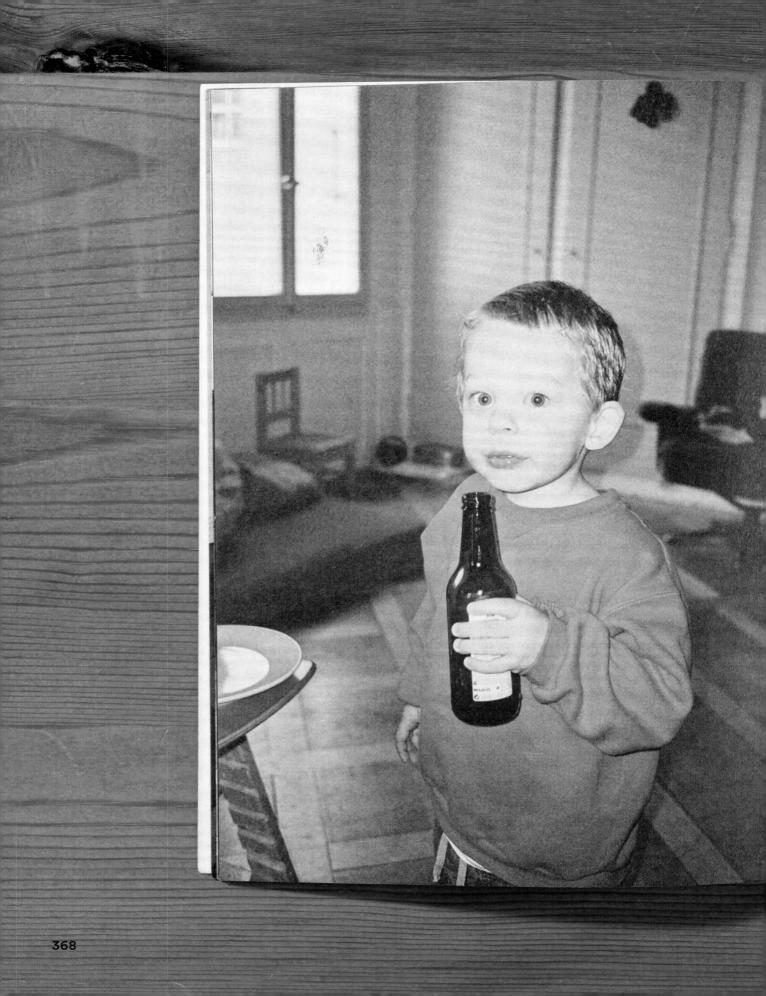

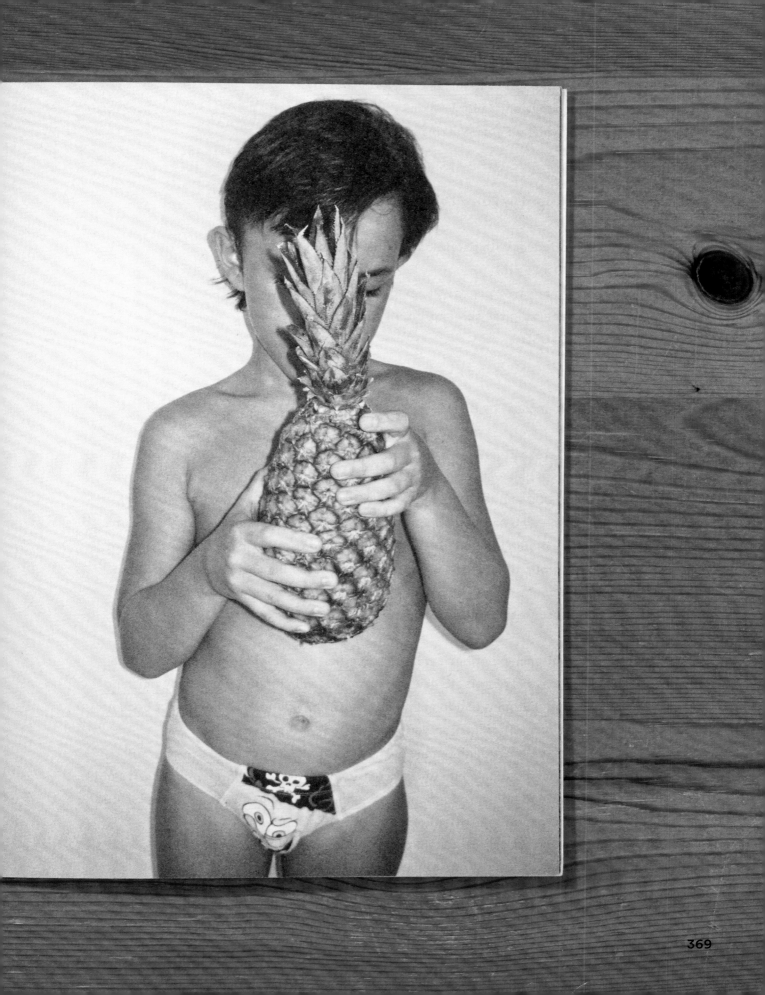

Title: <u>Index of Time</u>

Artists: <u>Tereza Zelenkova, Peter Watkins, and Oliver Shamlou</u>

Designers: Tereza Zelenkova and Peter Watkins

Editors: Tereza Zelenkova and Peter Watkins

Imprint: none

Printer: unknown

Publication date and place: July 2012 / London, UK

Edition: 100

Format and binding: softcover with gatefolds / saddle stitched

Size: 7 7/8 x 9 7/8 in. (20 x 25 cm)

Number of pages and images: 32 pages / 26 images

Type of printing and paper: digital, screenprint, risograph / unknown

Retail price: 20 GBP / 31 USD

Cost per unit: $$$

Book soundtrack: "Dark Entries" by Bauhaus

The Býčí skála Cave in Tereza Zelenkova's native Czech Republic has a mysterious history, allegedly including nineteen bejewelled remains from a Paleolithic settlement thought to have originated between 100,000 and 10,000 BCE. Zelenkova was intrigued by the legend and approached Peter Watkins—who had been photographing cave entrances in Germany—about a collaboration when they met in London in 2011. They agreed on aesthetic parameters, and set about engaging with a group of local speleologists who explored the cave in their spare time. The book is a poetic response to the story, with photographs of tools and the cave by Watkins and Zelenkova, as well as a set of three accompanying short stories by writer Oliver Shamlou.

Peter Watkins: It was quite an experience working together; from nights spent drinking by a campfire with the local cave explorers, to having our car stolen in Prague, to actually finishing the book and distributing it around London and Paris. It was only later that the project became an exhibition—as a direct result of the popularity of the book, I suppose.

Tereza Zelenkova: We made everything ourselves, from designing the book to screenprinting, cropping, and saddle stitching it on a nineteenth-century machine at my former college. It's not perfectly printed or high-end book production, but we made it ourselves with a reasonable budget, and still managed to capture the attention of quite a wide audience.

Peter Watkins: I think our work together went pretty smoothly, and it would seem our collaboration is continuing: we're expecting our first child later this year.

INDEX

of

TIME

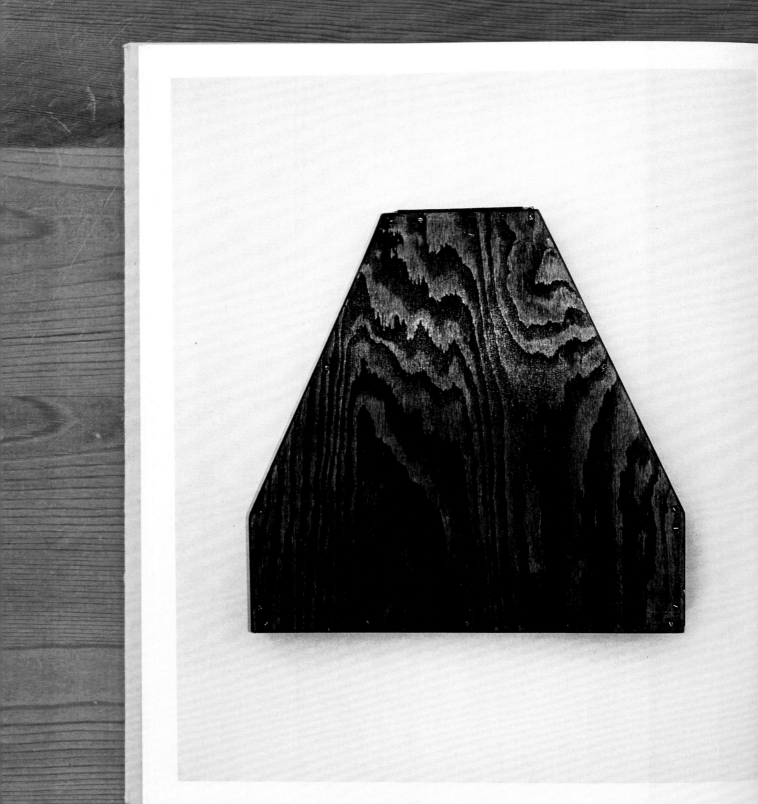

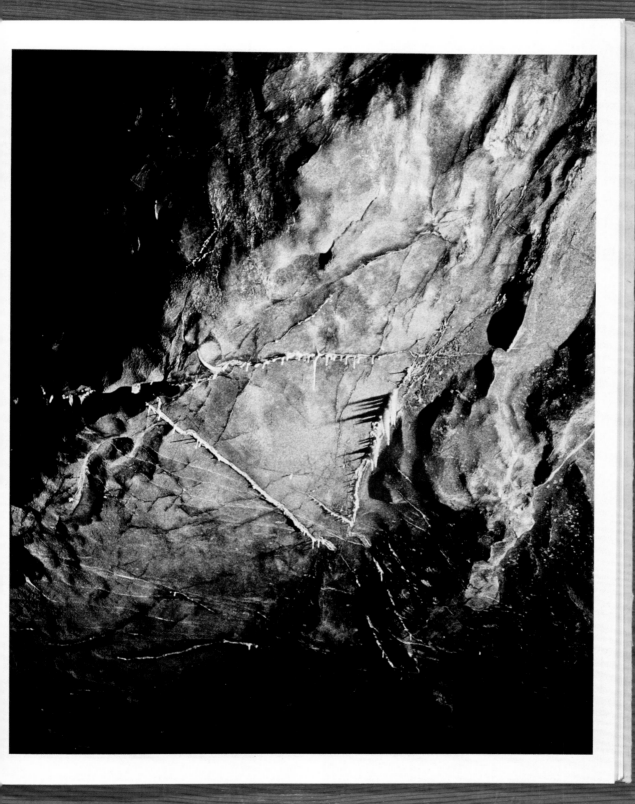

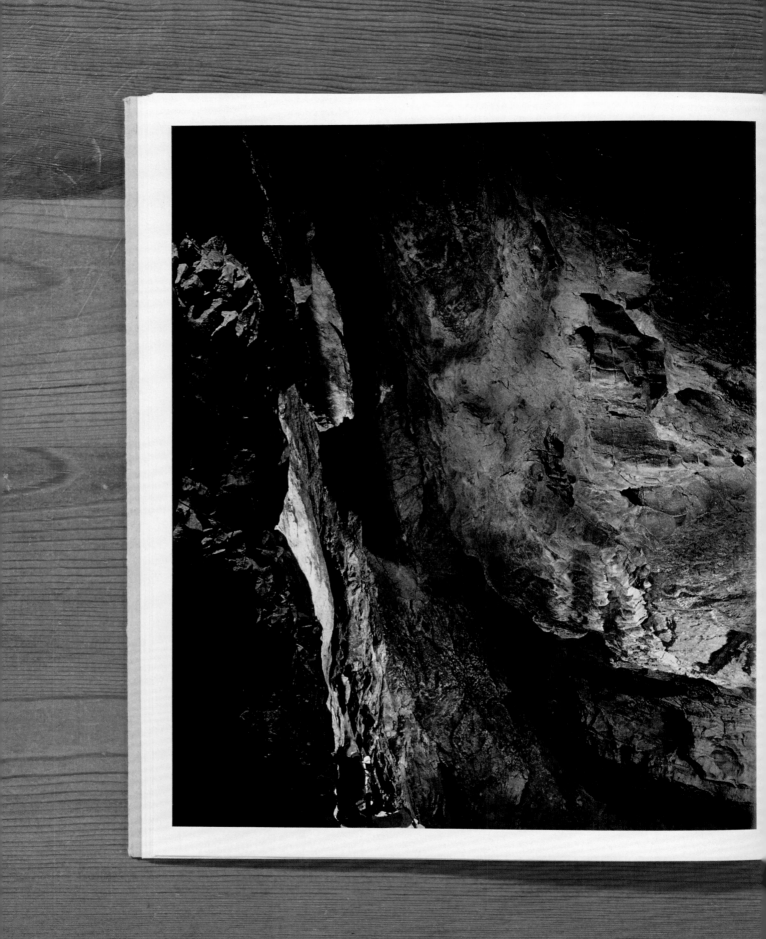

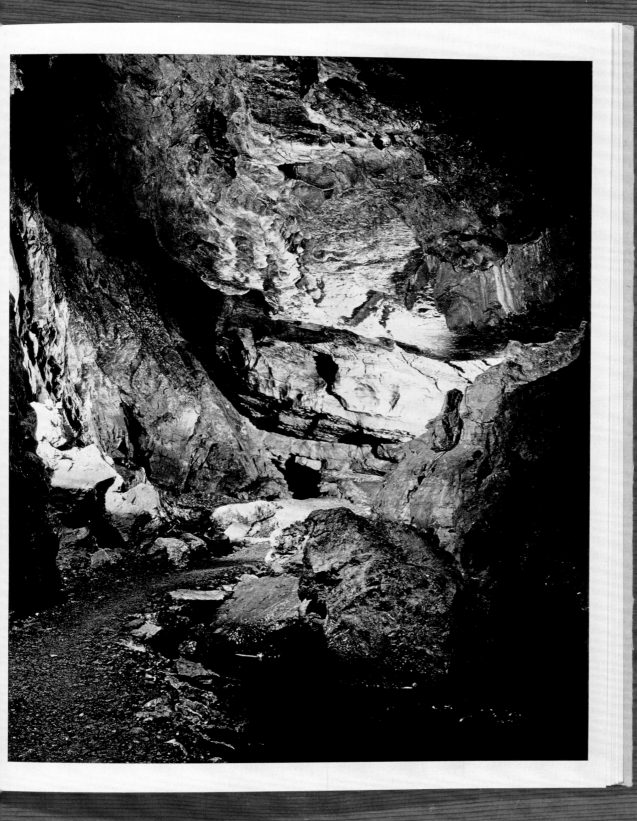

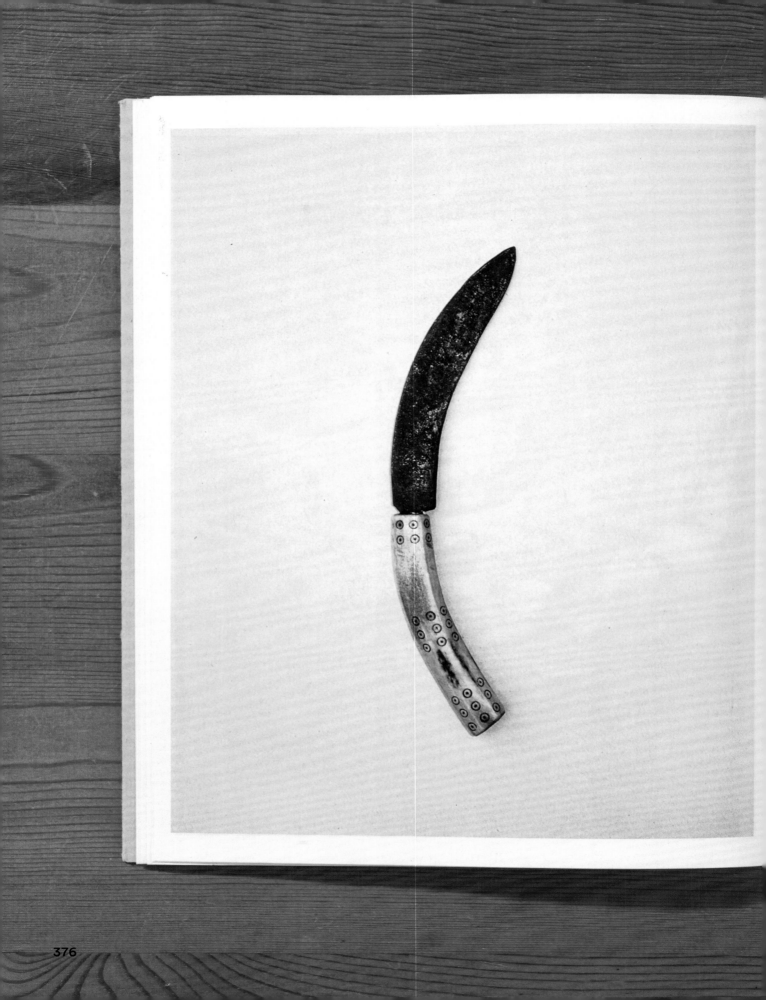

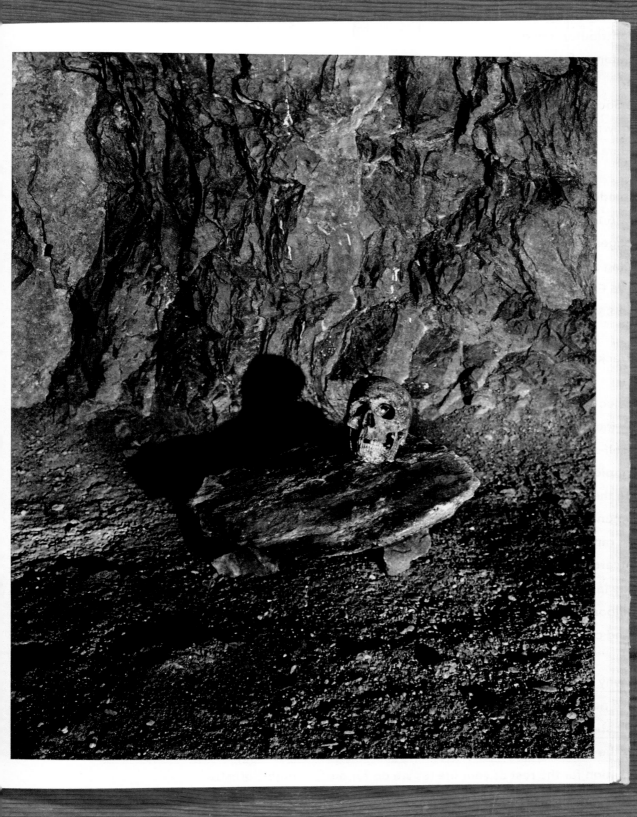

Title: Billboard Sochi Singers (Lilya/Olymp)

Artists: Rob Hornstra and Arnold van Bruggen

Additional contributor: none

Designers: Kummer & Herrman

Editor: none

Imprint: The Sochi Project

Printer: unknown

Publication date and place: 2013 / Utrecht, the Netherlands

Edition: 250

Format and binding: 42-piece billboard / unbound

Size: 11 6/8 x 16 1/2 in. (29.7 x 42 cm); complete size: 81 7/8 x 98 3/8 in. (208 x 250 cm)

Number of pages and images: 42 sheets in cardboard packaging / 2 images

Type of printing and paper: color offset / coated matte 135 gsm

Retail price: 25 EUR / 28 USD

Cost per unit: $$$$

Book soundtrack: "Buket iz belyh roz" by Viktor Korolev

The Sochi Project comprises photographer Rob Hornstra, journalist and filmmaker Arnold van Bruggen, and the design team Kummer & Herrman. In 2007, Hornstra and Van Bruggen embarked on a self-assigned project to document the area around Sochi, Russia, in advance of the 2014 Olympics. Following each trip, they self-published the resulting material as a way of disseminating their work, but also as a means of supporting the project and thanking the crowdfunding community that helped make each trip possible. The resulting output includes over twenty items, ranging from newsprint publications that double as exhibitions, to books of all formats, postcard sets, posters, and items such as this—Sochi Singers billboards. Printed on both sides, the individual, unbound stack of forty-two pieces of A3-sized paper can be assembled into a billboard-sized print, featuring one of the ever-present karaoke singers found in restaurants and cafés all over Sochi.

Ask yourself why you are making the work and who will be your audience. Strangely enough, the majority of publications are still made from a rather narcissistic perspective. Don't forget that the publication will be seen in hundreds of years, as well. Saving a couple hundred bucks, and reducing the quality of the work, really doesn't make sense. You will see the shortcomings of your publication for the rest of your life (as we do for ours). —Rob Hornstra

'We're leaving, but we'll come back to where the sun melts into the haze of autumn.'

THE SOCHI PROJECT
SOCHI SINGERS
42 PIECE BILLBOARD
208 X 252 CM.

74 /250

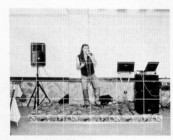

Restaurant Lilya, Lazarevskaya
© Rob Hornstra / The Sochi Project

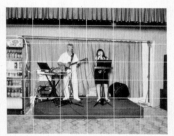

Restaurant Olymp, Novomikhailovsky
© Rob Hornstra / The Sochi Project

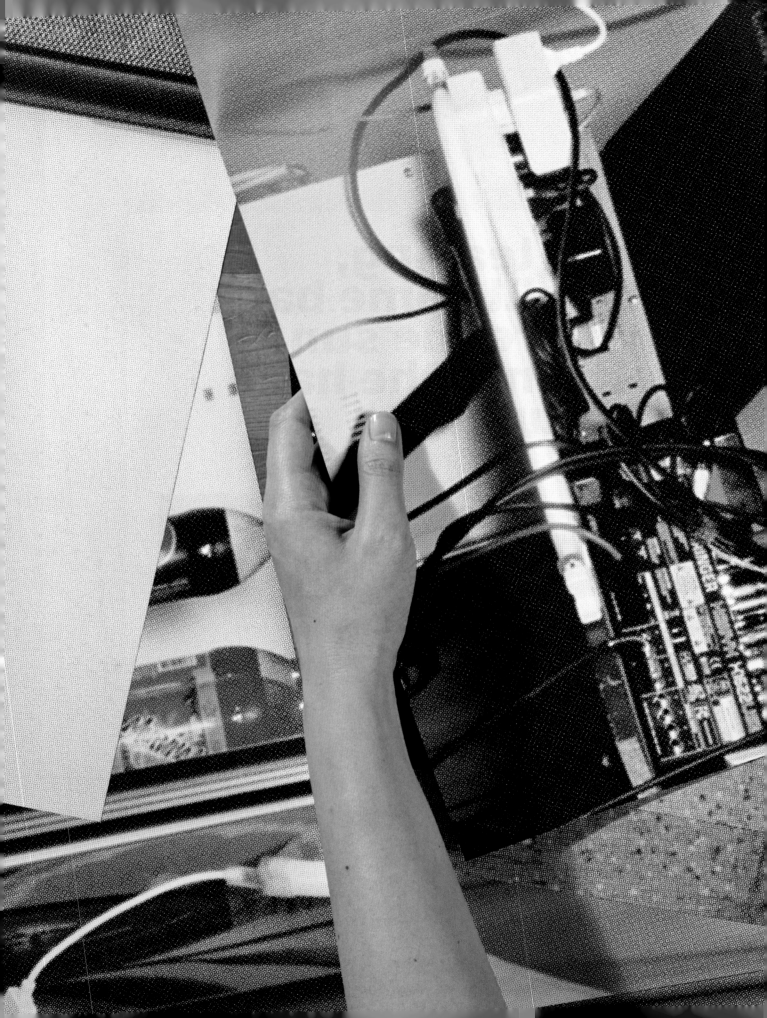

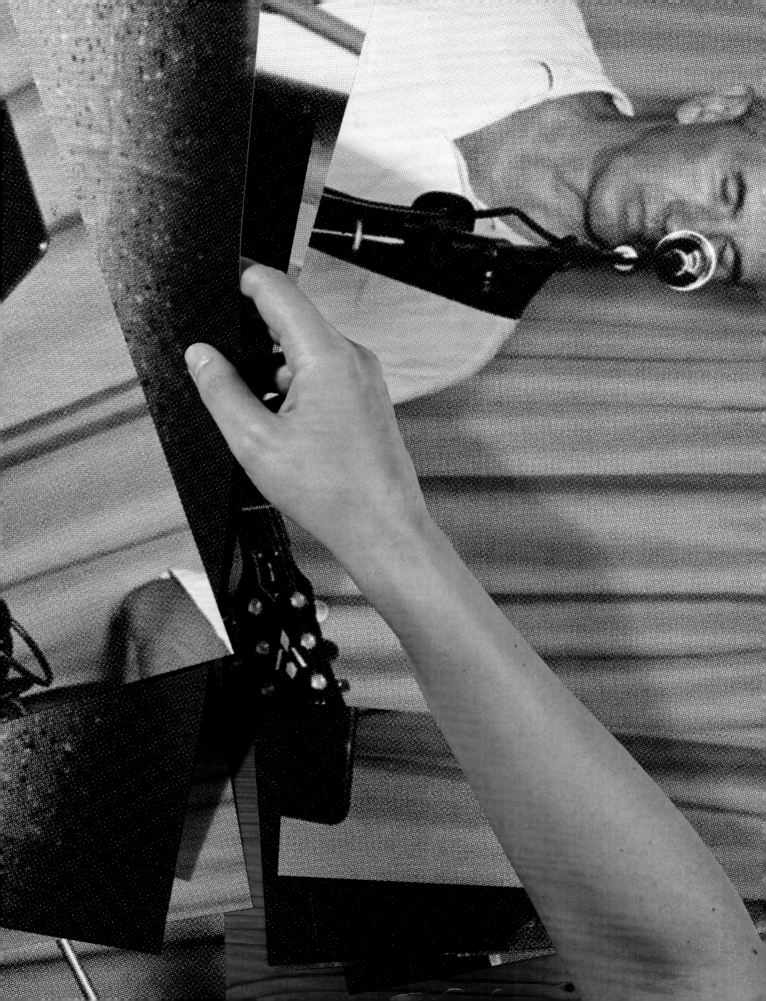

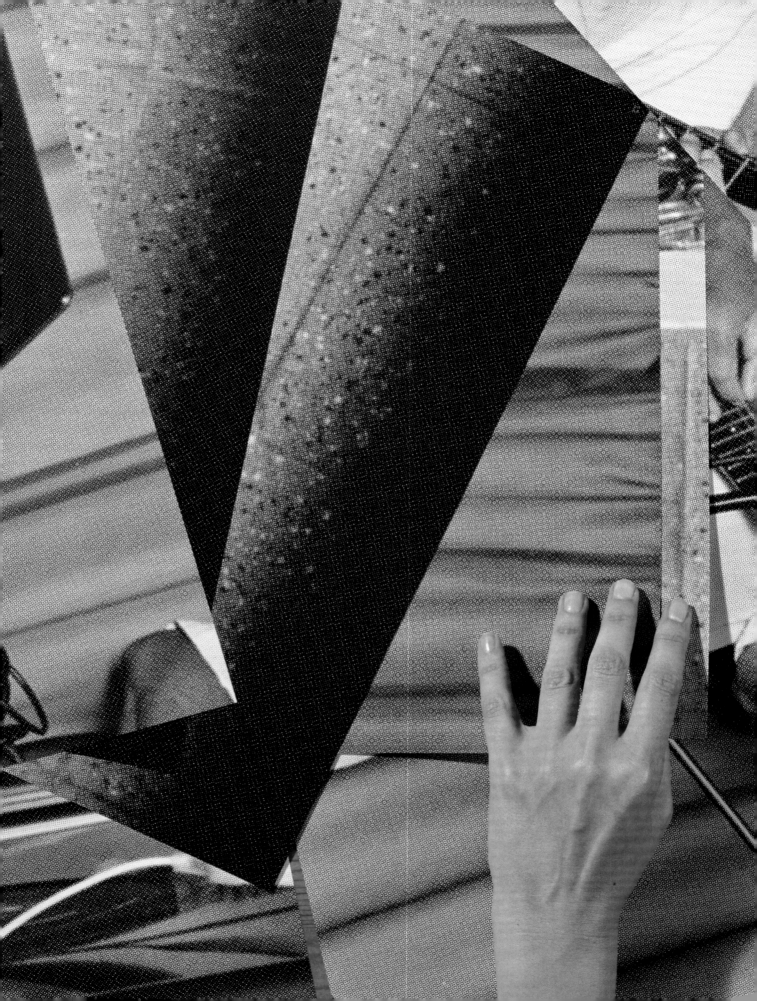

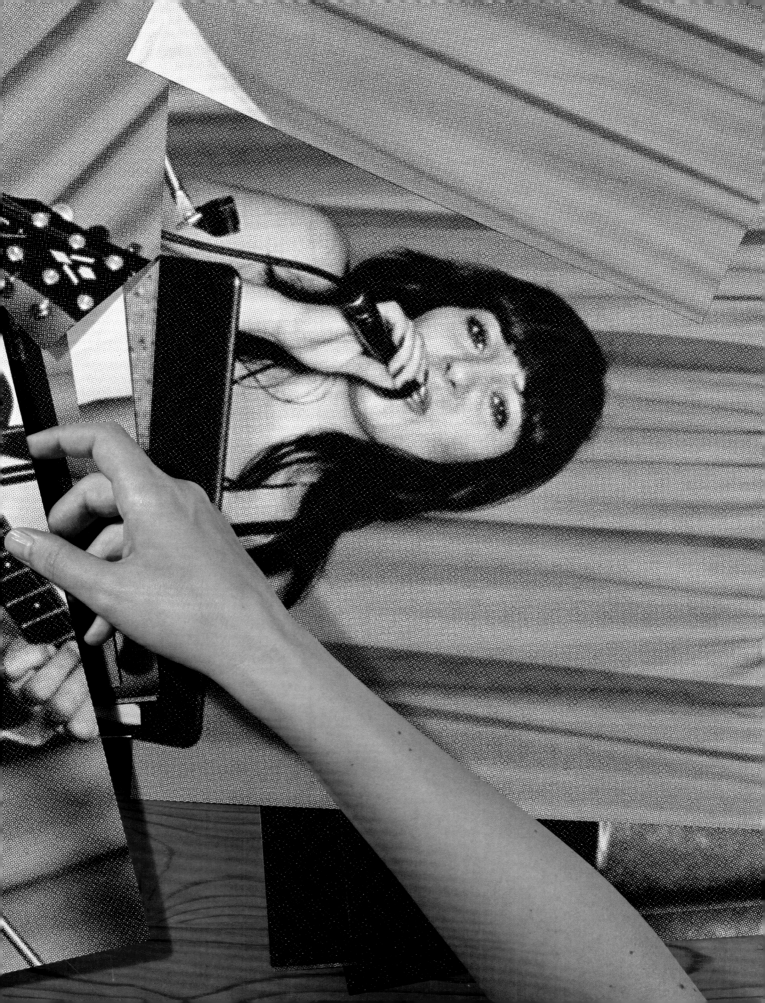

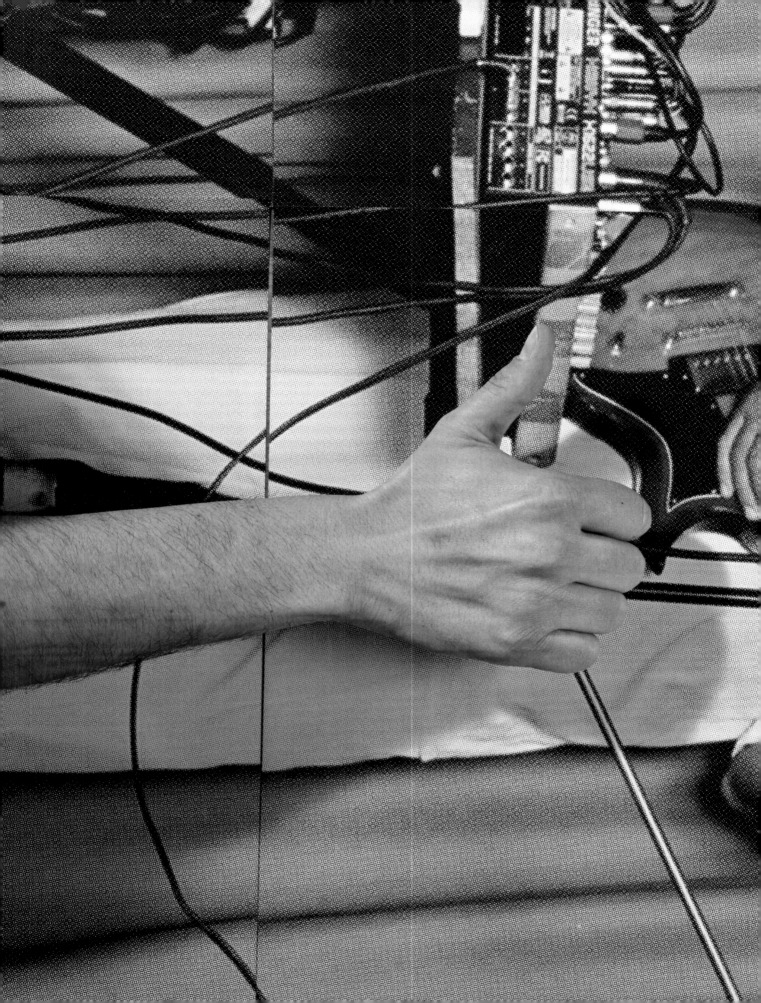

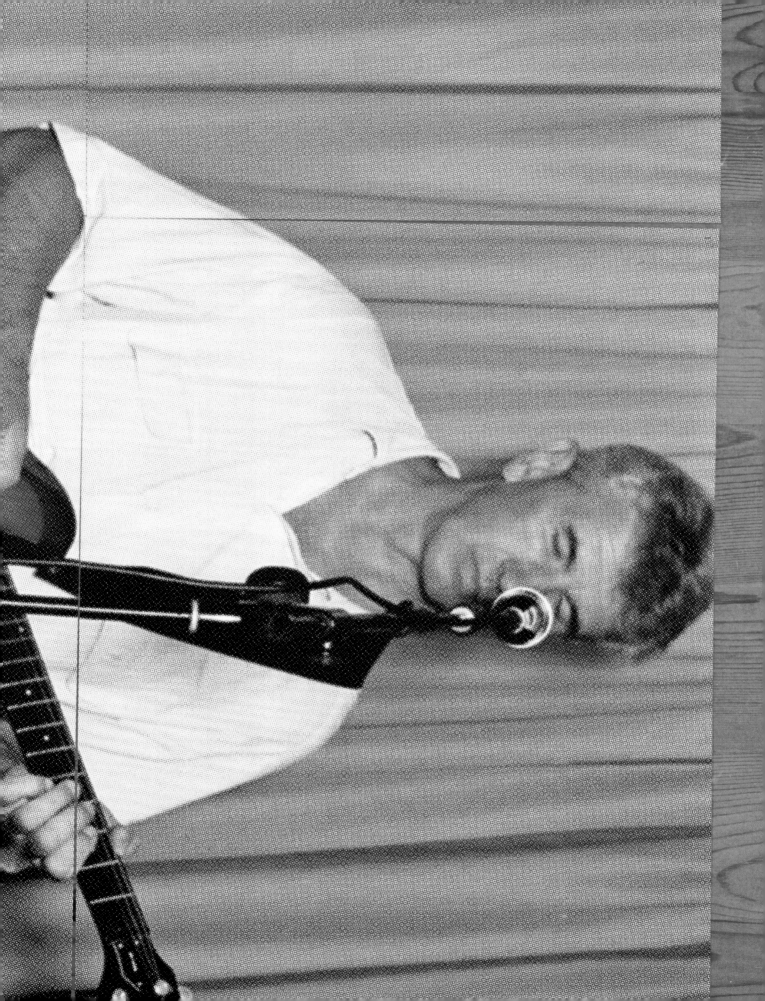

Self Publish, Be Crafty

Title: Effect Twin

Artists: Daisuke Yokota and Hiroshi Takizawa

Designers: Daisuke Yokota and Hiroshi Takizawa

Editors: Daisuke Yokota and Hiroshi Takizawa

Imprint: none

Printer: none

Publication date and place: May 2015 / London, UK

Edition: 75

Format and binding: softcover / aluminum clip binding

Size: 8 1/4 x 11 6/8 in. (21 x 29.7 cm)

Number of pages and images: 80 pages / 80 images

Type of printing and paper: Fuji Xerox DocuPrint C2250 / coarse laser paper with various materials added

Retail price: 150 GBP / 233 USD

Cost per unit: $$

Book soundtrack: "Right Here, Right Now" by Morning Musume '15

Daisuke Yokota has gained acclaim over the past few years for his abstract photographic works and live performances, employing substances such as acid. Hiroshi Takizawa has displayed a continued interested in raw materials, such as rock and concrete, as both subject and material in his practice. In a live performance at the Tate Modern, as a part of Self Publish, Be Happy's project space at Offprint London 2015, the two Japanese photographers put together a live performance in which they created a total of seventy-five unique photobooks, using experimental printing methods. Each artist had digital print-outs of his photographs, upon which he grated a different material in front of an audience—Yokota using rusted iron objects and Takizawa a block of cement—before sealing them with wax and glue and binding them together.

Bookmaking inspires me, and performance is an effective place to share that process with the audience. Even tiny unexpected happenings and events during the performance can be important to delivering a deeper understanding and appreciation of the work. —Daisuke Yokota

I regard the possibility of a book as a medium just like a sculpture or installation. Showing the process of making in the performance gives the audience the opportunity to understand that the book contains a linear timeline, with action, texture, and tactility. It is also a great way to establish the book as a three-dimensional object. —Hiroshi Takizawa

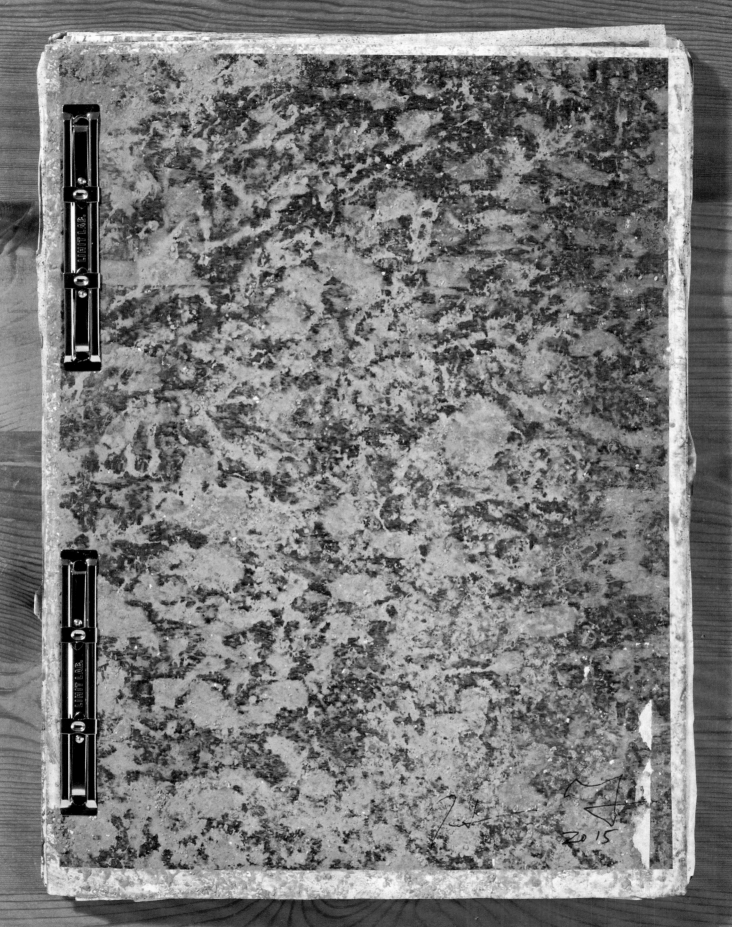

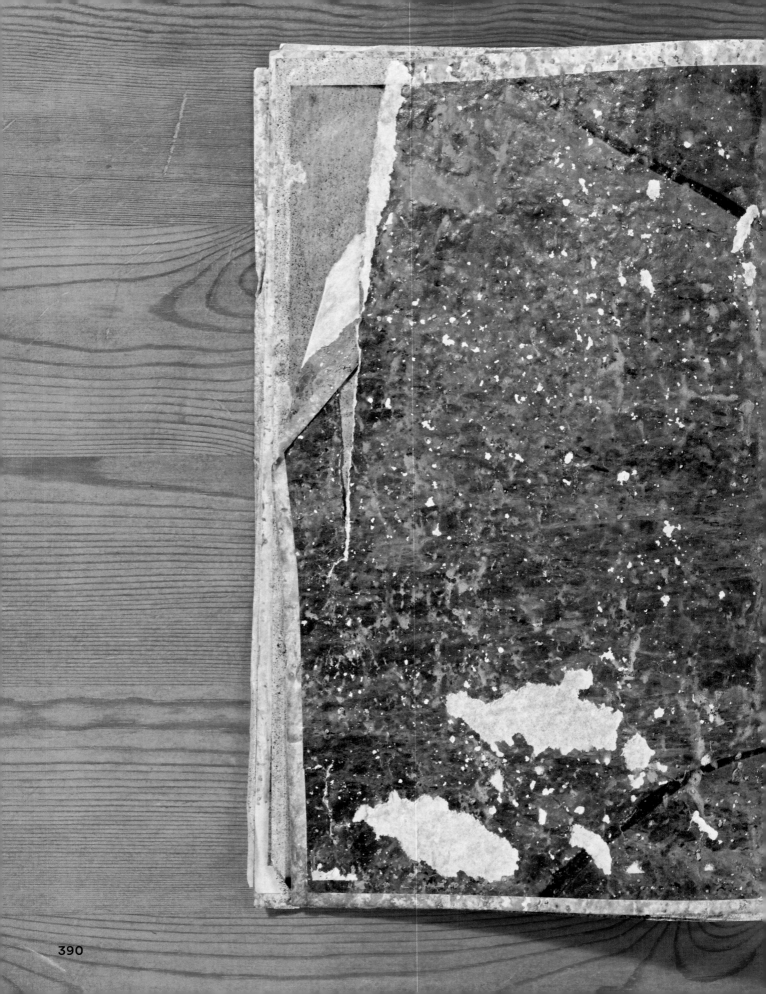

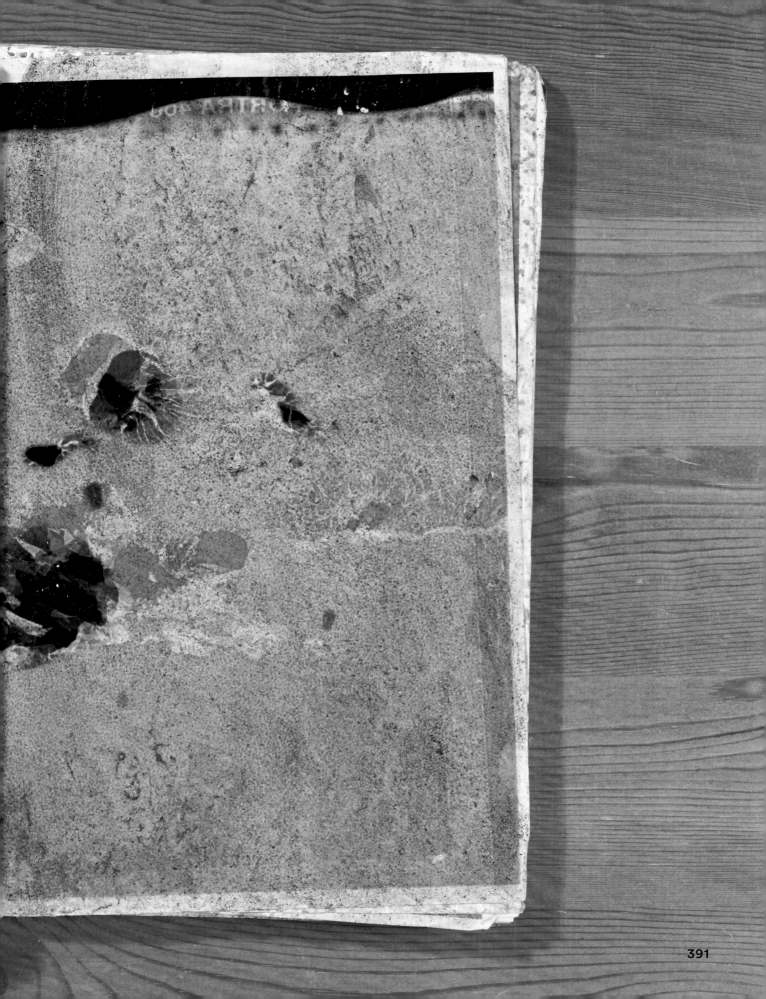

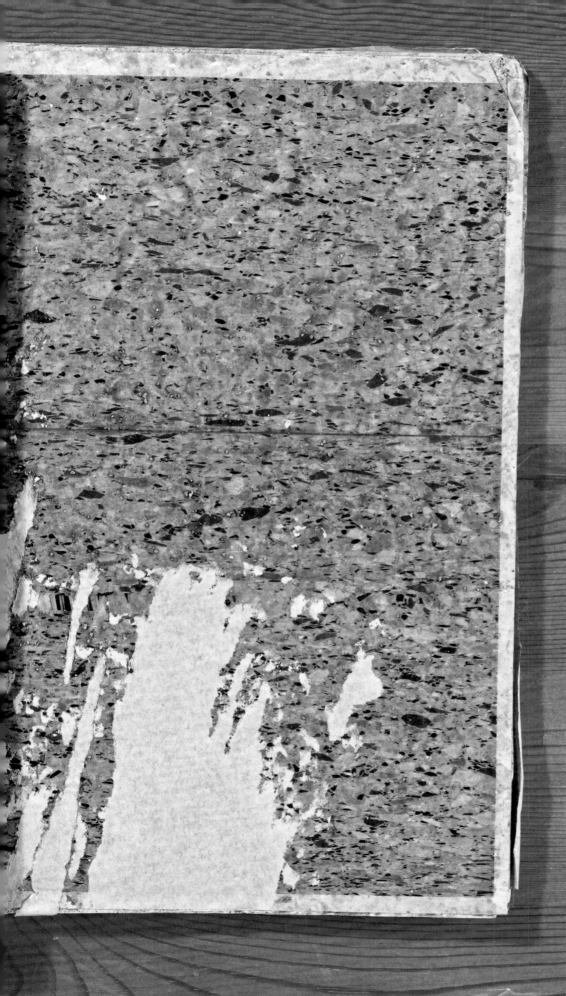

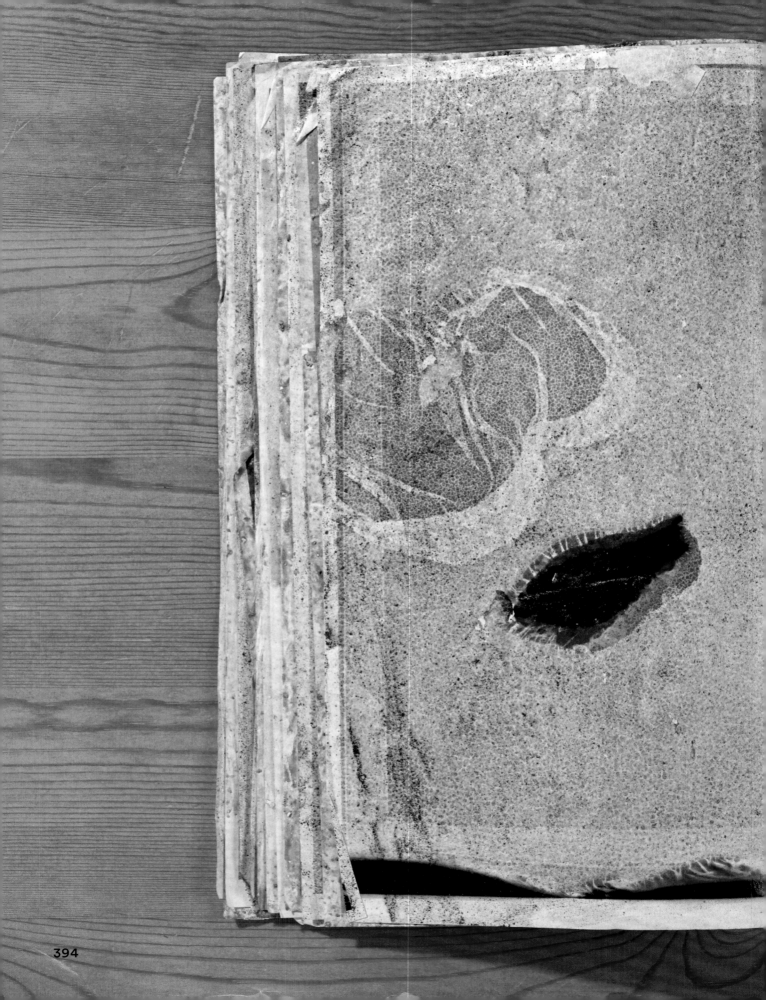

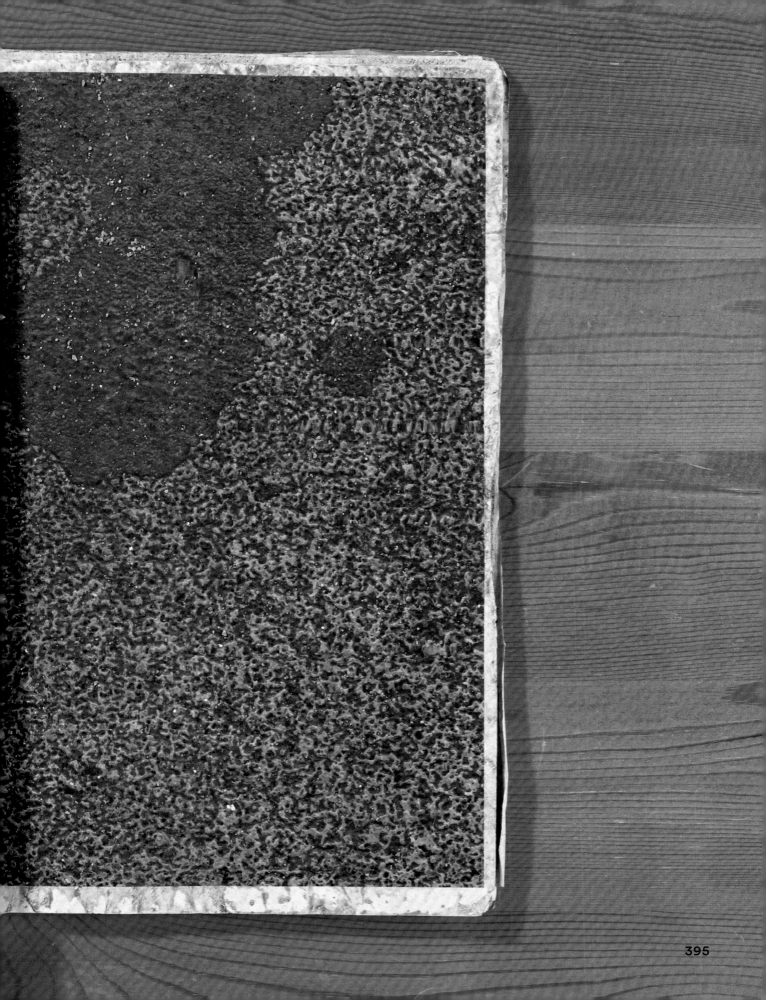

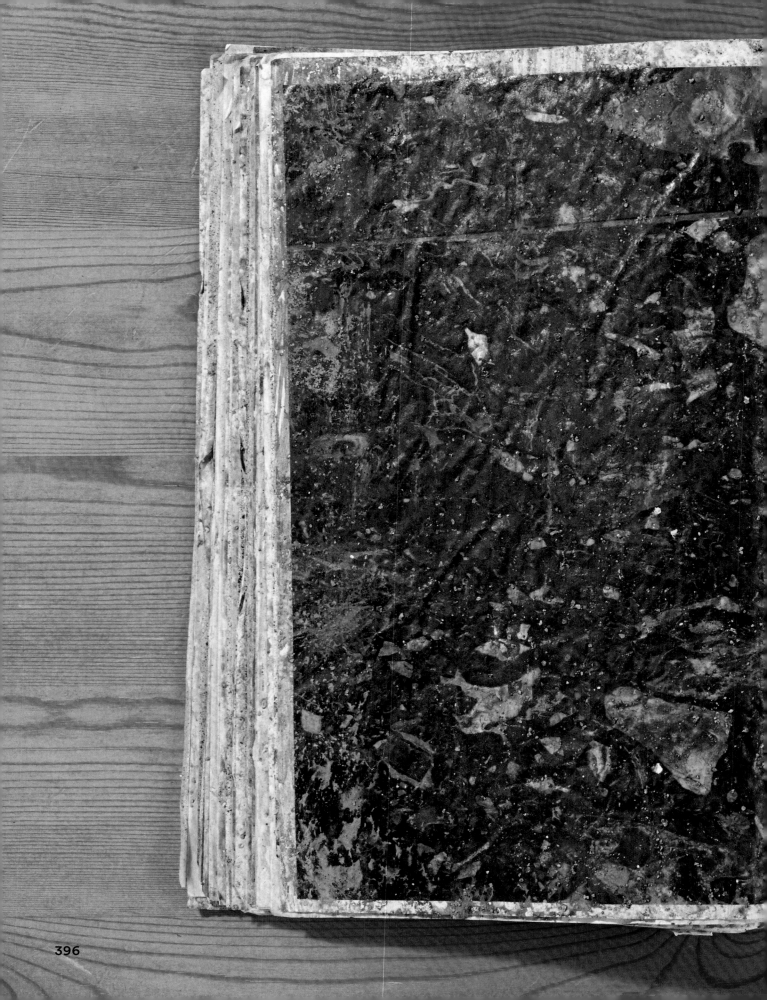

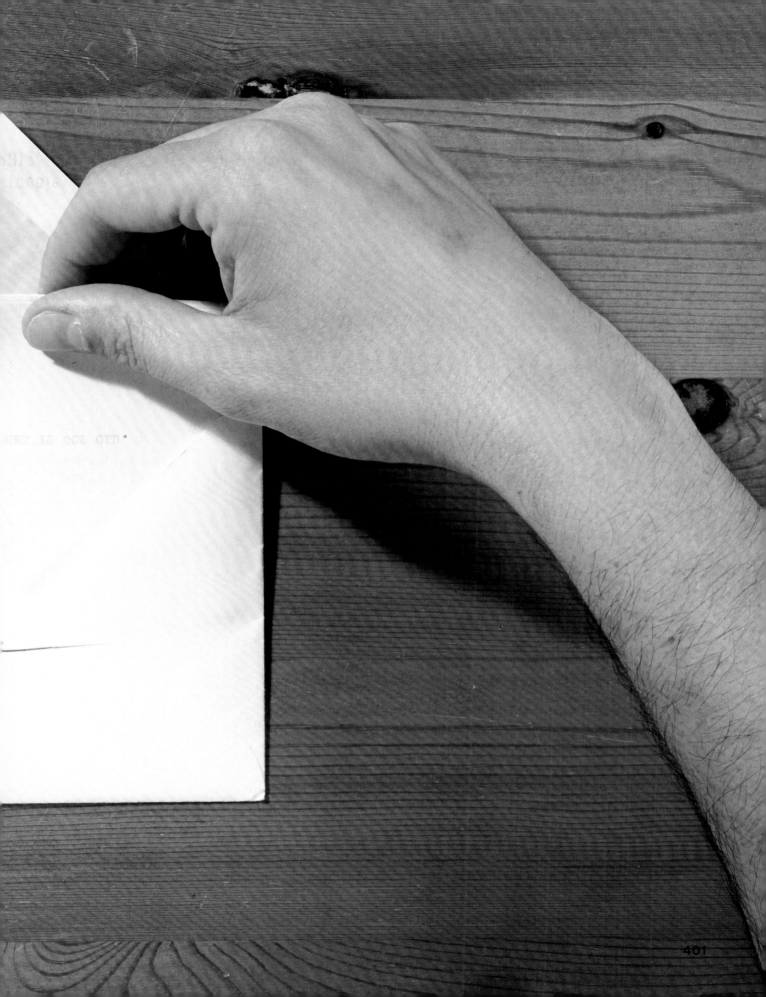

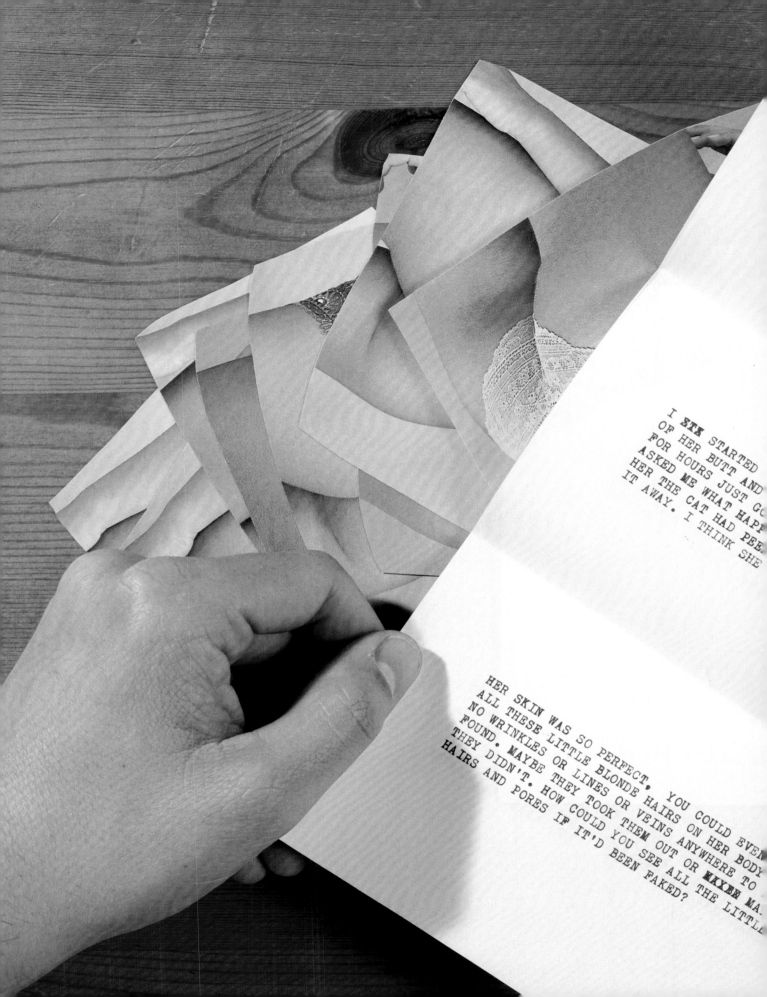

I STX STARTED AND
OF HER BUTT AND GO
FOR HOURS JUST GO
ASKED ME WHAT HAPP
HER THE CAT HAD PEE
IT AWAY. I THINK SHE

HER SKIN WAS SO PERFECT. YOU COULD EVEN
ALL THESE LITTLE BLONDE HAIRS ON HER BODY
NO WRINKLES OR LINES OR VEINS ANYWHERE TO
FOUND. MAYBE THEY TOOK THEM OUT OR MAYBE MA
THEY DIDN'T. HOW COULD YOU SEE ALL THE LITTLE
HAIRS AND PORES IF IT'D BEEN FAKED?

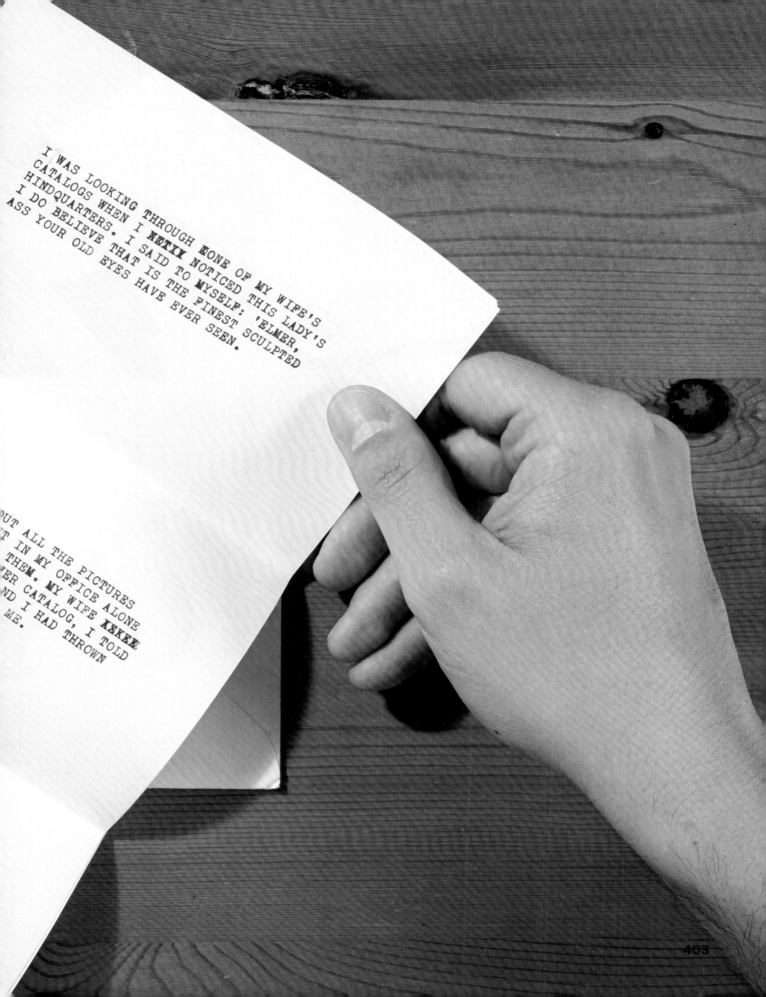

I WAS LOOKING THROUGH ⬛ONE OF MY WIFE'S
CATALOGS WHEN I ⬛⬛⬛⬛ NOTICED THIS LADY'S
HINDQUARTERS. I SAID TO MYSELF: 'ELMER,
I DO BELIEVE THAT IS THE FINEST SCULPTED
ASS YOUR OLD EYES HAVE EVER SEEN.

⬛UT ALL THE PICTURES
⬛T IN MY OFFICE ALONE
⬛ THEM. MY WIFE ⬛⬛⬛⬛
⬛ER CATALOG, I TOLD
⬛ND I HAD THROWN
⬛ ME.

403

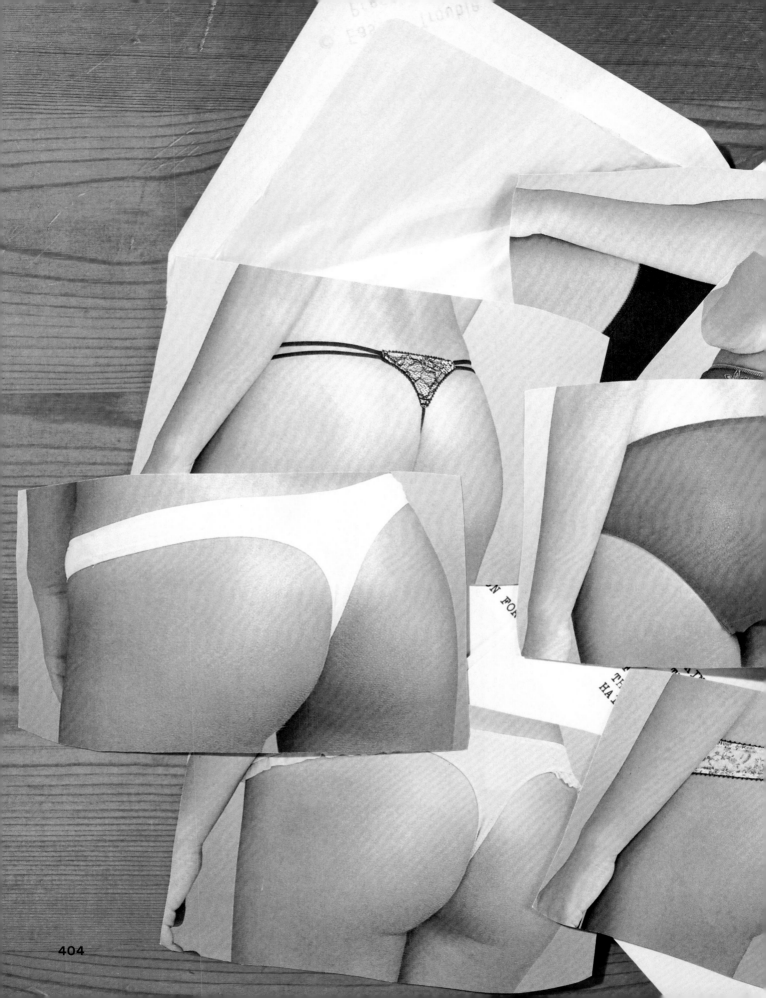

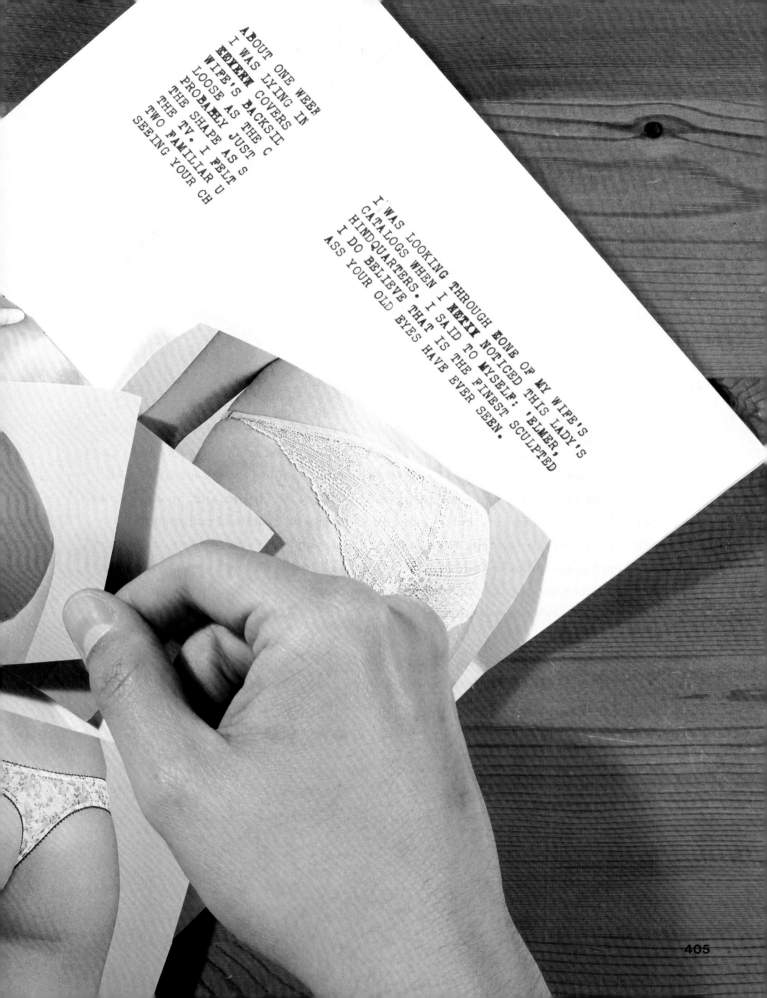

ABOUT ONE WEEK
I WAS LYING IN
EITHER COVERS
WIFE'S BACKSII
LOOSE AS THE C
PROBABLY JUST
THE SHAPE AS S
THE TV. I FELT
TWO FAMILIAR U
SEEING YOUR CH

I WAS LOOKING THROUGH EONE OF MY WIFE'S
CATALOGS WHEN I NOTXX NOTICED THIS LADY'S
HINDQUARTERS. I SAID TO MYSELF: 'ELMER,
I DO BELIEVE THAT IS THE FINEST SCULPTED
ASS YOUR OLD EYES HAVE EVER SEEN.

405

Title: *Fake Flowers in Full Colour*

Artists: Hans Gremmen and Jaap Scheeren

Designer: Hans Gremmen

Imprint: Fw: Books

Printer: Drukkerij Raddraaier, Amsterdam, the Netherlands

Publication date and place: 2009 / Amsterdam, the Netherlands

Edition: 500 (first printing) / 1,000 (second printing)

Format and binding: softcover / saddle stitched

Size: 9 1/2 x 13 3/8 in. (24 x 34 cm)

Number of pages and images: 40 pages / unknown

Type of printing and paper: offset / Royal Print, Tenax

Retail price: 12 EUR / 14 USD

Cost per unit: $$$

Book soundtrack: "Dead Flowers" by Townes Van Zandt

Working in tandem, Dutch photographer Jaap Scheeren and designer Hans Gremmen staged a series of still lifes of a bouquet of fake flowers. Each time, they painted the flowers one of four colors—cyan, magenta, yellow, or black—in order to create a "real-life" color separation. The book presents a documentation of the set-up, as well as each of the images, and, finally, a series of the images together in different combinations, building up a full palette of colors and tonalities as each color is overlayed on top of one another. The design includes a small color wheel on the border of each page, indicating which colors are active. Simple, creative, and playful, *Fake Flowers in Full Colour* operates as a meditation on the improbability and beauty of how images are rendered via the CMYK offset printing process.

Photography is nearly invisible in its purest form. It has no fixed medium. As an artist, you have to choose a medium to make it visible to the world. In the case of *Fake Flowers in Full Colour*, it had to become a book, since the final work could only exist by printing sixteen layers of ink (four of each full color) on top off each other in offset. —Jaap Scheeren

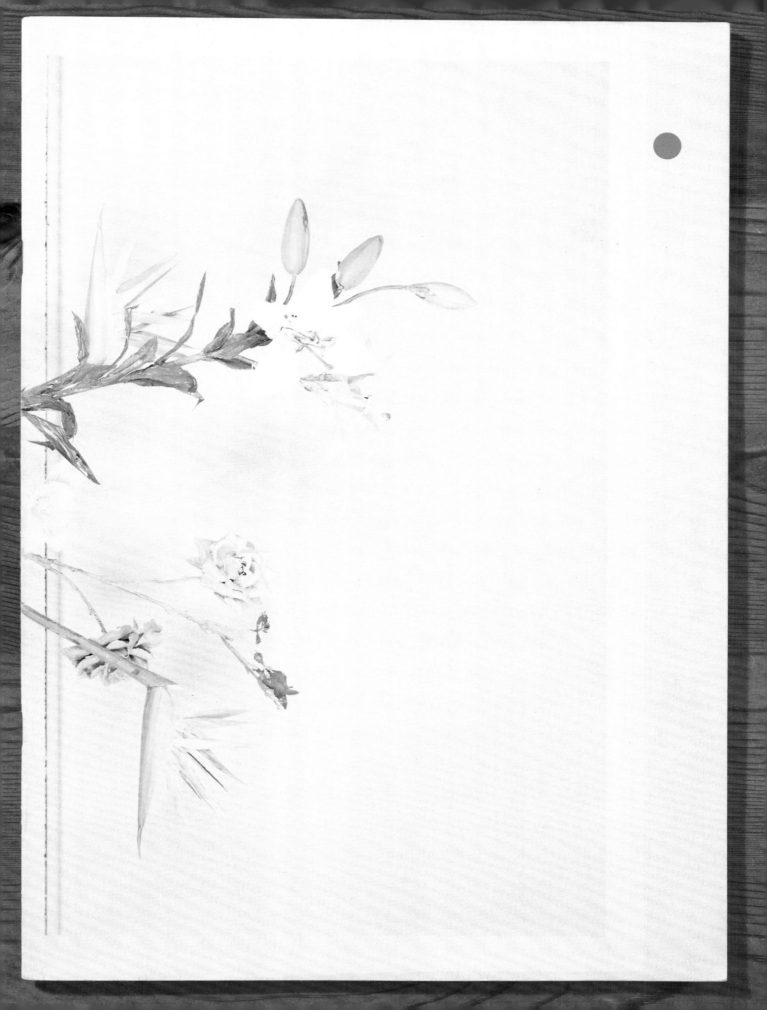

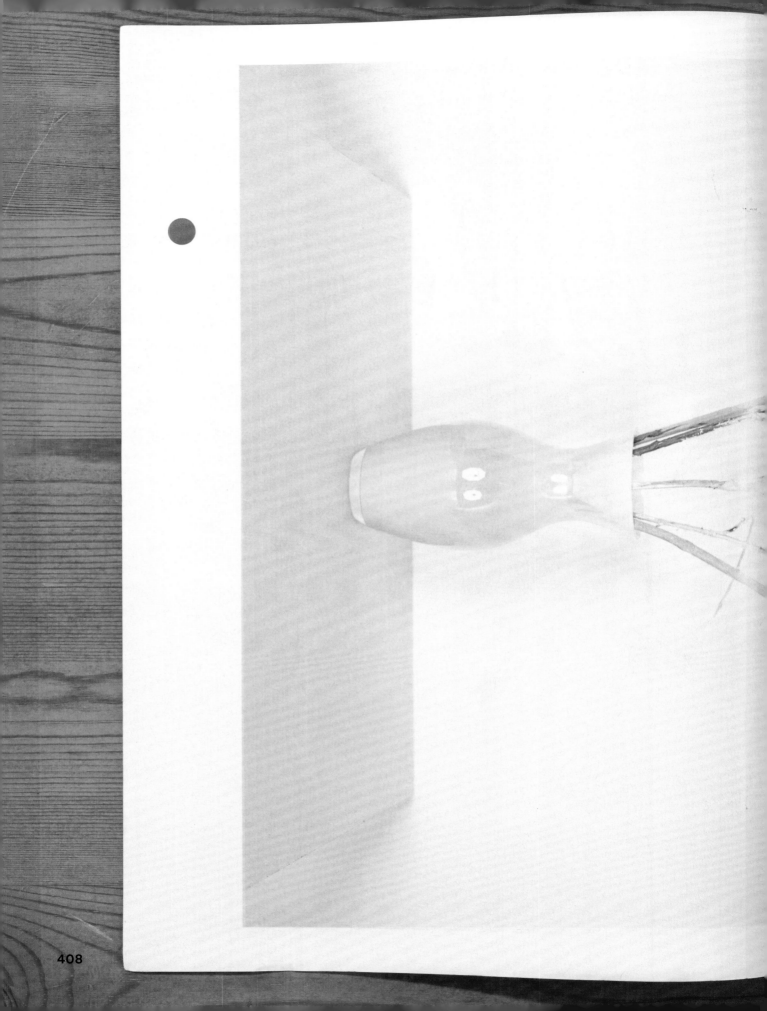

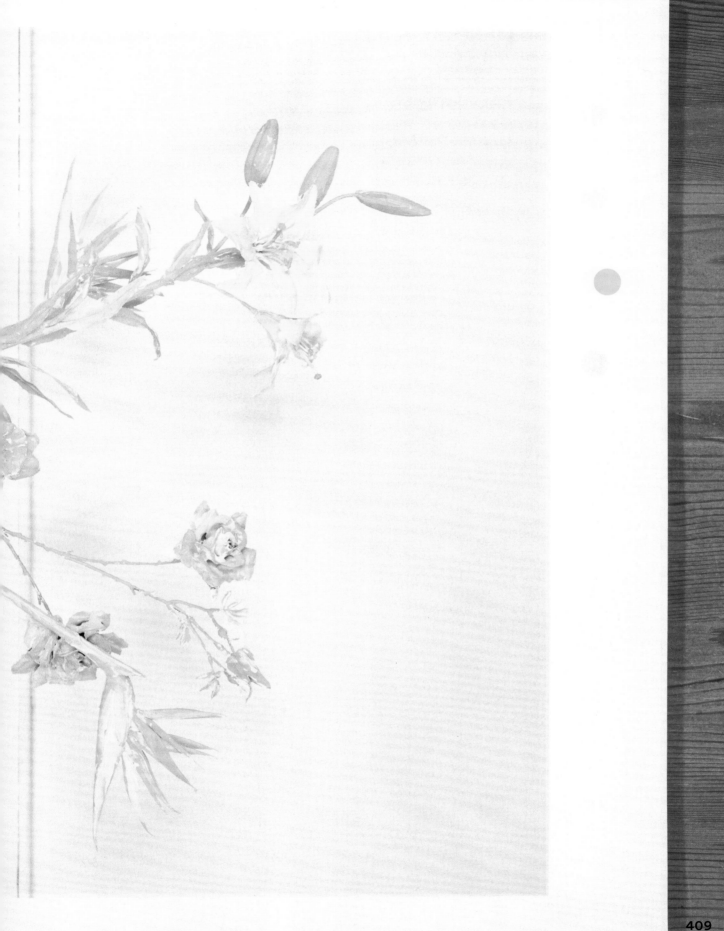

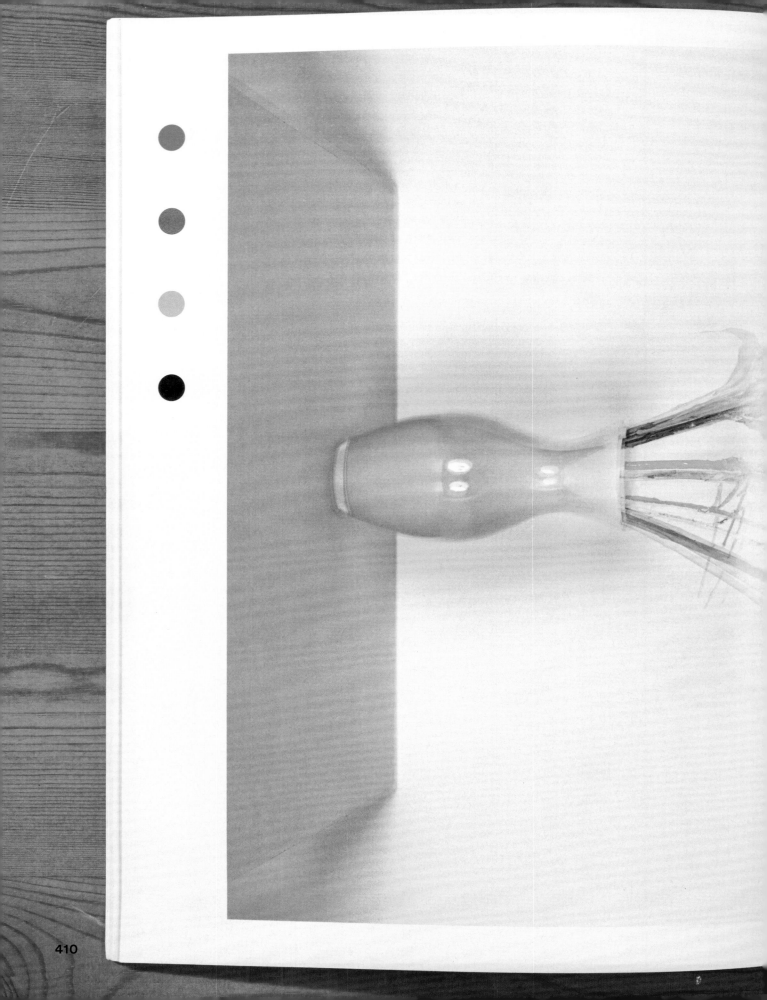

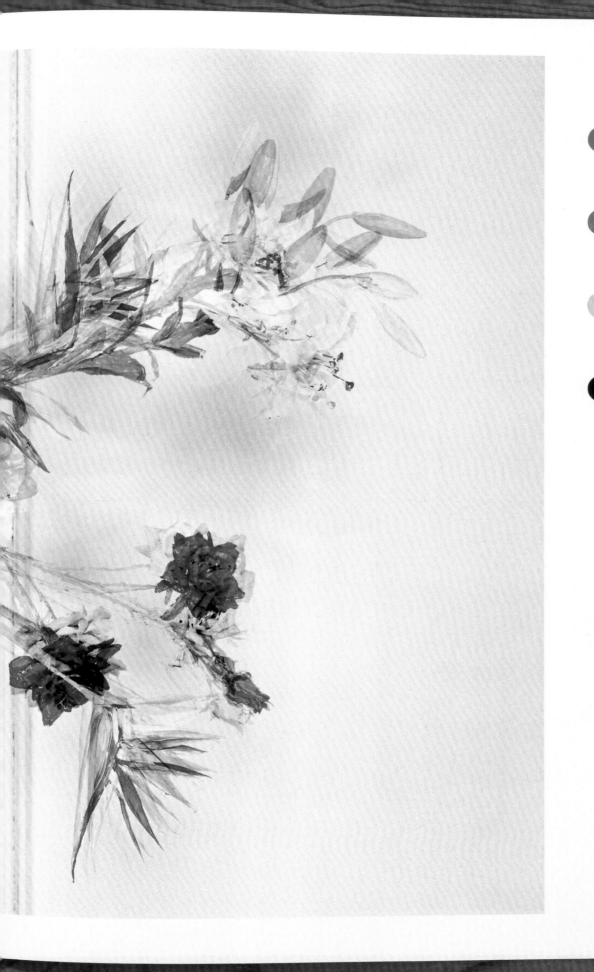

411

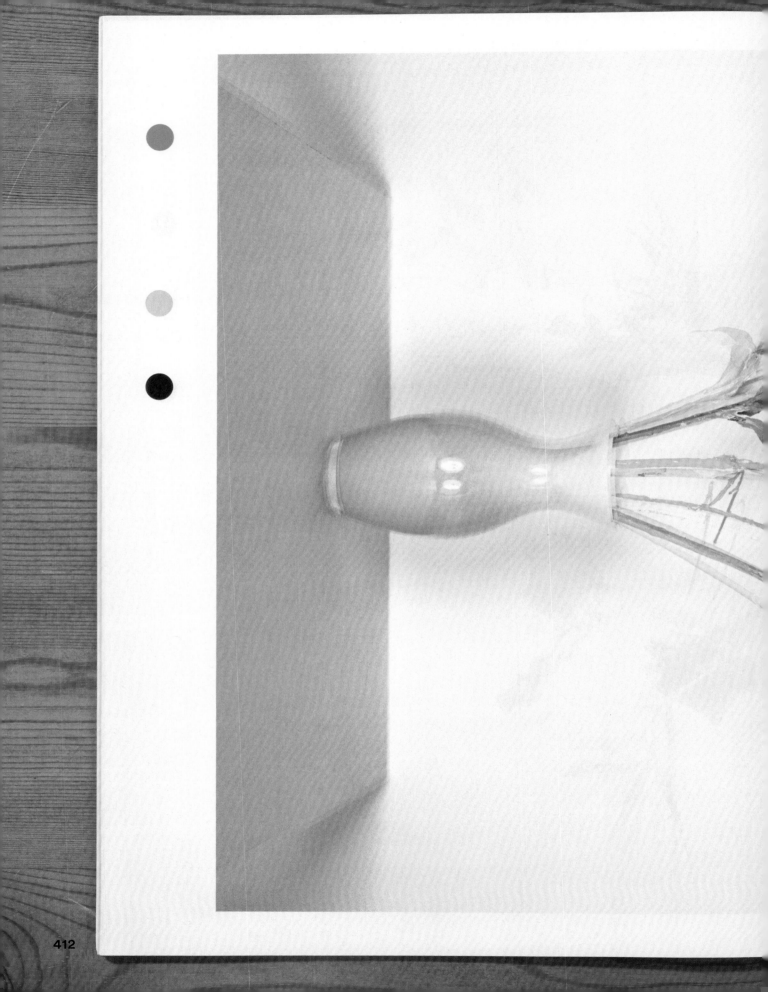

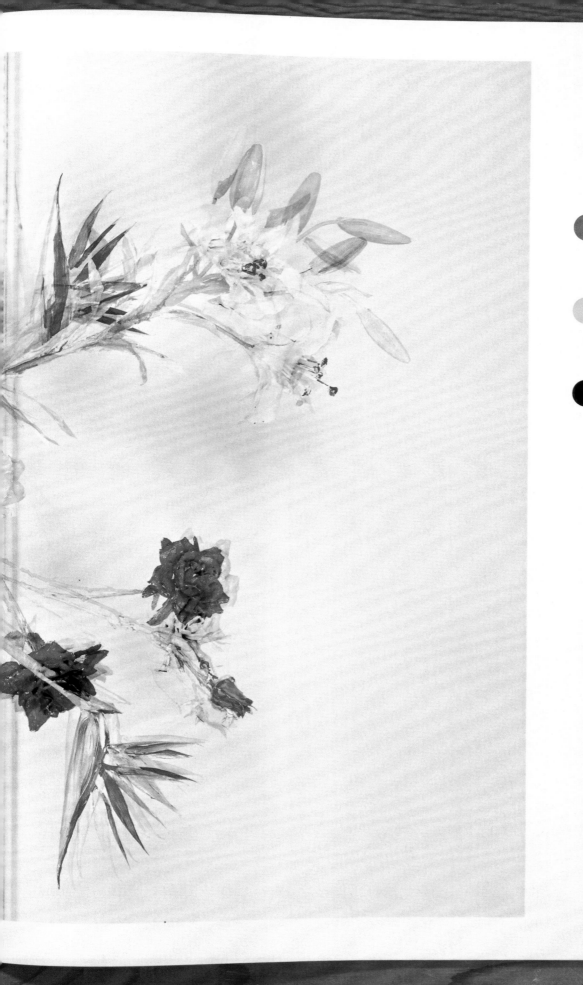

413

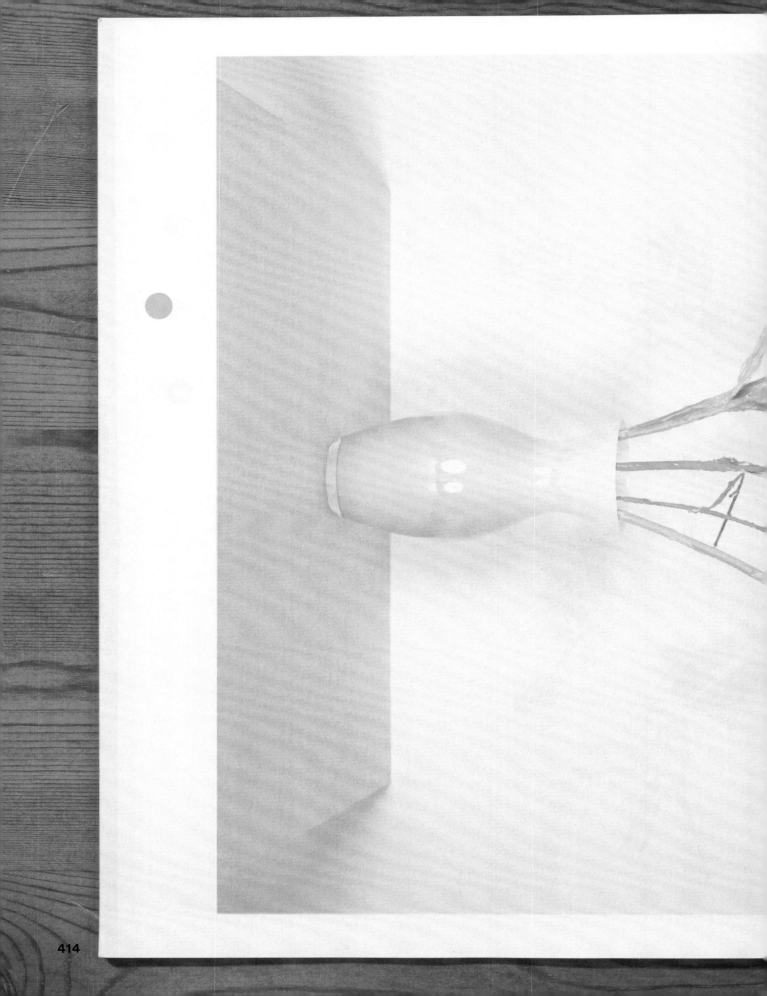

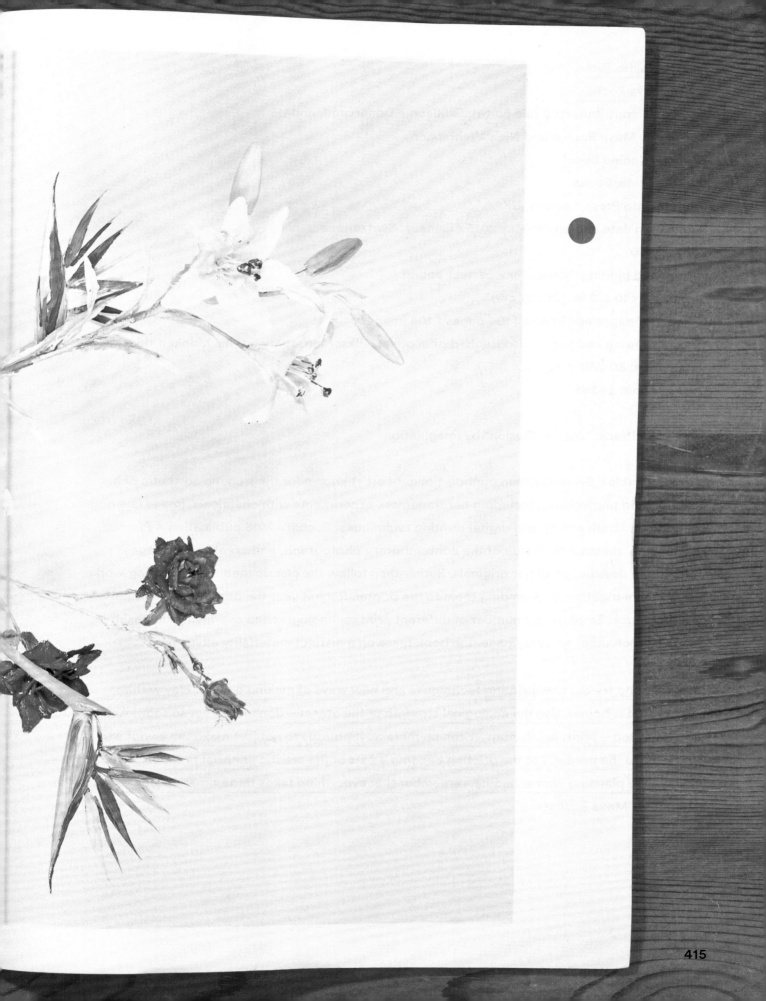

Title: A Plastic Tool

Artist: Maya Rochat

Additional contributors: Emile Barret, Guillaume Dénervaud, and U5

Designers: Maya Rochat and Niels Wehrspann

Editor: Delphine Bedel

Imprint: Meta/Books

Printer: Ditto Press, London, UK

Publication date and place: May 2015 / Geneva, Switzerland

Edition: 250

Format and binding: hardcover / perfect bound

Size: 8 1/4 x 10 5/8 in. (21 x 27 cm)

Number of pages and images: 104 pages / 104 images

Type of printing and paper: risograph, digital offset, silkscreen, spray paint / Munken 115gsm

Retail price: 80 CHF / 89 USD

Cost per unit: $$$$$

Book soundtrack: "Just an Illusion" by Imagination

Maya Rochat is a Swiss-German multidisciplinary artist known for the frenetic aesthetic of her artworks and photobooks, including her trademark experiments with chemicals, image layering, collages, and both analog and digital printing techniques. Rochat's 2015 publication *A Plastic Tool* aims to question the value of the contemporary photograph, and create new images through the destruction of her originals. Rather than follow the classic method of creating works, editing them together, and sending them to the printer, Rochat uses the printing stage as part of her practice. Employing a number of different print technologies and overlaying the results on top of each other on every page, the book takes on a distinct materiality all its own.

Take risks and try out new printing techniques and new ways of making a book. Play with the book after it is bound. Use the analogical strength of the object—don't let it rest so soon! And at the printer too—print, paint, print. It can be more adventurous to not just make the layout and send it off to the printer. Let the printing become a part of the artistic editorial practice. Also, when you're planning your schedule, remember that everything takes three times as long as you estimate! —Maya Rochat

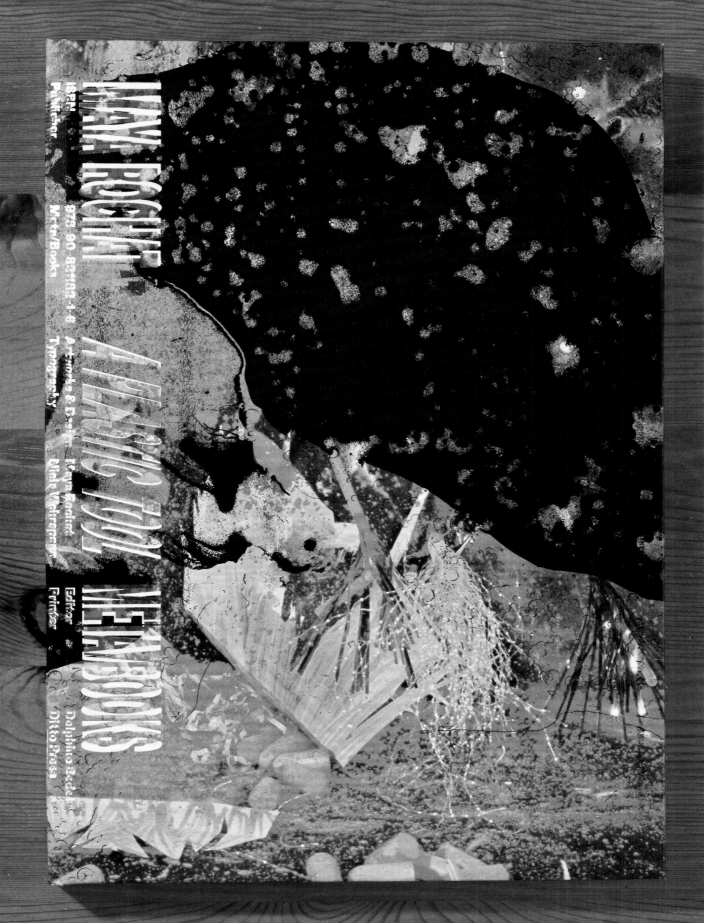

417

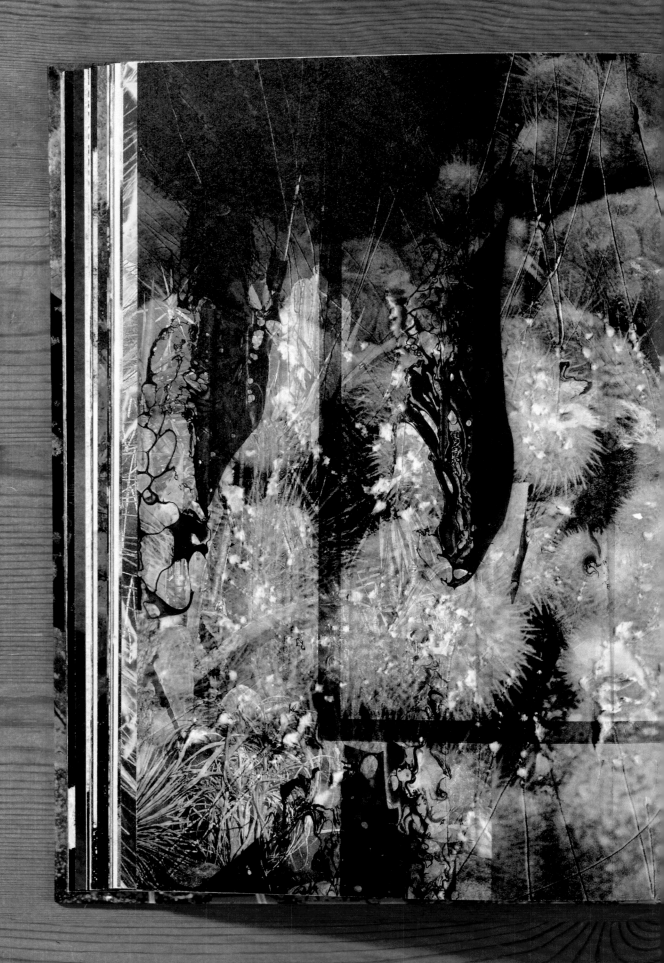

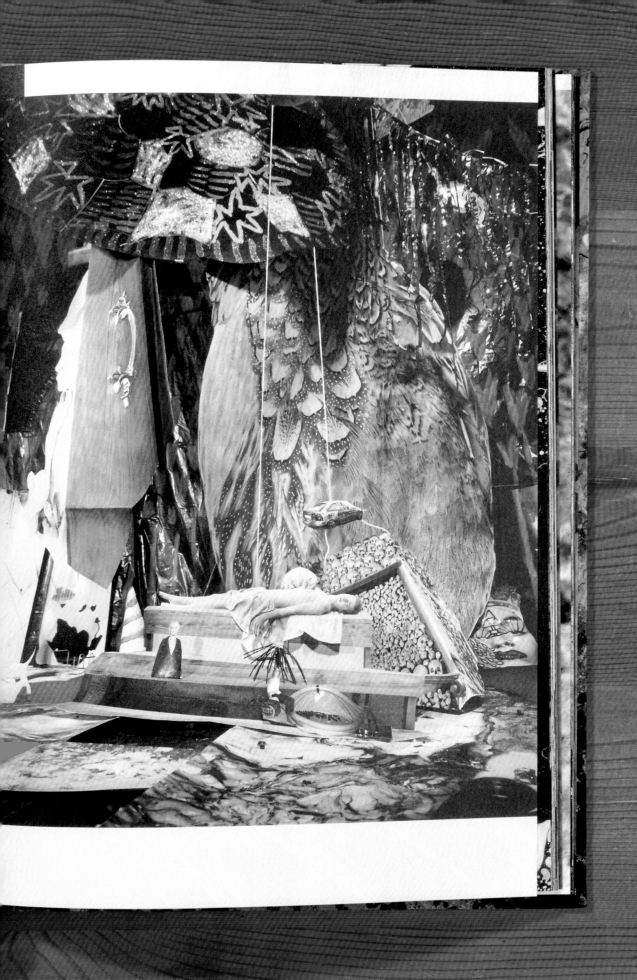

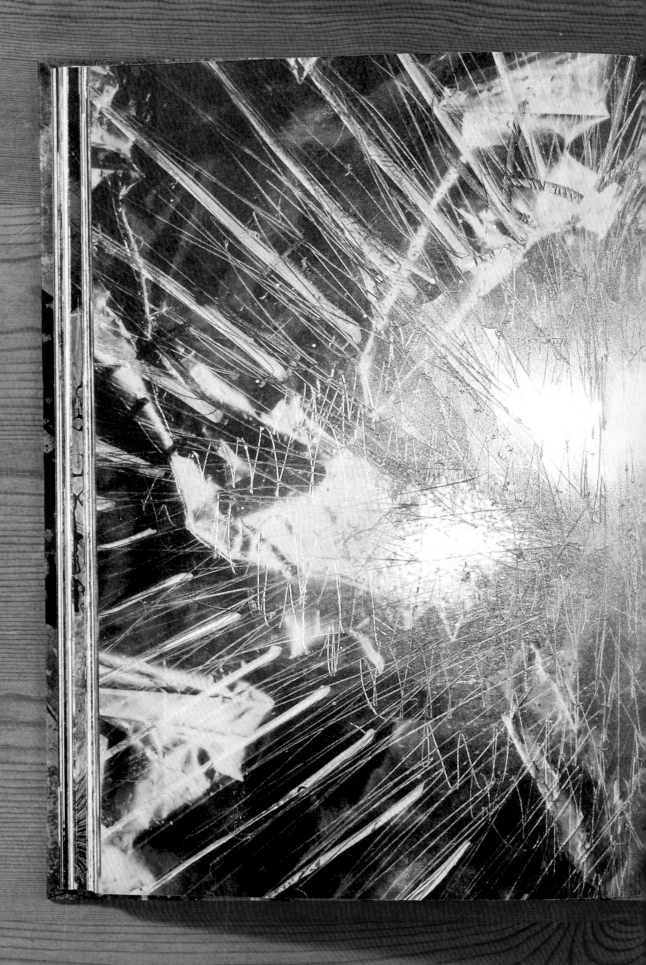

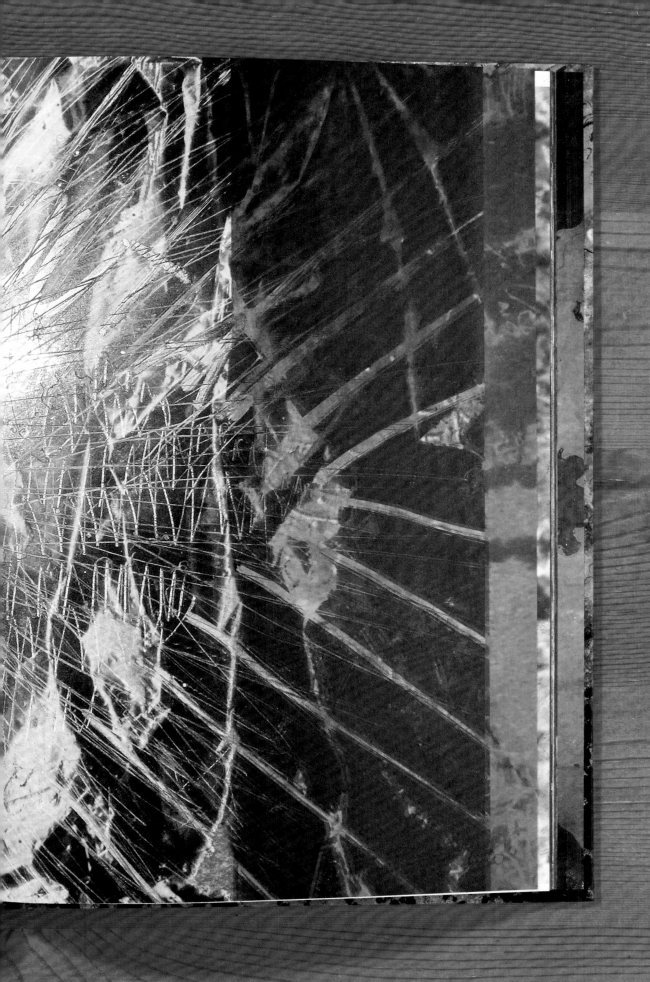

Title: Eyes that are like two suns
Artist: Luke Stettner
Additional contributor: Carmen Winant
Designer: Common Name
Printer: Haingraph, Seoul, South Korea
Publication date and place: September 2011 / New York, USA
Edition: 250
Format and binding: softcover / saddle stitched
Size: 8 1/2 x 11 in. (21.6 x 27.9 cm)
Number of pages and images: 47 pages / 34 images
Type of printing and paper: four-color offset / unknown
Retail price: 20 USD
Cost per unit: $$$

Luke Stettner's book *Eyes that are like two suns* was conceived in 2011 to coincide with a solo show of the same title at Kate Werble Gallery in New York. Stettner employs a range of different media in his work, and instead of a traditional show catalogue, he wanted to produce a publication that could be an extension of his practice. He compiled a series of photographs not included in the show, depicting graphic lines and shapes in shadow and light, and incorporated them into a design that uses folds throughout the book to create unexpected pairings. With texts reflecting on the content by writer and artist Carmen Winant, the publication becomes a sculptural addendum to the exhibition.

Folding the pages was an idea the designers Yoonjai Choi and Ken Meier had. It was really a way of forming abstract compositional pairings between disparate images, and made subtle allusion to some of photographs in the book. Sometimes you just need a simple, good idea.
—Luke Stettner

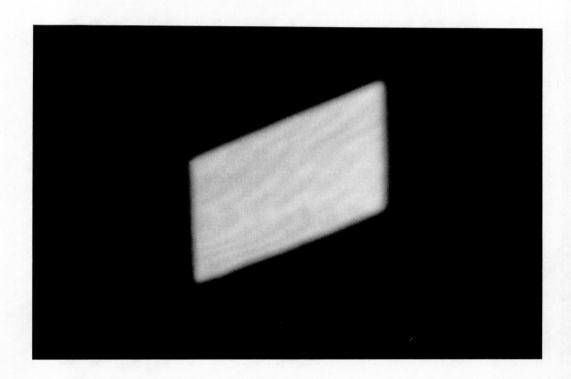

Eyes that are like two suns

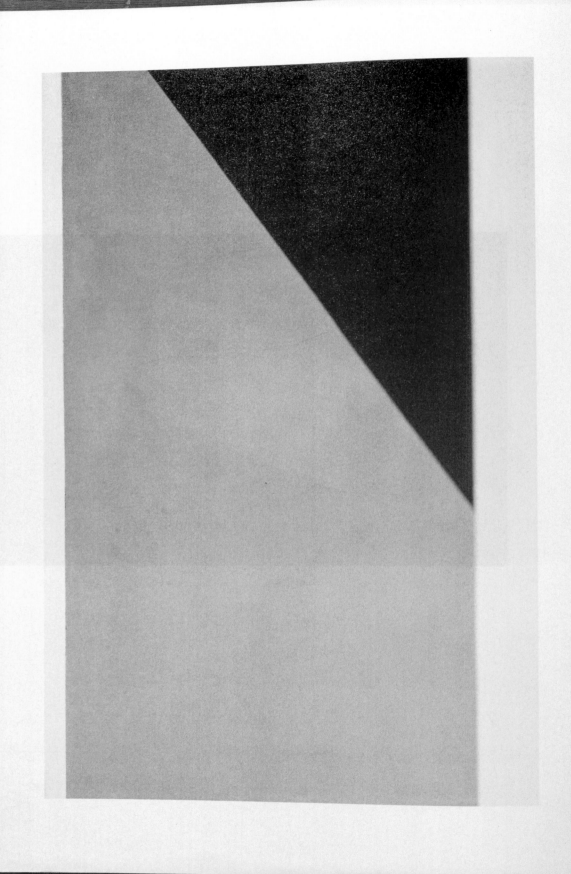

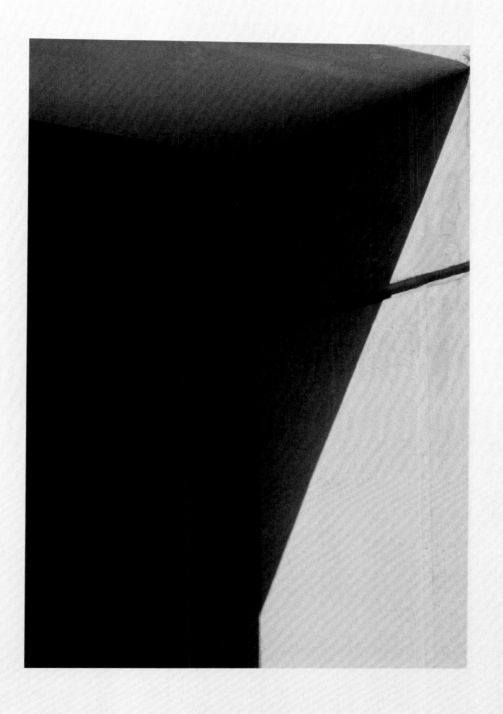

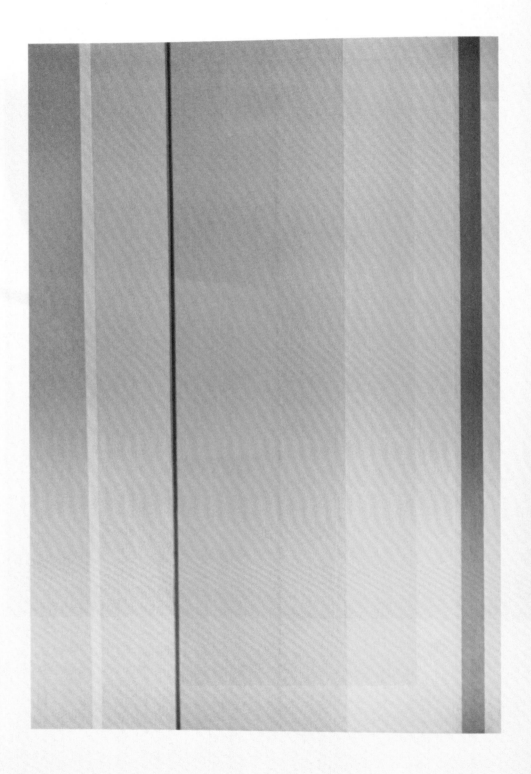

This comes as a re
does not prevent
'true' recognition
acknowledges our
to be relative and
and thereby unab
in the first place.
resisting, an onto
provokes connect
ledging the very l
threshold. Have y
ded to be blind in
desire to attempt
ness of our surro
partial experienc
In the moment of
ness, we enact th
condition of meta

ycho-
ne pro-
otograph
rd him
cent
s memory.
g in
nd refold-
story
nd page:
arrator
pes in
Though
each
foil and
fferent
sex
arily
never
ected.
cter
s directly
like
light.

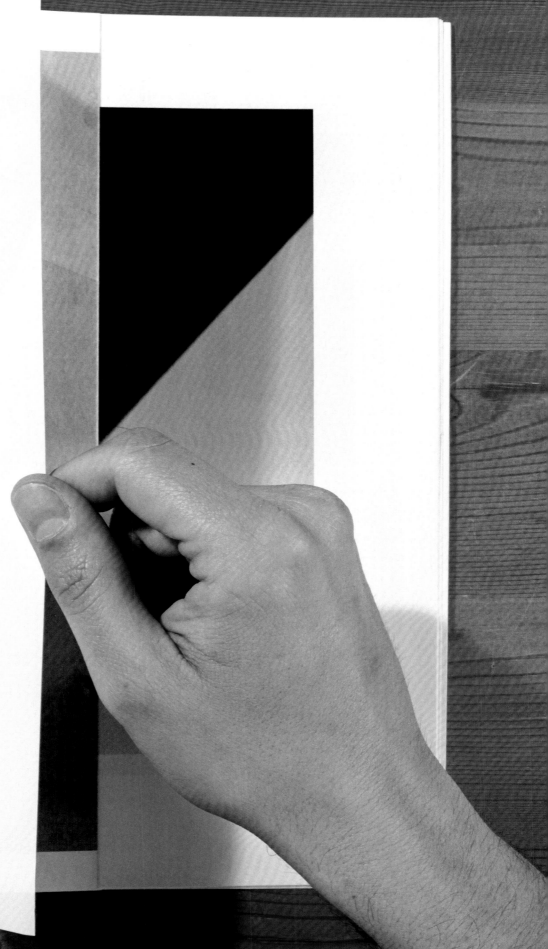

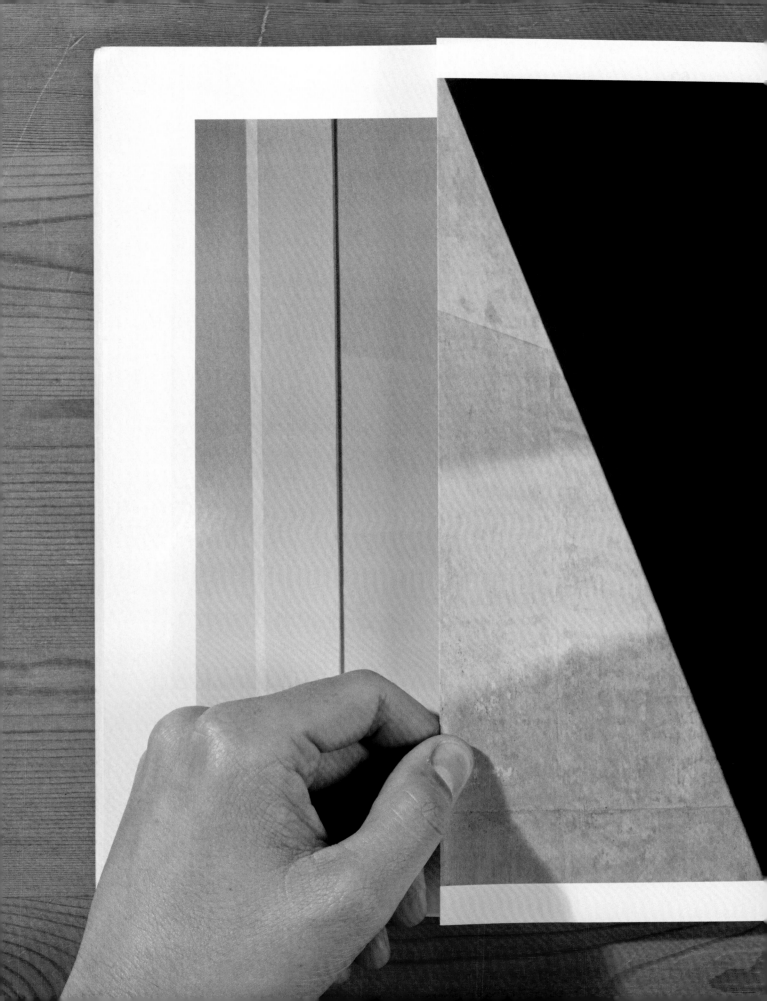

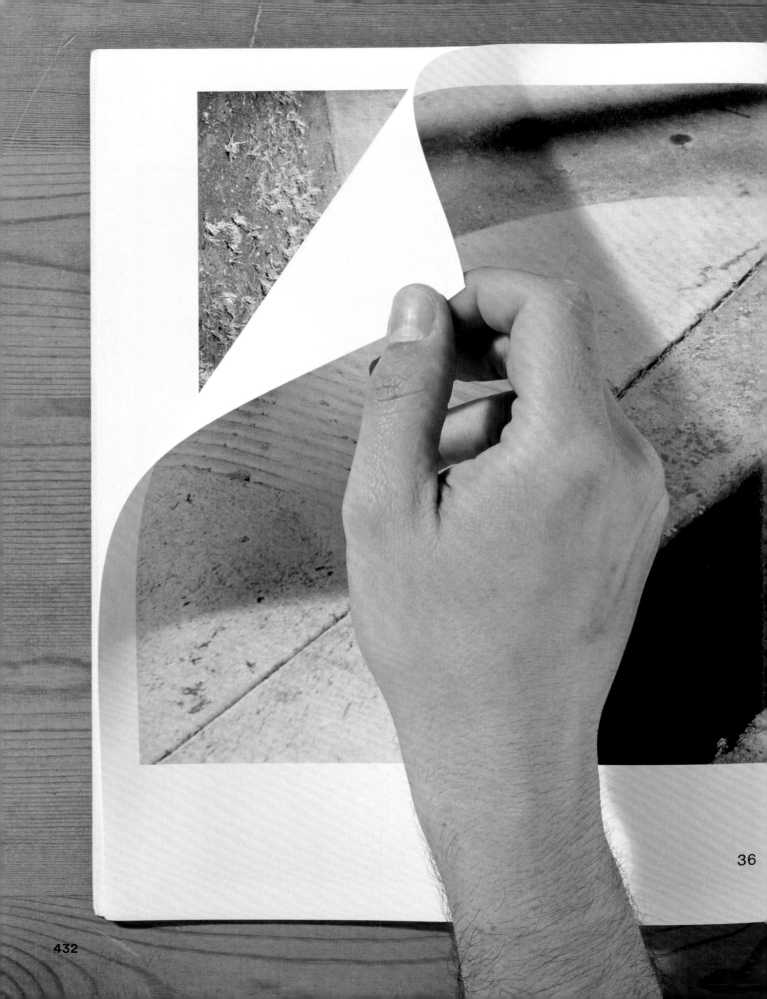

36

Title: The Photograph as Contemporary Art

Artist: Melinda Gibson

Additional contributors: Charlotte Cotton and Aaron Schuman

Designers: Kummer & Herrman

Editor: Melinda Gibson

Imprint: none

Printer: Robstolk, Amsterdam, the Netherlands

Publication date and place: September 2012 / Amsterdam, the Netherlands

Edition: 150

Format and binding: softcover / tapebound with linen spine

Size: 8 1/4 x 10 1/2 in. (21 x 26.7 cm)

Number of pages and images: 160 pages / 66 images

Type of printing and paper: offset / Munken Pure Rough 120gsm

Retail price: 125 GBP / 200 USD

Cost per unit: $$$$$

Book soundtrack: *Solo Piano* by Chilly Gonzales

Melinda Gibson takes an experimental and performative approach to artmaking. Her works are investigations, research-led and meticulous. Process is a fundamental part of her practice, and with previous live performances that saw her undertake such tasks as systematically smoking 250 books in a self-built smokehouse, it is clear there is an important labor-intensive undercurrent to her work. For *The Photograph as Contemporary Art*, Gibson took Charlotte Cotton's seminal 2004 photography theory book of the same name, and reworked and reappropriated it into an entirely new object. Slicing, splicing, cutting, and collaging, Gibson deconstructed the book again and again, in order to examine it both theoretically and conceptually. It was limited to a run of 150 copies, with each one taking three hours to complete. Mistakes and marks were left in, ensuring that each object was one-of-a-kind.

Performance plays an important role with my books, as a way to further consolidate the concept but also to present the medium in a new way—where tactility, labor, audience engagement, and the physical object are enhanced. You have to be open to new ideas that grow organically, expect the unexpected, and flourish in flexibility. Performances need planning; space, timing, and logistical constraints all need to be taken into account, while never losing sight of how this aids the book. A few questions I ask myself: is this contrived? Does it make sense conceptually? Does it enhance the visual pleasure of looking? —Melinda Gibson

THE PHOTO-GRAPH AS CONTEM-PORARY ART

Melinda Gibson

voyeurism. The infrequency with which other men appear (typically as clients or sexual partners of the women whom Araki photographs) is important in preserving this reading of the work. Sometimes the relationship between the photographer and his models is described as collaborative, to the extent that it is also suggested that Araki and his cameras are conduits for these women's sexual fantasies. Perhaps a more accurate description would be that the female subjects have a desire and curiosity to be in Araki's photo-shoots and to be part of his infamous oeuvre. Since his photography is considered to be a diary, one that promotes his genuine desire for these women, much of the potential debate about the possible pornographic and exploitative aspects of his work is curtailed. This shying away from obvious readings of Araki's images demonstrates how intimate photography can circumvent debates that surround so much other contemporary art photographers and photographic imagery in general.

American photographer and film director Larry Clark's (b. 1943) explicit portrayals of teenagers and young adults have, like the work of Goldin and Araki, been highly influential on contemporary photography. His books – *Tulsa* (1971), *Teenage Lust* (1983), *1992* (1992) and *The Perfect Childhood* (1993) – all

134. **Larry Clark**,
Untitled, 1972.

143

15

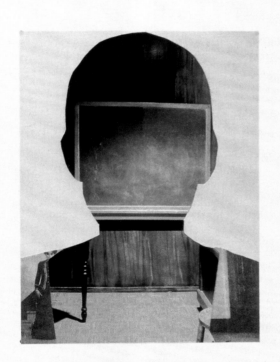

ıbstantial contribution to developing the phenomenological ffect of architectural tableau photography. Her photographs are ırge and backed onto (or directly printed onto) a canvas fabric ıat is pinned to gallery walls. *In the Course of Time, 6 (Factory, rakow)* [74] is over two metres in height and five metres in length. ı the presence of such a work, the viewer is offered an essentially ıysical relationship to the scene. The Polish factory is not life ze, but gives the viewer the feeling of approaching and being ɔout to enter the pictorial space. Another allusion could be to stage set moments before the performance begins. In the 1990s, ıuch of Collins's work was a meditation on post-Communist ɪrope. It traced the way contemporary life, shaped by both

22. Gillian Wearing.
Signs that say what you want them to say and not signs that say what someone else wants you to say,
1992–93.

30

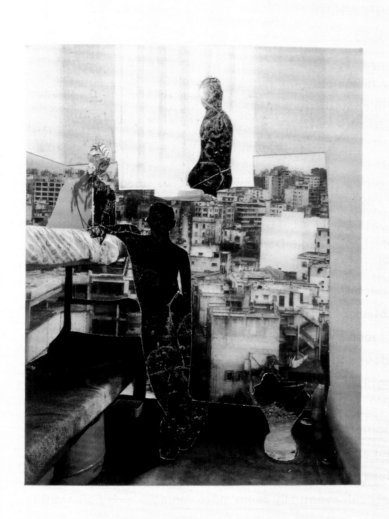

71

Title: The Book of Dictators

Artist: Nicolò Dante

Designers: Nicolò Dante and Heartfelt Studio

Editor: Corrado Cambiaghi

Imprint: Edizioni Scure

Printer: unknown

Publication date and place: 2011 / Milan, Italy

Edition: 300 copies

Format and binding: softcover / spiral bound

Size: 7 1/2 x 9 in. (19 x 23 cm)

Number of pages and images: 16 pages / 15 images

Type of printing and paper: silkscreen / uncoated 300gsm

Retail price: 22 EUR / 25 USD

Cost per unit: $$$

Book soundtrack: *Fresh Fruit for Rotting Vegetables* by Dead Kennedys

The Book of Dictators is the creation of designer Nicolò Dante, a satirical project conceived during the final year of Silvio Berlusconi's time in office. The form is simple: a spiral-bound, mix-and-match flipbook of dictators' faces which Dante sourced from various news archives and libraries. Each face is isolated against a black background and sliced into thirds so the reader can juxtapose the features of a variety of iconic dictators—Hitler's nose and signature moustache aligned with Kim Il-sung's pompadour and Castro's beard. The final page includes a template for you to paste in your own photograph—of yourself or your own "favorite" dictator.

The idea for *The Book of Dictators* was something I conceived years before its publication. I wrote it down in a notebook, then forgot about it. I rediscovered the notebook when I was moving. It's essential to collect all the ideas and inspiration you get, as very often something which does not persuade you immediately can eventually seem more valuable. —Nicolò Dante

THE BOOK OF DICTATORS

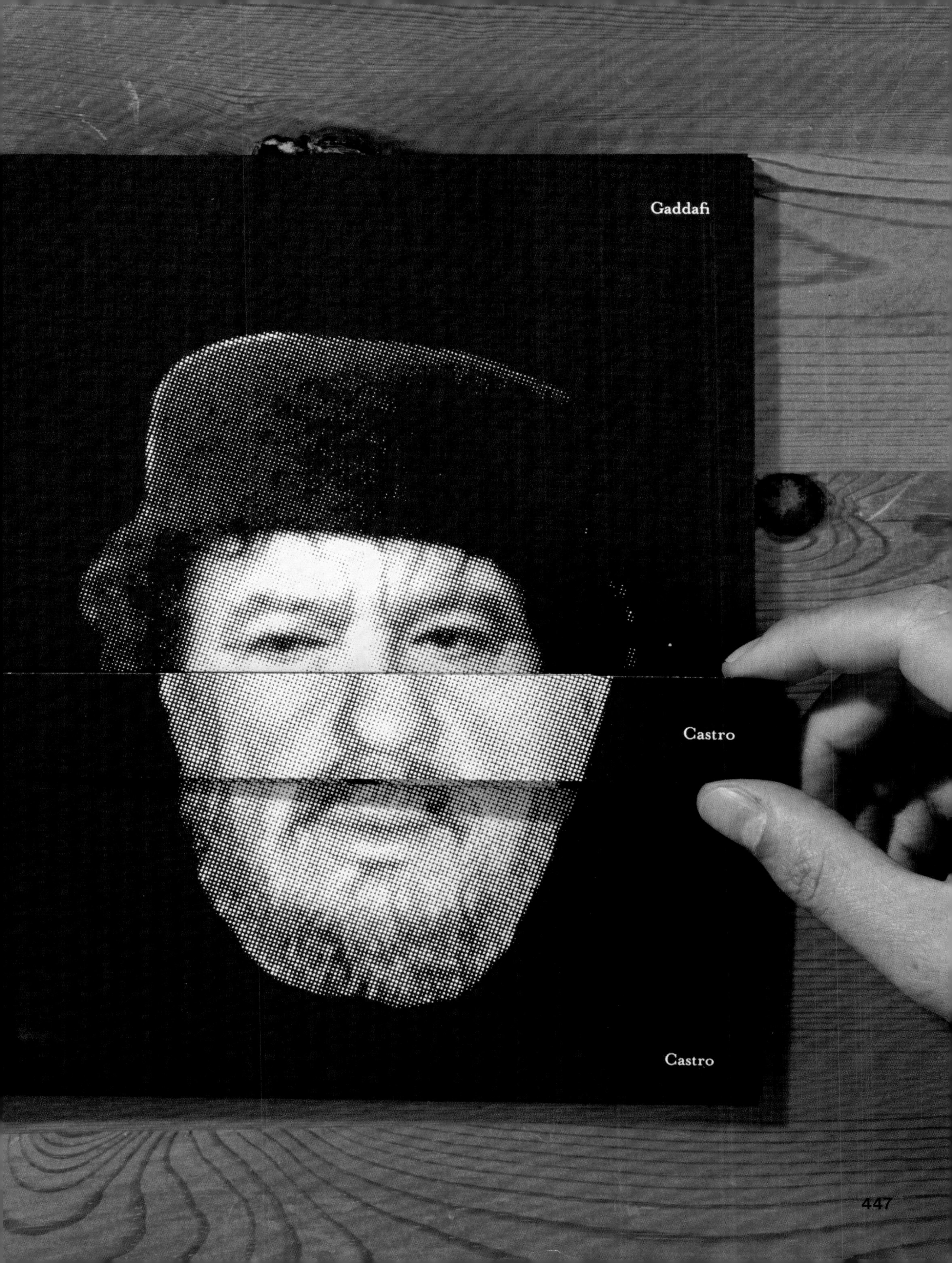

Gaddafi

Castro

Castro

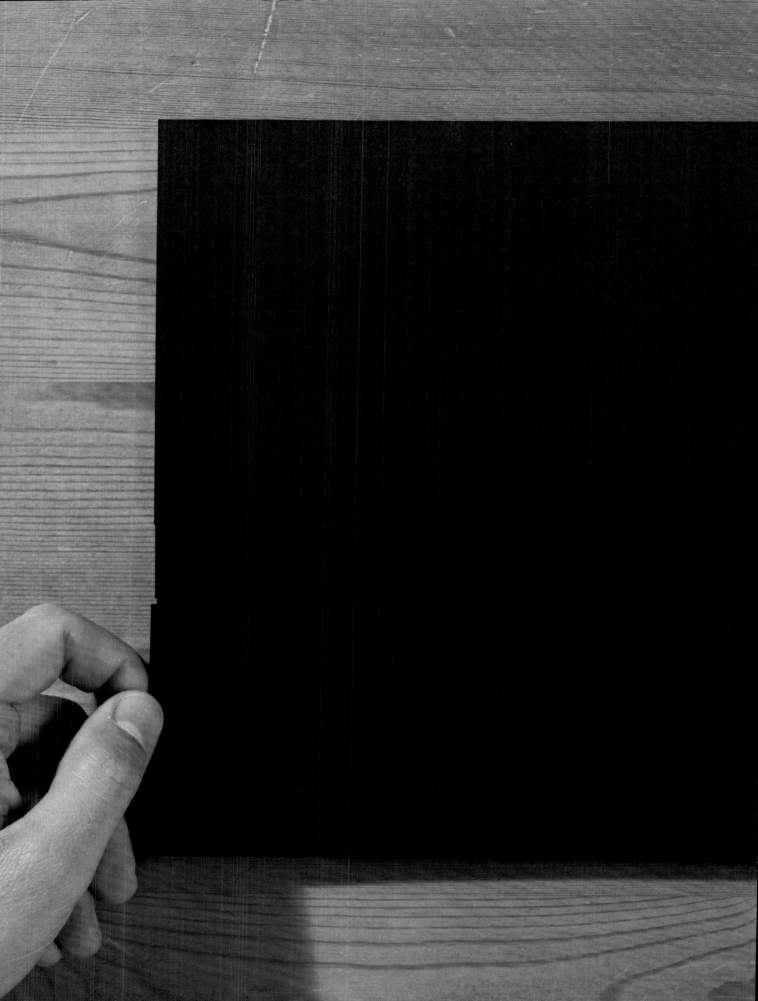

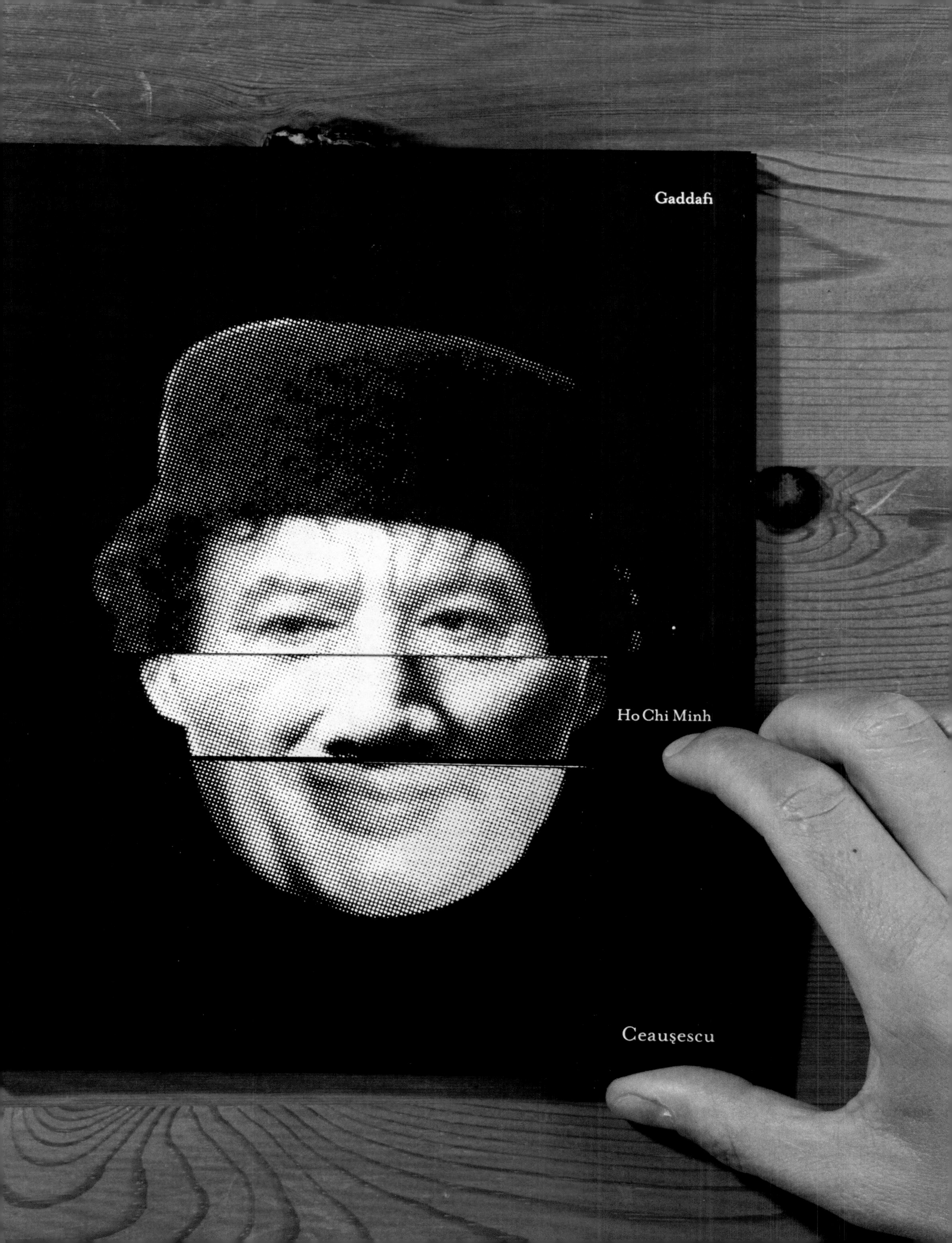

Gaddafi

Ho Chi Minh

Ceaușescu

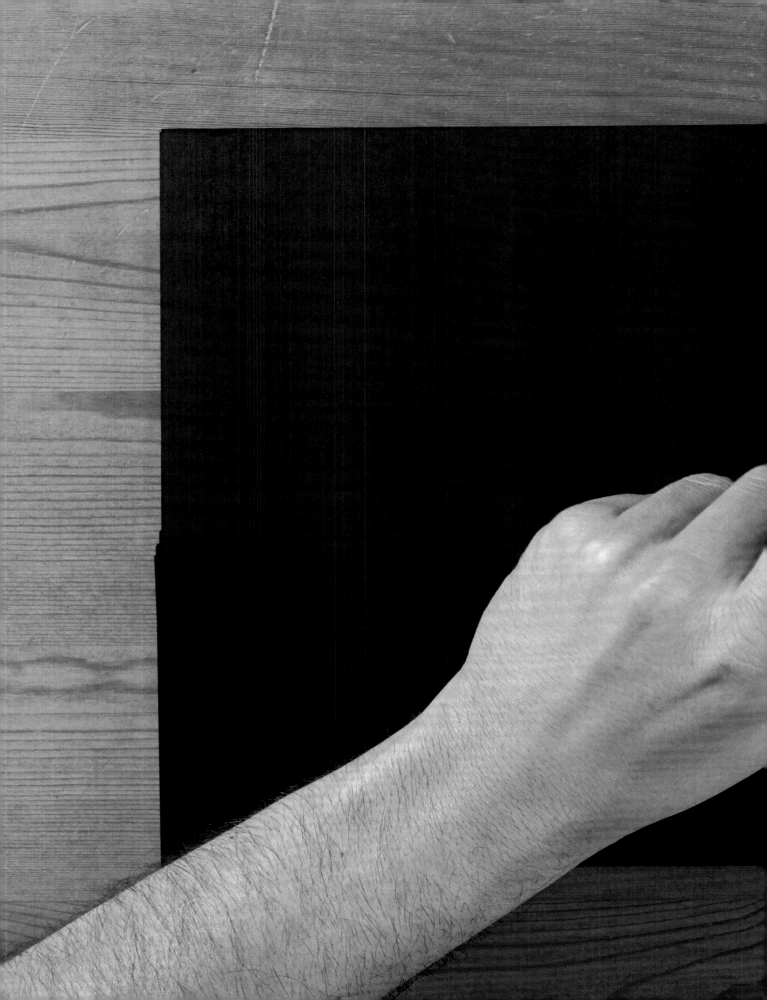

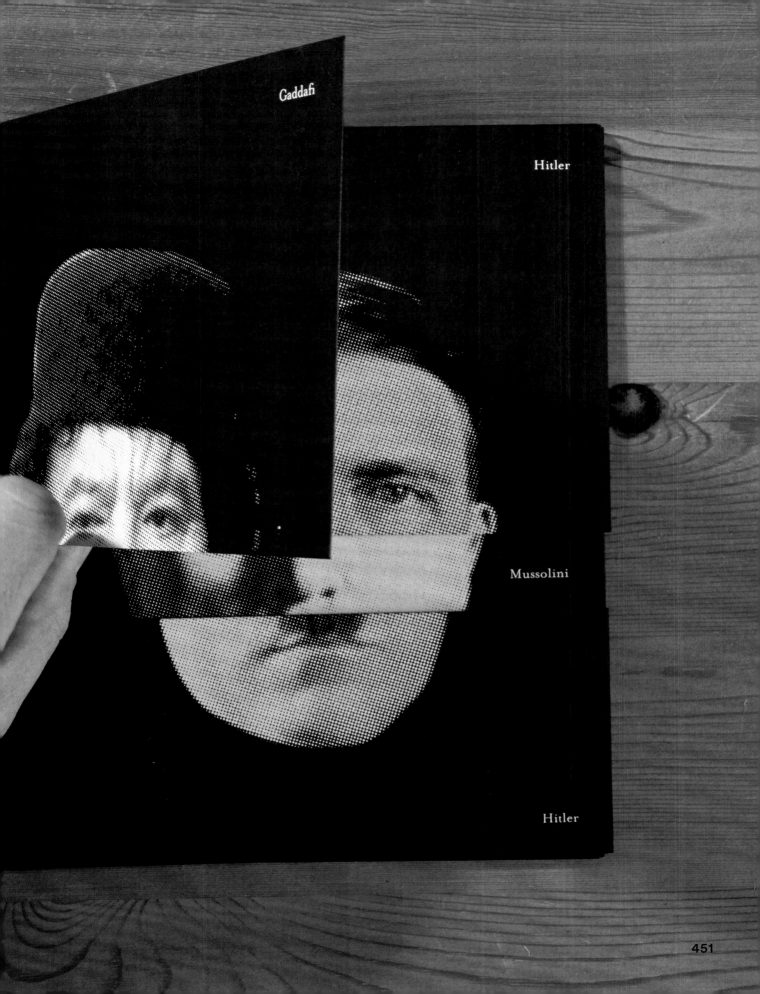

Gaddafi

Hitler

Mussolini

Hitler

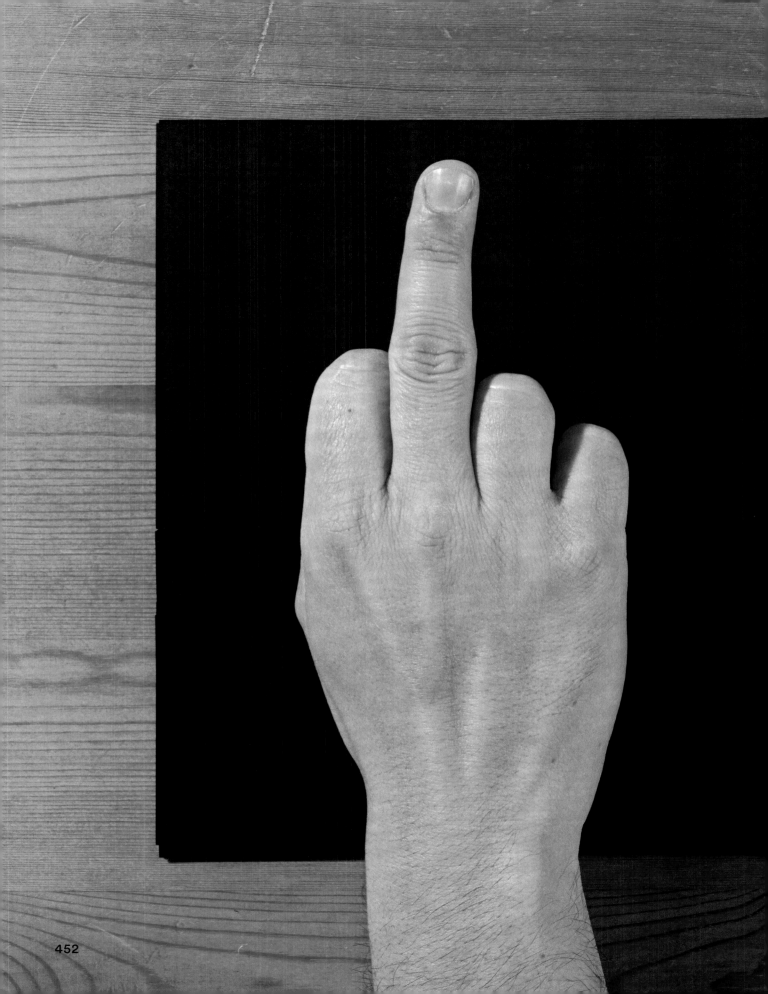

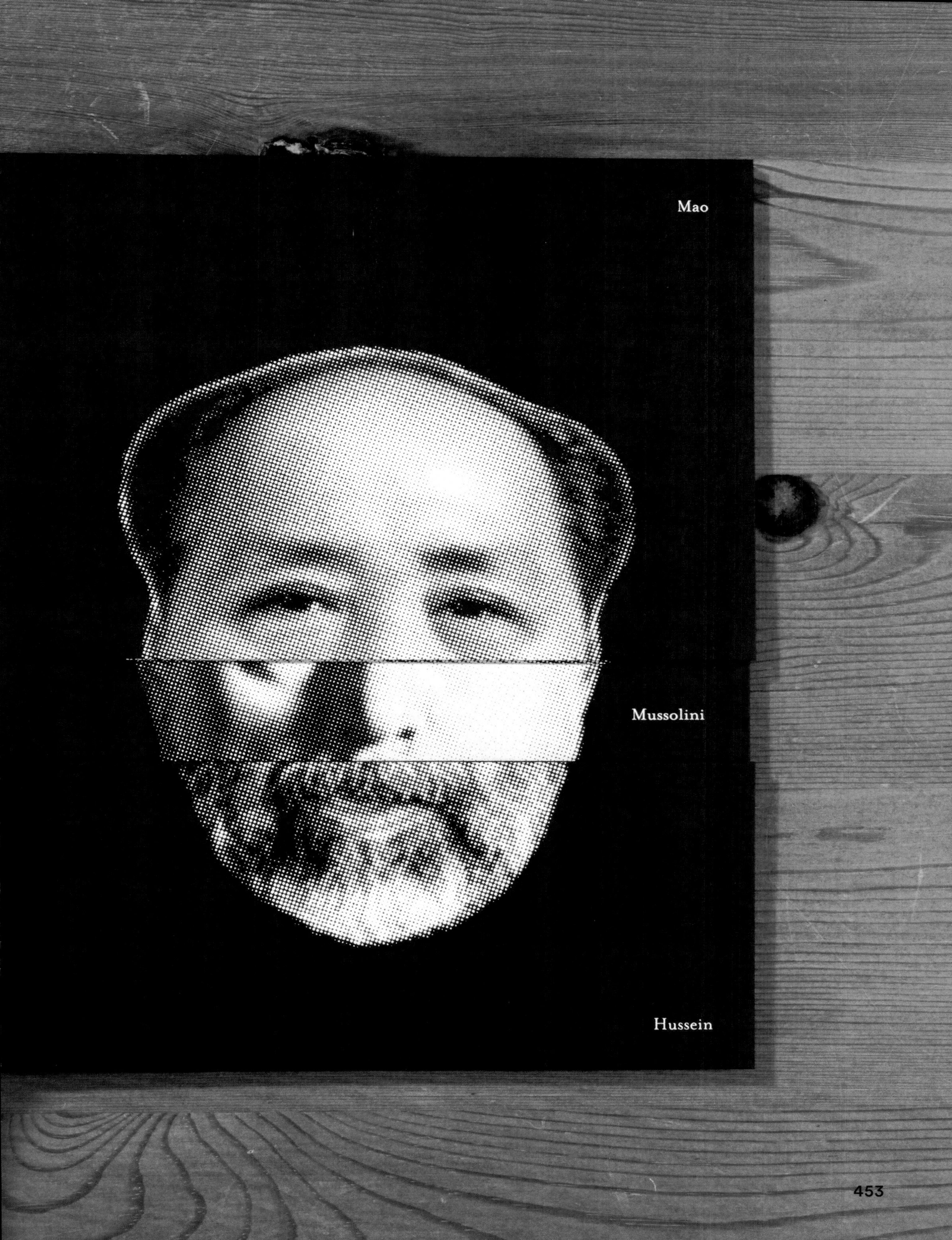

Mao

Mussolini

Hussein

Title: First Rate Second Hand 2012
Artists: Sophy Naess and Carmelle Safdie
Designers: Sophy Naess and Carmelle Safdie
Editors: Sophy Naess and Carmelle Safdie
Printer: Bridge Printing, Long Island City, New York, USA
Publication date and place: December 2011 / New York, USA
Edition: 190
Format and binding: wall calendar / spiral bound
Size: 11 6/8 x 8 1/4 in. (30 x 21 cm)
Number of pages and images: 28 pages / 16 images
Type of printing and paper: laser / unknown
Retail price: 20 USD
Cost per unit: $$

Book soundtrack: "Calendar Girl" by Neil Sedaka

Sophy Naess and Carmelle Safdie met at New York's Cooper Union in 2000, and have been creating an annual edition of their *First Rate Second Hand* calendar every year since 2006. Having spent time in different countries since graduating, they use the calendar as a way to continue their creative conversation despite the distance. Coming up with a seasonal sketch for each month, Naess and Safdie travel to different thrift stores in search of the items they need for costumes and props. Dressing up and being photographed in the outfits they put together, they use the store as their set, then return the articles of clothing to the rails—thus including the locations in their ongoing collaboration. The duo then collage themselves onto twelve different backdrops found online or in the New York Public Library Picture Collection, and produce a spiral-bound wall calendar.

These calendars mark time, and we are proud to look back at the ten years of our lives seen in this project. —Sophy Naess and Carmelle Safdie

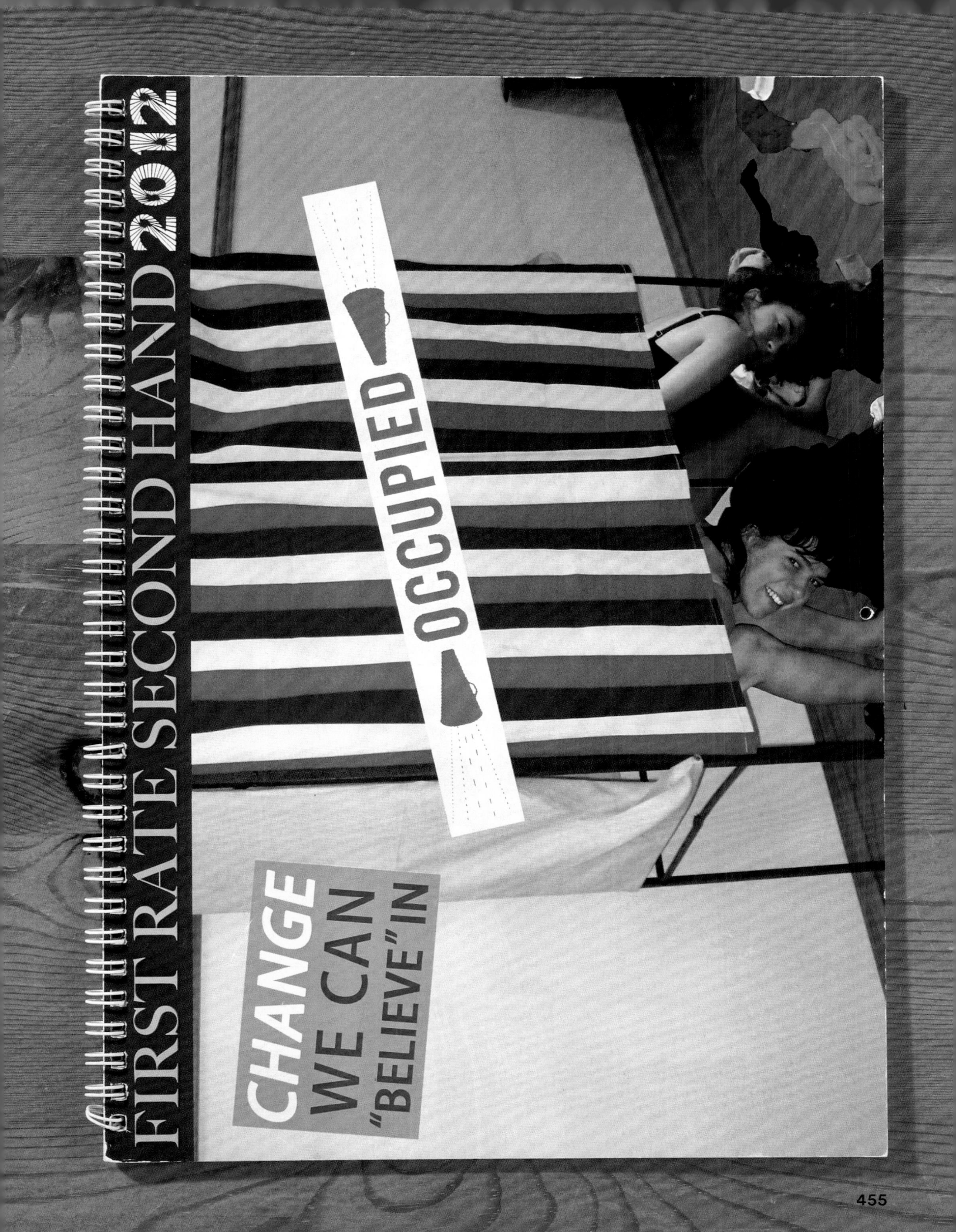

FIRST RATE SECOND HAND 2012

OCCUPIED

CHANGE WE CAN "BELIEVE" IN

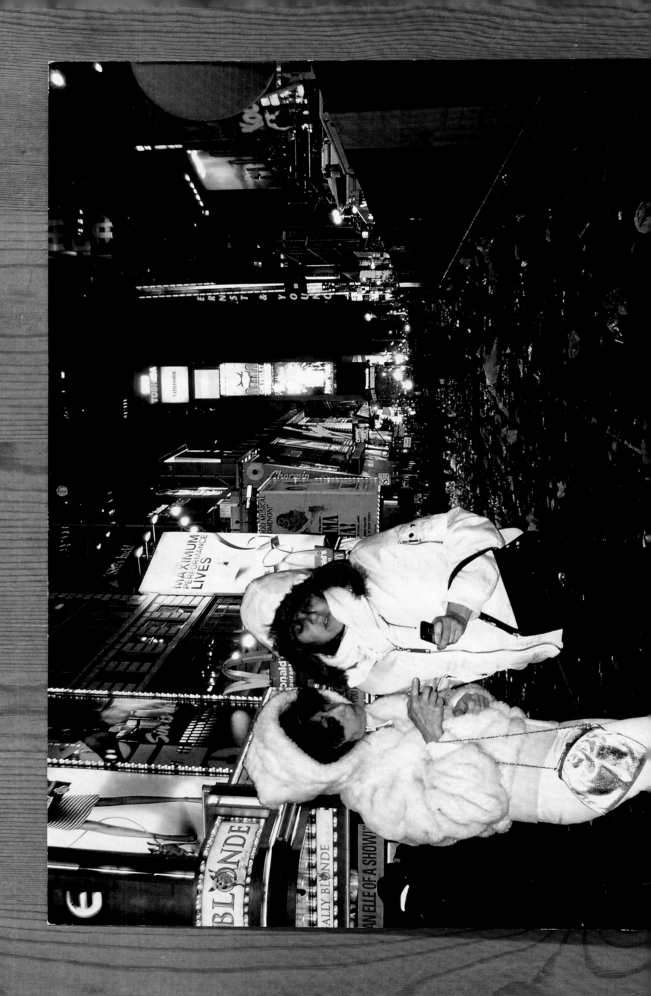

January

Sunday	Monday	Tuesday	Wednesday	Thursday	Friday	Saturday
1 *New Year's Day*	2	3	4	5	6	7
8	9	10	11	12	13	14
15	16 *Martin Luther King Day*	17	18	19	20	21
22	23 *Lunar New Year*	24	25	26	27	28
29	30	31				

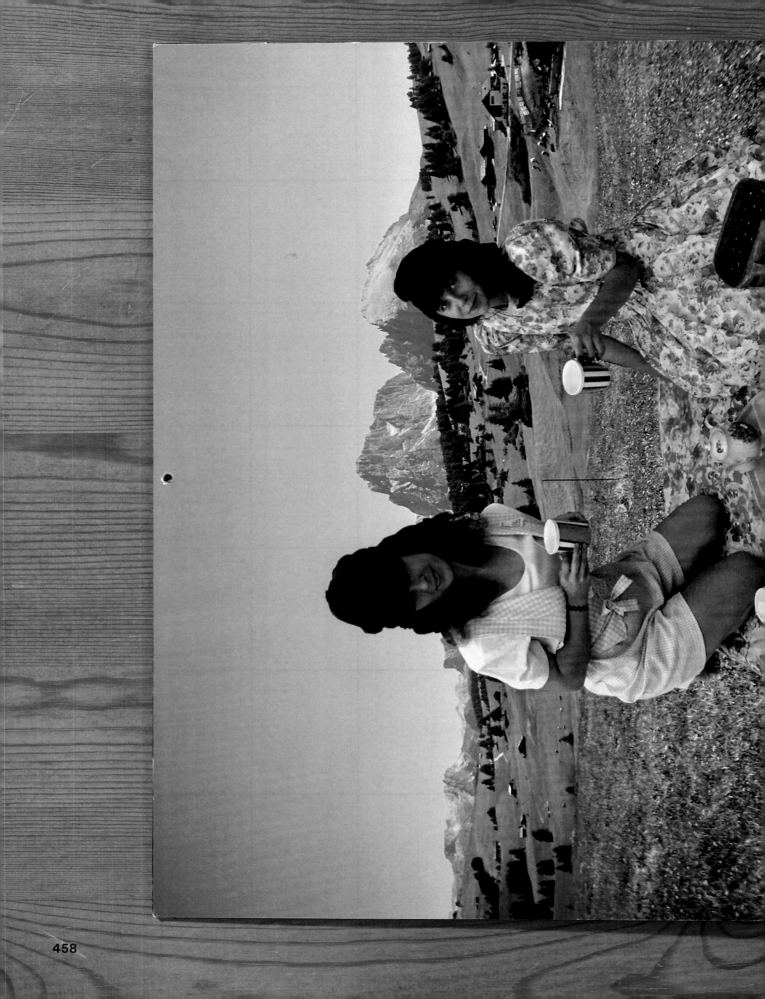

May

Sunday	Monday	Tuesday	Wednesday	Thursday	Friday	Saturday
		1	2	3	4	5 *Cinco de Mayo*
6	7	8	9	10	11	12
13 *Mother's Day*	14	15	16	17	18	19
20	21	22	23	24	25	26
27	28 *Memorial Day*	29	30	31		

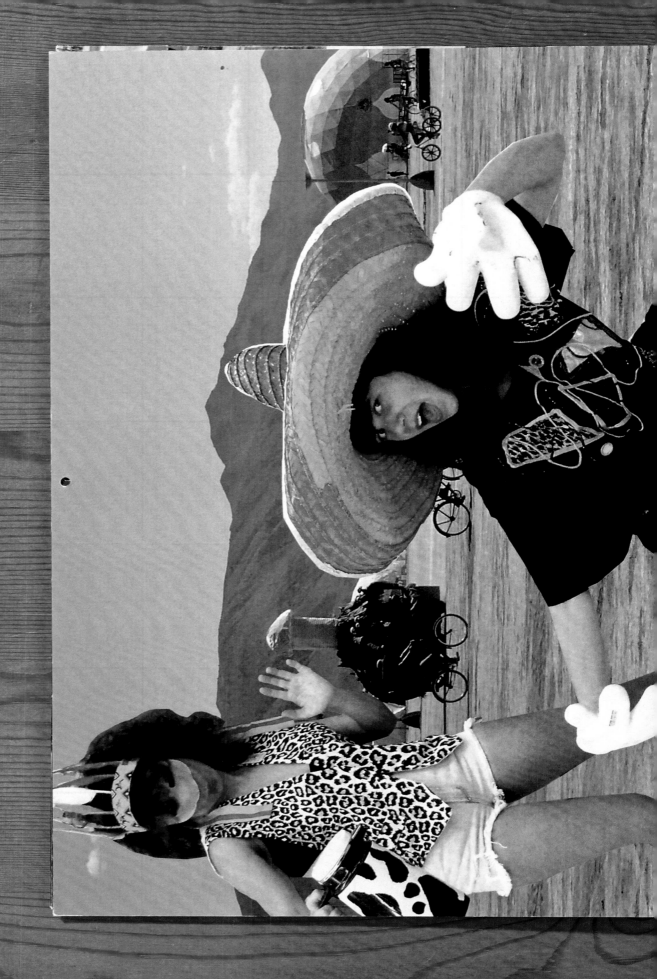

August

Sunday	Monday	Tuesday	Wednesday	Thursday	Friday	Saturday
			1	2	3	4
5	6	7	8	9	10	11
12	13	14 *Laylat al-Qadr*	15	16	17	18
19 *Eid-al-Fitr*	20	21	22	23	24	25
26	27	28	29	30	31	

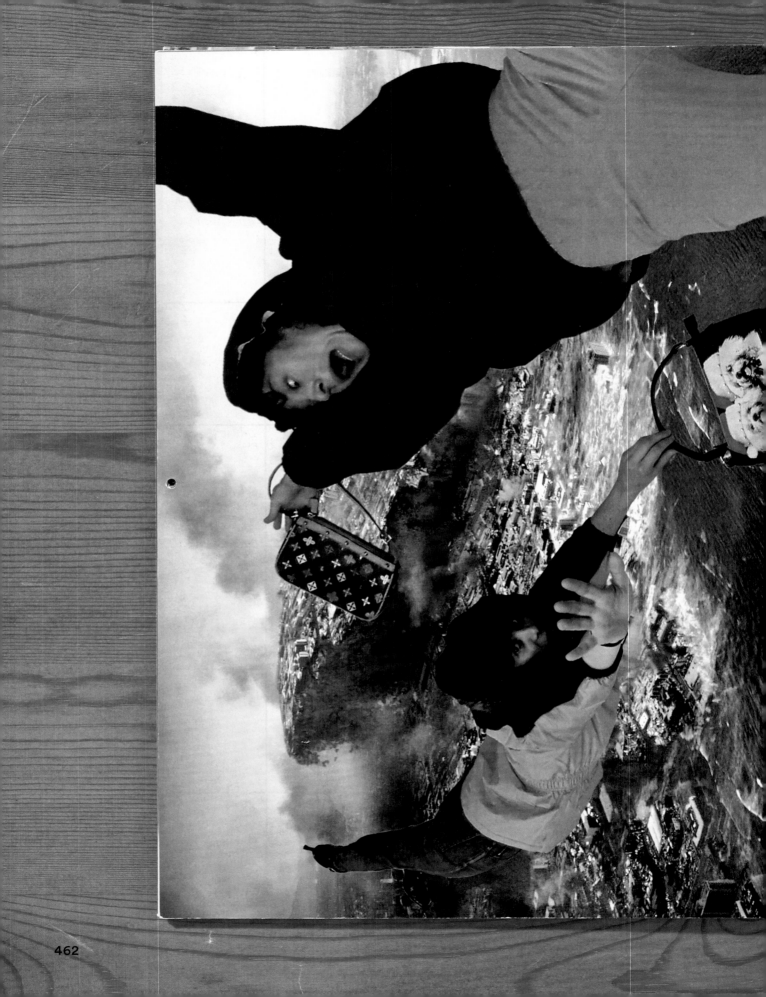

December

Sunday	Monday	Tuesday	Wednesday	Thursday	Friday	Saturday
						1
2	3	4	5	6	7	8
9 *First Day of Chanukah*	10	11	12	13	14	15
16 *Last Day of Chanukah*	17	18	19	20	21 LAST DAY OF MAYAN CALENDAR !!!!!!!! **HASTA LA VISTA BABY**	22
23	24 *Christmas Eve*	25 *Christmas Day*	26	27	28	29
30	31 *New Year's Eve*					

Title: 2013

Artist: Justin James Reed

Designer: Common Name

Editor: Ofer Wolberger

Imprint: Horses Think Press

Printer: self-printed

Publication date and place: May 2012 / New York, USA

Edition: 100

Format and binding: softcover with ultraviolet flashlight / unbound

Size: 9 1/2 x 13 in. (24 x 33 cm)

Number of pages and images: 24 pages / 16 images

Type of printing and paper: ink-jet with Firefly ink / Firefly dual-sided, non-OBA, warm white, matte, 220 gsm

Retail price: 75 USD

Cost per unit: $$$$$

Book soundtrack: BBC Radio 1—Friction mix by Blu Mar Ten

Printed using ultraviolet Firefly ink, *2013* requires a UV flashlight to illuminate the images on the white pages. Images of forests, landscapes, and abstractions are revealed, eerily appearing from the surface of the paper. From certain angles the images look almost 3-D—which Justin James Reed says was an unexpected element. The images' presentation not only comments on the instability of the photographic image, but also creates something of a photographic performance, which can only take place with the viewer's involvement. For Reed, the concept of book-as-object is important: for a 2014 book with a symbol for a title, he etched images into paper using a laser-engraving machine.

Finding a material that is directly related to the conceptual foundation of my work is crucial. In the case of *2013*, it was discovering ink that can only be viewed under an ultraviolet light source. It provided a platform for investigating many of the ideas I was thinking about at that time. The content of the book is almost entirely informed by its materials, and their uniqueness pushed me to reconsider the viewing experience itself. I see the book as a form open to interpretation; exploring the links between structure and concept is exciting, and a critical method for conveying ideas. —Justin James Reed

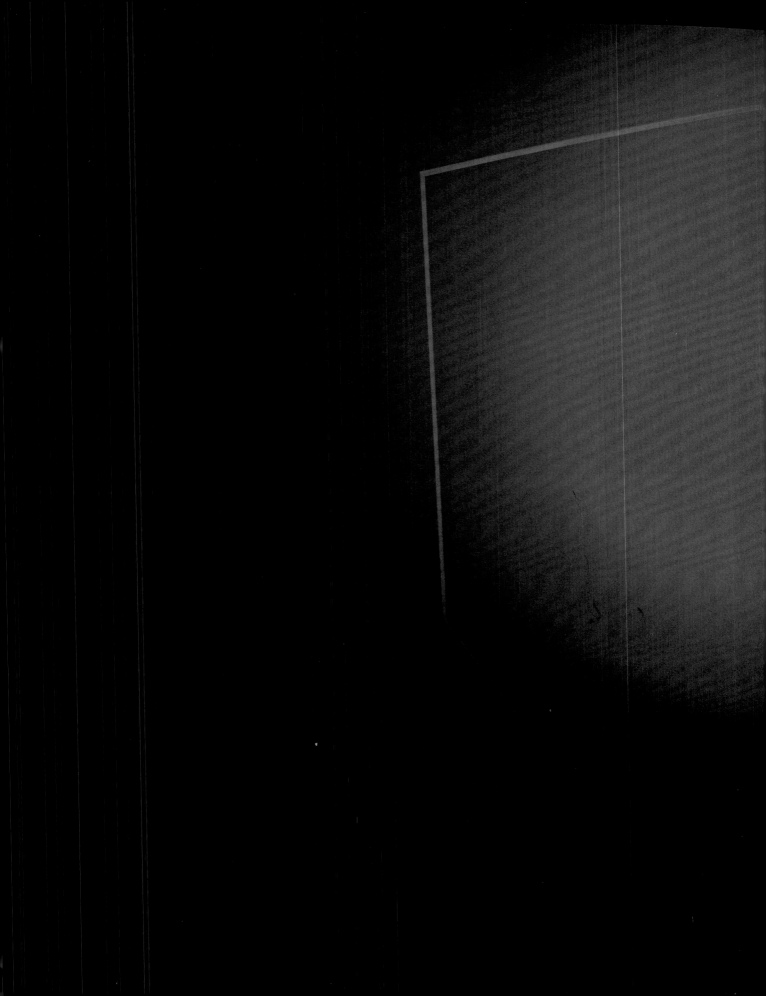

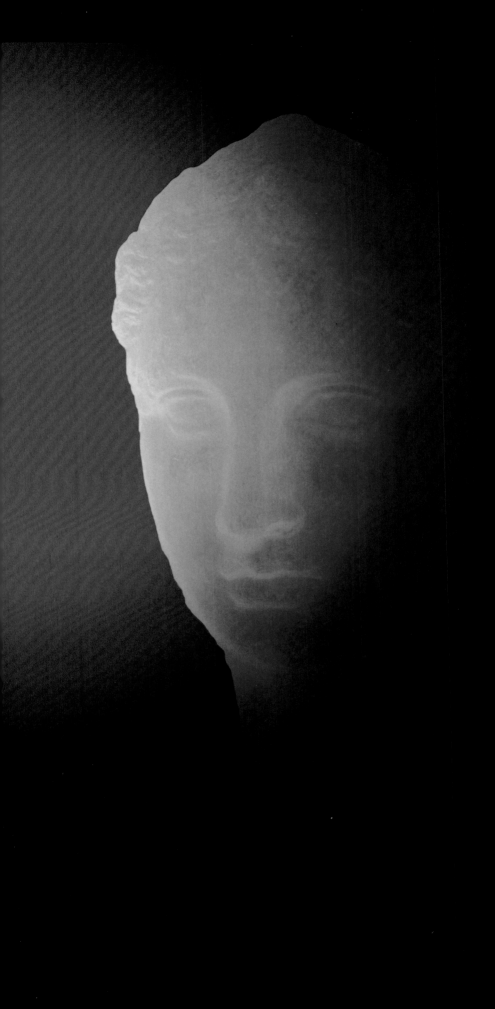

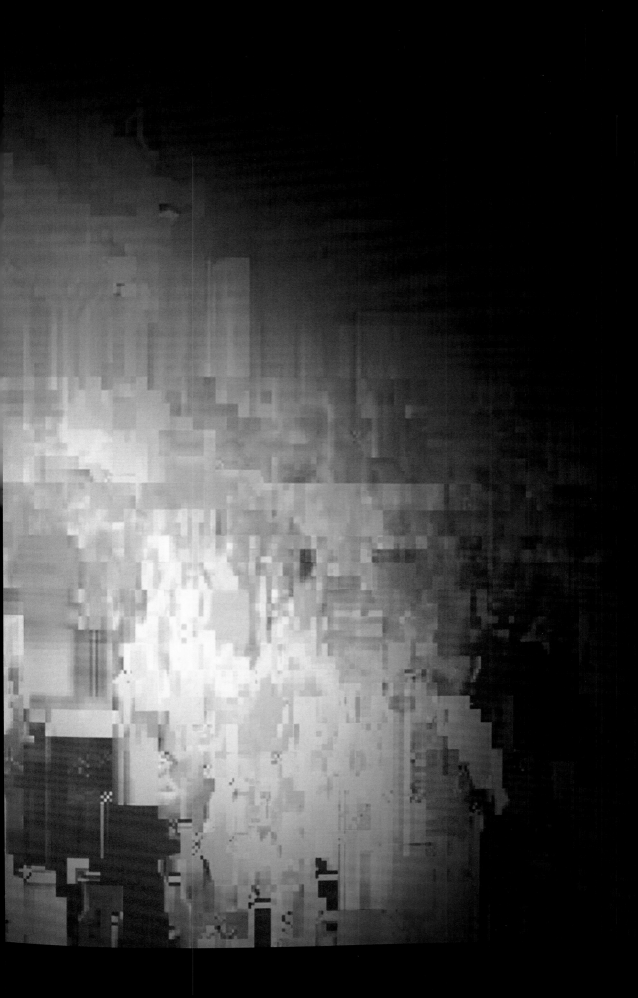

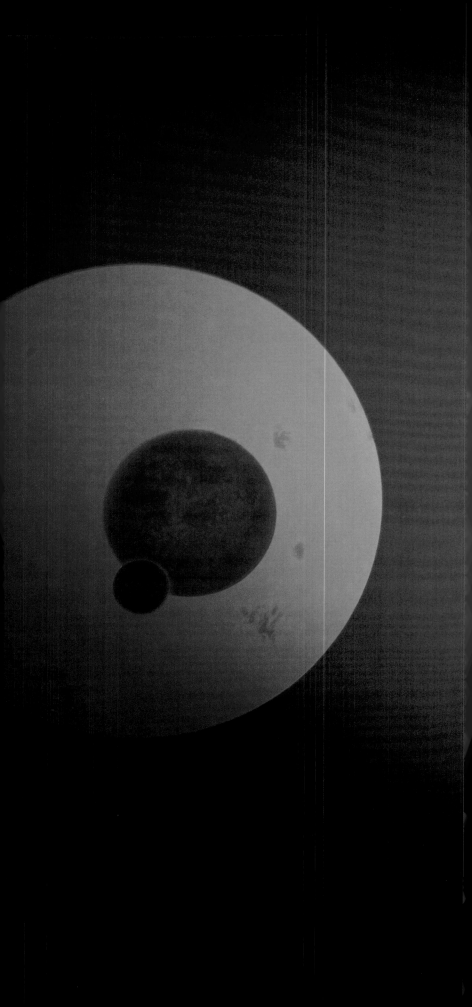

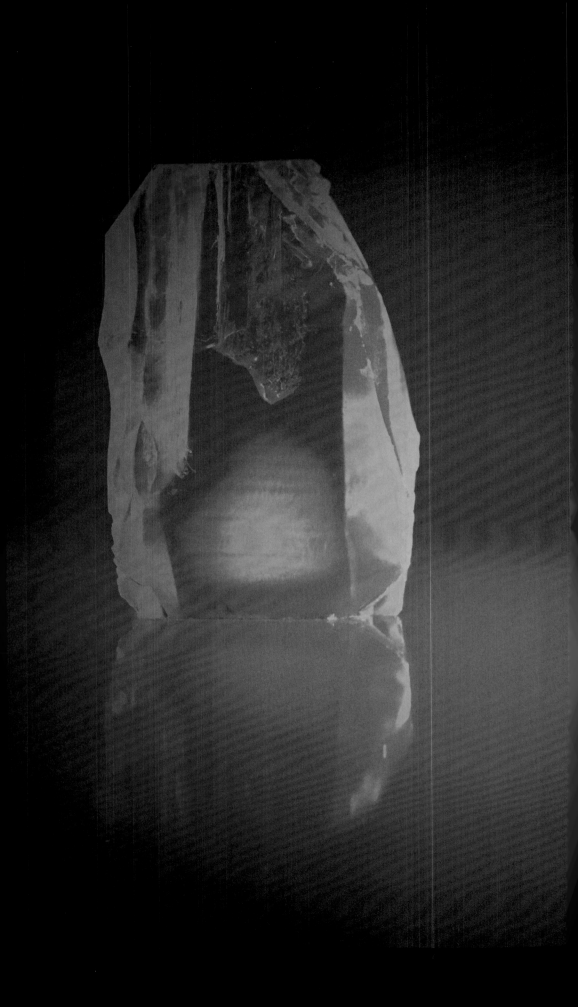

Title: Nudisme

Artists: Jason Fulford and Tamara Shopsin

Designers: Jason Fulford and Tamara Shopsin

Imprint: J&L Books

Printer: Speed Graphics, Scranton, Pennsylvania, USA

Edition: 250

Publication date and place: 2008 / Scranton, Pennsylvania, USA

Format and binding: softcover / saddle stitched

Size: 6 x 9 in. (15.2 x 22.9 cm)

Number of pages and images: 64 pages / 0 images

Type of printing and paper: offset / uncoated 118.4gsm

Retail price: 12 USD

Cost per unit: $

Book soundtrack: *4'33"* by John Cage

American photographer Jason Fulford is in the business of visual puzzles, pairing his photographs with slices of text in the form of riddles and stories for the reader to solve. As well as running his imprint J&L Books with cofounder Leanne Shapton, Fulford releases a high volume of photobooks, both self-published and otherwise. *Nudisme* is a playful object made in collaboration with his wife, the designer and writer Tamara Shopsin: a recreation of the book that appears in the hands of the protagonist in the opening scene of Jean Cocteau's classic 1950 film, *Orpheus*. As in the film, every page in the book is blank. In the film, another character explains the book to Orpheus, who calls the blank book "absurd." The other replies, "Less absurd than if it were full of absurd writing. No excess is absurd. Orpheus, your gravest fault is knowing how to get away with going too far."

We "printed" this book with an ornery man named Walter, who runs a small print shop in Scranton. He was a little confused by the book. He called it "Nude-Is-Me," and when we picked up the 250 copies, he said, "Good luck with that." —Jason Fulford

NUDISME

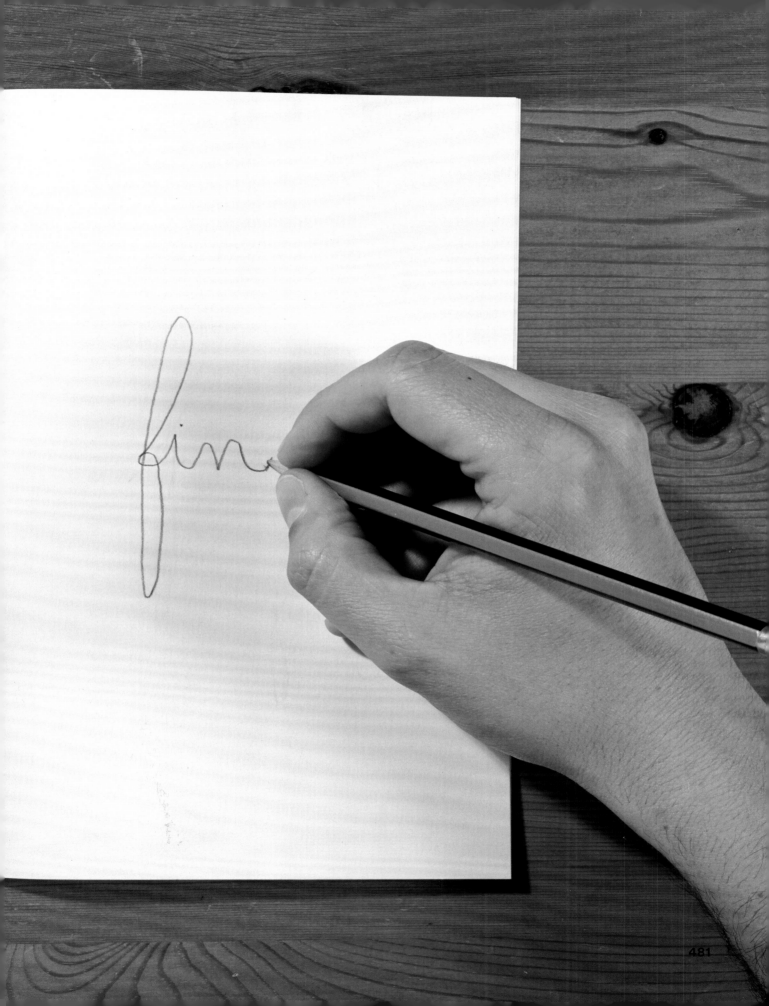

Self Publish, Be Happy Manual

by Bruno Ceschel

Photographs by Nicolas Haeni
and Thomas Rousset

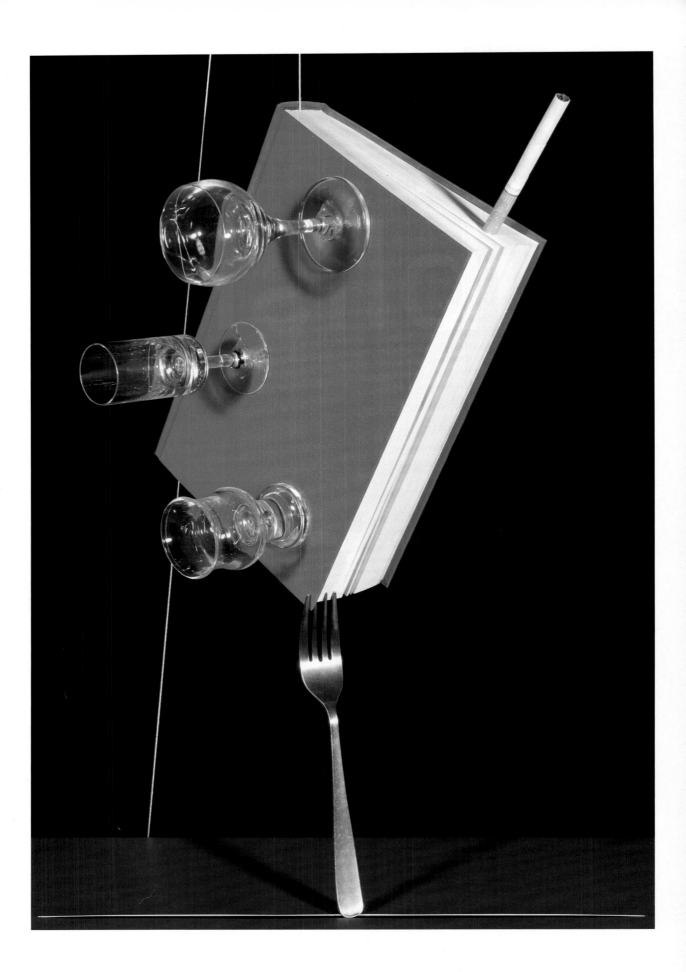

1

How on earth am I going to be able to make a photobook?

The first thing you must do is demystify the idea of the photobook. As soon as you demolish every single convention about what a photobook should be, you will free yourself to dream up something new, exciting, and—most important—completely doable.

Of course you love the classic, offset-printed, hardcover photobook! Who doesn't? But this love should not prevent you from making your own book. Any progress in society is cast against a preexisting set of norms or expectations. Artists are often at the forefront of cultural revolutions, challenging the status quo. Now more than ever, the tools you need are right in front of you. Digital tools for printing and disseminating offer easy (and cheap) means to make publications and get them out into the world.

The question here should really be: how on earth could I *not* make a photobook?

2
How to think of a book as a journey, not a destination

Think about the visceral pleasure of making a book, rather than being preoccupied with publishing something that will make money. Nor should you think about making something that will be selected for the next best-of list, propelling you to stardom. Making a book should be both challenging and fun. It should be an adventure that will make you aware of your own practice, ideas, knowledge, and skills. An adventure that might lead to creating something great—or not, which is also OK, so long as the journey was worthwhile.

Another thing you can do to free yourself from performance anxiety is think of your book as being in flux. Access to (high-quality, inexpensive) digital printing allows you to print a publication in quantities as small as just one at a time. And each time you print, the publication can change; you can experiment with different layouts, add photos, correct mistakes, and upload new photo files if they didn't print as hoped. You might as well embrace the technological possibilities, and conceive of your publication as a malleable object (p. 110).

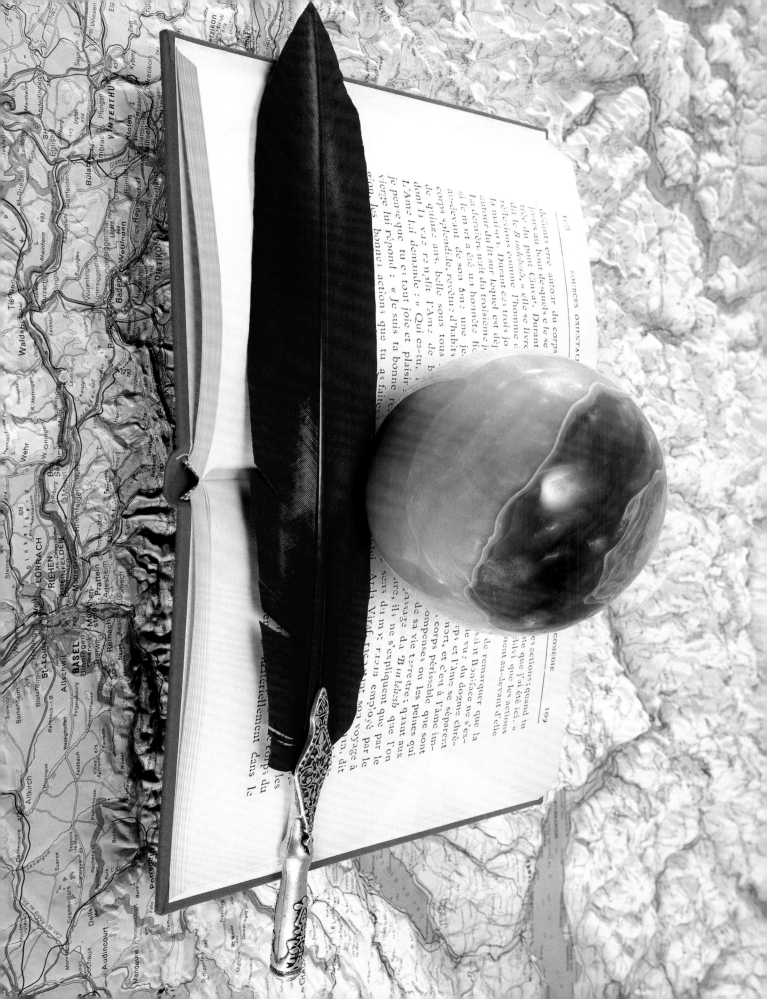

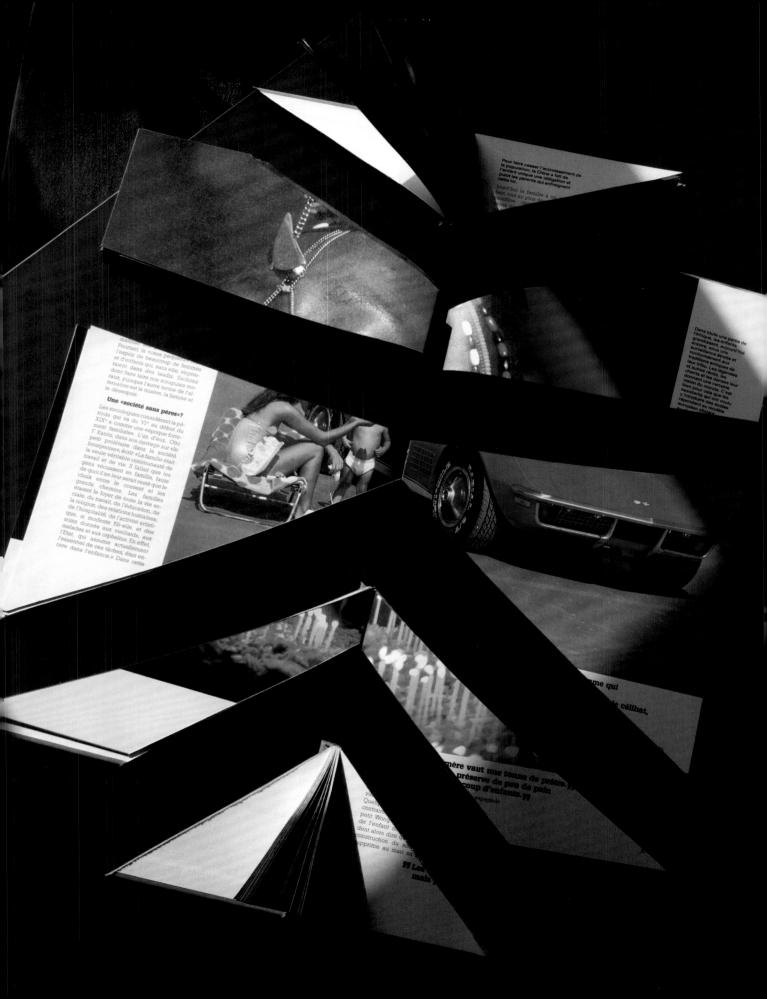

Pour faire cesser l'accroissement de la population, la Chine a fait de l'enfant unique une obligation et punit les parents qui enfreignent cette loi.

Dans toute une partie de l'Afrique, les enfants grandissent, aujourd'hui encore, sous une surveillance étroite et conforme aux traditions antiques de leur tribu. Les légendes et autres récits, les chants et les danses donnent une certaine vision du monde. C'est bien pour cela que les ecclésiastiques qui ont voulu y introduire des écoles répondant au modèle européen situent...

maintenant.

Pourtant, la «casa pequeña» l'espoir de beaucoup de femmes et d'enfants qui, sans elle, végéteraient dans des taudis. Sachons donc faire taire nos scrupules moraux, puisque l'autre terme de l'alternative est la misère, la famine et le désespoir.

Une «société sans pères»?

Les sociologues considèrent la période qui va du VI° au début du XIX° s. comme une époque fortement familiales. L'un d'eux, Otto F. Kanitz, dans son ouvrage sur «le petit prolétaire dans la société bourgeoise», écrit «La famille était la seule véritable communauté de travail et de vie. Il fallait que les gens vécussent en famille, faute de quoi il ne leur serait resté que le choix entre le couvent et les grands chemins. Les familles étaient le foyer de toute la vie sociale, du travail, de l'éducation, de la religion, des relations humaines, de l'hospitalité, de l'activité artistique, si modeste fût-elle, et des soins donnés aux vieillards, aux malades et aux orphelins. En effet, l'Etat, qui assume actuellement l'essentiel de ces tâches, était encore dans l'enfance.» Dans cette

...me qui

...é célibat,

...mère vaut une tonne de prêtre.
...préserve de peu de pain
...coup d'enfants.

espagnol

Quel...
contrai...
petit Wong...
de l'enfant n...
dent alors dire q...
construction du so...
supprime au mari es...

Le...
mais...

3
How to edit your photographs

Editing—meaning selecting which images will go in the book—is a cruel job, especially if you're the one who made the photographs. Sometimes it feels like a real sacrifice. Without getting too biblical about it, you have to be strong and brutal. You have to leave behind your emotional attachment to the images in order to serve the interest of your book project. It doesn't matter if you waited twenty years for the eclipse: if the photo you took of it doesn't work, just let it go.

To get going, group the photos by subject, theme, aesthetic, color, or composition. Group and regroup until you feel you have begun to make sense of the work. Dealing with hundreds of photos might feel overwhelming, but smaller groups are much easier to handle. The groups will also help you to see what you do or don't have, and help you see patterns emerge within and between your photographs. Then, start selecting the good ones. Keep two things in mind while you do this: the intrinsic quality of each photograph, and its function or role in the overall project. Sometimes a good photograph will simply not fit the message or concept you are trying to portray. Be willing to kill it.

Often self-published books suffer from self-indulgent photographers who cannot be objective and keep far too many photos in the edit, compromising the final result. If you feel you are one of those, ask for help from trusted colleagues, friends, or editors.

4
How to sequence your photographs

After editing the selection down to a manageable group of functional or meaningful pictures, it is time to create a sequence. If you think of the photobook as a film, and of the spreads as scenes, then you can think about how to create those individual scenes, and how they build the narrative of the book. I strongly recommend that you print out the images. They don't need to be photographic prints—just small print-outs that give the pictures a physicality. Start pinning them on the wall. If you are using strict criteria to order them chronologically (p. 172), conceptually (p. 74), or by following your visual instinct (p. 416), seeing the images on the wall will help you cement the sequence.

Often new and unexpected relationships emerge and new ideas can form. If you don't know where to start, then why not form groups of images like constellations (p. 82)? Don't stress out over creating a linear sequence. Just start exploring relationships between photographs.

Ideally, leave the sequence to breathe on your wall for a while; let it sit and return to it, maybe showing it to a few trusted people (but remember the old adage about "too many cooks!"). You will see that, very slowly, the sequence will begin to come together. When the sequence feels right, you are ready to think about how to turn it into a book!

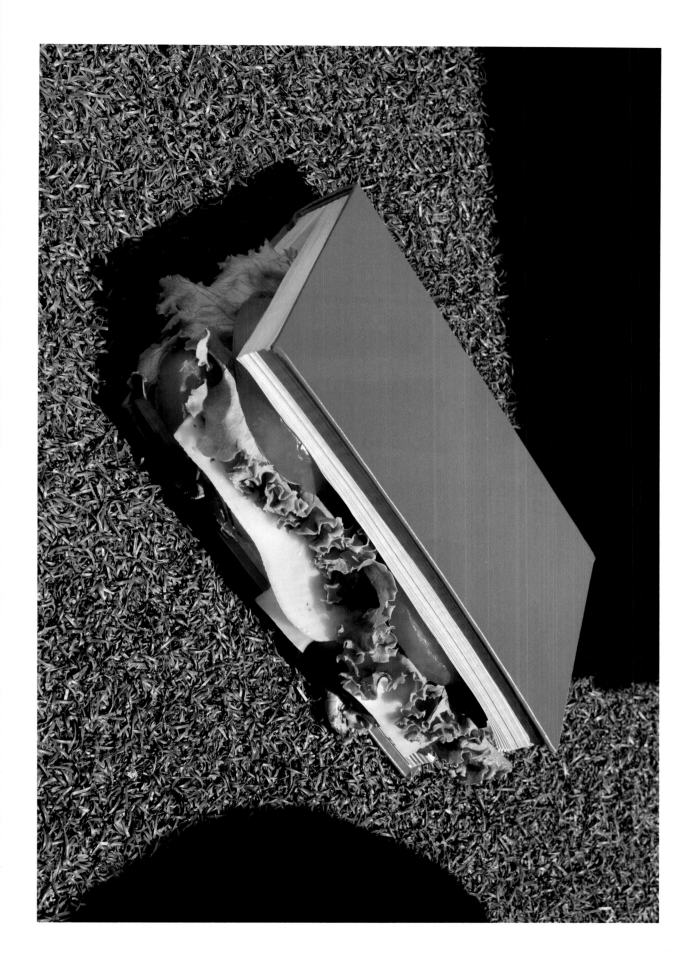

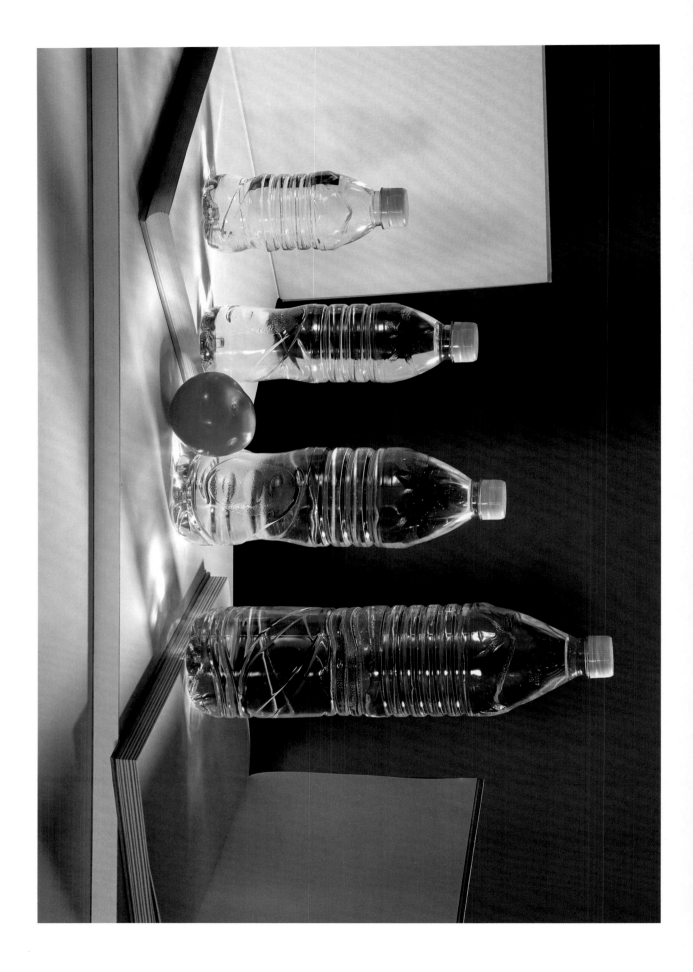

5
How to make the perfect book: size, binding, printing, and paper

You know what they say: it's not size that matters—it's what you do with it! Just flip though this book to see that great publications come in all shapes and sizes. The size should be determined by the material within: the photographs, text, and any other visual elements. Some books call for an intimate experience and smaller size (p. 120), while others require an XXL treatment (p. 378).

When it comes to binding, sometimes a project calls for simple staples (p. 258) or a PVC sleeve (p. 352) instead of the traditional case binding (p. 138) to hold it all together. Same goes for the choice of paper, whether it's matte or uncoated for a slightly raw, rough-and-ready feel (p. 286) or glossy for a slick look (p. 26), or even a combination of different types of paper (p. 276).

Printing can also offer all sorts of interesting opportunities. Classic (and expensive, if you are printing a limited number of copies) offset printing, more accessible digital printing, or alternative processes such as risograph (p. 416) or letterpress (p. 100) can all be great; each will give you a different feel for your book. It goes back to the principle of how you want to use them. Find a friendly printer and discuss your book project with them; show them your photos. Tell them what you want to do and ask for their recommendations, in terms of both the machine and paper to use. Sometime you don't need to look far for a printer, and it is better to stay local, visit the press, and befriend the technicians. Do not forget to ask them how to prepare the files for printing. It's important not to assume that the files you have prepared for ink-jet printing will translate directly to offset or any other kind of printing process. Each method of output will require a different type of file prepared specifically for that process. Don't be afraid to ask and test things out before you move ahead with printing the entire edition!

Ultimately, there isn't really a perfect format for your project. A set of photos can inhabit different skins: they can start as an immediate, cheap, and cheerful newsprint (p. 306), then find another life as an expensively printed hardcover book. Just evaluate your project, your skills, and your pocket before deciding!

6
How to think of a book as an object

Please do this experiment for me: close your eyes, touch the pages of this book, and bring it to your nose. Smell it!

This is to remind you that a book is an object—something that has weight, a smell, and communicates not only visually but also offers a tactile experience (p. 434). We have gotten so used to seeing photobooks online, we forget how important the physicality of a book can be. As a self-publisher, you will have to take that into consideration: what experience you want to give your readers, and especially how that experience might enhance or be in tune with the content of the book. If your book has a lot of text, and it requires time for reading, you want to make sure its format passes the toilet test: can it be read easily while in the lavatory? If a book needs a table to be opened, then forget about people falling asleep while reading it.

But the physicality of a book doesn't just have to do with functionality. In the chapter Self Publish, Be Crafty (p. 387) and throughout this book, you can see how artists have stretched and challenged the traditional book form to create objects that force the reader to engage and play—from images printed in invisible ink, only visible when using a special light (p. 464), to flip-though pages that can be mixed and matched (p. 444), or photographs that have to be buried (p. 92). The reader is invited to do more than passively look at photos—to literally get his or her hands dirty, and take part in the process of making meaning from a set of photographs.

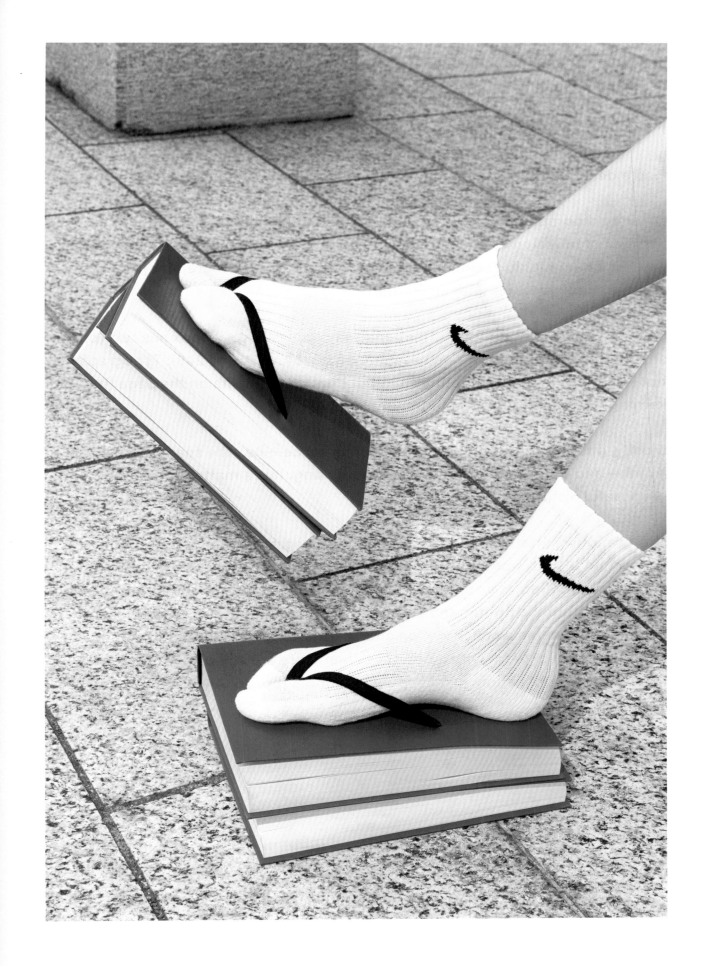

7

How to design a book

Find a designer!

Often photographers fancy themselves designers just because they have cracked versions of InDesign on their laptops. Imagine if it was the reverse: what would you think if a graphic designer called him or herself a photographer just because he or she took pictures with an iPhone?

Graphic design is an art form. This especially applies if your book has text (pp. 64 and 424), or requires inventive navigation (pp. 164, 230, and 248). Typography is not just about font choice, but also about how that font sits on the page (its size, kerning, etc.) and in relation to the image.

Mostly, photobook design is about negative space—i.e., the space not occupied by ink—and how that can make your photos sing. It is a matter of harmony, or purposeful disharmony.

The relationship between a designer and a photographer can bring a book to interesting places, pushing the project physically. You could create a book that could also function as an exhibition when the pages are overlaid (p. 82) or save the sheets from the printer and use them to exhibit (p. 406). Your relationship could even become a collaboration and coauthorship (p. 352). But if you do not want to or cannot work with a designer, then there are still plenty of ways to make a great publication: just keep things simple (pp. 36, 44, and 192).

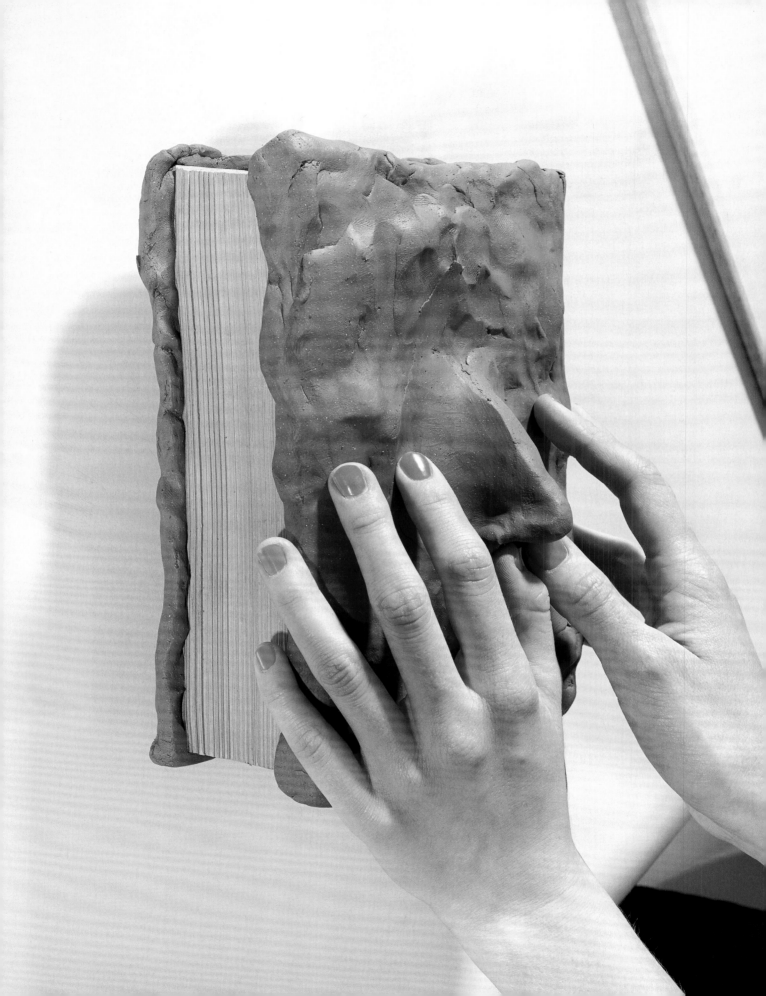

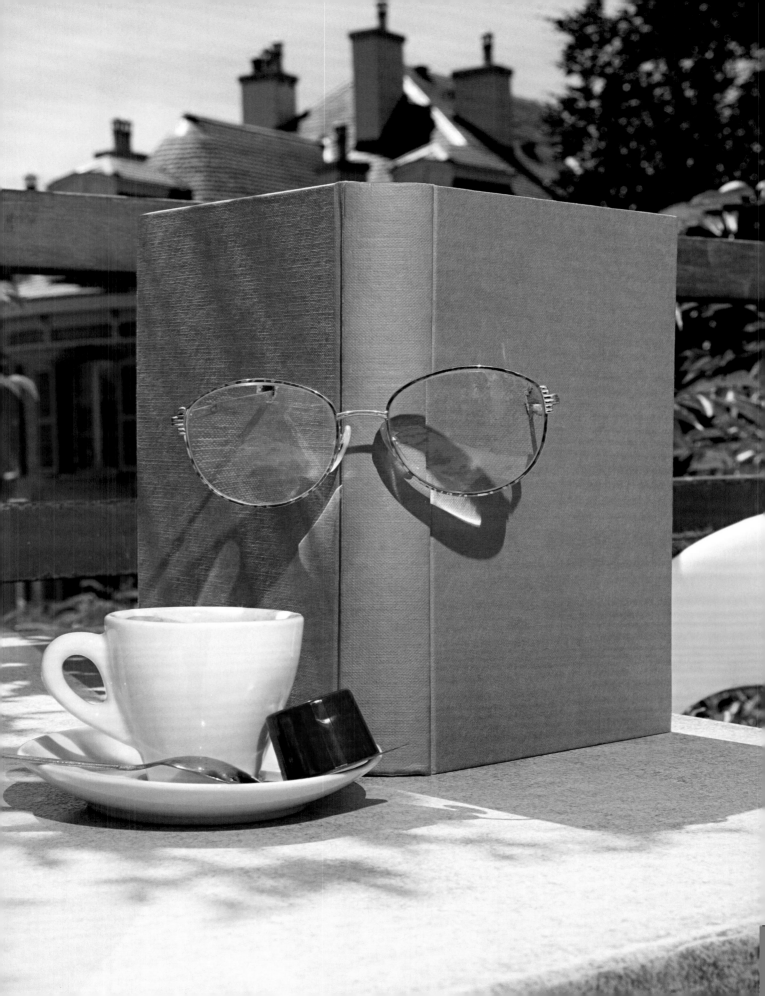

8
How to handle text

First things first, ask yourself: what is the text for? Does it complement the photos (p. 64)? Does it work as a parallel narrative to the one you are building with the photographs (p. 424)? How text and images play together can be very exciting—with one prompting the other, forming a second or third narrative, or a narrative that is ambiguous. The reader's job is to piece together the puzzle and make his or her own sense of it.

Ah, and a final word on text. If the text is an introduction, where you ask somebody to explain or to legitimize your book... *zzzzzzzzzz*

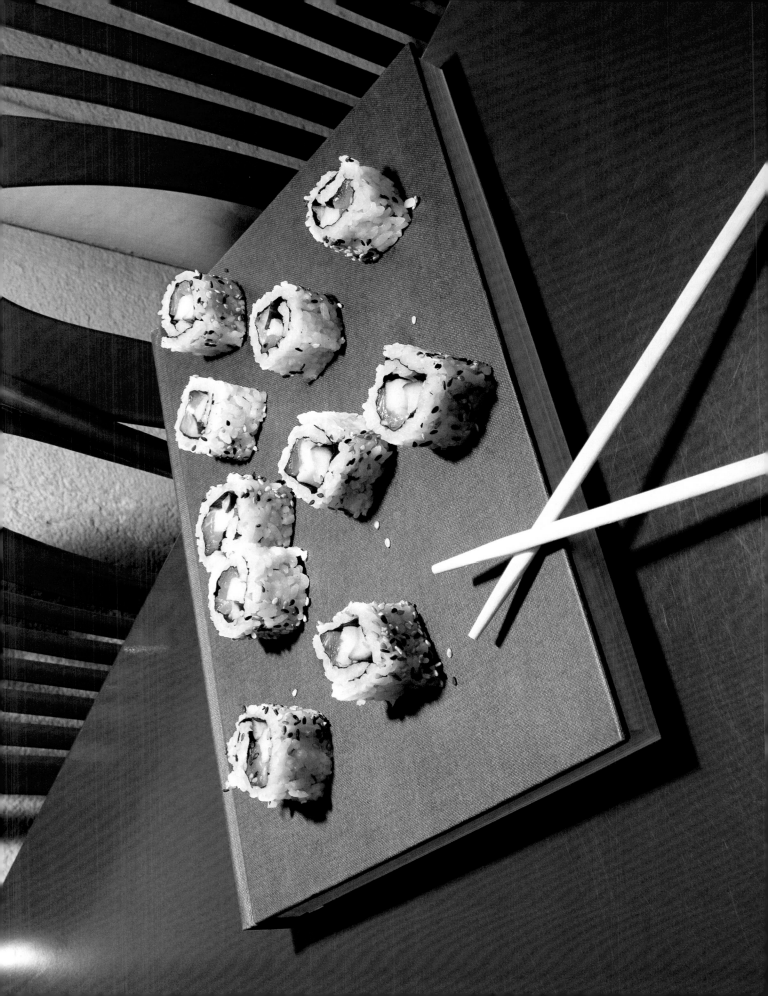

9

How to pick a good title and cover

Here, again, it is often best to keep it simple. Don't try to be too clever. If you try to show off with the title, you might just come across as a pretentious knob. A title should provide some kind of entry point to your work.

A good title is usually something that becomes iconic: it may be cheeky (pp. 26 and 248); bluntly descriptive (pp. 36, 54, 100, and 146); or poetic (pp. 74, 156, and 316).

Sometimes a good title will find you (p. 110) and it will magically, perfectly stick to your photos like they were always meant to be together (and they will live happily ever after).

10
How to find an audience

You are the audience of your book, first and foremost. You and your buddies. The long tradition of (fan)zines comes directly from the need to communicate with people like yourself—people who share your love for that band, that activity (I'm talking to you, skateboarders!), that lifestyle. A publication is another way to create a network, a community. In fact, traditionally, zines were often swapped instead of sold. That doesn't prevent a book or zine from reaching unexpected people and speaking to others. That is often not because a focus group was decided prior to the release, but because sometimes things can unpredictably capture the zeitgeist of a specific time.

There are also publications that, because of their content, aim to engage with a community outside of their creators' own—publications that deliver a specific message to specific people (p. 334). If yours is one of those, you have to pay attention to what kind of publication could engage your desired audience. What is important to them, and how much would they be willing to pay?

Think about a publication as a means to communicate. A book is very much like a message in a bottle: as soon as it starts circulating, who knows where it is going to go, who is going to see it, and when.

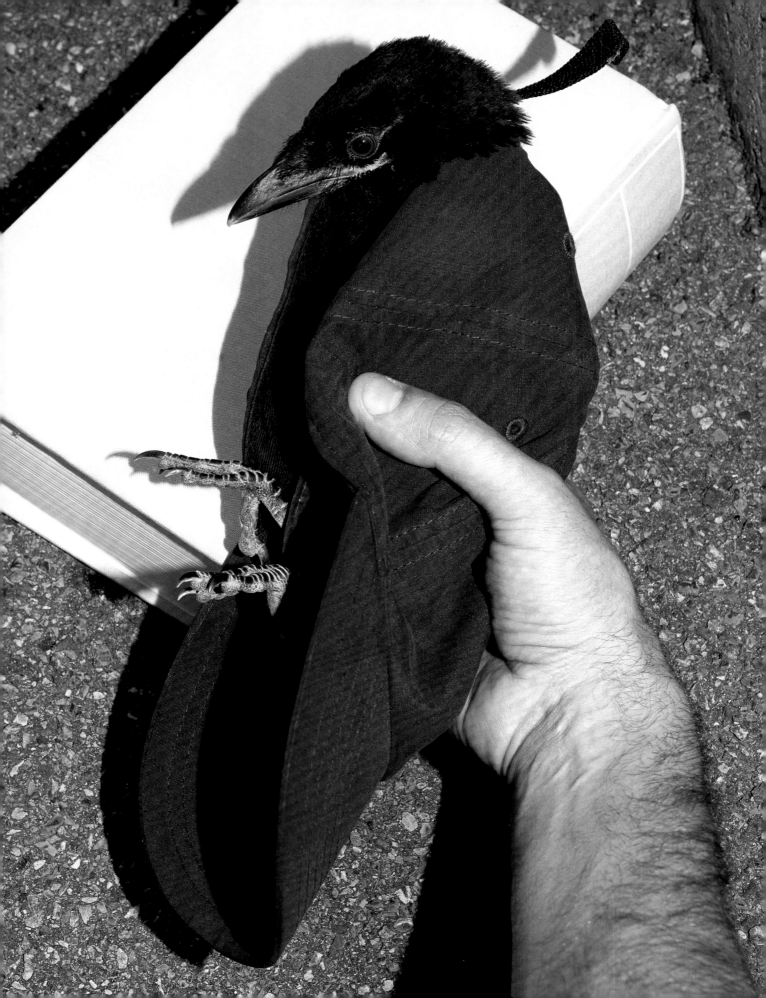

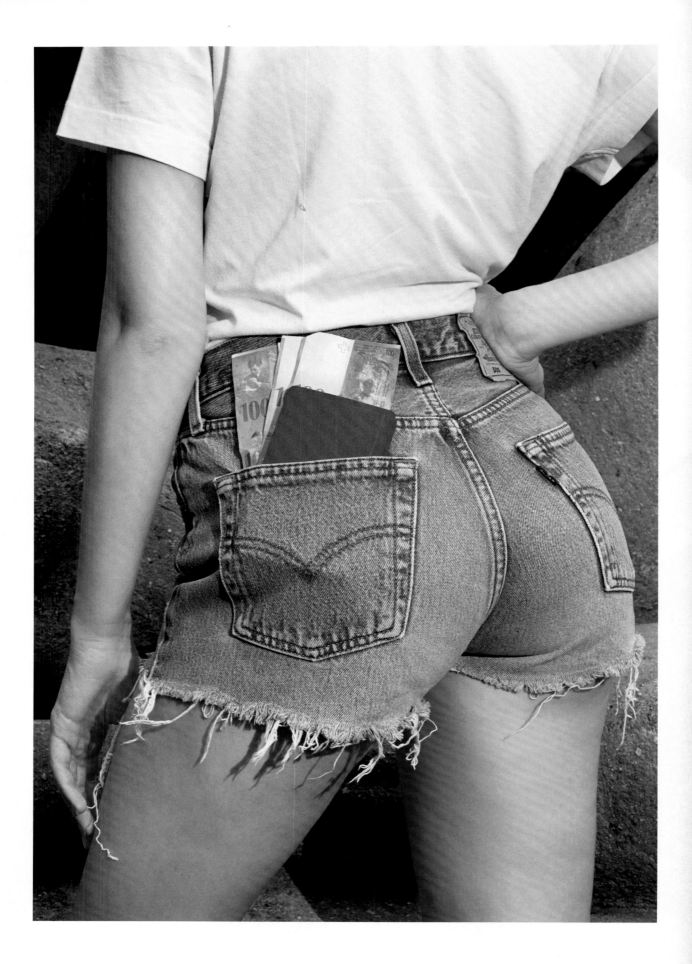

11

How to make $$$ with your book

Let me break it to you: if you are looking to make money, you are looking in the wrong place!

Photobooks don't really make much profit from sales. It is just too expensive to produce them (including their content, design, production, and printing). This means the margins are usually too low to make any serious profit, especially if you yourself are the primary means of selling your own book.

Here's how it usually works in traditional publishing: the publisher sells a book to a bookstore for 50 percent of the cover price, and another 20 to 30 percent goes to the distributor. Imagine a book sells for $50. A retailer will buy it for $25. The distributor may take up to $7.50 (30 percent), leaving the publisher with $17.50. The unit costs for the printing alone for most of the books featured here are between $10 and $30 per copy. That means that if a publisher sells that book via a distributor, he/she would end up with somewhere between $7.50 to negative $12.50 left after all is said and done.

The classic publishing formula is to multiply your unit cost by five to determine the cover price. Which means that if your book costs $20 per copy to produce, a traditional publisher would charge $100 per copy—which is, of course, an extraordinarily high price, and one that will make the book unsellable. Thankfully the traditional system of multiplying by five doesn't fit the business model of most self-published books, where some of the costs a normal publisher would have to take into account, including distribution, do not exist.

But you get the gist. The best way is to control costs, distribute and sell your book directly, and ideally fundraise to cover some of the costs of production. This can be done by applying for public or private grants, crowdfunding, or pre-selling copies of the book.

12
How to distribute

Get ready to have piles of book boxes in your bedroom. And prepare to become friendly with the people at the post office. That is what distribution is all about.

If you are your own distributor, you need to be good at handling orders, whether directly from visitors to your website (the real gold mine), or from the retailers that sell it for you. When people pay you money, they expect to get a book! The advantage of handling distribution yourself is that you are rewarded by direct communication with the people who love your book. The disadvantage is that it becomes a job.

The same thing applies to running a table (or half a table, or a quarter) at one of the many great book fairs around the world, or figuring out which of the great bookshops might like to sell your book, and who exactly you need to call in order to present the book to them for consideration.

One thing to always remember: before getting into business with somebody, do a bit of research about their line of credit. Another rule that will keep you out of trouble: money first, goods after. (That is, if you manage to convince a store to take the book on firm sale terms as opposed to consignment.)

Finally, the ultimate enemy is Amazon. If you bought this book there: shame on you! With its forced discount policy (often more than 52 percent off the suggested retail price), Amazon is destroying the industry, one art book at a time. Local bookstores and alternative online retailers are your friends—or, if they aren't now, make it your business to make them your friends.

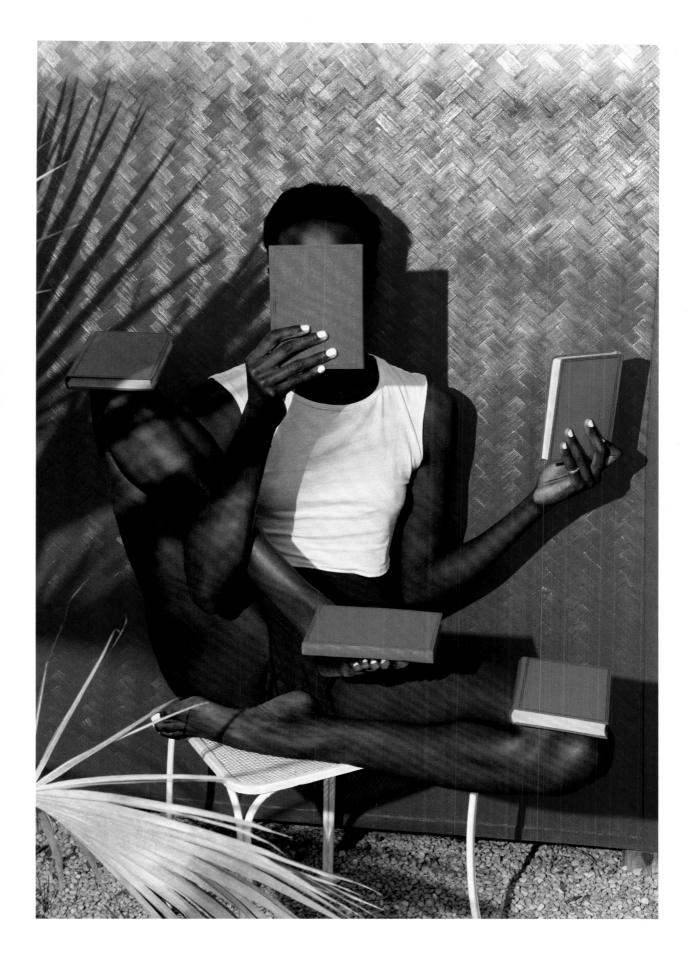

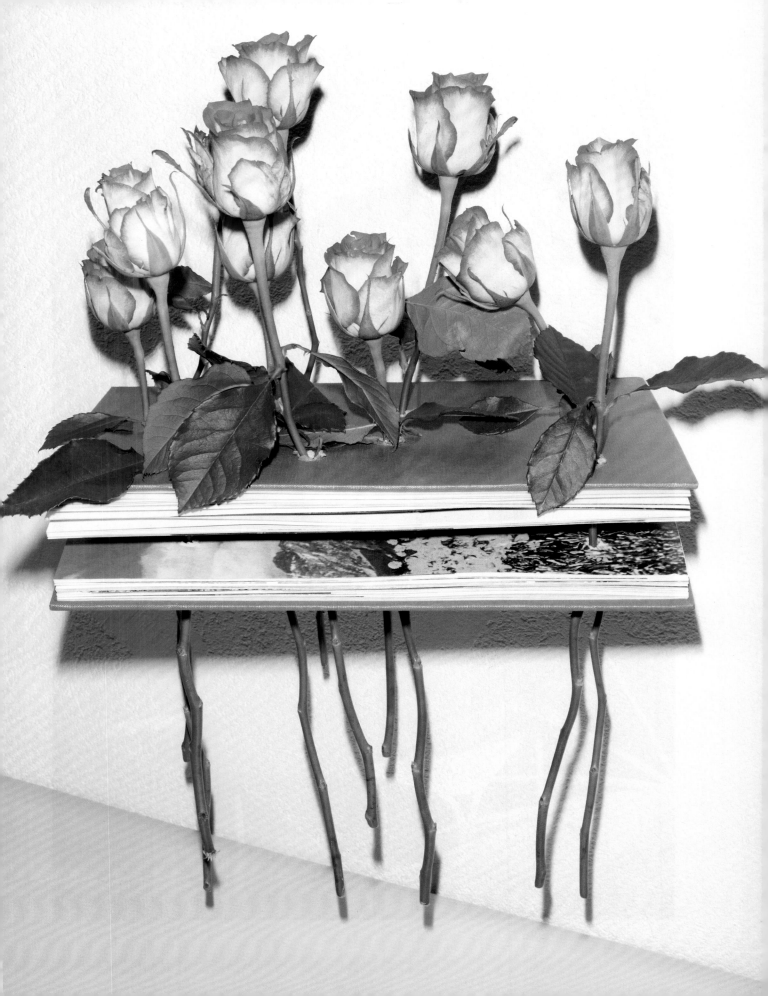

13

How to market your book

Start your book tour at your local pub (p. 268).

Engage your community, your people. Let them know you made a book.
The Internet is your friend (p. 326).

Get a few copies into the hands of people you admire, who you think would love
to have a copy. Do your research, and you will find a network of people who can
help you spread the word about your book via blogs, videos, and social media.

Buy other people's books. They will feel indebted to buy yours (and it's good
karma).

Send copies to competitions if you can afford it, and if you think they may
be receptive to what you do (p. 398).

Carry it everywhere (p. 156) and show it around.

If your book is good it will find its way—hopefully in your lifetime.

14

How to be happy

Whatever you have learned here and whatever anyone has said to you—including me or other self-publishers—*forget it*!

There is no formula for a great book. And the next amazing one will come from a totally unexpected place. You might know where that place is!